TONI MÖRWALD
STERNEKÜCHE

MÖRWALD

STERNEKÜCHE

STAR-AWARDED CUISINE ★ HAUTE CUISINE

TEXT HERBERT HACKER | **FOTOGRAFIE** MICHAEL ECKSTEIN

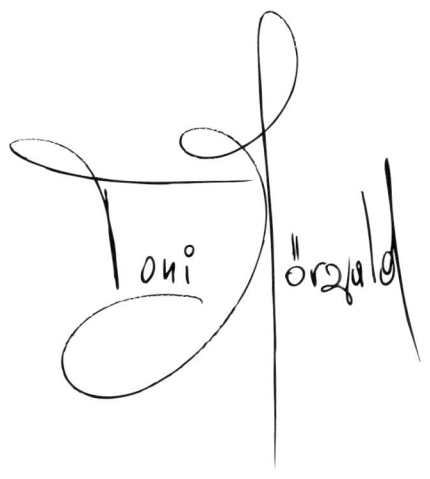

UMSCHAU

Worte vorab

TALENTIERTER KOCH UND GASTGEBER

Wie Hartnäckigkeit
und Begabung Toni Mörwald
zum Ziel bringen.

Liebe Leser,

eine Frage wird mir immer wieder gestellt: Wie wird man ein erfolgreicher Koch? Doch so kurz und knapp die Frage, so ausführlich und ausufernd könnte die Antwort ausfallen. Denn Koch zu sein ist heutzutage ein Beruf, der neben dem Hauptschauplatz Küche immer häufiger Kreativität und Engagement an zahlreichen Nebenschauplätzen verlangt. Und so braucht es neben Talent und handwerklichem Können vor allem Folgendes: Nur wer sein Ziel hartnäckig, mit großem Einsatz und mit begeisterter Kreativität verfolgt, schafft es, sich den Weg zu ebnen für eine erfüllendes, erfolgreiches Vorwärtskommen.
Toni Mörwald ist dafür ein gutes Beispiel. Er ist ein ausgesprochen vielseitiger und begabter Kollege, der sich mit unbeirrbarer Konsequenz ein kleines Imperium aufgebaut hat.
Manchmal erinnert er mich an Mozarts »Figaro«, wo immer man hinkommt, Toni Mörwald war schon da …
Seit vielen Jahren kreuzen sich Toni Mörwalds und meine Wege immer wieder. Daraus hat sich im Laufe der Zeit eine von großer Sympathie geprägte kollegiale Bekanntschaft entwickelt, mein großer Respekt vor seinen Leistungen ist ihm absolut sicher. So hat er in vielerlei Hinsicht bemerkenswertes erreicht, als Koch, aber auch als Gastgeber. Und in diesen seinen Paraderollen wird der geneigte Leser Toni Mörwald auch in seinem neuen Buch in vollem Einsatz erleben.

In kulinarischer Verbundenheit

Inhalt

8_Kloster Und
GÖTTLICHE FÜGUNG UND TALENTSCHMIEDE

104_Catering
LOGISTIK UND LANGUSTEN

122_Zur Traube
URSPRUNG UND TRADITION

148_Villa Katharina
GENIESSERHERBERGE UND GASTLICHKEIT

156_Toni M.
GOURMETOASE UND STERNETEMPEL

182_Kochschule
LEHRMEISTER UND MEISTERLEHRE

200_Weinbau Mörwald
WINZERTRADITION UND WEINREGION

210_Schloss Grafenegg
FÜRSTLICHE IDYLLE UND KUNSTGENUSS

232_m.kunst.genuss
KULINARIK UND KUNST

244_Persönlich
TELEFONIEREN UND KOCHEN

338_Wegbegleiter
TIEFE FREUNDSCHAFTEN UND KOLLEGIALES MITEINANDER

258_Alle Rezepte im Detail
REZEPTVERZEICHNIS UND ZUBEREITUNG DER REZEPTE

Appendix/Appendice
DETAILS OF PREPARATION IN ENGLISH ALONG WITH A LIST OF
ALL RECIPES CAN BE FOUND IN THE APPENDIX.

VOUS TROUVEREZ EN APPENDICE UNE VUE D'ENSEMBLE
ANSI QUE LA PRÉPARATION DES RECETTES FRANÇAISES.

Kloster Und

GÖTTLICHE FÜGUNG UND TALENTSCHMIEDE

Wo Mörwald
Jungköche fördert und
wo sich Gourmets
andächtig irdischen
Genüssen hingeben.

Für gewöhnlich dominieren in einem Kloster Entsagung und spartanische Lebensweise. Ob das immer so ist, sei dahingestellt, jedenfalls denken die meisten Menschen beim Wort Kloster mehr an dünne Suppen und meditative Lebensweise und nicht so sehr an Wachteln, Wein und Waller. Im Kremser Kloster Und ist das anders, dort wird ausgiebig gezecht und lustvoll getafelt.

Das Kloster Und ragt aber auch in anderer Hinsicht heraus. Es ist Mörwalds erfolgreichste Talentschmiede, in keinem seiner Restaurants haben junge Köche so schnell Karriere gemacht. Bestes Beispiel: Der junge Leonard Cernko erkochte im Kloster Und in kürzester Zeit höchste Auszeichnungen in praktisch allen wichtigen Gourmetführern. Die Folge: Cernko, von seinem Mentor Mörwald stets gefördert, erhielt Angebote aus der ganzen Welt. Und Mörwald ließ ihn ziehen. Cernko ist heute ein gefragter und hoch dotierter Küchenchef in Moskau. Die Küchenleitung hinterließ er seinem um zwei Jahre jüngeren Souschef Erwin Windhaber. Zur Überraschung aller Kritiker gelang Windhaber, was kaum jemand für möglich gehalten hätte: Er konnte das Niveau in der Küche nicht nur halten, er steigerte es noch. Der hoffnungsvolle Jungkoch Windhaber hat das Zepter in der Küche mittlerweile an das Duo Thomas Serret und Erwin Riedrich übergeben.

Mörwald betreibt das Restaurant im Kloster Und seit Mitte 2003. Gestaltet wurde es vom renommierten Wiener Architektenduo »Eichinger oder Knecht«. Es mag so manchem wie eine göttliche Fügung erscheinen, dass dieses kirchliche Kleinod nach einer bewegten Geschichte einer weltlichen Verwendung unter dem Zeichen von Genuss und Lebensfreude zugeführt wurde. Wo einst Mönche nach Enthaltsamkeit strebten, werden heute überirdisch gute Götterspeisen serviert.

So wechselhaft kann Geschichte sein. Mitte des 17. Jahrhunderts fiel das Kloster einem Brand zum Opfer. 1656 wurde es unter der Anleitung des Architekten Domenico Sciassia wieder neu errichtet und im Jahre 1796 auf Wunsch der Bürger von Krems säkularisiert.

Danach lag das Kloster lange Zeit brach, wurde zwischenzeitlich eher zweckentfremdet als Truppenspital und Wohnhaus genutzt. Ab 1987 beherbergte das Gebäude ein Weinkolleg.

Heute zählt das Relais-&-Châteaux-Kloster Und mit einem Michelin-Stern und drei Hauben im Gault Millau zu den höchst dekorierten Restaurants im gesamten Mörwald-Imperium – und damit auch zu den besten Restaurants Österreichs.

Neben einem prachtvollen Innenhofgarten mit Arkaden beinhaltet das gesamte Ensemble auch ein beeindruckendes Deckenfresko im Kirchenschiff aus dem Jahre 1756. Unter dieser malerischen Kuppel finden in regelmäßigen Abständen Festbanketts, Konferenzen und kulinarische Events statt.

Damit ist es Toni Mörwald gelungen, einem in Vergessenheit geratenen Architekturjuwel neues Leben einzuhauchen. Worüber auch der in Gourmetkreisen bekannte niederösterreichische Weinpfarrer Hans Denk immer wieder ins Schwärmen gerät: »Ich bin überzeugt«, meint der den Genüssen zugewandte Hochwürden, »dass mein Chef da oben die Entwicklung dieser himmlischen Bodenstation mit sehr viel Wohlgefallen betrachtet.«

Menü
Kloster Und

„ Vulcanoschinken, Baliklachs, Perlhendl und Kräutertopfen sind die Verführer des Abends. Von jedem ein Happen und die Sinne schwinden."

„ Drei grundverschiedene Knusperschnitten verlocken jeden Gourmet mit Gambas, Jungzwiebeln, Rindermark, Paradeisern und Rosmarin. "

27

„ Anmutig in Sulz gewickelt bezirzen die Flusskrebse die schmeichelnde Kerbelmousse."

„Sanft drängen sich feine **Trüffel** um flaumiges **Entenleberparfait**, begleitet von Bällchen aus Kohlrabipüree in einer krossen **Tramezzinihülle**."

Gemüse als Praline veredelt trifft auf ein Duett der Konsistenzen: **Kohlrabi** und **Kalb** ergänzen sich zu einem großartigen Geschmackserlebnis.

„ Scharfes

Wasabimousse

entlockt dem

Tatar vom Limousinrind

seine kulinarischen Geheimnisse. „

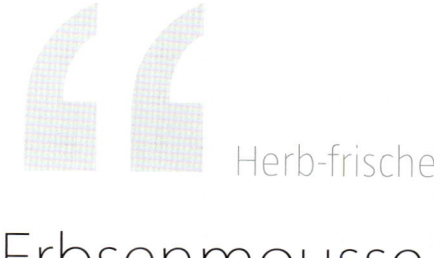

„Herb-frische **Erbsenmousse**, umspült vom **Hummerschaum**, zeigt Biss: Üppiger **Kaviar** komplettiert das lukullische Erlebnis."

„ Schmeichelndes **Kitz** in würziger Roulade wird umgarnt von der blutroten **Paradeiseressenz**. "

„Die kräftige Consommé vom **Waldviertler Fleckvieh** bekommt liebevolle Gesellschaft von würzigen **Milzschnitten**."

„Dreiklang von cremigem **Spinat**, knackigen **Flusskrebsschwänzen** und flüssigem **Wachtelei**. Der zarte **Ravioloteig** gibt den Takt vor."

„ Goldgelb panierte **Eier** betten sich auf cremigem **Spinat**, umringt von **Wiesenchampignons** und **Wurzelspeck**. "

„Kernige Tortelloni mit zarter Brokkolifülle werden umhüllt von pikanter Paradeis-Estragon-Butter."

„Vom betörenden Duft der weißen Trüffel überwältigt umschlingt das Erbsenpüree zärtlich ein pochiertes Ei."

„ Mit **Safran** verfeinerte **Miesmuscheln** kokettieren mit flaumigen **Gnocchi**. "

„ Zart marinierte **Jakobsmuscheln**
fächern ihr blütenweißes Fleisch über reinen **Mürbteig**. "

„ Entspannt genießen **Wallerfilets** und **Linsen** ihren Ausblick auf die verführerische **Riojabutter**. "

„ **Paradeisartischocken** und **Basilikumzwiebeln** buhlen um die Gunst des **St. Pierre**. "

„ Farbenfrohe **Kürbisgnocchis** und buntes **Gemüse** betten aufmunternd den bescheidenen **Steinbutt.** "

" Voller Kraft sprengt der **Meerwolf** seine **Salzkruste**, um sich auf knackigem **Gemüse** genussvoll zu entspannen. "

„Angeregt vom frischen Kerbel kokettiert das Kalbsbries mit den zurückhaltenden Wiesenchampignons."

„Galantine vom zart rosa Täubchen, angerichtet zwischen Apfelchutney und kecken Wagramer Dirndln."

„ Würzige Oliven-Paradeis-Kruste schmiegt sich an die weiche Brust vom Schwarzfederhuhn, eingebettet in orientalischem Piniencouscous. "

„Zarter **Kalbslungenbraten** im schützenden **Brotteigmantel** wird von geschmorten **Artischocken** umschwärmt."

„ Auf der Zunge zergehendes Kalbskotelett träumt auf feinen Nudeln von Olivenglace und Junglauch."

„Knuspriger Spanferkelrücken im Dialog mit Haxlravioli, erfrischt vom geschmorten Spitzkraut."

„ Kross und zart präsentieren sich **Kalbskrone** und **Kalbsbriesravioli** umschmeichelt vom nachhaltigen Aroma der **Petersilwurzelcreme** und **Petersilbutter**. "

„ Der Milchlammschlögel lässt sich von geschmortem Mangold und butterweichem Erdäpfelkuchen auf ein kulinarisches Fest begleiten. "

„ Rosa **Beiried** von Nina Metternich im Schlepptau von **Erdäpfelcrêpe** verführt weißen **Solospargel** im Sauce-Béarnaise-Kleid. „

„ Kerniges **Rindsfilet** aus dem Attergau, schwungvoll umgeben von **Sellerie** und gebratener **Gänseleber**.

„ Knusprig gebackene **Rehleber** liebäugelt mit sinnlich purpurfarbenem **Rübencarpaccio** und scharfer **Krenvinaigrette**. "

83

„Gebettet auf körnigem Gries und begleitet von knackigem Kürbiskernconfit fühlt sich der sanft gegarte Rehrücken besonders wohl."

„Zartes **Kitz** im Schutz einer feinen Panier, nur in Gesellschaft von zart mariniertem **Erdäpfelsalat**, mit **Rucola** garniert."

„ Leidenschaftlicher **Wildschweinschlögel** umwirbt zarte **Briochepalfyknödel** in hinreißend deftiger **Linsen-Speck-Sauce**. "

„In goldbraunem Teig lässt sich der **Hirschlungenbraten** von fruchtigen **Gnocchi** umwerben."

„ Wie in einem Märchen aus „Tausendundeiner Nacht" verführt das rassige Waldbeerengelee die zarte Vanillecreme.

„ Lockerer **Marillenschaum** und leichter **Marillenröster** versuchen kühles **Mandeleis** und zartes **Marillensorbet** zum Schmelzen zu bringen. "

„ Innig verschlungen ruhen weißes **Schokoladenparfait** und schwarze **Schokoladencreme** auf weichem **Biskuit**, bedeckt nur mit einem Hauch von geschäumter **Whiskymousse** "

„**Nougatmousse** und **Zitronengelee** gehen eine zärtliche Verbindung ein und verhelfen dem **Bananenpüree** zu einem stolzen Auftritt.

„ Kirschen schmiegen sich sanft an **Pfirsichmarmelade** und kühlen ihre Leidenschaft am **Pfirsichsorbet**. "

„Menage à cinq – knackig schokoladige **Küchlein** mit einem süßen Hauch von Nichts treffen exotisch verführerische **Cremes** in fruchtigen Cocktailkleidern."

Catering

LOGISTIK UND LANGUSTEN

Wie Mörwald als Manager, Koch und Caterer seit Jahren eine gewachsene Stammklientel mit edler Kulinarik versorgt.

Die Gäste sind alle schon eingetroffen, es wird Champagner serviert. Nach einiger Zeit bittet der Hausherr zu Tisch und ersucht um Aufmerksamkeit. Er will jenen Mann vorstellen, den er eigens engagiert hat: Es ist Toni Mörwald, der die erlauchte Feinschmeckerrunde an diesem Abend ganz privat bekochen soll.
Das Menü entspricht dem eines gehobenen Gourmetrestaurants: *Hummerschaumsuppe mit Flusskrebsen, Glacierte Gänseleber à la Provence, Pochierter Heilbutt mit Fenchelgemüse* und als Hauptgang *Filet von der Ente à l'orange*. Zum Dessert gibt es *Nougatmousse mit Minze und frischen Erdbeeren.*
Der Auftritt hat seine Wirkung nicht verfehlt. Den Anwesenden läuft das Wasser im Munde zusammen und auch die Gastgeber wirken völlig entspannt. Statt in der Küche selbst Hand anzulegen, können sie sich den ganzen Abend ihren Gästen widmen. Auch das Servieren der Speisen wird von einem Mörwald-Mitarbeiter erledigt. Gegen Mitternacht erscheinen dann Küchen- und Servierprofis noch einmal vor der begeisterten Runde und genießen den Applaus.

»Rent a Cook« nennt sich diese Dienstleistung, bei der sich Feinschmecker in den eigenen vier Wänden von einem Profi bekochen lassen können – ohne sich selbst die Schürze umbinden zu müssen und in einer Qualität, wie man sie nur von feinen Gourmettempeln kennt.
Das Rent-a-Cook-Business boomt. Ambulante Kocheinsätze von prominenten Herdvirtuosen sind in Mode gekommen – mit stetig steigender Nachfrage. »Unsere Auftragsbücher sind voll«, sagt Mörwald. »In den vergangenen Jahren hat sich dieser Dienstleistungsbereich zu einem echten Renner entwickelt.«
Mörwald hat diesen Service innerhalb seines gesamten Kulinarik-Imperiums schon vor Jahren zu einem eigenen Geschäftszweig gemacht – mit offizieller Preisliste und fixen Tarifen. Der umtriebige Gastronom kommt sogar mit eigens dafür ausgestatteten Autos angereist, erledigt den gesamten Einkauf und bringt auf Verlangen auch Geschirr, Gläser und alle notwendigen Küchenutensilien mit. »Wir schauen uns vorher die Küche an und bringen

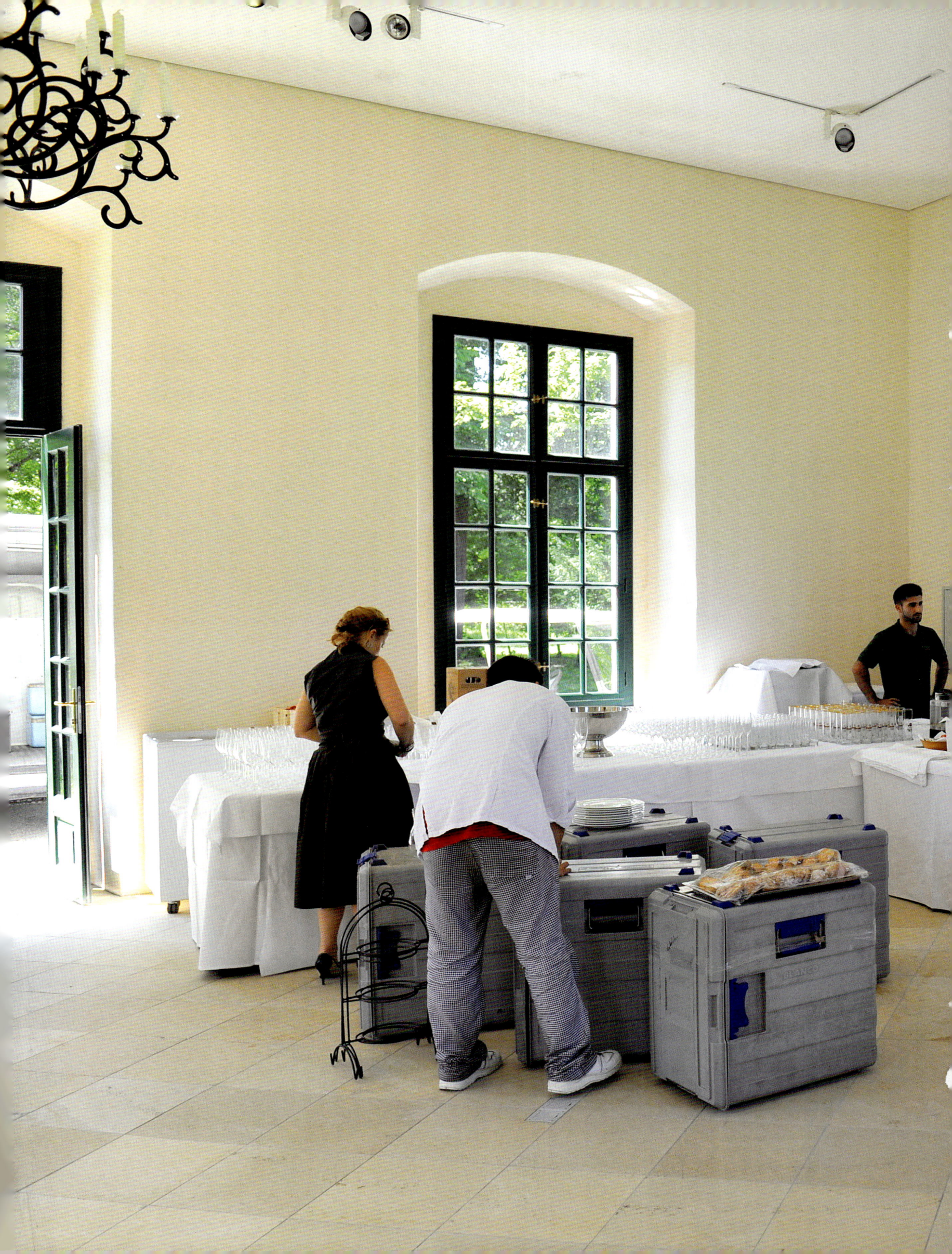

dann mit, was fehlt«, erklärt Mörwald. »Notfalls haben wir in unserem Wagen sogar eine vollständige Kücheneinrichtung dabei.«
Rent a Cook ist jedoch nur ein Teil des Mörwald-Cateringservices. Neben Einsätzen in privaten Haushalten steht das Team um Mörwald auch für Veranstaltungen jeder Art zur Verfügung. Ob Empfänge, Cocktails oder Galamenüs – das Mörwald-Team liefert und erledigt praktisch alles, was nötig ist. Vom Essen bis zur Ausstattung, vom Wein bis zur Dekoration, von der Küchentechnik bis zu den Servietten, nichts wird dem Zufall überlassen.

Nicht nur die Sterneküche hat sich im Laufe der Zeit deutlich verändert. Auch die Ansprüche an ein modernes Catering sind heute ganz anders als früher. Mit durchschnittlicher Qualität kann man in diesem heiß umkämpften Markt schon lange nicht mehr reüssieren.

Toni Mörwald weiß das und hat schon früh erkannt, dass Catering mehr ist als lediglich die Verpflegung möglichst vieler Menschen auf einer Party oder einem Fest. Als Sternekoch bürgt er allein schon mit seinem Namen für eine außergewöhnliche Qualität, für eine Kulinarik, die auch den Ansprüchen verwöhnter Gaumen gerecht wird und nicht bloß den Hunger stillt.

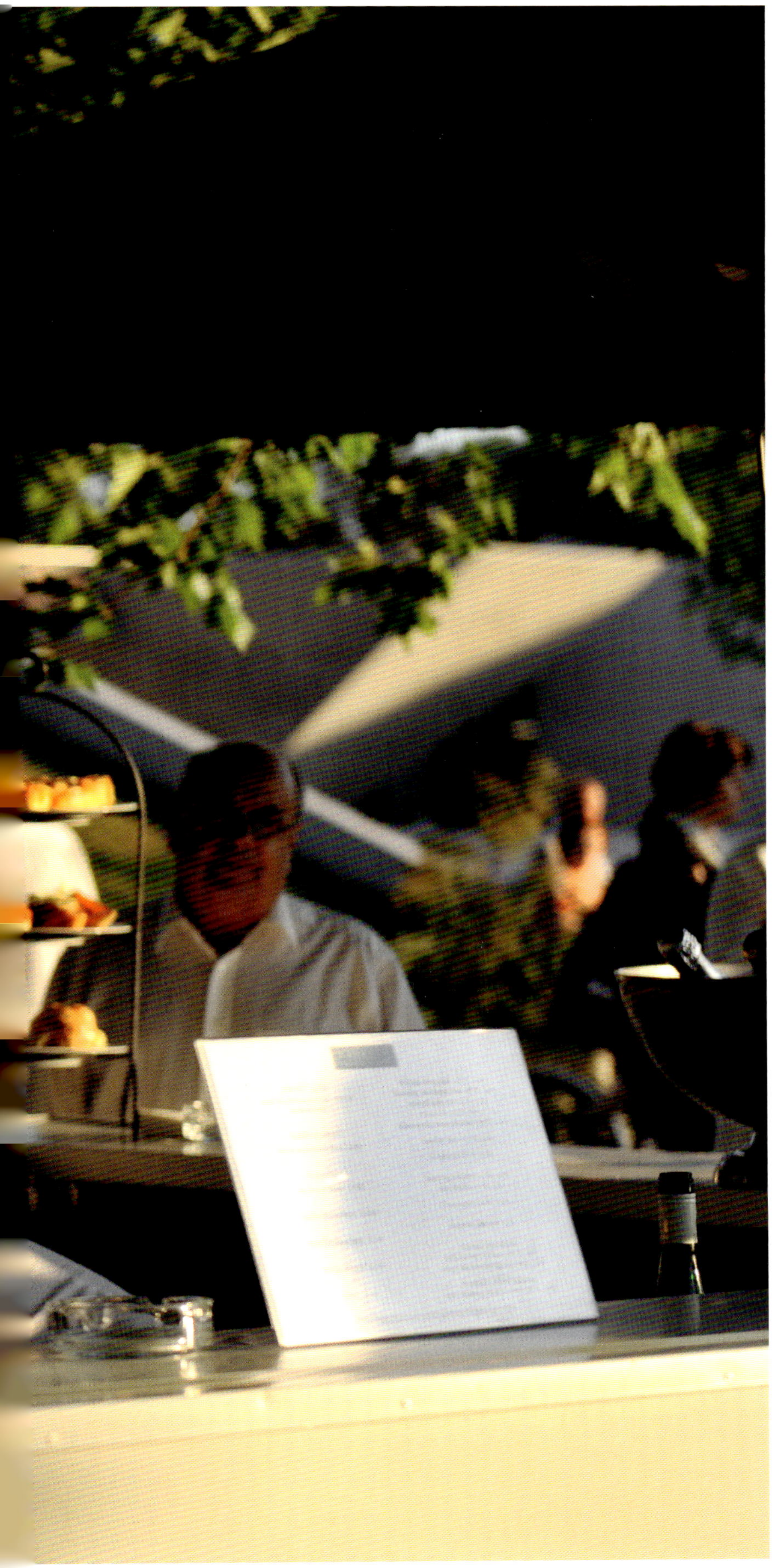

enuss.Mobil überholen Sie vielle
ber unsere Qualität nicht!“
ÖRWALD
ww.moerwald.at

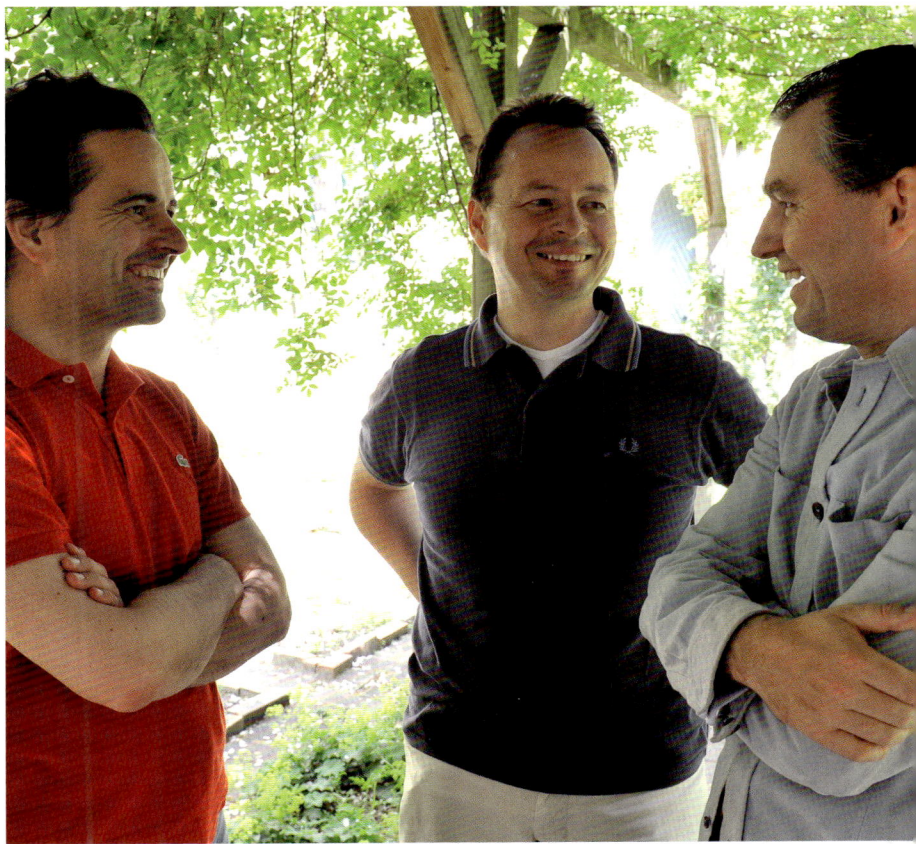

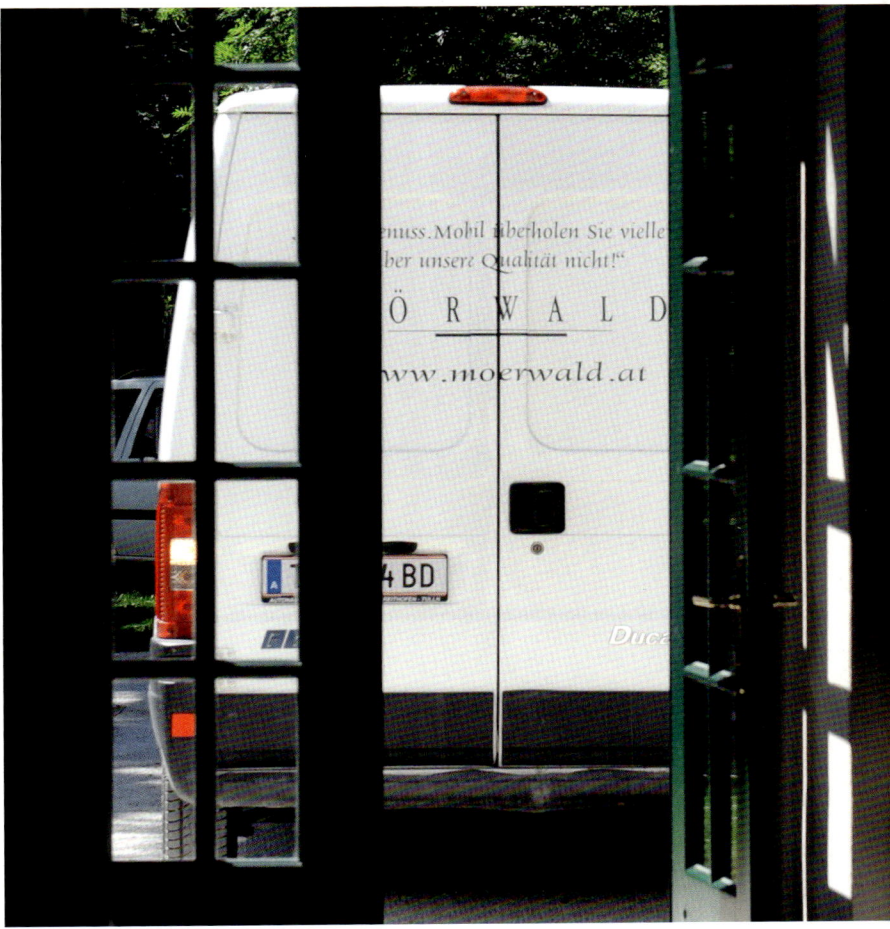

Menü
Catering

„Fruchtige **Limetten** und sommerlicher **Weißwein** konkurrieren um die Gunst der in Teig gehüllten **Crevetten**."

„ Unterschiedlichste Aromen und Konsistenzen finden in **Herz** und **Lunge** ihre gemeinsame Vollendung. "

„Unter knackiger Glasur findet der Gaumen eine zart fruchtige Cremefüllung, um schließlich in knusprigem Blätterteig auf sanften Schaum zu stoßen."

Zur Traube

URSPRUNG UND TRADITION

*Wo Mörwalds
Karriere begonnen hat
und wo er sich noch
heute von Traditionen
inspirieren lässt.*

Feuersbrunn in Niederösterreich wäre wohl ohne den Namen Mörwald nicht viel mehr als ein kleines idyllisches Dorf geblieben. Heute ist die 700-Seelen-Gemeinde ein Treffpunkt für Feinschmecker aus dem In- und Ausland. Von überall reisen Gourmets an und genießen die Mischung aus ländlicher Idylle und gastronomischen Highlights. Durch den Namen Mörwald hat Feuersbrunn eine neue, unverwechselbare Identität erhalten, für die Leute im Ort ist Toni Mörwald der große Zampano des Genießens geworden, einer, in dessen Reich die Leckerbissen niemals ausgehen.

Genau hier in Feuersbrunn begann seine Karriere, von hier aus gelang es ihm in Rekordzeit ein gastronomisches Imperium aufzubauen, mit mehreren Spitzenrestaurants, einer erfolgreichen Kochschule und einem profitablen Cateringbetrieb. Für seine Feinschmeckerlokale erhielt Mörwald nicht weniger als insgesamt sieben Hauben im Gault Millau und zwei Sterne im Guide Michelin. Seine Zielstrebigkeit im Verwirklichen von Ideen brachte ihm so begehrte Titel wie »Wirt des Jahres«, »Gastronom des Jahres« oder »Grande Chef de Cuisine Europe« ein.

Eigentlich hat seine Tante Rikki an allem Schuld. Sie führte in Feuersbrunn lange Zeit ein einfaches Dorfwirtshaus. Bis ein Landwirt aus dem Waldviertel auftauchte, sie ehelichte und in das raue Klima seiner Heimat entführte. Feuersbrunn war plötzlich ohne Dorfwirtshaus – eine veritable Katastrophe.

Daraufhin bedrängte die Dorfgemeinschaft den Schwager der abtrünnigen Wirtsfrau: Toni Mörwalds Vater. Er solle so schnell als möglich die verwaiste Gaststätte übernehmen, denn ein Dorf ohne Dorfwirt sei doch kein Zustand.

Nach mehreren Überredungsversuchen sprang die Familie Mörwald tatsächlich ein. Vater Mörwald ließ das Gasthaus von Grund auf umbauen, seine Frau Erika übernahm das Kommando in der Küche und die Großmutter stand tagsüber hinter der Schank.

In diesem Umfeld wuchs der junge Toni Mörwald auf und war von den Kochkünsten seiner Mutter schon im zarten Kindesalter fasziniert. Es war eine Welt der Düfte und Geschmäcker, die unweigerlich dazu führte, dass für ihn nur ein Beruf in Frage kam: der des Kochs.

Mörwald lernte sein Handwerk unter anderem bei Österreichs Starkoch Reinhard Gerer, sammelte aber auch wertvolle Erfahrungen in Frankreich, Monaco, Italien, Spanien und China. 1989 übernahm er schließlich das Gasthaus Zur Traube von den Eltern. Kurze Zeit später erhielt er als damals jüngster Koch Österreichs die erste Haube vom Gault Millau.

Die herausragenden Leistungen des aufstrebenden Küchenchefs führten schon bald dazu, dass die Traube über Wochen ausgebucht war. Ganz Feuersbrunn wunderte sich nun, wo plötzlich all die Leute herkamen.

Mehrere Umbauphasen führten dazu, dass der Betrieb heute mit einem verzweigten aber zeitgemäßen Ambiente aufwarten kann. Neben dem klassischen Gasthausbereich, dem gediegenen Gourmetrestaurant Toni M., einem Kräuterzimmer, einem Gartensaal, drei Gartenzimmern, einem Wintergarten und einem Festsaal bietet das Restaurant noch eine gut sortierte, reichhaltig gefüllte Vinothek und eine hochmoderne Küche, in der nahezu jeden Mittwoch Kochseminare abgehalten werden. Dennoch verfügt die Traube in manchen Räumen noch immer über die sympathische Aura eines bodenständigen Landgasthauses. Darauf legt der Hausherr auch großen Wert. Denn die Traube dient Mörwald auch dazu, seine kulinarischen Wurzeln nicht aus den Augen zu verlieren. Hier, wo alles begonnen hat, tischt heute der Küchenchef François Laliberté exklusive, österreichische Gerichte auf – eine ideale Ergänzung zur internationalen Gourmetküche von Toni Mörwalds kulinarischem Imperium.

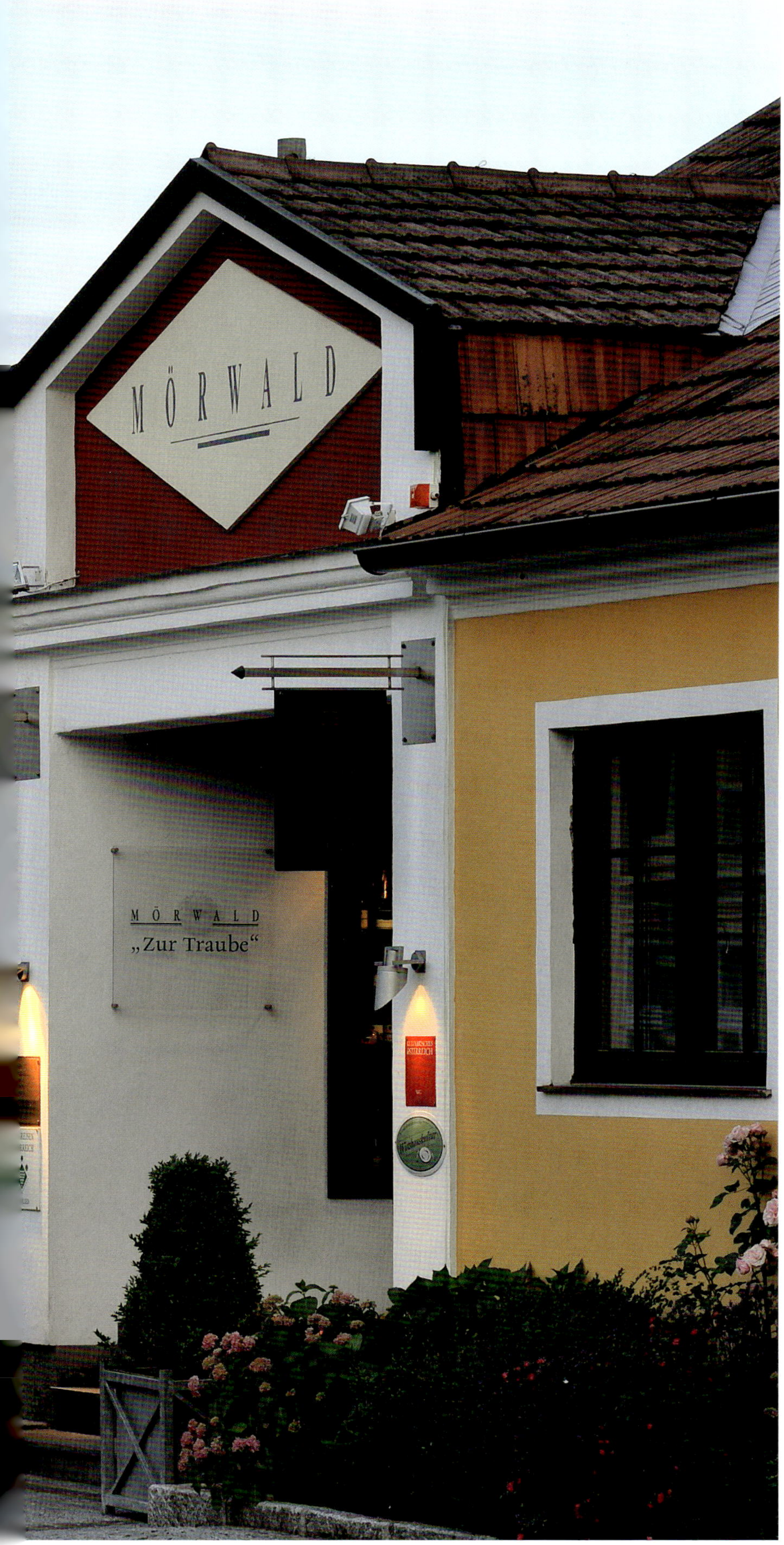
MÖRWALD
MÖRWALD
„Zur Traube“

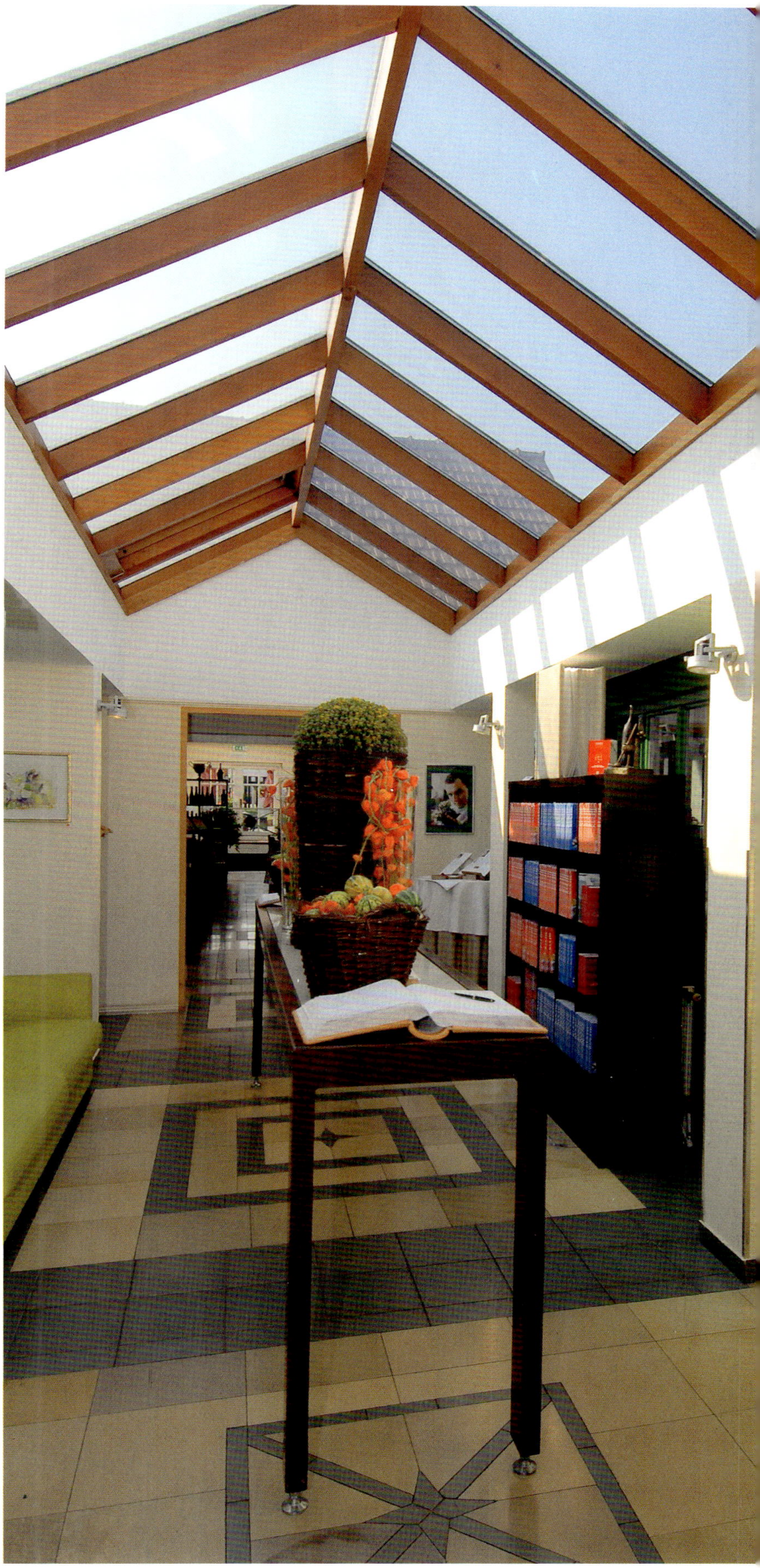

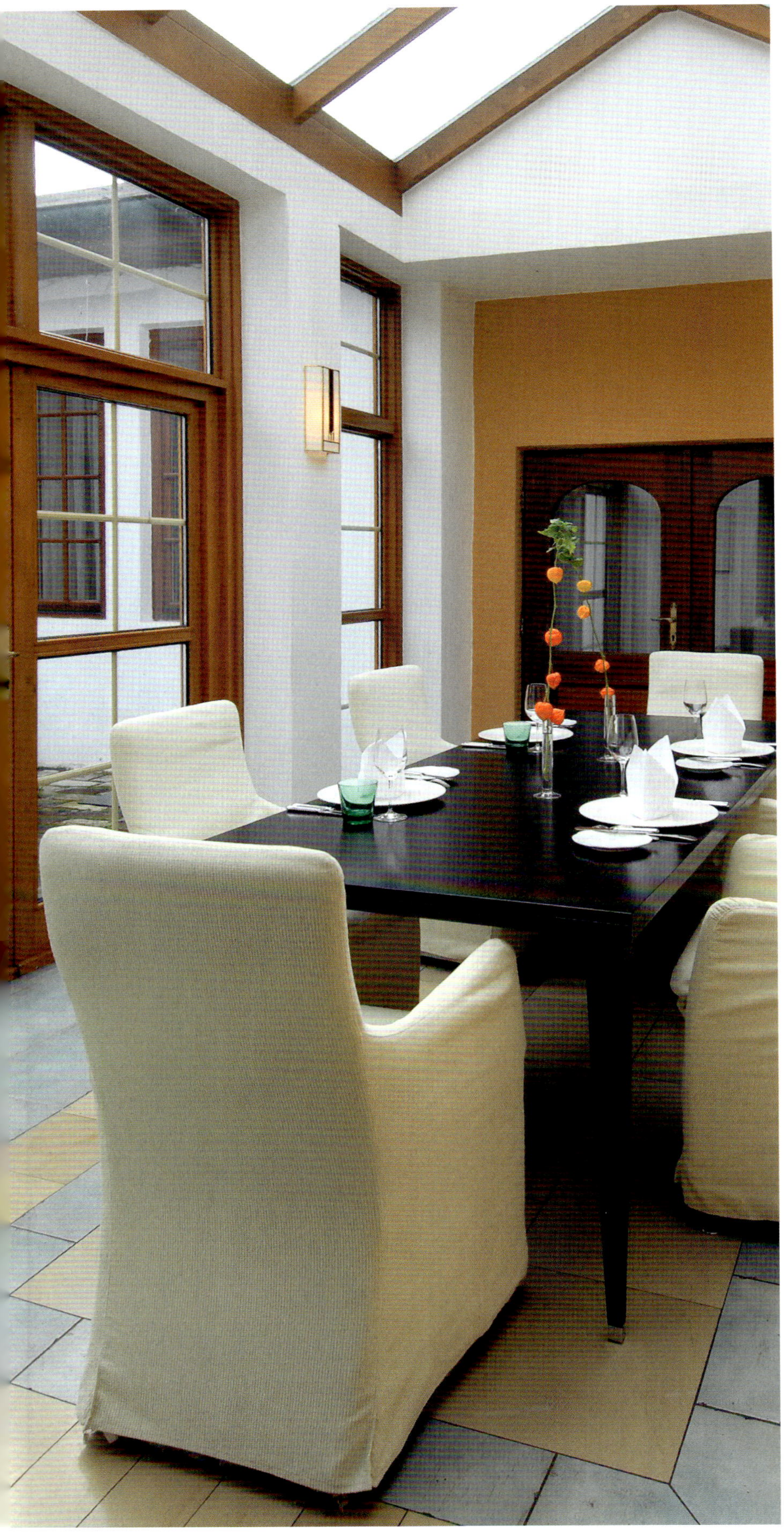

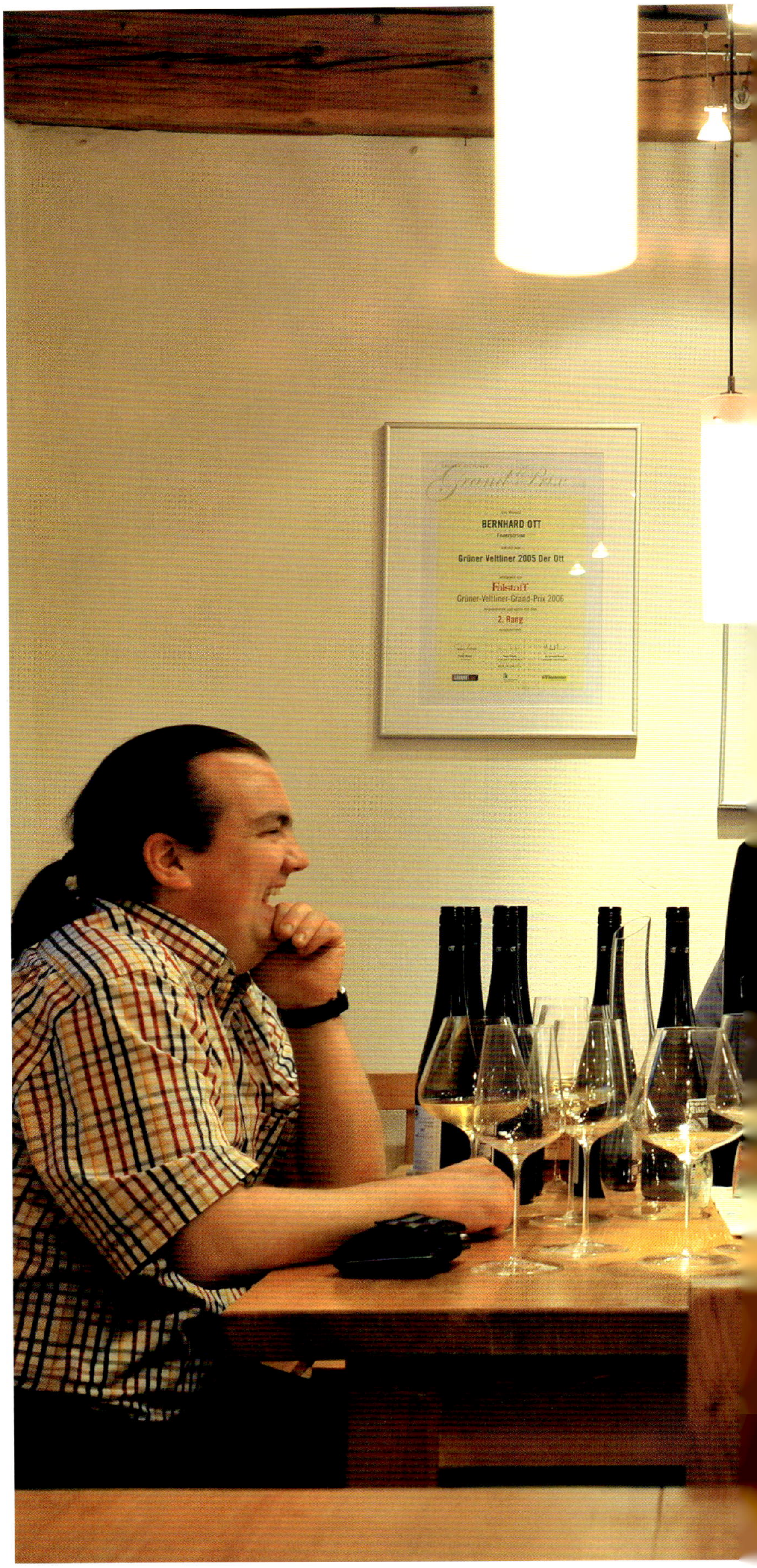
Grand Prix
BERNHARD OTT
Grüner Veltliner 2005 Der Ott
Falstaff
Grüner-Veltliner-Grand-Prix 2006
2. Rang

131

Menü
Zur Traube

„ Der feurige **Kren** bringt die **Kalbszunge** zum Lodern. Einen kühlen Kopf bewahrt dagegen das zarte, fein marinierte **Wurzelwerk**. "

„Dreierlei knackiges **Gemüse** konkurriert um das Wohlwollen üppiger **Meeresfrüchte**."

„ Samtweiche **Kastanien** in Begleitung fruchtig-knuspriger **Speckpflaumen**. "

„ Noch grün hinter den Ohren bereiten **Pappardelle** und **Kohlrabi** dem **Wildsaibling** ein sanftes Bett. "

„Leicht beschwipste Kalbsvögerl genießen ihr erfrischendes Bad in pikant-scharfem Kapernsud."

„Das würzige **Kraut** macht aus seiner Begegnung mit dem schmucken **Entlein** ein wahres Fest."

„Cremig gefüllte **Palatschinken** brauchen für ihre Darbietung lediglich ein paar wilde **Früchtchen**."

Villa Katharina

GENIESSERHERBERGE UND GASTLICHKEIT

Wo Mörwald seinen Besuchern ein feines Hotel mit dörflicher Gastfreundlichkeit bietet.

Die Villa Katharina ist ein echtes Genießerhotel und befindet sich direkt gegenüber dem Mörwald-Stammhaus Zur Traube in Feuersbrunn. Damit ist diese Feinschmeckerherberge ein strategisch ungemein günstig gelegener Ausgangspunkt für viele kulinarische Touren. Die erste Adresse ist natürlich die nahe gelegene Traube mit sämtlichen Einrichtungen – von den rustikalen Stuben des Landgasthauses bis zum edlen Feinschmeckerbereich Toni M. – einem vom Ambiente her modern und außergewöhnlich gestalteten Restaurant im Restaurant.

Die Villa Katharina ist aber auch ein idealer Ort, um von hier aus die gesamte Weinbauregion Wagram zu erkunden – mit den romantischen Kellergassen und zahlreichen Spitzenwinzern, deren Weine in jüngster Zeit für viel Anerkennung gesorgt haben. Nicht zuletzt auch deshalb hat Toni Mörwald jedes der zehn Zimmer nach einer speziellen Rebsorte benannt, Rebsorten die in dieser Region eine tragende Rolle spielen: vom Grünen Veltliner über Riesling bis zum Chardonnay.

Feuersbrunn liegt aber auch nahe der berühmten Wachau, weshalb viele der Gäste die Gelegenheit nutzen, von hier aus die einzigartige Kulturlandschaft an der Donau aufzusuchen. Die Wachau ist nicht nur UNESCO-Weltkulturerbe, sondern gehört zu den schönsten und faszinierendsten Gegenden Österreichs. Sie ist reich an kulinarischen Hotspots mit vielen Spitzenrestaurants, aber auch an Winzern von internationalem Ruf. Viele der Wachauer Weinmacher sind weltberühmt, nicht wenige davon sind mit Toni Mörwald persönlich befreundet, der deshalb für seine Gäste auch immer wieder Exkursionen unter dem Motto »Wagram trifft Wachau« organisiert.

Wer ein Genusswochenende in der Villa Katharina bucht, wird in Sachen Kulinarik und Wein in jedem Fall auf seine Kosten kommen. Die Liste der Aktivitäten dabei ist lang und beginnt meist mit Morgensport in Feuersbrunn: Joggen durch eine der Kellergassen und über den Weinberg. Anschließend wird ein Feinschmeckerfrühstück in der Traube mit Riesling-Sekt und guten Würsten serviert. Tagsüber können die Gäste auf Wunsch Weingärten besichtigen und Winzer besuchen, zu Mittag steht ein ausgiebiges Essen im Gasthaus mit bodenständiger Landhausküche auf dem Programm.

Und schließlich wartet Toni Mörwald am Abend noch mit einem Überraschungsmenü »Cuisine Freestyle« im Korab-Speisezimmer der Traube auf. Der Ausklang findet dann meist in der Vinothek bei Kerzenlicht statt – mit erlesenen Weinen, versteht sich.

Toni M.

GOURMETOASE UND STERNETEMPEL

Wo Mörwald ein Restaurant im Restaurant betreibt und dafür Jahr für Jahr höchste Auszeichnungen erhält.

Salat von wilden Karotten, Sellerie und Limousinrinderfilet. Eierspeise mit schwarzen Trüffeln. Kraftsuppe vom Fasan mit Gansl-Ravioli. Rieslingsbeuschel vom Kalb mit Wachtelei. Brüstchen von der Wildente mit Wildschweinbraten auf zarten Belugalinsen mit Wurzelspeckwürfel. Soufflé von Kastanien und Walnüssen mit Schaffenburger-Schokolade auf Eiswein-Sabayon.

Das sind nur einige Gerichte, die typisch sind für das Restaurant Toni M. in Feuersbrunn. Toni M. steht für eine gänzlich eigenständige Küchenlinie, für kulinarische Genüsse auf allerhöchstem Niveau. Wer im eleganten Toni M. diniert, der kann davon ausgehen, dass jedes einzelne Gericht vom Meister höchstpersönlich kreiert und auf Qualität überprüft wurde. Schon allein durch das architektonisch außergewöhnliche Ambiente hebt sich dieser Raum deutlich ab. Ein elegantes und zeitgemäßes Luxusrestaurant inmitten eines Landgasthauses, ein Restaurant im Restaurant. Das ist das Konzept – ungewöhnlich, aber erfolgreich. Dafür wird Toni Mörwald seit Jahren von der Gourmetkritik mit höchsten Auszeichnungen bedacht.

Für sein Toni M. hat Mörwald eine eigene Fusionsküche entwickelt, ein Begriff, der aber auch missverstanden werden könnte. Denn hier geht es nicht darum, verschiedenste Küchenstile aus allen Ecken der Welt nach Tageslaune zu kombinieren. Ganz im Gegenteil: Mörwald bewegt sich ausschließlich im Kanon der österreichischen Kochkultur und fusioniert die Grundidee der großen Klassik mit einer modernen Zubereitungsphilosophie. Ihm geht es dabei vor allem um Leichtigkeit, Raffinesse und Eleganz, um einen modernen Kochstil, basierend auf regionalen Grundprodukten von erlesener Qualität.

Es gehört zu den herausragenden Eigenschaften Toni Mörwalds, immer wieder neue Lieferanten regionaler Delikatessen aufzustöbern. Es sind Idealisten wie etwa Alexander Quester mit seinem Mariazeller Wildsaibling oder der niederösterreichische Käsespezialist Robert Paget. Schnecken bezieht Mörwald von Züchtern südlich von Wien und sogar seine Teigwaren wie Spaghetti oder Tagliolini stammen nicht mehr nur aus Italien, sondern von einem Produzenten aus dem Waldviertel.

Für seine Lieferanten ist Mörwald mehr als nur ein gewichtiger Geschäftspartner. Indem er regionale Spezialitäten in seinem Restaurant Toni M. zu deliziösen Gerichten verarbeitet, bringt er die Namen und Produkte der Erzeuger in aller Munde – im wahrsten Sinne des Wortes.

Menü
Toni M.

"Graziöse **Froschschenkel** genießen umgeben von jungem **Gemüse** die Frische von **Kren** und **Zitrone**."

„ Umgeben von berauschenden **Schnecken** räkelt sich das edle **Ei**. "

„ Frischer **Hummer**

vergnügt sich mit knusprigen

Erdäpfeln und zartem **Blattspinat**. "

„ Schüchterne

Kalbsnierchen

bringen zum Schäferstündchen mit den

Eierschwammerln

knackige Verstärkung mit. "

„ Bodenständiges **Schwein** trifft auf maritimen **Kaisergranat**. Eng aneinandergeschmiegt ergründen sie ihre Harmonie. "

„Gemeinsam entdecken **Rauke** und **Erdapfel** ihre Vorliebe für feines **Rindsbackerl**."

„Luftig leicht beschließt das Soufflé in fruchtiger Gesellschaft das Mahl."

Kochschule

LEHRMEISTER UND MEISTERLEHRE

Wo Mörwald als
Küchenlehrmeister
interessierte Hobbyköche
eine kulinarische
Meisterlehre
absolvieren lässt.

Landgasthaus Zur Taube in Feuersbrunn: Der Hausherr Toni Mörwald erscheint pünktlich um 17 Uhr. Eine Gruppe von knapp zehn Leuten wartet bereits gespannt auf den prominenten Küchenchef. Wie nahezu jeden Mittwoch um diese Zeit treffen hier einander Hobbyköche, um herauszufinden, wie man Suppen macht, einen Wildfond ansetzt, Saucen montiert, Fische filetiert oder Wachteln und Hühner zerteilt – all das zeigt Mörwald bei seinen regelmäßigen Kochseminaren. In der Traube steht dort eigens zu diesem Zweck eine ultramoderne Hochglanzküche bereit. Mörwald: »Wir haben hier alles, was wir brauchen, da kann sich jeder nach Herzenslust austoben.«

Kochschulen wie diese stehen hoch im Kurs. Die Nachfrage ist enorm. Ob Frauen, Männer, Studenten, Bankangestellte, Manager oder Wirtschaftsbosse aus der Chefetage, sie alle brutzeln und schmoren, was die Töpfe hergeben, und buchen inzwischen Kochkurse so selbstverständlich wie ein Wochenende in einem Wellnesshotel.

Toni Mörwald ist auf diesem Gebiet in Österreich führend. Er hält mit Abstand die meisten Seminare ab, seit über 20 Jahren hat er jede Woche ein anderes Thema im Angebot. Das breit gefächerte Spektrum reicht von der *Mittelmeerküche* bis zur typischen *Wiener Küche,* ein anderes Mal geht es um *Salzwasserfische und Krustentiere,* um die *Cuisine Naturelle* oder um das *Biolandhendl gekocht, gebraten, gefüllt und am Punkt gegart*.

Diesmal steht *Sushi und Japan Cuisine* auf dem Programm. Bevor es ans Eingemachte geht, binden sich alle erwartungsvoll die Küchenschürzen um und nippen leicht nervös am Champagnerglas. Prost, es kann losgehen.

Das erste Gericht lautet *Thuna-Sushi mit Chili-Sauce und grünem Pfeffer,* Mörwald zeigt jeden einzelnen Schritt: Wie ein Fisch richtig geschnitten, eine Chilisauce zubereitet und der richtige Reis gemacht wird. Anschließend präsentiert er den Biolachs für ein *Wildlachs-Sashimi in Wasabi*. Das prachtvolle Flossentier wird von allen Seiten bestaunt und gleich hernach filetiert.

Mörwalds Kochkurse sind ein Renner. Manche Teilnehmer buchen immer wieder einen Kurs, manche haben schon 20 oder 30 Seminare besucht. »Wichtig ist für mich«, sagt Mörwald, »dass die Leute Spaß am Kochen haben und Techniken lernen, mit denen sie spielerisch umgehen können.«

Mit mehreren Tausend Kursen ist die Mörwaldsche Kochschule wohl das renommierteste Institut im Vermitteln von Basiswissen und Tipps und Tricks, die das Hantieren am Herd für Hobbyköche leichter machen und bei den Teilnehmern eine neue Kochlust entstehen lassen.

Sämtliche Gerichte werden im Anschluss an die Kurse von den Teilnehmern an Ort und Stelle verspeist, Mörwald serviert dazu die passenden Weine. Und schließlich erhält jeder der Kocheleven eine Rezeptmappe, eine Schürze und eine Urkunde für zu Hause – eine Auszeichnung, die inzwischen unter Hobbyköchen fast schon so begehrt ist wie Hauben und Sterne unter den professionellen Herdvirtuosen.

Menü
Kochschule

„ Pikantes Rendezvous von nobel-blassen **Zitronennudeln** und herb dunklem **Ossietrakaviar** gebettet auf köstlichem **Rahm**. "

„Scharf gebratenes **Maishendl** sucht Erfrischung im **Ribiselessig**. Cremige Begleitung erhält das Hendl durch das anschmiegsame **Risotto**."

„Die heißen **Apfelröster** bringen das **Eis** zwischen **Sauerrahm** und luftiger **Buchtel** zum Schmelzen."

Weinbau Mörwald

WINZERTRADITION UND WEINREGION

Wo Mörwalds Familie
erlesene Weine
nach traditionellen
Methoden keltert.

Der Wagram ist eine Weinbauregion, in der sich die Menschen eine gewisse Gelassenheit bewahrt haben. Nichts fürchten sie mehr als einen Tourismus, der ihnen ihre Identität rauben könnte. Und so ist die Beschaulichkeit dieser bezaubernden Gegend bis heute erhalten geblieben. Klimatisch begünstigt gedeihen hier großartige Weine, die international vielleicht noch nicht so bekannt sind wie jene der nahe gelegenen Wachau. Doch auf den mächtigen nach Süden abfallenden Lösslagen entstehen inzwischen einige der besten Grünen Veltliner des Landes.

Der Weinbau hat hier jahrhundertelange Tradition, viele der uralten Kellerhäuser sind noch heute erhalten. In dieser sympathischen Region betreibt auch die Familie Mörwald seit Generationen Weinbau, genauer gesagt seit 1860. Heute wird das Weingut von Bruder Erhard und seiner Frau Angelika geführt. Der Familienbetrieb verfügt über 14 Hektar Weingärten und eine 40 Hektar große Landwirtschaft, in der auch der Obstbau für die zahlreichen Edelbrände des Hauses seinen Standort hat.

Das önologische Angebot der Mörwalds ist alles andere als klein: Für die Weißweine stehen die Rebsorten Grüner Veltliner, Frühroter Veltliner, Sauvignon blanc, Weißburgunder, Riesling und Gelber Muskateller zur Verfügung, für die Rotweine sind es Blauer Zweigelt, Cabernet Sauvignon, Merlot und Blauburgunder.

Tonis Bruder Erhard Mörwald ist ein feinsinniger Weinmacher mit viel Gespür für die richtige Mischung aus traditionellen Methoden und moderner Kellertechnik. Sämtlichen Weinen ist deshalb eine ganz spezielle Charakteristik eigen.

Die Weine des Wagram sind wie alle Weine stark von den geologischen Gegebenheiten geprägt. Vor allem der Grüne Veltliner gedeiht auf den tiefen Lössböden des Wagram prächtig, zu den regionalen Spezialitäten zählt aber auch der Rote Veltliner. Riesling hingegen wächst auf den höher gelegenen schotterigen Böden, was wiederum die Aromenbildung der Trauben positiv beeinflusst. Nicht zuletzt ist der Wagram aber auch für Rotweine von besonders feingliedriger Textur bekannt.

Neben den Weinen bietet das Haus Mörwald auch eine Vielzahl an Edelbränden und Hausschnäpsen an. Das Sortiment ist riesig und reicht von Marille über Williamsbirne, Apfel und Vogelbeere bis zu Himbeere und Edelkirsche. Einige der hochwertigen Destillate wurden immer wieder mit einschlägigen Preisen ausgezeichnet, so etwa der herausragende Veltlinerbrand im Holzfass.

Und weil bei den Mörwalds in allen Bereichen neben der Innovation auch die Tradition nicht zu kurz kommt, vergisst Erhard Mörwald nicht seine guten alten Hausschnäpse. Denn sollte es etwa den legendären Nussschnaps – egal ob als Edelbrand oder Likör – plötzlich nicht mehr geben, würden viele Stammgäste der Mörwalds sofort einen Aufstand organisieren.

Schloss Grafenegg

FÜRSTLICHE IDYLLE UND KUNSTGENUSS

Wo Mörwald ein
edles Schlossrestaurant
für Besucher eines
internationalen
Musikfestivals betreibt.

Es war eine Königsidee eines Fürsten. Als Fürst Franz Albrecht Metternich Sandor Anfang der 1990er-Jahre einen erfahrenen Spitzengastronom für sein Schlossrestaurant Grafenegg in Niederösterreich gewinnen wollte und bei Toni Mörwald anfragte, lehnte dieser zunächst ab. Doch die anfängliche Skepsis wich schon bald einer wachsenden Begeisterung für ein letztlich doch außerordentlich reizvoll erscheinendes Abenteuer. Schließlich ist Schloss Grafenegg in Niederösterreich alles andere als ein beliebiger Ort. Was der Fürst zu bieten hatte, erschien bei genauerer Betrachtung durchaus eindrucksvoll: ein großer, weitläufiger Park. Im Hintergrund ein prachtvolles Schloss, dass ein wenig an ein französisches Château erinnert. Gegenüber ein elegantes Restaurant mit einem wunderbaren Garten. Ein faszinierendes Kleinod mitten in Niederösterreich. Ein derartiges Ensemble findet man für gewöhnlich nur in Frankreich, dort sind solche Plätze, die auch gastronomisch genutzt werden, keine Seltenheit.

Fazit: Mörwald sagte zu. Heute ist Schloss Grafenegg aber nicht nur ein Treffpunkt für anspruchsvolle Gourmets, inzwischen bietet der Ort seinen Besuchern auch ein über die Grenzen hinaus berühmtes Musikfestival. So befindet sich gleich neben Mörwalds Schlosstaverne der technisch hochmoderne Konzertsaal »Auditorium« sowie schräg gegenüber die futuristische Open-Air-Bühne »Wolkenturm«. Jedes Jahr treten dort renommierte Ensembles und weltberühmte Solisten auf. Das internationale Musikfestival Grafenegg ist in kürzester Zeit zu einem hochkarätig besetzten und innovativen Kulturevent geworden.

Ein Restaurant an einem solchen Ort bietet damit einen außergewöhnlichen Rahmen. Die Schlosstaverne mit ihrem aristokratischen Charme ist aber auch noch in anderer Hinsicht bemerkenswert. Toni Mörwalds Team, unter der Leitung des Küchenchefs Thomas Törpel, bietet hier eine geradlinige und schnörkellose Regionalküche, für die ausnahmslos österreichische Grundprodukte verwendet werden: kein Atlantik-Steinbutt sondern Mariazeller Wildsaibling, kein argentinisches Beef sondern Waldviertler Limousinrind, selbst der Kaviar stammt von einem Salzburger Störzüchter statt aus Russland oder dem Iran.

Von der Gourmetkritik wurde diese strenge Küchenlinie stets gewürdigt und so erhielt die Schlosstaverne in Grafenegg auch 2009 wieder eine Haube im Gault Millau und 80 von 100 Punkten im österreichischen Falstaff-Restaurantguide.

Inzwischen ist auch ein Hotel mit modern und komfortabel gestalteten Zimmern hinzugekommen, wodurch für Konzertbesucher und Restaurantgäste die Möglichkeit besteht, den Aufenthalt über ein ganzes Wochenende auszudehnen. Und wer das Glück hat, bei schönem Wetter in Grafenegg zu verweilen, der kann auch noch ein Picknick im Freien buchen – mitten im gepflegten Schlosspark mit kulinarischen Spezialitäten und einer Kulisse, die er so schnell nicht vergessen wird.

Schloss Grafenegg, das ist eine unvergleichliche Symbiose aus Kunst und Kulinarik – und wie man sieht, eine echte Königsidee eines Fürsten.

„ Sämig-sahnige **Kutteln** finden ihre Vollendung in knusprig ausgebackenen **Flusskrebserln**. "

„Zander und Lachsforelle treffen sich auf cremigem Petersilpüree, um ihre Vollendung in heißer Beurre blanc zu finden."

„ Zart-rosa

Kalbsleber

hat ihren großen Auftritt vor jubelnden

Erdäpfeln

und **Eierschwammerln**.

Im Background wird sie von knackigen

Kirschen

begleitet. "

Die Trüffel lässt sich von allerlei Getier hofieren: **Wachteln** und **Gänseleber** verhelfen ihr zur Krönung.

„ Schicht für Schicht gerät der Genießer in Verzückung. Die mürb-cremige

Torte Metternich

ist leichtes Vergnügen und üppige Sünde gleichermaßen. "

m.kunst.genuss

KULINARIK UND KUNST

Wie Mörwald
mit seiner m.-Linie
Museumsgäste und Radiomitarbeiter
mit einer schnellen und
zeitgemäßen Küche versorgt.

Mit seinen Hauben- und Sternerestaurants Zur Traube, Schloss Grafenegg und Kloster Und bedient Toni Mörwald vorwiegend eine Feinschmeckerklientel mit hohem kulinarischem Anspruch.

Genießen lässt sich's aber nicht nur in feinen Gourmettempeln. Es muss ja auch nicht jeden Tag Hummer und Kaviar sein. Deshalb hat Mörwald die schlanke m.-Linie konzipiert. Dabei geht es um Betriebe, die der Nachfrage nach einer schnellen, preiswerten aber dennoch hoch qualitativen Küche gerecht werden.

Das Café-Restaurant in der Kunsthalle Krems entspricht voll und ganz diesem Konzept. Im m.kunst.genuss wird unter der Ägide von Michael Mayr weit mehr geboten, als man von einer reinen Kantine in einem Museum erwarten würde. So harmoniert etwa das Ambiente ideal mit der Architektur des Museums, aber auch in kulinarischer Hinsicht wird den Ausstellungsbesuchern eine perfekt auf ihre Bedürfnisse abgestimmte Küche geboten. Frühstück, Snacks, preisgünstige Menüs und eine Vielzahl an mediterranen Gerichten sowie Kaffee und Mehlspeisen umfasst das breit gefächerte Angebot – und das alles auf einem hohen Qualitätsniveau.

Mit seiner Betriebsküche m.hitradio.genuss verwöhnte Mörwald von 2003–2008 auch das Team von »Ö3« – Österreichs bekanntestem Radiosender. Dazu war es ebenfalls notwendig, in kulinarischer Hinsicht innovative Wege zu gehen. Denn bei einem Lokal im Haus eines Radiosenders geht es noch viel mehr um Tempo, Kreativität und gastronomische Innovation. Mörwald sagt dazu: »Was manche Airlines beim Bordservice geschafft haben, wollten wir im Bereich der Betriebsküchen erreichen. Das ist ein gastronomisch noch völlig unterschätztes Gebiet.«

Der dritte Betrieb der m.-Linie ist der bodenständigste: das Gasthaus m.wirts.haus im Stammhaus in Feuersbrunn. Mörwald will hier dokumentieren, dass eine traditionelle Wirtshausküche mit regionalen Produkten gleichzeitig auch nach zeitgemäßen Kriterien vermarktet werden kann. So wird dem Gast eine ländliche Küche mit regionalen Spitzenprodukten geboten, die preiswert ist, aber auch im Fall des Falles schnell zubereitet und serviert werden kann.

Wer hingegen viel Zeit mitbringt, der kann sich ganz bedächtig der behaglichen Landgasthaus-Atmosphäre hingeben und jedes Gericht nach Herzenslust genießen.

Menü
m.kunst.genuss

„Sanft vom Frühlingsboten **Bärlauch** aromatisiert schwelgen die Tascherln in lockerleichter **Kerbelsabayon**."

> Mürb geworden lässt der **Gamspfeffer** sich auf ein Stelldichein mit der grazilen **Pasta** und ihren leidenschaftlichen **Pilzen** ein.

243

Persönlich

TELEFONIEREN UND KOCHEN

Wie es Toni Mörwald schafft,
als Spitzenkoch und Manager
eines Kulinarik-Imperiums Kraft zu tanken,
um nach den Sternen zu greifen.

Toni Mörwalds Lieblingsbeschäftigung ist das Telefonieren. Kaum ein Zeitpunkt, an dem er nicht mit einem Handy am Ohr gesichtet wird. Doch bloß mit einem Mobiltelefon zu hantieren genügt ihm in den meisten Fällen nicht. Oft genug hat er auch noch ein weiteres am anderen Ohr und telefoniert mit zwei Leuten gleichzeitig. Mörwald ist ein Meister im Synchrontelefonieren und hat in dieser Disziplin im Laufe der Zeit ein hohes Maß an Virtuosität entwickelt. Sein Motto lautet: Was du nicht sofort erledigen kannst, geschieht meistens nie. Also kommt mindestens ein Telefon fast permanent zum Einsatz, nicht selten sind es gleich zwei.

Ähnlich kompromisslos ist Mörwald beim Autofahren. Um sein weitverzweigtes Genuss-Imperium mit mehreren Restaurants und Lokalen in Niederösterreich und Wien sowie einer Kochschule und einem Cateringbetrieb am Laufen zu halten, muss er gezwungenermaßen eine enorme Zeit in einem seiner Autos verbringen. Bis zu 500 Kilometer legt er an manchen Tagen zurück und es liegt die Vermutung nahe, dass er auch während der Fahrt die Segnungen des Mobilfunks nutzt.

Von bedächtiger Fahrweise hält er wenig. Wer mit Toni Mörwald im Auto fährt, wird den Eindruck nicht los, dass es sich hierbei mehr um fliegen denn um fahren handelt. Die Zeitspanne zwischen Start und Landung sucht Mörwald jedenfalls so kurz wie möglich zu halten, in solchen Momenten wird aus dem feinsinnigen Sternekoch ein unerschrockener Pilot und aus seinem Gefährt ein Kampfjet an der Grenze zur Überschallgeschwindigkeit.

Doch für Toni Mörwald ist das alles ganz normal. Er ist eben kein Zauderer, keiner, der halbe Sachen macht. Mörwald ist ein Schneller, ein Energiebündel, wie es nur wenige gibt. Doch wie hält sich so jemand permanent auf Trab, wie tankt er Kraft und wie gelingt es ihm, den enormen Stress auszugleichen?

Eine der Hauptenergiequellen ist wohl seine Familie. Seine Frau Eva und seine drei Töchter Antonia, Johanna und Theresia sind für Toni Mörwald der Lebensmittelpunkt. »Ein intaktes Familienleben ist für mich wichtiger als alles andere«, sagt Mörwald, »das ist die Erdung, die ich brauche, meine innere Mitte.«

Kraft tankt Mörwald aber auch im Beruf selbst. Es mag zunächst absurd anmuten, dass gerade einer, der ständig von Termin zu Termin hetzt, seinen Gästen immer wieder predigt: »Nehmt euch Zeit zum Genießen, denn Essenszeit ist die beste Lebenszeit.« Doch gerade in diesem scheinbaren Widerspruch liegt das Phänomen Mörwald. Das permanente Verwirklichen von Ideen schafft immer wieder neue Motivation – und das in einer Branche, in der Genuss die wichtigste Ware ist. Und so verschwimmen bei Toni Mörwald die Grenzen zwischen Beruf und Privatem. Selbst an Tagen, an denen es besonders hektisch zugeht, kann es vorkommen, dass er sich Zeit für ein ausgiebiges Mittagessen nimmt – aus beruflichen wie aus privaten Gründen. Auch in seinen eigenen vier Wänden in der Nähe von Feuersbrunn zelebriert er jenen Lebensstil, den er so erfolgreich vermarktet. In seinem Haus genießt er es, im Kreise seiner Familie mit Freunden Feste zu feiern. An diesem Ort entstehen aber auch regelmäßig Aufnahmen für diverse Fernsehsendungen. Toni Mörwald ist ein Genussmensch durch und durch. Im Unterschied zu vielen anderen ringt er sich aber das Genießen nicht mühsam ab, sondern lebt davon – als Manager, als Koch und als Privatmensch.

Rezepte
Alle Rezepte im Detail

Rezeptverzeichnis

KLOSTER UND

262_Gebackene Topfen-Kräuter-Bällchen

262_Baliklachs mit Buttermilchmousse,
Blini und grünem Kaviar vom Fliegenfisch

263_Perlhendlroulade
mit Selleriecreme und Erdäpfelbaumkuchen

264_Grüne Roulade mit Sauerrahm und Vulcanoschinken

264_Rosmarintoast
mit Paprika, Paradeisern und grünem Spargel

265_Crostini mit Gambas, Melone und Gurke

265_Geröstetes Schwarzbrot mit Jungzwiebeln und Rindermark

266_Flusskrebsterrine mit Kerbelmousse

267_Cannelloni von der Entenleber
mit Kohlrabipüreebällchen und Madeiragelee

268_Roh mariniertes Kalb mit Gemüsepraline und Friséesalat

269_Tatar vom Waldviertler Limousinrind
in gelierter Rindskraftsuppe mit Wasabimousse

270_Hummerschaumsuppe mit Erbsensoufflé und Ossietrakaviar

271_Kitz-Paradeis-Essenz mit Paradeisroulade

272_Consommé vom Waldviertler Fleckvieh mit Milzschnitten

273_Flusskrebsravioli mit Wachtelei und Eierschwammerl

273_Ei »Wiener Art«
mit Spinat, Wurzelspeck und Wiesenchampignons

274_Brokkolitortellini mit Paradeis-Estragon-Butter

274_Erbsengnocchi mit pochiertem Ei und weißem Trüffel

275_Ausgelöste Miesmuscheln in Weißwein mit Safran und Gnocchi

276_St- Jacques à la St. Germain

277_Medaillons vom Waller mit Dijonlinsen und Riojabutter

278_St. Pierre mit Paradeisartischocken und Basilikumzwiebeln

279_Schnitte vom Steinbutt
mit Kürbisgnocchi, Sommertrüffel und Zimt

280_Wolfsbarsch im Ganzen in der Salzkruste

281_Kalbsbries
mit Erdäpfelnudeln, Wiesenchampignons und Kerbel

282_Taubengalantine mit Apfelchutney und Wagramer Dirndln

283_Schwarzfederhuhn
in Oliven-Paradeis-Kruste und Piniencouscous

284_Kalbslungenbraten im Brotteig mit geschmorten Artischocken

285_Kalbskotelett
auf feinen Nudeln mit schwarzen Oliven und Junglauch

286_Spanferkel mit Waldviertler Kümmel,
Haxlravioli und geschmortem Spitzkraut

287_Kalbskrone mit Kalbsbriesravioli,
Petersilwurzelcreme und Petersilbutter

288_Milchlammschlögel
mit geschmortem Mangold und Erdäpfelkuchen

289_Rosa Beiried vom Milchstier
mit Spargel, Erdäpfelcrêpe und Sauce béarnaise

290_Attergauer Rindsfilet mit Sellerie und gebratener Gänseleber

291_Gebackene Rehleber
mit Rote-Rüben-Carpaccio und Krenvinaigrette

292_Rehrücken mit Kürbiskernconfit und Grießschnitten

293_Gebackenes Kitz auf Erdäpfelsalat und Rucola

294_Hirschlungenbraten
im Baumkuchen mit Maroni-Dörrzwetschken-Gnocchi

295_Wildschweinschlögel mit Linsen-Speck-Sauce und Palfyknödeln

296_Millefeuille mit Joghurtmousse und Waldbeeren

297_Dessert von Marille, Kardamom und Mandeln

298_Schokoladenvariation mit Whiskymousse und Kaffeeparfait

300_Nougatbarren mit
Matchatee-Eis und Bananenkompott

302_Kirschentarte, Pfirsich und Pistazien

304_Schokoladenpralinen mit Nougatkrokant

304_Cheesecaketörtchen mit Ananas und Kokos

305_Macarons

305_Orangenküchlein

306_Brioche mit Vanillecreme

CATERING

307_Crevetten-Ricotta-Ravioli

308_Rieslingsbeuschel vom Kalb

309_Punschkrapferl mit Nougatkrokant

309_Schaumrollen

ZUR TRAUBE

310_Lauwarm marinierte Kalbszunge mit Wurzeln, Kren und Kernöl

310_Bohnensalat mit Langostino und Weingartenpfirsich

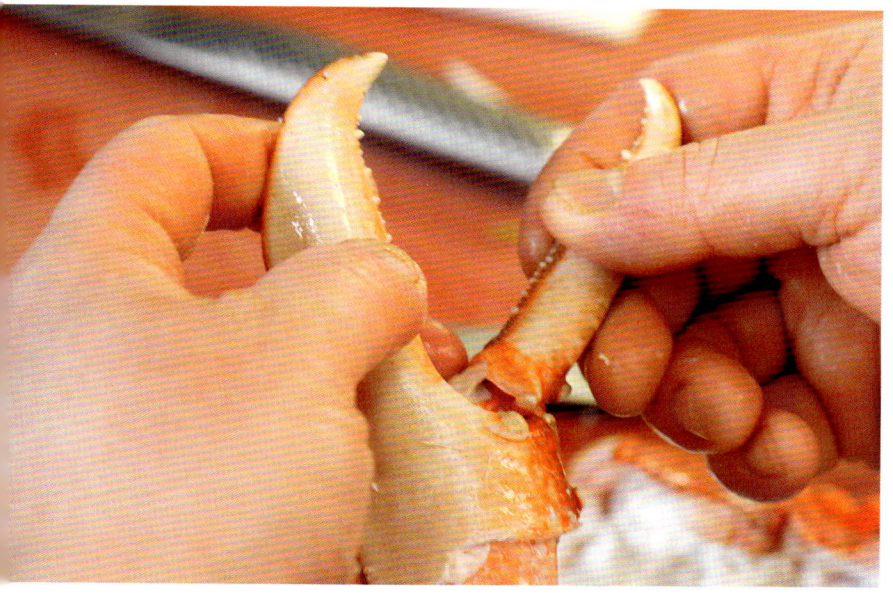

311_Kastanienvelouté mit Zwetschken in Speck

312_Mariazeller Wildsaibling
mit Petersilpappardelle und Rahmkohlrabi

313_Kalbsvögerl
in Senf-Kapern-Sauce mit Champignons und Basmatireis

314_Wildentenbrust und -keule auf süßsaurem Liebstöckelkraut

315_Soufflierte Topfenpalatschinken

TONI M.

316_Froschschenkel
mit Zitronenconfit und Velouté von geräuchertem Kren

317_Weinbergschnecken in Burgunderreduktion mit pochiertem Ei

318_Hummer mit Pomelo-Honig-Reduktion,
Blattspinat und Pommes Maxim

319_Kalbsniere
mit Frühlingsspitzkraut, Eierschwammerl und Sauce Robert

320_Schweinsbauch mit Kaisergranat und Erbsensalat

321_Rindsbackerl,
Schalotten, Kamptaler Wurzelspeck, Rucolajus und Powidl

322_Limettensoufflé mit Himbeersorbet und Amarettosabayon

KOCHSCHULE
322_Feine Zitronennudeln mit Ossietrakaviar

323_Maishendlbrust
mit Eierschwammerlrisotto und schwarzem Ribiselessig

324_Waldviertler Mohnbuchteln mit Apfelröster und Sauerrahmeis

SCHLOSS GRAFENEGG
325_Mariazeller Flusskrebserl mit Erdäpfelstroh auf Kalbskutteln

326_Zanderroulade mit Petersilpüree und Gemüse-Beurre-blanc

327_Rosa Kalbsleber
mit Essigkirschen, Eierschwammerln und Erdäpfelpüree

328_Wachtelcrépinette mit Gänselebertrüffel und kleinem Wiesensalat

329_Haustorte »Metternich«

M.KUNST.GENUSS
330_Frischkäsebärlauchtascherl mit Spargel und Kerbelsabayon

331_Gamspfeffer mit Preiselbeeren und Pilznudeln

332_Grundrezepte

Gebackene Topfen-Kräuter-Bällchen

Zutaten für circa 45 Bällchen ❙ Foto Seite 24

Topfen-Kräuter-Bällchen
45 g weiche Butter
2 Eigelb
1 Ei
125 g Semmelbrösel
400 g Topfen

70 g gehackte Kräuter (nach Geschmack, z. B. Petersil, Schnittlauch, Estragon, Kerbel)
150 g Semmelbrösel
Öl zum Ausbacken
Salz, Pfeffer, Muskat

Topfen-Kräuter-Bällchen
Die Butter schaumig schlagen, nach und nach Eigelb und Ei einrühren. Semmelbrösel und Topfen untermischen, mit den Gewürzen und Kräutern abschmecken. Bällchen von circa 15 Gramm abdrehen, in den Semmelbröseln wälzen und in heißem Fett ausbacken.

Baliklachs mit Buttermilchmousse, Blini und grünem Kaviar vom Fliegenfisch

Zutaten für circa 30 Happen ❙ Foto Seite 24

Blinis
40 g Weizenmehl
20 g Roggenmehl
50 ml lauwarme Milch
1 Ei
5 g frische Germ
1 Prise Zucker
1 Msp. Salz
2 EL Öl zum Backen

Buttermilchmousse
200 ml Buttermilch
50 g Crème fraîche
Saft von ½ Zitrone
3 Blatt Gelatine
125 ml Obers
Salz, Pfeffer, Cayennepfeffer

Anrichten
300 g geräucherter Baliklachs
30 g grüner Fliegenfischkaviar
rote Kresse zum Garnieren

Blinis
Alle Zutaten gut miteinander verrühren und bei 35 Grad circa 30 Minuten gehen lassen. Das Öl in einer beschichteten Pfanne erhitzen, den Teig ½ Zentimeter hoch hineingießen und von beiden Seiten goldgelb braten. So verfahren bis der gesamte Teig aufgebraucht ist. Abkühlen lassen und Kreise ausstechen.

Buttermilchmousse
Buttermilch und Crème fraîche miteinander verrühren, Zitronensaft beigeben und mit Salz, Cayennepfeffer und Pfeffer abschmecken. Gelatine einweichen, gut ausdrücken und kurz erhitzen bis sie flüssig wird und unter die Buttermilch rühren. Obers schlagen, unterheben und die Mousse kalt stellen.

Anrichten
Den Lachs dünn aufschneiden und die einzelnen Scheiben zwischen Klarsichtfolie plattieren. Buttermilchmousse aufspritzen und einrollen, sodass Rouladen mit gleichem Durchmesser wie die Blinis entstehen. In eine Frischhaltefolie schlagen und kalt stellen.
Vor dem Anrichten in Scheiben schneiden und auf dem Blini anrichten. Mit dem grünen Kaviar vom Fliegenfisch und der Kresse dekorieren.

Perlhendlroulade mit Selleriecreme und Erdäpfelbaumkuchen
Zutaten für circa 30 Rouladen ▮ Foto Seite 24

Erdäpfelbaumkuchen
100 g mehlige Erdäpfel
35 g weiche Butter
3 Eigelb
3 Eiweiß
10 g Zucker
20 g Mehl
50 g Maisstärke
Salz, Pfeffer, Muskat

Perlhendlroulade
150 ml Obers
150 g Hühnerfleisch
35 g Tramezzinibrot
2 Eier
25 g Petersil,
blanchiert und passiert
2 Perlhuhnbrüste
Salz, Pfeffer

Selleriecreme
½ Sellerieknolle
250 ml Obers
Salz, Pfeffer

Anrichten
Gartenkresse zum Garnieren

Erdäpfelbaumkuchen
Erdäpfel mit der Schale weich kochen, pellen und durch ein feines Sieb passieren. Die Butter schaumig schlagen und mit dem Eigelb zur Erdäpfelmasse geben, gut verrühren. Eiweiß mit Zucker zu Schnee schlagen und unter die Erdäpfelmasse heben. Mehl und Stärke vorsichtig untermischen. Den Ofen auf 180 Grad Oberhitze vorheizen. Einen Teil der Masse auf ein mit Backpapier ausgelegtes Backblech circa 1 Millimeter hoch aufstreichen und hellbraun backen. Danach eine weitere Schicht darüberstreichen, wieder hellbraun backen. Den Vorgang so lange wiederholen, bis der Teig etwa 5 Millimeter hoch ist.

Perlhendlroulade
Obers, Hühnerfleisch, Tramezzinibrot, Eier und Petersil in den Cutter geben, mit Salz und Pfeffer abschmecken und fein mixen.
Die Perlhendlbrüste zwischen Klarsichtfolie ganz dünn plattieren. Mit der Farce bestreichen, einrollen, in Klarsichtfolie einschlagen, dann mit Alufolie umwickeln und bei 75 Grad 20 Minuten pochieren.

Selleriecreme
Sellerie in gobe Würfel schneiden, circa 10 Minuten garen, mit den restlichen Zutaten in einen Cutter geben, sehr fein mixen und durch ein feines Sieb passieren. In einen Dressiersack füllen und kalt stellen.

Anrichten
Aus dem Baumkuchen etwa 30 Kreise vom Durchmesser der Roulade ausstechen, die Roulade in circa 30 Scheiben teilen, auf die Baumkuchenkreise legen, mit Selleriecreme und Kresse dekorieren.

Grüne Roulade mit Sauerrahm und Vulcanoschinken

Zutaten für circa 30 Rouladen ❙ Foto Seite 24

Sauerrahmmousse
60 g Sauerrahm
Saft und Zesten von ¼ Limette
1 Blatt Gelatine
50 ml Obers
Salz, Pfeffer

Crêpes
90 ml Milch
40 g Mehl
1 Ei
5 g Kräuter nach Geschmack, blanchiert und passiert
Öl zum Braten

Anrichten
12 Scheiben Vulcanoschinken
Kresse zum Dekorieren

Sauerrahmmousse
Sauerrahm, Limettensaft, Limettenzesten, Salz und Pfeffer in einer Schüssel gut verrühren. Die eingeweichte Gelatine gut ausdrücken und kurz erhitzen und geschmolzen mit der Sauerrahmmasse verrühren. Obers schlagen, unterheben und mit Salz und Pfeffer abschmecken.

Crêpes
Alle Zutaten zu einem glatten Teig verrühren. Etwas Öl in einer Pfanne erhitzen, wenig Teig gleichmäßig darin verteilen und beidseitig braten, insgesamt 6 Crêpes zubereiten.

Anrichten
Die Crêpes halbieren, mit etwas Sauerrahmmousse bestreichen, mit Vulcanoschinken belegen und eine weitere Schicht Mousse auftragen. Einrollen, vorsichtig in eine Klarsichtfolie einschlagen und kalt stellen. Vor dem Anrichten in feine Scheiben schneiden und mit etwas Kresse dekorieren.

Rosmarintoast mit Paprika, Paradeisern und grünem Spargel

Zutaten für 4 Personen ❙ Foto Seite 26

Rosmarintoast
1 gelbe Paprika
2 Tomaten
2 EL Olivenöl
2 Spritzer Balsamico
1 Knoblauchzehe
1 Rosmarinzweig
2 KL gehackte Petersil
4 Spitzen grüner Spargel
4 Toastbrotscheiben
1 EL Butter
Salz, Pfeffer

Rosmarintoast
Paprika und Tomaten würfeln und in Olivenöl anschwitzen, würzen, mit Balsamico ablöschen. Vom Herd nehmen, Knoblauch hineinpressen, fein gehackten Rosmarin und Petersil zugeben. Die Spargelspitzen in Salzwasser bissfest kochen. Toastbrot in Rechtecke schneiden. Butter in einer Pfanne erhitzen und das Toastbrot darin beidseitig goldbraun braten. Auf Küchenpapier abtropfen lassen.

Anrichten
Das Gemüse auf die noch warmen Brotscheiben häufen, mit den Spargelspitzen garnieren und servieren.

Crostini mit Gambas, Melone und Gurke

Zutaten für 4 Personen | Foto Seite 26

Crostini

¼ Honigmelone
½ Salatgurke
1 EL weißer Balsamico
2 EL Joghurt
4 EL Olivenöl
Saft von 1 Zitrone
4 Scheiben Toskanabrot
oder 8 Scheiben Baguette
8 Garnelen
Salz, Pfeffer, Cayennepfeffer

Anrichten

8 Minzeblätter

Crostini

Honigmelone und Gurke schälen, entkernen, in kleine Scheiben schneiden und in eine Schüssel geben. Balsamico, Joghurt, 2 Esslöffel des Olivenöls, Salz und Pfeffer dazugeben und verrühren. Mit Cayennepfeffer und Zitronensaft abschmecken und einige Minuten marinieren lassen. Die Brotscheiben in etwas Olivenöl von beiden Seiten goldbraun braten und auf einem Küchenpapier abtropfen lassen.

Garnelen schälen, Darm entfernen, salzen und pfeffern und im restlichen Olivenöl 4 Minuten beidseitig braten.

Anrichten

Auf die noch warmen Brotscheiben den Melonen-Gurken-Salat geben und mit Garnelen ausgarnieren. Minze in Streifen schneiden und darüberstreuen.

Geröstetes Schwarzbrot mit Jungzwiebeln und Rindermark

Zutaten für 4 Personen | Foto Seite 26

Schwarzbrot

2 Scheiben Schwarzbrot
60 g Rindermark
2 Jungzwiebelstangen
Maldonsalz
schwarzer Pfeffer, geschrotet

Schwarzbrot

Schwarzbrot in 4 Rechtecke schneiden und in einer Pfanne ohne Fett knusprig rösten. Rindermark in Salzwasser pochieren, kurz abschrecken und im lauwarmen Zustand in Scheiben schneiden. Jungzwiebeln putzen und in feine Ringe schneiden.

Anrichten

Schwarzbrot mit Markscheiben belegen, Zwiebelringe darüberstreuen und mit Maldonsalz und Pfeffer vollenden.

Flusskrebsterrine mit Kerbelmousse

Zutaten für 1 Terrinenform (Dreiecksform: Länge 40 Zentimeter, Breite 5 Zentimeter) | Foto Seite 28

Gelee

300 g Wurzelgemüse
2 Schalotten
2 Paradeiser
¼ l Fischfond
2 Eiweiß
1 Lorbeerblatt
5 weiße Pfefferkörner
2 Wacholderbeeren
700 ml Noilly Prat
14 Blatt Gelatine
Salz, Cayennepfeffer

Flusskrebssulz

10 große Flusskrebse
200 g Blattspinat
Kümmel, Dille, Salz

Kerbelmousse

100 g Kerbel
50 g Sauerrahm
1 ½ Blatt Gelatine
100 g Crème légère
Pernod zum Abschmecken
Salz, Cayennepfeffer

Sauerrahmmousse

Saft von 1 Zitrone
3 Blatt Gelatine
250 g Sauerrahm
200 g Crème légère
reduzierten Noilly Prat
zum Abschmecken (siehe Gelee)
Salz, Cayennepfeffer

Anrichten

gemischter Salat zum Garnieren
einige Topfen-Kräuter-Bällchen
(siehe Seite 262)

Gelee

Wurzelgemüse, Schalotten und Paradeiser faschieren, mit dem Fischfond, ¼ Liter Wasser und dem Eiweiß in einem Topf gut vermengen. Lorbeerblatt, Pfefferkörner und Wacholderbeeren dazugeben, unter geringer Hitzezufuhr langsam aufkochen lassen und anschließend auf kleinster Flamme etwa 2 Stunden ziehen lassen. Den Noilly Prat in einem Topf auf ein Viertel einreduzieren, um damit später abzuschmecken. Den noch heißen Fond durch ein Passiertuch seihen. Die Gelatine in kaltem Wasser einweichen, aus dem Wasser nehmen, ausdrücken und im Fond auflösen. Mit Salz, Cayennepfeffer und etwas reduziertem Noilly Prat abschmecken. Etwa die Hälfte der Masse beiseitestellen und warm halten (damit sie flüssig bleibt), die andere Hälfte abkühlen lassen. Ein Blech mit Klarsichtfolie möglichst glatt auslegen, es darf keine Flüssigkeit auslaufen. Die Größe des ausgelegten Blechs ist von den Maßen der Terrinenform abhängig, es sollte mindestens 50 x 50 Zentimeter groß sein, damit die Terrine zweimal ausgelegt und einmal abgedeckt werden kann. Die abgekühlte Masse circa 3 Millimeter hoch auf das Blech gießen und im Kühlschrank kalt stellen.

Flusskrebssulz

Flusskrebse in kochendem Wasser mit Salz, etwas Kümmel und Dille kochen. Die Schwänze und die Scheren der Flusskrebse ausbrechen und getrennt voneinander aufbewahren.

Die Flusskrebsschwänze etwas abtrocknen und in einer dreieckigen Terrinenform (sie sollte kleiner sein als die spätere Form) legen. Von der beiseitegestellten, warm gehaltenen Geleemasse 2–3 Esslöffel weiterhin warm halten, den Rest etwas abkühlen lassen und die Krebsschwänze in der Form gerade damit bedecken und gut durchkühlen lassen.

Den Blattspinat putzen, gut waschen, in kochendem Salzwasser blanchieren und in Eiswasser abschrecken.

Einige Blätter beiseitelegen, die restlichen Blätter dachziegelartig auf ein Tuch geben, sodass eine dichte Spinatmatte entsteht. Diese mit einem Tuch trocken tupfen und anschließend mit der beiseitegestellten restlichen Geleemasse bepinseln.

Die bereits gestockte dreieckige Flusskrebssulz aus der Form nehmen, in die getrocknete Spinat-Gelee-Matte einwickeln, in Klarsichtfolie schlagen und erneut kalt stellen.

Kerbelmousse

Den Kerbel klein schneiden und mit dem Sauerrahm fein pürieren (wenn nötig, etwas Wasser beigeben) und durch ein feines Sieb streichen. Einen kleinen Teil (etwa 2–3 Esslöffel) erwärmen. Die Gelatine in Wasser einweichen, ausdrücken, in der warmen Masse auflösen und mit der restlichen Masse verrühren. Die Crème légère halb steif schlagen und unter die Kerbelmasse heben. Mit Salz, Cayennepfeffer und einem Schuss Pernod abschmecken.

Die noch klebrige Geleematte (vom Blech) in 3 Teile schneiden: 2 gleich große Stücke, um die Terrine auszukleiden, und 1 Stück, um die Form abschließend zu bedecken.

Die Kerbelmousse dünn und gleichmäßig auf eines der beiden gleich großen Stücke streichen und anstocken lassen. (Falls nicht die ganze Mousse benötigt wird, kann man später zum Anrichten einige Nocken ausstechen.) Die beiseitegelegten Spinatblätter darauf verteilen und die zweite Geleematte darauflegen.

Sauerrahmmousse

Den Zitronensaft erwärmen und die in kaltem Wasser eingeweichte und ausgedrückte Gelatine darin auflösen. Den Sauerrahm glatt rühren und zügig mit der Gelatine vermengen. Die Crème légère halbfest schlagen und unter den Sauerrahm heben. Mit Salz, Cayennepfeffer und reduziertem Noilly Prat abschmecken.

Terrine fertigstellen

Eine passende Terrinenform mit Öl ausstreichen. Die mit Kerbelmousse bestrichene Geleeplatte vorsichtig auf eine Klarsichtfolie geben und mit der Folie nach unten in die Form einlegen. Die Form in einen Behälter mit Eiswasser stellen. Die Hälfte der Sauerrahmmousse einfüllen. Die Krebssulz im Spinatmantel in die Mousse drücken. Mit der restlichen Sauerrahmmousse auffüllen und mit dem letzten Stück Gelee bedecken. Die Terrine gut durchkühlen lassen.

Anrichten

Die Terrine aus der Form nehmen, die Folie entfernen und die Flusskrebsterrine in 2 Zentimeter breite Stücke schneiden.
Etwas Salat auf den Tellern verteilen, eventuell Kerbelmoussenocken, die Terrinenstücke, Topfen-Kräuter-Bällchen und die Krebsscheren ansetzen.

Cannelloni von der Entenleber mit Kohlrabipüreebällchen und Madeiragelee

Zutaten für 4 Personen ▎ Foto Seite 30

Entenleberparfait
600 g Entenleber
ca. 1 l Milch
10 g Pökelsalz
12 g Fleur de Sel
3 KL reduzierter weißer Portwein
1 KL reduzierter Noilly Prat
1 KL reduzierter Madeira
2 cl Cognac
300 g grüner Speck
(Pastetenspeck)
Pfeffer

Kohlrabipüreebällchen
125 ml Noilly Prat
1 Kohlrabi
70 ml Obers
1 Blatt Gelatine
1 Ei
2 EL Mehl
1 Scheibe Tramezzinibrot
Öl zum Backen
Salz, Pfeffer

Madeiragelee
300 ml Rindsconsommé
5 Blatt Gelatine
2 EL reduzierter Madeira
1 EL Trüffeljus
Salz, Pfeffer

Entenlebercannelloni
200 g des Entenleberparfaits
20 g Sommertrüffel

Entenleberparfait

Von der Entenleber die Haut entfernen, in nussgroße Stücke schneiden und die Adern auslösen. Die geputzte Leber in ein hohes Gefäß geben und mit Milch bedeckt 24 Stunden kalt stellen. Die Leber anschließend in einem hohen schmalen Gefäß mit Pökelsalz, Fleur de Sel, Pfeffer, Portwein, Noilly Prat, Madeira und Cognac gut verschlossen 24 Sunden marinieren. Eine Terrinenform (15 x 4 x 4 Zentimeter) mit Pastetenspeck auslegen und die Gänseleber mit der Marinade einfüllen, Speck darüberschlagen, abfolieren und den Terrinendeckel daraufgeben. Bei 85 Grad auf eine Kerntemperatur von 42 Grad pochieren. Das Parfait einpressen, um so das ganze Fett herauszudrücken. Anschließend 24 Stunden durchkühlen lassen.

Kohlrabipüreebällchen

Noilly Prat auf 30 Milliliter reduzieren. Kohlrabi schälen, weich kochen, fein mixen, mit Obers vermengen und mit Salz, Pfeffer und dem reduzierten Noilly Prat abschmecken. Püree durch ein feines Sieb passieren. Gelatine einweichen, auflösen und mit 60 Gramm des Pürees verrühren. Etwas stocken lassen und zu 4 gleich großen Kugeln formen. Püreekugeln nun mit Mehl, Ei und fein gewürfeltem Tramezzinibrot panieren, im Tiefkühler 10 Minuten anfrieren lassen und anschließend ausbacken.

Madeiragelee

Die Consommé erhitzen und die eingeweichte Gelatine darin auflösen. Mit Salz, Pfeffer, Madeira und Trüffeljus abschmecken, circa 1 ½ Millimeter hoch auf ein mit Folie ausgelegtes Blech gießen, gelieren lassen.

Entenlebercanneloni

Entenleberparfait mithilfe einer Klarsichtfolie zu 4 Rollen à 50 Gramm formen. Diese Rollen mit gehobeltem Trüffel belegen und in das Madeiragelee einrollen.

Anrichten

Das Kohlrabipüree mittig anrichten, Cannelloni und gebackene Kohlrabibällchen anlegen.

Roh mariniertes Kalb mit Gemüsepraline und Friséesalat

Zutaten für 10 Personen ▎ Foto Seite 32

Kalbsfilet
1 kg Kalbsfilet

Gemüsepraline
1 Kohlrabi, 1 Karotte
100 ml Obers
1–2 Blatt Gelatine
2 Eier
100 g Mehl
50 g altbackenes Toastbrot
Öl zum Ausbacken

Salat
1 Friséesalat
1 Prise Zucker
1 EL Zweigeltessig
2 EL Nussöl
Salz, Pfeffer

Kalbsfilet

Kalbsfilet von Fett und Haut befreien und in circa 10 Zentimeter lange Stränge schneiden. Die Stränge so dünn wie möglich mit einem scharfen Messer aufrollen. Gleichmäßig plattieren, eine dünne Schicht Kohlrabicreme darauf verteilen, wie eine Schnecke fest einrollen. Mit Klarsicht- und Alufolie nachdrehen und tiefkühlen.

Gemüsepraline

Kohlrabi und Karotte schälen, die Rundungen mit einer feinen Reibe wegreißen und in Wasser einlegen. Das Gemüse in 2 Millimeter große Würfel schneiden und in Salzwasser blanchieren. Das gerissene und das gewürfelte Gemüse in eine Pfanne geben, Obers zugießen, einmal aufkochen lassen und mit Salz und Pfeffer abschmecken.
Die Masse in einen Messbecher gießen, pro 100 Milliliter 1 Blatt Gelatine in kaltem Wasser einweichen und in der heißen Masse auflösen. Die Masse kalt stellen. Sobald die Masse gut geliert ist, kann man daraus kleine Kugeln formen.
Die Kugeln doppelt in Mehl und Ei panieren und einmal in circa 5 Millimeter kleinen entrindeten Toastbrotwürfeln wälzen. Vor dem Anrichten die Pralinen in heißem Fett herausbacken.

Salat

Den Friséesalat waschen und trocken schleudern. Anschließend mit Salz, Pfeffer, Zucker, Zweigeltessig und Nussöl marinieren.

Anrichten

Das angetaute Kalb mit einem scharfen Messer oder der Aufschnittmaschine dünn auf einen Teller aufschneiden. Mit Salz und Pfeffer nachwürzen. Den Salat auf dem Kalb anrichten und die gebackene Gemüsepraline daraufsetzen.

Tatar vom Waldviertler Limousinrind in gelierter Rindskraftsuppe mit Wasabimousse

Zutaten für 4 Personen | Foto Seite 34

Tatar in Rindskraftsuppe

¼ l Rindskraftsuppe
4 Blatt Gelatine
1 Schalotte
200 g Rindsfilet
2 kleine Essiggurken
3 Kapernbeeren
1 KL Dijonsenf
5 KL Ketchup
2 EL Olivenöl
1 Spritzer Worcestershiresauce
1 Spritzer Zitronensaft
2 EL gehackter Petersil
Tabasco nach Geschmack
Salz, Pfeffer

Wasabimousse

20 g Wasabi
½ Blatt Gelatine
100 ml Obers

Rote Rübe

1 Rote Rübe
2 EL Himbeeressig
1 EL Nussöl
Zucker
Kümmel
Salz, Pfeffer

Tatar

Die Suppe erhitzen, die in kaltem Wasser eingeweichte Gelatine darin auflösen, abschmecken und durch ein feines Sieb seihen. Die Ringformen (Durchmesser 7,5 Zentimeter, 3 Zentimeter Höhe) mit Folie bespannen, sodass nichts auslaufen kann.

Das Gelee bis circa 5 Millimeter unter den Rand füllen und stocken lassen. Sobald es fest ist, aus der Form nehmen und mit einem kleineren Ausstecher das Gelee in der Mitte ausstechen. Das ausgestochene Gelee wieder leicht erwärmen, sodass es flüssig wird, und den Boden der Formen dünn damit bedecken. Ist es etwas fester, aber noch klebrig, die ausgestochene Form aufsetzen. Das restliche Gelee zum Bedecken der Formen beiseitestellen.

Die Schalotte in feine Würfel schneiden und blanchieren. Das Rindsfilet, die Essiggurken und die Kapernbeeren fein hacken. Schalottenwürfel, Dijonsenf, Ketchup, Olivenöl, Worcestershiresauce, Zitronensaft und den gehackten Petersil dazugeben und kräftig verrühren. Mit Salz, Pfeffer und Tabasco abschmecken. Das Tatar in die ausgelierten Ringformen füllen, glatt streichen, mit dem restlichen abgekühlten Gelee bedecken und kalt stellen.

Wasabimousse

Das Wasabi mit der in kaltem Wasser eingeweichten und ausgedrückten Gelatine leicht erwärmen, bis die Gelatine sich gelöst hat, und durch ein feines Sieb streichen. Kurz vor dem Stocken das Obers schlagen, unterheben und mit etwas Salz abschmecken. Die Mousse kalt stellen.

Rote Rübe

Rote Rübe in mit Essig, Salz, Zucker und Kümmel gut abgeschmecktem Wasser weich kochen. Dann die Rübe in gleichmäßige Würfel schneiden und mit Himbeeressig, Nussöl, Salz, Pfeffer und Zucker abschmecken.

Anrichten

Das Tatar auf der Tellermitte anrichten, eine Wasabimoussenocke aufsetzen und Rote-Rüben-Würfel um das Tatar dekorieren.

Hummerschaumsuppe mit Erbsensoufflé und Ossietrakaviar

Zutaten für 4 Personen | Foto Seite 36

Suppe

1–2 Hummerkarkassen
1 EL Butter
1 EL Olivenöl
½ Sellerieknolle
2 cl Cognac
2 cl Pernod
¼ l Sauvignon Blanc
½ l Hummerfond
½ l Obers
2–3 nussgroße Butter-
oder Hummerbutterstücke
Salz, weißer Pfeffer

Soufflé

100 g Erbsenpüree
(siehe Grundrezept Seite 332)
50 ml Milch
50 ml Obers
2 Eier
Butter zum Ausstreichen
Salz, Pfeffer

Anrichten

40 g Ossietrakaviar

Suppe

Die Hummerkarkassen in kleine Stücke brechen, in einem Topf mit Butter und Olivenöl rösten. Sellerie schälen, fein würfeln, beigeben und mitrösten. Mit Cognac und Pernod ablöschen und flambieren. Mit Weißwein auffüllen, auf die Hälfte reduzieren lassen, Hummerfond dazugeben, erneut auf die Hälfte reduzieren lassen, Obers beigeben, mit Salz und weißem Pfeffer abschmecken, durch eine feines Sieb seihen und mit Butter oder Hummerbutter aufmontieren.

Soufflé

Alle Zutaten miteinander vermengen und abschmecken. Souffléförmchen mit Butter ausstreichen, Masse etwa 4 Zenitmeter hoch einfüllen mit hitzebeständiger Klarsichtfolie abdecken und im Wasserbad circa 30 Minuten pochieren.

Anrichten

Soufflé stürzen, mit Kaviar garnieren und mit der Suppe umgießen.

Kitz-Paradeis-Essenz mit Paradeisroulade

Zutaten für 6 Personen | Foto Seite 38

Essenz

1 kg Kitzknochen
200 g Wurzelwerk
1 EL Paradeismark
½ l Rotwein
125 ml Sherry
5 Wacholderbeeren
1 Lorbeerblatt
400 g Klärfleisch vom Kitz
6 Eiweiß
Salz, weißer Pfeffer

Kitzfarce

150 g Kitzschulter, gewolft
150 ml Obers
35 g Toastbrot, entrindet
1 Ei
1 EL Paradeismark
Salz, Pfeffer

Roulade

50 g Mehl
50 ml Milch
1 Ei
100 g Kitzfarce (Rezept s. oben)
1 Prise Salz

Essenz

Die Knochen und das Wurzelwerk anrösten, Paradeismark beigeben und mit Rotwein und Sherry ablöschen. Einreduzieren lassen, mit 2 Liter kaltem Wasser auffüllen. Für 2–3 Stunden köcheln lassen, nach der Hälfte der Kochzeit Wacholderbeeren und Lorbeer dazugeben. Nach Ende der Kochzeit abseihen und kalt stellen.

Wenn der Fond kalt ist, das Fett abschöpfen, Klärfleisch und Eiweiß in den Fond geben. Wieder zustellen und unter Rühren langsam aufziehen lassen, nicht kochen! Wenn die Suppe klar ist, langsam durch ein Sieb abseihen. Mit einem Papiertuch das letzte Fett von der Suppe entfernen, mit Salz und Pfeffer abschmecken.

Kitzfarce

Alle Zutaten der Farce im Cutter fein mixen und mit Salz und Pfeffer abschmecken.

Rouladen

Aus Mehl, Milch, Ei und Salz einen glatten Teig herstellen. Palatschinken backen und mit der Farce bestreichen. Sehr fest einrollen, in Alufolie wickeln und bei 90 Grad im Wasserbad 10 Minuten ziehen lassen. Folie entfernen und die Einlage in Scheiben schneiden.

Anrichten

Die Kitz-Paradeis-Essenz mit der Einlage in Tellern oder kleinen Kaffeetassen anrichten.

Consommé vom Waldviertler Fleckvieh mit Milzschnitten

Zutaten für 4 Personen | Foto Seite 40

Consommé

2 Karotten
½ Lauchstange
1 Gelbe Rübe
1 Selleriestange
1 Zwiebel
1 Tafelspitz (ca. 1–2 kg) vom Waldviertler Fleckvieh
1 Bund Liebstöckel
½ Bund Petersil
1 Bund Schnittlauch
5 Pfefferkörner
1 Lorbeerblatt

Klären

½ kg Rindsfaschiertes
1 Karotte
1 Gelbe Rübe
½ Sellerieknolle
5 Eiweiß

Milzschnitte

160 g Milz, fein geschabt
3 Eier
1 Prise Majoran
1 EL gehackter Petersil
1 KL fein gehackter Knoblauch
4 Toastbrot- oder Weißbrotscheiben
2 EL Öl
4 EL Mehl
Salz, Pfeffer

Consommé

Karotten, Lauch, Gelbe Rübe und Sellerie putzen und grob zerteilen. Die Zwiebel halbieren und die Schnittfläche in einer heißen Pfanne bräunen.

In einem großen Topf 5 Liter Wasser erhitzen, den Tafelspitz und die restlichen Zutaten (bis auf Pfeffer und Lorbeer) ins kochende Wasser geben. Das Ganze einmal aufkochen und bei kleiner Hitze 2–3 Stunden sieden lassen. Nach der Hälfte der Kochzeit Lorbeerblatt und Pfefferkörner dazugeben. Aufsteigenden grauen Schaum zwischendurch mit einem Schaumlöffel abschöpfen. Die Suppe über Nacht kalt stellen.

Klären

Das Faschierte mit den restlichen Zutaten im Cutter grob mixen und in die kalte Suppe geben. Langsam unter Rühren zum Sieden bringen, das Klärfleisch soll sich nicht anlegen. Circa 2 Stunden sieden lassen und danach durch ein feines Sieb abseihen.

Milzschnitte

Milz, 2 der Eier, Kräuter und den Knoblauch vermengen, mit Salz und Pfeffer abschmecken. Masse fingerdick auf 1 Brotscheibe streichen, eine zweite Scheibe auflegen, erneut mit der Masse bestreichen, so auch mit der dritten Scheibe verfahren, mit dem vierten Brot abschließen.

Öl in einer geräumigen Pfanne erhitzen. Das gefüllte Brot mehlieren, durch das verbliebene, verquirlte Ei ziehen und von beiden Seiten im heißen Fett goldgelb backen. Aus der Pfanne heben, abtropfen lassen und in gewünschte Stücke schneiden.

Anrichten

Die Rindssuppe durch ein Sieb und durch ein Passiertuch abgießen, abschmecken und mit der Einlage servieren.

Flusskrebsravioli mit Wachtelei und Eierschwammerl

Zutaten für 4 Personen ❙ Foto Seite 42

Ravioli
100 g Nudelteig
(siehe Grundrezepte Seite 335)
1 Ei zum Bestreichen
16 KL Cremespinat
(siehe Grundrezept Seite 332)
16 Wachteleigelb
8 Flusskrebse
Butter zum Sautieren

Sauce
500 ml Fischfond
(siehe Grundrezept Seite 333)
250 ml Obers
1 EL kalte Butter
Salz, Pfeffer

Anrichten
100 g Eierschwammerl
Butter zum Sautieren
1 Erdapfel
Fett zum Frittieren

Ravioli
Nudelteig mit der Maschine dünn ausrollen. Teig mit Ei bestreichen und Cremespinat darauf verteilen, eine kleine Mulde machen und je ein Wachteleigelb hineingeben. Flusskrebse abkochen, ausbrechen, Schwänze halbieren, ebenfalls zu Spinat und Wachtelei geben. Sehr vorsichtig eine weitere Platte Nudelteig darüberlegen und gut andrücken. Ravioli mit dem Eigelb nach oben in kochendem Salzwasser garen. Butter in einer Pfanne schmelzen und die Ravioli darin schwenken.

Sauce
Den Fischfond noch leicht einkochen. Das Obers beifügen, nicht zu stark aufkochen, die kalte Butter beigeben und aufmixen. Mit Salz und Pfeffer abschmecken.

Anrichten
Eierschwammerln putzen, in etwas Butter sautieren, anrichten und mit Sauce übergießen. Ravioli aufsetzen, als Garnitur frittierte Erdapfelwürfel darübergeben.

Ei »Wiener Art« mit Spinat, Wurzelspeck und Wiesenchampignons

Zutaten für 4 Personen ❙ Foto Seite 44

Eier
4 Eier
1 Schuss Essig
1 Ei
50 g Mehl
50 g Weißbrotsemmelbrösel
Öl zum Backen
Salz, Pfeffer

Beilagen
200 g Spinat
1 KL Butter
80 g Wurzelspeck
120 g Wiesenchampignons

Eier
Die Eier in Essigwasser 4 Minuten kochen, herausheben, abschrecken und schälen. Mit Salz und Pfeffer würzen, leicht mehlieren, durch das verquirlte Ei ziehen und mit Semmelbrösel panieren. Öl erhitzen und die Eier darin schwimmend goldgelb backen.

Beilagen
Spinat waschen, die Butter in einer Pfanne erhitzen und den Spinat darin anschwitzen, mit Salz, Pfeffer abschmecken. Wurzelspeck in Streifen schneiden und in einer beschichteten Pfanne braun rösten. Champignons keilförmig einschneiden und mitrösten.

Anrichten
Spinat anrichten und das Ei daraufsetzen. Mit dem Speck und den Champignons umrunden, je einen Champignon auf das Ei geben.

Brokkolitortellini mit Paradeis-Estragon-Butter

Zutaten für 4 Personen I Foto Seite 46

Tortellini
350 g Brokkoli
2 EL Béchamelsauce
2 Eier
1 Eigelb
40 ml Obers
25 g flüssige Butter
200 g Nudelteig
(siehe Grundrezept Seite 335)

Paradeis-Estragon-Butter
100 ml Weißwein
2 cl Sherry
1 Schalotte
½ l Hühnerfond
200 ml Obers
30 g Butter
Estragon (nach Geschmack)
2 EL Paradeiswürfel
Salz

Anrichten
braune Butter zum Sautieren
Grana Padano oder Bergkäse

Tortellini
Brokkoli putzen und blanchieren. Im Mixer mit Béchamelsauce, einem Ei, Eigelb, Obers und Butter zu einer feinen Farce mixen, gegebenenfalls pürieren. Mit Salz und Pfeffer abschmecken.
Den Nudelteig per Hand oder mit der Maschine dünn ausrollen und mit dem zweiten, verquirlten Ei bestreichen. Die abgekühlte Brokkolimasse portionsweise auf eine Teigplatte geben. Eine zweite darüberlegen, gut andrücken und Ravioli ausstechen. Die fertigen Ravioli in leicht kochendem Salzwasser etwa 4 Minuten gar ziehen lassen.

Paradeis-Estragon-Butter
Weißwein, Sherry und die fein gewürfelte Schalotte aufkochen, mit dem Hühnerfond auffüllen und auf ein Viertel reduzieren. Obers und Butter zugeben, 10 Minuten leicht köcheln lassen, durch ein feines Sieb passieren und im Mixer aufschlagen, mit Estragon und Salz abschmecken. Kurz vor dem Servieren die Paradeiswürfel unterrühren.

Anrichten
Die gekochten Tascherln in brauner Butter schwenken. Die Paradeis-Estragon-Butter auf die Teller geben und die Tascherln darauf anrichten. Grana Padano oder Bergkäse grob hobeln und darübergeben.

Erbsengnocchi mit pochiertem Ei und weißem Trüffel

Zutaten für 6 Personen I Foto Seite 48

Pochierte Eier
6 Eier
2 EL Essig

Erbsengnocchi
500 g Erbsen
2 Blatt Gelatine
1 KL Trüffelbutter
100 g gekochte mehlige Erdäpfel

50 g Erdäpfelstärke
20 g flüssige Butter
1 Eigelb
50 ml Obers
Salz

Anrichten
1 kleine weiße Trüffel
100 ml Trüffelsauce

Pochierte Eier

Eier aufschlagen und jeweils 1 Ei vorsichtig auf einen Teller oder in eine Schüssel geben. Wasser auf circa 80 Grad erhitzen. Den Essig dazugeben und mit einem Schneebesen so lange rühren, bis ein Strudel entsteht. Nacheinander 2–3 Eier am Rand in den Topf gleiten lassen und circa 2 Minuten pochieren. Mit den restlichen Eiern ebenso verfahren. In Eiswasser abschrecken, zuputzen und beiseitestellen.

Erbsengnocchi

Erbsen in Salzwasser weich kochen, in Eiswasser abschrecken, pürieren und durch ein feines Sieb streichen.

Gelatine in kaltem Wasser einweichen. 100 Gramm des Pürees erwärmen, mit Trüffelbutter und Salz abschmecken und die Gelatine einrühren. Ein kleines Blech oder einen großen Teller mit Frischhaltefolie auslegen. Das Püree circa. 5 Millimeter hoch aufstreichen und stocken lassen.

200 Gramm des Pürees mithilfe eines Passiertuchs ausdrücken, bis es fast keine Flüssigkeit mehr enthält. Aus diesem trockenem Püree, den passierten Erdäpfeln, Stärke, Butter, Eidotter und Salz einen glatten Teig herstellen. Daraus 42 Gnocchi formen. Das gelierte Püree in 5 Millimeter kleine Würfel schneiden und die Gnocchi damit füllen.

Anrichten

Restliches Erbsenpüree mit Obers erhitzen, abschmecken und in tiefen Tellern anrichten. Erbsengnocchi in heißem Wasser 2 Minuten ziehen lassen, in Butter schwenken und um das Püree verteilen. Pochierte Eier in der Trüffelsauce erwärmen, mittig auf das Püree setzen. Trüffelsauce nun schäumen, damit das Ei nappieren und weißen Trüffel darüberhobeln.

Ausgelöste Miesmuscheln in Weißwein mit Safran und Gnocchi
Zutaten für 4 Personen ∎ Foto Seite 50

Miesmuscheln

1 kg Miesmuscheln
3–4 Schalotten
2 EL Olivenöl
10 Safranfäden
½ l Weißwein
½ l Fischfond oder leichte Suppe
100 g kalte Butter
Salz, weißer Pfeffer

Gnocchi

100 g passierte Erdäpfel
20 g Erdäpfelstärke
1 Eigelb
1 EL flüssige Butter
Salz, Muskat

Anrichten

6 Junglauchstangen
Butter zum Anschwitzen

Miesmuscheln

Die Miesmuscheln säubern, mit einem Messer den Bart der Muscheln entfernen, offene oder an der Schale beschädigte Muscheln aussortieren. Die Schalotten fein würfeln. Einen Topf mit Olivenöl erhitzen, Muscheln, Schalotten und Safran beigeben, den Deckel aufsetzen und kurz durchschwenken. Mit etwas Weißwein ablöschen, aufkochen, die Muscheln herausnehmen, geschlossene erneut aussortieren. Den restlichen Weißwein in den Topf geben und vollständig reduzieren, Fischfond hinzufügen, aufkochen, mit Salz und Pfeffer abschmecken und mit kalter Butter montieren. Die Muscheln aus der Schale lösen und zurück in den Topf geben.

Gnocchi

Alle Zutaten zu einem glatten Teig verkneten, Gnocchi formen, in heißem Salzwasser 2 Minuten garen, dann in Butter schwenken.

Anrichten

Junglauch grob schneiden und in Butter anlaufen lassen. Die Gnocchi auf Tellern verteilen, die Muscheln mit dem Safransud darauf anrichten. Mit Junglauch garnieren.

St. Jacques à la St. Germain

Zutaten für 4 Personen | Foto Seite 52

St. Jacques (Jakobsmuscheln)
8 Jakobsmuscheln
2 EL Olivenöl
Meersalz

Rahmsauce
100 g Sauerrahm
Saft und Zesten
von ½ Limette
Salz, Pfeffer

Mürbteig
1 Eigelb
45 g Butter
25 g geriebener
Parmesan
60 g Mehl
Salz, Pfeffer

Anrichten
Kresse und Limettenzesten
zum Dekorieren

St. Jacques
Pro Portion 2 Jakobsmuscheln in insgesamt 8 Scheiben schneiden und mit Olivenöl und Meersalz marinieren.

Rahmsauce
Alle Zutaten miteinander glatt verrühren und kalt stellen.

Mürbteig
Den Ofen auf 160 Grad vorheizen. Eigelb und Butter miteinander verquirlen, Parmesan, Salz, Pfeffer und Mehl unterrühren und zu einem geschmeidigen Teig verarbeiten. In Klarsichtfolie einschlagen und mindestens 1 Stunde im Kühlschrank rasten lassen. Anschließend zwischen 2 Backpapierbögen ausrollen und kalt stellen. Wenn die Masse hart ist, Kreise (circa 10 Zentimeter Durchmesser) ausstechen und auf ein mit Backpapier ausgelegtes Blech geben. Im Ofen circa 10 Minuten backen. Auskühlen lassen und vorsichtig umschichten.

Anrichten
Vor dem Anrichten die Jakobsmuscheln etwas temperieren. Die Sauerrahmsauce auf dem Teller verteilen, einen Teigkreis ansetzen und die Jakobsmuscheln darauf gefächert anrichten. Mit Kresse und Limettenzesten ausgarnieren.

Medaillon vom Waller mit Dijonlinsen und Riojabutter

Zutaten für 4 Personen ❙ Foto Seite 54

Dijonlinsen
100 g Belugalinsen
3 Schalotten
2 Scheiben Bauchspeck
1 KL Olivenöl
¼ l Geflügelfond
¼ l Obers
2 KL Dijonsenf
1 Schuss Balsamico
1 EL gehackter Petersil
Salz, Pfeffer

Riojabutter
4 Schalotten
1 Rosmarinzweig
1 EL Butter
1 EL Kristallzucker
½ l Rioja
kalte Butter zum Binden

Waller
12 Wallermedaillons à 50 g
Maiskeimöl
Salz, Pfeffer

Dijonlinsen
Linsen in Wasser einweichen. Schalotten und Speck fein würfeln und in etwas Olivenöl leicht anrösten. Linsen in Salzwasser 2 Minuten blanchieren, abgießen, abschrecken und zum Speck geben. Geflügelfond aufgießen und einkochen lassen. Obers beigeben und ebenfalls etwas einkochen. Die Linsen mit Dijonsenf, Balsamico, Salz und Pfeffer abschmecken. Kurz vor dem Anrichten gehackten Petersil unterrühren.

Riojabutter
Schalotten fein würfeln und mit Rosmarin in etwas Butter anschwitzen. Kristallzucker beigeben und leicht karamellisieren. Mit Rioja auffüllen, auf ein Drittel einkochen lassen und abseihen. Kurz vor dem Anrichten mit einem Schneebesen kalte Butter einrühren bis die Reduktion leicht bindet.

Waller
Wallermedaillons mit Salz und Pfeffer würzen. In einer beschichteten Pfanne Maiskeimöl erhitzen, Waller mit der Hautseite nach unten in die Pfanne legen und knusprig braten. Danach umdrehen, die Hitze reduzieren und den Waller nachziehen lassen bis er glasig ist.

Anrichten
Linsen in der Mitte eines Tellers anrichten, je 3 Wallermedaillons daraufsetzen und die Riojabutter an der Seite anrichten.

St. Pierre mit Paradeisartischocken und Basilikumzwiebeln

Zutaten für 4 Personen | Foto Seite 56

Paradeisartischocken
2 Paradeiser
4 Artischockenherzen
2 EL Olivenöl
Lorbeerblatt und Thymian
(nach Geschmack)
1 Knoblauchzehe
25 g kalte Butter
Salz, Pfeffer

Basilikumzwiebeln
2 weiße Zwiebeln
2 EL Olivenöl
1 Basilikumzweig
6 cl Weißwein
Salz, Pfeffer

St. Pierre
400 g St.-Pierre-Filet
1 EL Butter
Salz

Anrichten
4 Erdäpfelrosetten
Basilikumpesto

Paradeisartischocken
Den Ofen auf 150 Grad vorheizen. Paradeiser in kochendem Wasser blanchieren, kalt abschrecken, die Haut abziehen und würfeln. Artischockenherzen in Stifte schneiden. In einer Pfanne Olivenöl erhitzen und die Artischocken anschwitzen, nach 2 Minuten die Paradeiser, Gewürze und den fein gewürfelten Knoblauch beigeben, mit Alufolie abdecken und im Ofen 15 Minuten schmoren lassen, anschließend mit Butter binden.

Basilikumzwiebeln
Zwiebel halbieren und in feine Streifen schneiden. In Olivenöl langsam sehr weich schwitzen. Mit etwas Salz, Pfeffer und Weißwein abschmecken. Zum Schluss fein geschnittenen Basilikum unterheben.

St. Pierre
St. Pierre in 4 gleiche Portionen teilen, salzen und in Butter 4–5 Minuten glasig braten.

Anrichten
Die Paradeisartischocken auf die Tellermitte geben, den Fisch daraufgeben und die Basilikumzwiebeln darauf anrichten. Mit einer frittierten Erdäpfelrossette und etwas Basilikumpesto garniert servieren.

Schnitte vom Steinbutt mit Kürbisgnocchi, Sommertrüffel und Zimt

Zutaten für 6 Personen | Foto Seite 58

Gnocchi

200 g gekochte
mehlige Erdäpfel
100 g Kürbispüree
(siehe Grundrezept Seite 334)
4 EL Erdäpfelstärke
2 Eier
Butter zum Schwenken
Salz

Sauce

10 EL Kürbiswürfel
1 EL Butter
40 g schwarze Trüffel
2 EL Rosinen
1 Schuss Trüffeljus
100 ml Madeira
100 ml Kalbsfond
100 ml Trüffeljus
100 ml Obers
Muskat, Zimt, Pfeffer

Steinbutt

600 g Steinbuttfilet
1 EL Butter
Salz

Anrichten

Champagner-Fisch-Nage
(siehe Grundrezept Seite 332)
etwas Trüffel bei Wunsch

Gnocchi

Die Erdäpfel passieren und mit Kürbispüree, Stärke, Eiern und etwas Salz zu einem glatten Teig verarbeiten und rasten lassen.
Vom Erdäpfel-Kürbis-Teig Gnocchi abdrehen, in gut gesalzenem Wasser kochen und mit Butter durchschwenken.

Sauce

Kürbiswürfel in Butter angehen lassen, gehackte Trüffel, Zimt und Rosinen beigeben, mit etwas Trüffeljus ablöschen, einkochen und dann abschmecken.
Madeira, Kalbsfond, Trüffeljus zusammen auf 100 Milliliter einkochen, mit Obers aufgießen und mit Salz und Pfeffer abschmecken und zu den Kürbiswürfel geben.

Steinbutt

Den Steinbutt in Butter braten und etwas salzen.

Anrichten

Gnocchi und Sauce nebeneinander anrichten, den Steinbutt auflegen, die aufgeschäumte Champagner-Fisch-Nage anlegen und bei Wunsch etwas Trüffel darüberhobeln.

Wolfsbarsch im Ganzen in der Salzkruste

Zutaten für 4 Personen | Foto Seite 60

Wolfsbarsch

1 Wolfsbarsch
(ca. 1,2 kg)
4 Eiweiß
1 Bund Thymian
2 Knoblauchzehen
2 kg grobes Meersalz
Miesmuscheln

Anrichten

blanchierter Spinat
(nach Bedarf)

Wolfsbarsch

Den Fisch waschen und trocknen. Die Bauchhöhle mit Thymian und den ganzen Knoblauchzehen auslegen. Den Backofen auf 220 Grad vorheizen und das Meersalz mit dem Eiweiß vermengen. Wenn die Masse zu hart ist, noch etwas Wasser beigeben. Ein Backblech mit Alufolie auslegen und den Fisch daraufgeben. Mit der Salzmasse den Fisch abdecken und mit den Händen fest andrücken, sodass die Form eines Fisches entsteht. Den Rand der Alufolie aufrollen und den Fisch für 20 Minuten in den Backofen stellen.

Anrichten

Die Salzkruste aufbrechen und herunternehmen, den Fisch filetieren und mit einer geeigneten Beilage (zum Beispiel mit blanchiertem Spinat) servieren.

Kalbsbries mit Erdäpfelnudeln, Wiesenchampignons und Kerbel

Zutaten für 4 Personen | Foto Seite 62

Erdäpfelnudeln
50 g mehligkochende Erdäpfel
200 g Mehl
1 Ei (nach Bedarf)
2 EL Weizengrieß
Salz

Kalbsbries
200 g Kalbsbries (geputzt, gewässert und gezupft)
2 EL Mehl
1 EL Öl
1 EL Butter
Salz, Pfeffer

Wiesenchampignons
300 g Wiesenchampignons
1 EL Butter
2 Knoblauchzehen
100 ml Kalbsfond
1 EL gehackter Kerbel
Salz, Pfeffer

Anrichten
frischer Kerbel

Erdäpfelnudeln
Die Erdäpfel in der Schale kochen, kurz ausdämpfen lassen, schälen und noch heiß durch die Presse drücken. Das Mehl dazugeben und alles mit 100 Milliliter kaltem Wasser zu einem festen glatten Teig verkneten. Ist der Teig zu fest, ein Ei hinzugeben, verkneten und sofort weiterverarbeiten.
Den Teig portionsweise mit der Nudelmaschine (ohne Mehl) 1–2 Millimeter dick ausrollen und zu etwa 1 Zentimeter breiten Streifen schneiden. Zwischen den Händen zu kleinen Schupfnudeln drehen, im Weizengrieß wenden und auf einem Blech etwas trocknen lassen. Die Nudeln in kochendem Salzwasser bissfest kochen.

Kalbsbries
Die Kalbsbriesröschen mehlieren und würzen. In einer Pfanne in Öl und Butter goldbraun braten. Die Röschen aus der Pfanne nehmen und warmstellen.

Wiesenchampignons
Die Champignons putzen, Butter in die Pfanne geben und die Champignons gemeinsam mit dem fein gehackten Knoblauch anschwitzen. Mit Salz und Pfeffer würzen, den Kalbsfond angießen, Kerbel unterheben. Das Kalbsbries zugeben und kurz ziehen lassen.

Anrichten
Die Erdäpfelnudeln in tiefe Teller geben. Kalbsbries und Wiesenchampignons darauf verteilen. Mit frischem Kerbel ausgarnieren.

Taubengalantine mit Apfelchutney und Wagramer Dirndln

Zutaten für 6 Personen | Foto Seite 64

Taubengalantine

2 Tauben
200 g Geflügelfarce
(siehe Grundrezept Seite 334)
1 EL Karottenwürfel
1 EL Gelbe-Rüben-Würfel
1 EL Selleriewürfel
2 Taubenfilets
2 EL gehackte Eierschwammerl
oder Morcheln
1–2 EL Obers
1 l kräftiger Geflügelfond
Salz, Pfeffer

Apfelchutney

1 Apfel
1 EL Honig
1 Spritzer Weißweinessig
Salz, Pfeffer

Anrichten

24 eingelegte
Wagramer Dirndln
Blattsalate der Saison

Taubengalantine

Die Tauben auslösen und zwischen 2 befeuchteten Folien plattieren. Die Geflügelfarce mit Gemüsewürfeln, den klein geschnittenen Taubenfilets und den Eierschwammerln vermischen und mit ein wenig Obers verdünnen. Mit Salz und Pfeffer abschmecken.

Die Masse auf die Taube streichen, fest einrollen, in ein sauberes und gewässertes Stofftuch einschlagen und mit Küchengarn fest verschließen. Die Taubengalantine in einem kräftigen Geflügelfond bei 80 Grad circa 30 Minuten pochieren.

Die Galantine nach dem Garen im Fond unbedingt kalt stellen, so bekommt sie noch mehr Geschmack.

Apfelchutney

Den Apfel schälen, entkernen und in feine Würfel schneiden. In einer Pfanne den Honig karamellisieren, Apfelwürfel dazugeben, durchschwenken und mit Weißweinessig ablöschen. Bei mittlerer Hitze weich schmoren und mit Salz und Pfeffer abschmecken.

Anrichten

Die Wagramer Dirndln und den Salat auf die Teller geben. Vom Apfelchutney Nocken stechen und die Galantinescheiben anlegen.

Schwarzfederhuhn in Oliven-Paradeis-Kruste und Piniencouscous

Zutaten für 4 Personen | Foto Seite 66

Schwarzfederhuhn

4 Schwarzfederhuhnbrustfilets à 150 g
1 EL Öl
150 g Paradeiser
2 EL Olivenöl
60 g Oliven
60 g getrocknete Paradeiser
1 Thymianzweig
80 g Semmelbrösel
Salz, Pfeffer

Piniencouscous

80 g Couscous
½ Bund Basilikum
2 EL Olivenöl
2 EL geriebener Parmesan
40 g geröstete Pinienkerne
Salz, Pfeffer

Anrichten

Hühnerjus

Schwarzfederhuhn

Ofen auf 180 Grad vorheizen. Hendlbrüste mit Salz, Pfeffer würzen und auf beiden Seiten in einer Pfanne scharf anbraten. Im Ofen circa 5 Minuten braten.

Die Paradeiser häuten, in Würfel schneiden, in Olivenöl anschmoren, mit Salz und Pfeffer würzen und kühl stellen.

Ofen auf 220 Grad Oberhitze vorheizen. Oliven und getrocknete Paradeiser in Würfel schneiden, Thymianblättchen fein hacken, alles unter die abgekühlten Paradeiswürfel mischen. Brösel zugeben, bis die Masse geschmeidig und streichbar ist, abschmecken.

Kruste auf die Hendlbrüste streichen, im Ofen goldbraun überbacken.

Piniencouscous

Couscous in kaltem Wasser einweichen. Basilikum mit Olivenöl, 2 Esslöffeln Wasser und Parmesan zu einem feinen Pesto mixen. Couscous abseihen, in einem breiten Topf mit Pinienkernen und Pesto einkochen und mit Salz und Pfeffer abschmecken.

Anrichten

Couscous auf den Tellern platzieren und die Schwarzhuhnbrüste darauf anrichten, mit Hühnerjus garnieren.

Kalbslungenbraten im Brotteig mit geschmorten Artischocken

Zutaten für 4 Personen | Foto Seite 68

Kalbslungenbraten

600 g Kalbslungenbraten
150 g Tramezzinibrot
50 g Kalbsfarce
Öl zum Anbraten
100 ml Kalbssauce
Salz, Pfeffer

Artischocken

2 Paradeiser
2 EL Olivenöl
2 Artischockenherzen
Lorbeerblatt und Thymian
1 Knoblauchzehe
12 g kalte Butter
Salz, Pfeffer

Anrichten

Petersilbutter
(siehe Grundrezepte Seite 335)
Artischockenchips
(siehe Grundrezepte Seite 332)

Kalbslungenbraten

Den Backofen auf 180 Grad vorheizen. Den Kalbslungenbraten zuputzen, portionieren und würzen. Das Tramezzinibrot mit dem Nudelholz dünn ausrollen, mit Farce bestreichen und den Kalbslungenbraten daraufsetzen. Fest einrollen und in Fett rundherum anbraten, bei 180 Grad im Ofen 5 Minuten garen und weitere 5 Minuten bei 80 Grad rasten lassen.

Artischocken

Den Ofen auf 150 Grad vorheizen. Paradeiser in kochendem Wasser blanchieren, häuten und in kleine Würfel schneiden. In einer Pfanne Olivenöl erhitzen und die gewürfelten Artischocken anschwitzen, Paradeiser, Gewürze und fein gewürfelten Knoblauch beigeben, mit Alufolie abdecken und im Ofen 15 Minuten schmoren lassen. Aus dem Ofen nehmen und mit Butter binden.

Anrichten

Kalbslungenbraten in 4 Portionen teilen, mittig anrichten, etwas Petersilbutter anlegen und mit den Artischocken und Artischockenchips servieren.

Kalbskotelett auf feinen Nudeln mit schwarzen Oliven und Junglauch

Zutaten für 6 Personen ∎ Foto Seite 70

Kalbsrücken

1 kg Kalbsrücken mit Knochen
1 frischer Rosmarinzweig
Schweineschmalz zum Anbraten
1 EL Butter
Salz, weißer Pfeffer

Nudelteig

200 g glattes Mehl
1 EL Olivenöl
1 Ei, 3 Eigelb
Salz

Olivenglace

12 Junglauchstangen
½ EL Butter
60 ml Gemüsefond
60 g schwarze Oliven ohne Stein
¼ l Kalbsglace
40 g kalte Butter

Kalbsrücken

Den Ofen auf 180 Grad vorheizen. Kalbsrücken von Sehnen befreien, mit Salz und Pfeffer würzen. In einer Pfanne mit dem Rosmarinzweig in heißem Schmalz anbraten, für 25 Minuten mit der Butter in den Ofen geben. Anschließend bei 85 Grad 10 Minuten ziehen lassen.

Nudelteig

Alle Zutaten zu einem glatten Teig kneten und 1 Stunde kühl stellen. Den Nudelteig mit der Nudelmaschine dünn ausrollen und feine Nudeln herstellen. Die Nudeln in kochendem Salzwasser bissfest garen.

Olivenglace

Den Junglauch putzen und in grobe Stücke schneiden. In der Pfanne mit Butter angehen lassen und mit etwas Fond ablöschen. Die Oliven in feine Streifen schneiden. Kalbsglace aufkochen, mit kalter Butter montieren und mit den Oliven verfeinern.

Anrichten

Die Nudeln mit einer Fleischgabel aufdrehen, Fleisch in 4 Stücke schneiden, anlegen, Junglauch auflegen und mit Olivenglace umgießen.

Spanferkel mit Waldviertler Kümmel, Haxlravioli und geschmortem Spitzkraut

Zutaten für 4 Personen | Foto Seite 72

Spanferkelrücken
800 g ausgelöster Spanferkelrücken, mit Schwarte
1 Rosmarinzweig
1 Thymianzweig
1 Lorbeerblatt
2 Knoblauchzehen
Olivenöl zum Beträufeln
Waldviertler Kümmel
Salz, Pfeffer

Haxlravioli
2 Schweinshaxln
8 Pfefferkörner
2 Lorbeerblätter
200 g Wurzelgemüse (Karotten, Gelbe Rüben, Sellerie)
1 Zwiebel
2 EL Sonnenblumenöl
½ l Weißwein
50 g kalte Butter
200 g Nudelteig (siehe Grundrezept Seite 335)
Butter zum Sautieren
Kümmelsamen, Salz

Spitzkraut
400 g Spitzkraut
80 g Butter
Salz, Pfeffer

Spanferkelrücken
Die Schwarte mit einem scharfen Messer einschneiden, mit Salz und Pfeffer rundum würzen. Die Fleischseite mit etwas Kümmel bestreuen, mit Rosmarin, Thymian, Lorbeer, angedrücktem Knoblauch belegen und mit Olivenöl beträufeln.

Gewürzten Spanferkelrücken vorsichtig in einen Vakuumiersack geben, auf höchster Stufe vakuumieren und im Wasserbad bei maximal 75 Grad 3 ½–4 Stunden garen. Wer keinen Vakuumierer zu Hause hat, kann den Rücken mit den Gewürzen auch beim Fleischer vakuumieren lassen. Spanferkelrücken aus dem Vakuumierbeutel nehmen, trocken tupfen und mit der Schwarte nach unten auf der Grillplatte oder in einer großen Pfanne knusprig braten. Warm stellen.

Haxlravioli
Den Ofen auf 200 Grad vorheizen. Schweinshaxln mit Wasser bedecken, mit Pfefferkörnern, Lorbeer, Kümmel und Salz circa 1 Stunde köcheln lassen. In einer Schmorpfanne grob geschnittenes Wurzelgemüse und gewürfelte Zwiebel in Sonnenblumenöl bräunen. Haxln aus dem Sud nehmen, trocken tupfen, zum Gemüse geben und kurz mitrösten. Mit Weißwein ablöschen und im Ofen circa 40 Minuten schmoren. Haxln aus der Schmorpfanne nehmen, die sulzige Haut mit einem kleinen Messer abschaben und klein hacken. Das Fleisch von den Haxln lösen und ebenfalls klein hacken. Die Hälfte des Schmorgemüses in einer Schüssel mit einer Gabel zerdrücken. Haxlfleisch, Haut und Gemüse vermengen, mit Salz und Pfeffer abschmecken.

Für eine Sauce den Rest des Wurzelgemüses mit den Knochen nochmals kräftig rösten, 2 Liter Wasser aufgießen und 20 Minuten köcheln lassen. Fond durch ein feines Sieb abseihen und auf circa ¼ Liter reduzieren, mit Salz und Pfeffer abschmecken und mit der Butter montieren.

Nudelteig mit der Nudelmaschine so dünn wie möglich ausrollen. Eine Hälfte des Teigs mit wenig Wasser bestreichen, Haxlfülle häufchenweise darauf verteilen, mit der zweiten Hälfte bedecken, andrücken und Ravioli ausstechen, in Salzwasser circa 2 Minuten kochen und in einer Pfanne mit Butter schwenken.

Spitzkraut
Statt Spitzkraut können Sie auch normales Weißkraut verwenden, es ist aber in Geschmack und Struktur nicht so fein wie Spitzkraut.

Das Kraut in einzelne Blätter teilen, Strünke entfernen und in Fleckerl von circa 3 x 3 Zentimeter schneiden. In einer breiten Pfanne die Hälfte der Butter erhitzen, Krautfleckerl beigeben und leicht anrösten. Mit 60 Milliliter Wasser ablöschen, restliche Butter beigeben und zu einer sämigen Konsistenz einkochen. Mit Salz und Pfeffer abschmecken.

Anrichten
Das Spitzkraut auf den Tellern anrichten, das Spanferkel portionieren und auf das Kraut setzen. Ravioli und Sauce anlegen.

Kalbskrone mit Kalbsbriesravioli, Petersilwurzelcreme und Petersilbutter

Zutaten für 4 Personen ▮ Foto Seite 74

Kalbskrone

1 ½ kg Kalbskrone mit Knochen
2 EL Öl
1 Salbeizweig
2 EL Butter
Salz, Pfeffer

Ravioli

160 g Weizenmehl (Type 550)
160 g Hartweizendunst
2 Eier
2 Eigelb
15 ml Olivenöl
Hartweizendunst zum Ausrollen
20 kleine Kalbsbriesröschen
1 Eigelb
2 EL Butter

Petersilwurzelcreme

300 g Petersilwurzel
50 g gebräunte Butter
100 ml Obers
Salz

Petersilbutter

100 g Blattpetersil
75 g Butter
Salz

Anrichten

Eierschwammerl
Jungzwiebel
Butter zum Sautieren

Kalbskrone

Den Ofen auf 200 Grad Ober- und Unterhitze vorheizen. Die Kalbskrone mit Salz und Pfeffer würzen. Öl in einer Pfanne erhitzen und das Fleisch rundum scharf anbraten. Im Ofen circa 40 Minuten rosa braten.
Bei 60 Grad 10–15 Minuten ruhen lassen. Danach die Butter in einer Pfanne bräunen, den Salbei beigeben, die Kalbskrone kurz nachbraten.

Ravioli

Aus Mehl, Hartweizendunst, Eiern, Eigelben und Olivenöl einen geschmeidigen Teig kneten, bei Bedarf Wasser hinzufügen.
Abgedeckt etwa 1 Stunde im Kühlschrank rasten lassen. Den Teig mit einer Nudelmaschine dünn ausrollen und dabei immer wieder mit etwas Dunst bestreuen.
Die Kalbsbriesröschen für einige Minuten pochieren, aus dem Topf herausnehmen und abtropfen lassen. Die Röschen in etwa 4 Zentimeter Abstand auf die eine Hälfte des ausgerollten Nudelteigs setzen, die Ränder mit dem Eigelb bestreichen. Mit der zweiten Nudelteighälfte bedecken, die Ravioli ausstechen und die Ränder fest andrücken.
Die Kalbsbriesravioli in einem großen Topf etwa 2 Minuten kochen lassen, abschütten und in einer Pfanne mit etwas Butter schwenken.

Petersilwurzelcreme

Die Petersilwurzel schälen, in grobe Stücke zerteilen, im leicht gesalzenem Wasser weich kochen und abgießen. Gebräunte Butter mit Obers zu der gekochten Petersilwurzel geben, mixen, mit Salz abschmecken und durch ein feines Sieb streichen.

Petersilbutter

Petersil waschen, klein zupfen und kurz blanchieren. Abschrecken, mit Butter, Salz und 20 Milliliter Wasser in einer Küchenmaschine zu einer Paste verarbeiten und durch ein feines Sieb streichen. Die Paste sanft erwärmen und mit einem Schneebesen oder dem Stabmixer emulgieren.

Anrichten

Die Eierschwammerln und Jungzwiebeln in Scheiben kurz in Butter sautieren. Die Kalbskrone portionieren, auf die Teller geben, mit der Petersilbutter umgeben. Ravioli und Petersilwurzelcreme ansetzen und mit Eierschwammerl servieren.

Milchlammschlögel mit geschmortem Mangold und Erdäpfelkuchen

Zutaten für 6 Personen | Foto Seite 76

Milchlammschlögel
1 Milchlammschlögel
1 EL Pommerysenf
1 Rosmarinzweig
1 Thymianzweig
1 EL Olivenöl
1 EL Butter
1 EL Sonnenblumenöl
Salz, Pfeffer

Erdäpfelkuchen
5 Erdäpfel
1 Bund roter Mangold
1 Schalotte
1 Knoblauchzehe
2 EL Butter
4 EL passierte Erdäpfel
1 Ei
1 Eigelb zum Bestreichen
Salz, Pfeffer, Muskat

Anrichten
¼ l Lammsauce

Milchlammschlögel
Den Schlögel salzen und pfeffern, mit Senf, den gehackten Kräutern und Olivenöl einreiben. In einen Vakuumsack geben, vakuumieren (kann auch der Fleischer übernehmen) und in 72 Grad heißem Wasser 3 Stunden ziehen lassen. Herausnehmen und in Butter und Öl nachbraten.

Erdäpfelkuchen
Den Ofen auf 200 Grad Heißluft vorheizen. Aus den Erdäpfeln 12 Blätter für eine Ringform hobeln. Die restlichen Erdäpfel in kleine Stifte schneiden. In Salzwasser kochen und in Eiswasser abschrecken.
Den Mangold in feine Streifen schneiden. Schalotte und Knoblauch fein würfeln und in Butter anschwitzen. Den Mangold dazugeben, würzen und bei kleiner Hitze schmoren, bis er weich und die Flüssigkeit fast verkocht ist. Etwas Mangold zum Anrichten beiseitelegen.
Die restliche Masse mit passierten Erdäpfeln binden, das Ei dazugeben und abschmecken.
Auf den Boden einer Ringform ein Erdäpfelblatt geben, die Wände der Form mit den Stiften auskleiden, die Mangoldmasse einfüllen und mit einem weiteren Erdäpfelblatt verschließen. Mit Ei bestreichen und im Ofen 15 Minuten backen.

Anrichten
Die beiseitegestellte Mangoldmasse auf den Tellern anrichten, den Lammschlögel aufschneiden, auf dem Mangold anrichten und mit den Erdäpfelkuchen und der Lammsauce servieren.

Rosa Beiried vom Milchstier mit Spargel, Erdäpfelcrêpe und Sauce béarnaise

Zutaten für 4 Personen | Foto Seite 78

Ochsenbeiried

ca. 800 g Ochsenbeiried
im Ganzen
Dijonsenf zum Einstreichen
1 Thymianzweig
Salz, weißer Pfeffer

Solospargel

18 Stangen Solospargel
Saft von ½ Zitrone
1 Semmel
Salz, Zucker

Erdäpfelcrêpe

4 mittelgroße Erdäpfel
4 Eigelb
1 EL weiche Butter
Öl zum Braten
Salz, Pfeffer

Sauce béarnaise

4 Eigelb
1 EL Weißwein
2 EL Rindssuppe
1 EL Obers
Saft von ½ Zitrone
300 g lauwarme geklärte Butter
2–3 EL Estragon
1 Msp. Cayennepfeffer
Salz

Ochsenbeiried

Den Ofen auf 160 Grad vorheizen. Die Beiried mit Salz und weißem Pfeffer aus der Mühle würzen, mit Senf einstreichen und mit dem Thymianzweig in einer heißen Pfanne rundum anbraten. Circa 1 Stunde in den vorgeheizten Backofen geben.

Solospargel

Den Spargel sorgfältig schälen und mit dem Zitronensaft, der Semmel und etwas Salz und Zucker 1 Minute kochen lassen, vom Herd nehmen und 2 Stunden ziehen lassen.

Erdäpfelcrêpe

Die Erdäpfel kochen, schälen und durch die Erdäpfelpresse drücken. Mit den Eigelben, Salz und Pfeffer zu einer glatten Masse rühren. Die Butter unterrühren und in einer Pfanne mit heißem Fett goldbraune Dukaten braten.

Sauce béarnaise

Eigelbe mit Weißwein, Rindssuppe, Obers und Zitronensaft verrühren und über Wasserdampf schaumig schlagen. Die Butter unter fortwährendem Schlagen beigeben, anschließend mit Salz und Cayennepfeffer würzen und den fein gehackten Estragon dazugeben.

Anrichten

Beiried portionieren, auf die Teller geben, den Solospargel anlegen, mit Sauce béarnaise nappieren und mit den Dukaten servieren.

Attergauer Rindsfilet mit Sellerie und gebratener Gänseleber

Zutaten für 4 Personen | Foto Seite 80

Filet
600 g Rindsfilet
1 EL Butter
Salz, Pfeffer

Sellerie
1 Sellerieknolle
1 Staudenselleriestange
250 ml Kalbsfond
150 ml Obers
Salz, Pfeffer
Muskat

Gänseleber
4 Gänselebern à 50 g
Mehl zum Wenden
Sonnenblumenöl
zum Braten
Salz, Pfeffer

Anrichten
60 ml Kalbsglace

Filet
Rindsfilet zuputzen, in 4 Stücke portionieren und würzen, mit Butter von beiden Seiten langsam braten, bis das Fleisch medium ist. Nun 1–2 Minuten rasten lassen.

Sellerie
Knollen- und Staudensellerie schälen. Beide in nussgroße gleichmäßige Stücke schneiden, die ungleichmäßigen restlichen Abschnitte des Knollenselleries beiseitestellen. Zuerst die Knollenselleriestücke in Kalbsfond halb garen, dann den Staudensellerie dazugeben, beide weich kochen und aus der Flüssigkeit nehmen. Nun die beiseitegestellten Abschnitte des Knollenselleries weich kochen, mit dem Obers fein mixen und mit Salz, Pfeffer und Muskat abschmecken.

Gänseleber
Gänseleber würzen, in Mehl wenden und in einer beschichteten Pfanne mit etwas Öl beidseitig je circa 1 ½ Minuten braten.

Anrichten
Die Kalbsglace in einem Topf erhitzen. Das Selleriepüree auf den Tellern verstreichen, Filet mittig platzieren und mit dem Gemüse umranden. Mit Gänseleber krönen und mit der Kalbsglace umgießen.

Gebackene Rehleber mit Rote-Rüben-Carpaccio und Krenvinaigrette

Zutaten für 4 Personen | Foto Seite 82

Carpaccio
4 Rote Rüben
(gleich groß)
2 EL Dijonsenf
1–2 Spritzer Balsamico
1–2 Spritzer Olivenöl
reichlich Kümmel
(nach Geschmack)
Salz, Pfeffer

Rehleber
400 g Rehleber
100 g Mehl
1 Ei
100 g Semmelbrösel
Butterschmalz zum Ausbacken
Pfeffer

Anrichten
Erdäpfelpüree (siehe Seite 327)
frisch gerissener Kren

Carpaccio
Rote Rüben schälen und in Wasser mit reichlich Kümmel weich kochen. Abkühlen lassen und mit einer Aufschnittmaschine feine Scheiben von circa 1 Millimeter schneiden. 100 Gramm Rübenreste mit 200 Milliliter Kochfond, Dijonsenf, einigen Spritzern Balsamico und Olivenöl kurz zu einer sämigen Konsistenz mixen.

Rehleber
Die Rehleber häuten, von den Adern befreien, in 3 Zentimeter dicke Scheiben schneiden, nur pfeffern. In Mehl, Ei und Semmelbrösel panieren und goldgelb herausbacken. Danach auf einem Küchenpapier gut abtropfen lassen.

Anrichten
Die Roten Rüben schuppenartig auf Teller auflegen, mit der sämigen Sauce beträufeln und mit Kren nach Geschmack bestreuen. Das Erdäpfelpüree in einem Ring anrichten, darauf die Leberscheiben geben und sofort servieren.

Rehrücken mit Kürbiskernconfit und Grießschnitten

Zutaten für 4 Personen | Foto Seite 84

Rehrücken
4 Rehrückenstränge à 140 g
2 EL gehackter Petersil
5 Wacholderbeeren
1 EL Öl
300 ml Wildfond
50 g Preiselbeeren
1 KL Butter
Salz, Pfeffer

Kürbiskernconfit
200 g Kürbisfleisch
½ Zwiebel
2 EL Olivenöl
50 g Honig
50 g Kürbiskerne
Salz, Pfeffer

Grießschnitten
¼ l Milch
125 ml Obers
125 ml Gemüsefond
150 g Weizengrieß
10 g kalte Butter
10 g geriebener Parmesan
1 EL Olivenöl
Salz, Pfeffer, Muskat

Rehrücken
Den Backofen auf 180 Grad vorheizen. Die Rehrücken mit Salz, Pfeffer, Petersil und zerdrücktem Wacholder würzen. In heißem Öl von beiden Seiten scharf anbraten. Im Backofen circa 5 Minuten fertig garen, anschließend aus der Pfanne nehmen und warm stellen. Den Bratenrückstand mit Wildfond ablöschen, durch ein Sieb passieren, einkochen lassen, die Preiselbeeren beigeben und mit etwas Butter binden.

Kürbiskernconfit
Das Kürbisfleisch würfeln und mit der gehackten Zwiebel im heißen Olivenöl anschwitzen. Mit Salz und Pfeffer würzen, Honig dazugeben, etwas einköcheln lassen danach die gerösteten und gehackten Kürbiskerne unterheben.

Grießschnitte
Milch, Obers und Gemüsefond mit Salz, Pfeffer und Muskat würzen, einmal aufkochen, Grieß hinzufügen und einkochen lassen. Vom Herd nehmen, Butter und Parmesan unterrühren, etwa 1 ½ Zentimeter dick auf ein Blech streichen und 2–3 Stunden gut durchkühlen lassen.
Die Grießschnitten rund ausstechen oder in Rauten schneiden. Eine Alufolie mit Olivenöl einpinseln, auf den Grill legen und die Schnitten darauf von beiden Seiten braten.

Anrichten
Griesschnitten auf den Tellern platzieren, den Rehrücken darauf anrichten und mit dem Kürbiskernconfit und etwas Sauce servieren.

Gebackenes Kitz auf Erdäpfelsalat und Rucola

Zutaten für 4 Personen | Foto Seite 86

Erdäpfelsalat

400 g Erdäpfel
2 EL Weißweinessig
3 EL Sonnenblumenöl
1 Zwiebel
Zucker
Salz, weißer Pfeffer

Kitz

400 g Kitz (Schlögel oder Teile des Rückens)
frisch gehackter Petersil
100 g Mehl
1 Ei
100 g Weißbrotbrösel
Schweineschmalz
Salz, Pfeffer

Anrichten

200 g Rucola

Erdäpfelsalat

Die Erdäpfel waschen und kochen, leicht auskühlen lassen, pellen und in Scheiben schneiden. Aus Essig, Öl, Salz, Pfeffer und Zucker eine Vinaigrette herstellen. Die Zwiebeln fein würfeln und mit der Vinaigrette zu den Kartoffeln geben. Gut verrühren und ½ Stunde ungekühlt ziehen lassen, danach nochmals abschmecken, da die Erdäpfel sehr viel vom Geschmack aufnehmen.

Kitz

Kitz portionieren und plattieren, mit Salz, Pfeffer und Petersil würzen. Nacheinander durch das Mehl, das verquirlte Ei und die Brösel ziehen und im heißen Schmalz ausbacken.

Anrichten

Den Erdäpfelsalat auf einem Teller anrichten, das Kitz darauflegen und mit Rucola garnieren.

Wildschweinschlögel mit Linsen-Speck-Sauce und Palfyknödeln

Zutaten für 8–10 Personen | Foto Seite 88

Schlögel
1 Wildschweinschlögel
1 EL Wacholderbeeren
2 EL Öl
2 Zwiebeln, 4 Karotten
3 Petersilwurzeln
2 Thymianzweige
1 Lorbeerblatt
2 EL Sherry
1 EL Honig
1 l Wildfond
Pfeffer

Petersilwurzeln
4 Petersilwurzeln
2 EL Olivenöl
1 cl Weißweinessig
6 cl Rindsfond
50 g Petersil
Salz, Pfeffer

Linsen-Speck-Sauce
100 g geräucherter Bauchspeck
3 Schalotten
1 Knoblauchzehe
4 cl Balsamico
¼ l Gemüsefond
¼ l Obers
20 g Butter
90 g rote Linsen
1 EL gehackter Petersil
Salz, Pfeffer

Palfyknödel
250 g altbackenes Brioche
150 ml Milch
100 ml Obers
½ Zwiebel
40 g Butter
4 Eier
15 g geschlagenes Obers
Salz, Pfeffer, Muskat

Schlögel
Den Ofen auf 220 Grad vorheizen. Den Schlögel mit Salz, Pfeffer und gehackten Wacholderbeeren einreiben. In einer Bratenpfanne das Öl erhitzen und den Schlögel von beiden Seiten scharf anbraten. Im Backofen 30 Minuten braten lassen.

Zwiebeln, Karotten und Petersilwurzeln schälen und in grobe Stücke schneiden. Gemüse und Gewürze zum Schlögel geben, etwas Wildfond dazugeben und die Hitze auf 180 Grad reduzieren. In etwa 1 Stunde fertig garen, das Fleisch dabei regelmäßig mit dem eigenen Saft begießen. Falls notwendig, noch etwas Wildfond angießen.

Den Schlögel herausnehmen, 10 Minuten warm stellen und die Hitze im Backofen auf 250 Grad erhöhen. Den Bratenfond entfetten, mit etwas Wasser ablöschen und kräftig einkochen lassen. Durch ein Sieb gießen und mit Sherry abschmecken. Den Schlögel mit Honig bestreichen, zurück in die Bratenpfanne geben und im Backofen einige Minuten glasieren. Mit frisch gemahlenem Pfeffer würzen.

Petersilwurzeln
Die Petersilwurzeln schälen und in Stifte schneiden. Das Olivenöl erhitzen und die Petersilwurzeln anbraten. Mit Weißweinessig ablöschen, mit Salz und Pfeffer würzen. Rindsfond zugeben und weich dünsten. Vor dem Servieren den gehackten Petersil unterheben.

Linsen-Speck-Sauce
Speck, Schalotten und Knoblauch würfeln, Speck kurz anbraten, Schalotten und Knoblauch beigeben und glasig anschwitzen, mit Balsamico ablöschen und reduzieren. Gemüsefond und Obers zugießen und mit Salz und Pfeffer würzen. Erneut einkochen lassen. Mit dem Schneebesen die Butter einrühren. Die Linsen einweichen, dann abtropfen lassen und mit dem gehackten Petersil vor dem Servieren unterheben.

Palfyknödel
Brioche in Würfel schneiden, mit Milch und Obers mischen. Fein gehackte Zwiebel in Butter glasig anschwitzen. Die Eier in einer Schüssel verquirlen und gemeinsam mit dem geschlagenen Obers unter die Briochewürfel heben. Mit Salz, Pfeffer und Muskat würzen. Gut durchkneten und ½ Stunde rasten lassen. Die Masse zu kleinen Knödel formen, in kochendem Salzwasser 12 Minuten bei kleiner Hitze ziehen lassen.

Anrichten
Wildschweinschlögel portionieren, die Linsen anlegen und mit Knödel und Petersilwurzelstiften servieren.

Hirschlungenbraten im Baumkuchen mit Maroni-Dörrzwetschken-Gnocchi

Zutaten für 4 Personen | Foto Seite 90

Hirschlungenbraten

600 g Hirschlungenbraten
150 g Baumkuchen
50 g Kalbsfarce
4 Strudelteigblätter
2 EL Öl
Salz, Pfeffer, Wacholder

Gnocchi

100 g Erdäpfel
100 g Maronipüree
20 g Erdäpfelstärke
1 EL Butter
1 Eigelb
25 g Dörrzwetschken
Salz, Pfeffer

Anrichten

glacierte Quitten
Wildnage
(siehe Grundrezepte Seite 335)
250 ml Hirschsauce

Hirschlungenbraten

Den Ofen auf 180 Grad vorheizen. Den Hirschlungenbraten zuputzen, in 4 gleich große Teile schneiden und würzen. Den Strudelteig auf 4 Stücke zu 15 x 15 Zentimeter zuschneiden, den Baumkuchen dünn aufschneiden und gefächert auflegen. Jeweils mit Farce bestreichen und den Hirschlungenbraten daraufsetzen. Einrollen und in Öl rundherum anbraten, anschließend im Ofen 5 Minuten garen, die Temperatur auf 80 Grad reduzieren und 5 Minuten rasten lassen.

Maroni-Dörrzwetschken-Gnocchi

Die Erdäpfel in der Schale kochen, kurz ausdämpfen lassen, pellen, noch heiß durch die Presse drücken, mit dem Maronipüree vermischen. Stärke, Butter und Eigelb dazugeben und zu einem Teig verkneten. Die Dörrzwetschken fein hacken, zu kleinen Kugeln formen und tiefkühlen. Sobald sie fest sind, Gnocchi formen und mit den Dörrzwetschkenkugeln füllen. In heißem Salzwasser einige Minuten gar ziehen lassen.

Anrichten

Die Maroni-Dörrzwetschken-Gnocchi mit den glacierten Quitten und der Wildnage auf dem Teller anrichten, den Hirschlungenbraten mittig platzieren und mit Hirschsauce umgeben.

Millefeuille mit Joghurtmousse und Waldbeeren

Zutaten für 10 Personen | Foto Seite 92

Crème-brûlée-Eis
375 ml Obers
375 ml Milch
2 Vanilleschoten
7 Eigelb
60 g Zucker
50 g brauner Zucker

Joghurtmousse
250 g Joghurt
25 g Zucker
2 Blatt Gelatine
125 ml Obers

Vanillecreme
125 g Zucker
60 g Puddingpulver
100 g Eigelb
500 ml Milch
250 ml Obers

Waldbeerengelee
250 g Walderdbeerenmark
25 g Zucker
2 Blatt Gelatine

Waldbeerensauce
200 g Waldbeeren
25 g Zucker
Saft von 1 Zitrone

Teig
500 g Blätterteig
Zucker und Staubzucker
 zum Bestreuen

Anrichten
frische Beeren

Crème-brûlée-Eis
Den Ofen auf 90 Grad vorheizen. Obers, Milch, ausgekratztes Vanillemark und Vanilleschote aufkochen. Eigelb und Zucker weiß schlagen und unter die Obers-Milch-Mischung rühren. Die Schote herausnehmen und die Masse in ein hohes Blech gießen. Im Ofen circa 1 Stunde backen. Danach mit braunem Zucker bestreuen und mit einem Flambierbrenner oder einer Lötlampe karamellisieren. Die Crème brûlée in eine Schüssel geben und gut durchmixen. In Pacojetformen füllen und tiefkühlen. Vor Gebrauch mit Pacojet aufmixen.

Joghurtmousse
Joghurt mit Zucker verrühren. Die Gelatine einweichen, ausdrücken und auflösen, zum Joghurt geben und gut vermischen. Obers schlagen und unterheben, Cocktailgläser halb mit der Mousse füllen und kalt stellen.

Waldbeerensauce
Früchte und Zucker in einem zugedeckten Topf erhitzen und weich kochen. Gut mixen, den Zitronensaft beigeben und die Sauce durch ein feines Sieb streichen.

Teig
Den Ofen auf 175 Grad vorheizen. Den Blätterteig circa 3 Millimeter dick ausrollen, auf ein mit Backpapier ausgelegtes Backblech geben und mit etwas Zucker bestreuen. Im Ofen circa 20–25 Minuten backen. Nach der Hälfte der Backzeit den Teig mit einem Blech beschweren. Anschließend kalt stellen und in 4 ½ x 4 ½ Zentimeter große Stücke schneiden. Die einzelnen Blätter trennen, mit etwas Staubzucker bestreuen und mit dem Flambierbrenner oder einer Lötlampe karamellisieren (circa 10 Blätter pro Portion).

Vanillecreme
Zucker, Puddingpulver und Eigelb aufschlagen, bis die Masse hell und dicklich ist. Die Milch aufkochen und über die Masse gießen, in einen Topf geben, erneut aufkochen und anschließend kalt stellen. Das Obers schlagen und unter die abgekühlte Masse heben. In Dressiersack mit glatter Tülle füllen und erneut kühl stellen.

Waldbeerengelee
Das Waldbeerenmark und den Zucker aufkochen, die eingeweichte Gelatine beigeben und gut verrühren. Auf ein mit Backpapier ausgelegtes Backblech gießen und kalt stellen. Mit einer kleinen runden Ausstechform insgesamt 50 Kreise ausstechen.

Anrichten
Die Waldbeeren vor dem Servieren mit einem Teil der Waldbeerensauce marinieren. Blätterteigblätter und Vanillecreme abwechselnd montieren und bei jedem zweiten einen Waldbeerengeleekreis dazugeben. Teller nach Belieben mit der Waldbeerensauce dekorieren und das Eis auf das Millefeuille geben. Die Beeren schön auf der Mousse dressieren.

Dessert von Marille, Kardamom und Mandeln

Zutaten für 10 Portionen | Foto Seite 94

Kardamomkruste
100 g brauner Zucker
250 g Mehl
125 g Butter
1 Eigelb
frisch gemahlener Kardamom

Hippen
30 g Butter
100 g brauner Zucker
50 g Eiweiß
75 g Mehl

Marillenröster
20 frische Marillen
25 g Butter
25 g Zucker
1 KL Honig
frisch gemahlener Kardamom

Brioche
1 Brioche
25 g Butter
1 Prise Zucker

Mandelmousse
200 ml Milch
100 g Marzipanrohmasse
50 g Calisson (südfrz. Konfekt)
2 Blatt Gelatine
2 Tropfen Bittermandelaroma
125 ml Obers

Marillensorbet
500 g reife Marillen
160 g Zucker
50 g Glukose
Saft von 1 Zitrone

Mandeleis
500 ml Milch
185 g Zucker
6 Eigelb
150 g geröstete gem. Mandeln
100 ml Obers

Marillen-Kardamom-Schaum
200 g Marillenmark
25 g Zucker
1 Prise Kardamom
1 Blatt Gelatine
100 g Crème légère

Kardamomkruste
Alle Zutaten in einen Mixer mit flachem Einsatz geben und zu einem Pulver verarbeiten. Auf ein mit Backpapier ausgelegtes Backblech verteilen und kalt stellen.

Hippen
Den Ofen auf 180 Grad vorheizen. Die Butter schmelzen und leicht bräunen. Zucker, Eiweiß und Mehl mit der Butter vermengen. Mithilfe eines Spachtels dünn auf ein mit Backpapier ausgelegtes Backblech streichen (3 x 18 Zentimeter), darauf die Kardamomkruste geben und im Ofen backen, bis die Hippen braun werden. Die noch heißen Hippen auf ein Nudelholz rollen.

Marillenröster
Marillen entsteinen und achteln, Butter in der Pfanne schmelzen, Zucker und Honig dazugeben und leicht karamellisieren lassen. Marillen ebenfalls in die Pfanne geben, mit Kardamom überstreuen, weich dünsten und anschließend kalt stellen.

Brioche
Das Brioche in 5 Millimeter dicke Scheiben schneiden und Ringe mit dem Durchmesser der Hippen ausstechen. In leicht gezuckerter Butter ausbraten.

Mandelmousse

Die Milch erhitzen, Marzipan und Calisson beigeben. Gelatine einweichen, ausdrücken und dazugeben. Aroma beigeben, alles mixen und kalt stellen, bis es leicht anzieht. In die noch flüssige Masse das geschlagene Obers heben.
In einen Rahmen (8 x 20 Zentimeter) gießen. Kalt stellen, bis die Masse fest wird, und in der Größe des Brioches ausstechen.

Marillensorbet

Marillen entkernen, in einen Topf geben, Zucker und Glukose dazugeben. Wenn die Marillen weich gekocht sind, Zitronensaft beigeben, fein mixen und durch ein Sieb streichen. In eine Pacojetform geben und tiefkühlen. Vor Gebrauch mit Pacojet mixen.

Mandeleis

Milch und Zucker aufkochen, die Eigelbe beigeben und bei 84 Grad im heißen Wasserbad unter ständigem Rühren eine englische Creme herstellen. Mandeln und Obers beimengen, verrühren, in Pacojetform geben und tiefkühlen. Vor Gebrauch mit Pacojet mixen.

Marillen-Kardamom-Schaum

Marillenmark aufkochen, Zucker, Kardamom und die eingeweichte Gelatine beigeben. Gut verrühren, dann kalt stellen. Die Crème légère unter die Masse rühren und in eine Isi-Flasche füllen.

Anrichten

Schaum zum fertiggestellten Brioche in die Hippe geben, Marillenröster daraufsetzen und mit dem Marillenschaum bedecken. Die Mandelmousse in ein kleines Gefäß füllen und mit Eis und Sorbet anrichten.

Schokoladenvariation mit Whiskymousse und Kaffeeparfait
Zutaten für 10 Portionen ❘ Foto Seite 96

Schokoladenbiskuit
150 g Butter
100 g Bitterschokolade mit 66 % Kakaoanteil
120 g Ei
180 g Zucker
80 g Mehl

Schokoladenganache
250 ml Obers
175 g Schokolade „Pure Caraibe"

Karamellisierte Filoblätter
3 Blätter Filoteig
50 g Butter
20 g Staubzucker
10 g Kakaopulver

Schokoladencreme
25 g Zucker
50 g Eigelb
125 ml Milch
125 ml Obers
140 g Jivara-Milchschokolade

Whiskymousse
25 g Zucker
25 g Eigelb
125 ml Milch
1 Blatt Gelatine
65 ml Obers
15 ml Whisky

Kaffeeparfait
150 g weiße Schokoladenkuvertüre
20 g Zucker
40 g Eigelb
100 ml Milch
100 ml Obers
1 Blatt Gelatine
5 g lösliches Kaffeepulver

Zuckerhippe
75 g Fondant
75 g Glukose
75 g Isomalt
1 Tonkabohne

Schokoladenbiskuit

Den Ofen auf 180 Grad vorheizen. Butter und Schokolade im Wasserbad schmelzen. Eier und Zucker leicht aufschlagen. Die zwei Massen miteinander verrühren, das Mehl beigeben und etwa 2 Zentimeter hoch auf ein gebuttertes und gemehltes Backblech streichen. Im Ofen circa 12 Minuten backen, in 6 x 6 Zentimeter große Stücke schneiden.

Schokoladenganache

Obers aufkochen und über die Schokolade gießen. Alles gut verrühren bis die Schokolade geschmolzen ist und eine homogene und geschmeidige Masse entsteht. Erkalten lassen und in einen Dressiersack mit glatter Tülle geben.

Karamellisierte Filoblätter

Den Ofen auf 160 Grad vorheizen. Blätter in insgesamt 20 Quadrate von 8 x 8 Zentimeter Größe schneiden. Die Butter schmelzen, mit Staubzucker und Kakaopulver vermischen und die Teigstücke damit bestreichen. Auf ein mit Backpapier ausgelegtes Backblech geben, mit einem zweiten Stück Backpapier bedecken und mit einem weiteren Blech beschweren. Im Ofen backen, bis die Blätter schön karamellisiert sind.

Schokoladencreme

Zucker und Eigelb aufschlagen, bis die Masse hell und dicklich ist. Die Milch mit dem Obers aufkochen, über die Zucker-Ei-Masse gießen, in einen Topf geben und bei 86 Grad erneut erhitzen. Die Schokolade dazugeben, verrühren, schmelzen lassen und gut durchmixen. Kalt stellen und zum Dressieren in einen Spritzsack mit einer sternförmigen Tülle füllen.

Whiskymousse

Zucker und Eigelb aufschlagen, bis die Masse hell und dicklich ist. Die Milch aufkochen, über die Zucker-Ei-Masse gießen, in einen Topf geben und auf 86 Grad erhitzen. Die eingeweichte Gelatine, Obers und Whisky beigeben, gut verrühren und in eine Isi-Flasche füllen.

Kaffeeparfait

Die weiße Schokolade schmelzen. Zucker und Eigelb aufschlagen, bis die Masse hell und dicklich ist. Die Milch mit dem Obers aufkochen, über die Zucker-Ei-Masse gießen, in einen Topf geben und auf 86 Grad erhitzen. Die eingeweichte Gelatine und die Schokolade unterrühren. Das lösliche Kaffeepulver dazugeben und alles gut verrühren. Zylinder (Durchmesser 3 Zentimeter, Höhe 5 Zentimeter) mit Backpapier auslegen und die Masse einfüllen. Zylinder tiefkühlen.

Zuckerhippe

Den Ofen auf 190 Grad vorheizen. Fondant, Glukose und Isomalt in einen Topf geben und auf 165 Grad erhitzen. Auf eine Silikonmatte streichen und trocknen lassen. Die Masse zerbröseln und im Blender fein mixen. Erneut auf einer Silikonmatte verteilen und mit einer Muskatreibe die Tonkabohne darüberreiben. Im Ofen backen bis der Zucker gut geschmolzen ist. Fest werden lassen und in gewünschte Stücke schneiden.

Anrichten

Die Ganache auf den Biskuitboden auftragen. Ein Filoblatt darauflegen und eine Schicht Schokoladencreme daraufdressieren. Mit einem weiteren Filoblatt bedecken und eine weitere Schicht Schokoladencreme auftragen. Das Parfait daraufsetzen, mit den Hippen dekorieren und die Whiskymousse aufspritzen.

Nougatbarren mit Matchatee-Eis und Bananenkompott

Zutaten für 10 Personen ❙ Foto Seite 98

Haselnussdacquoise

85 g Staubzucker
85 g geriebene Haselnüsse
100 g Eiweiß
30 g Zucker

Nougatbarren

100 ml Milch
2 Blatt Gelatine
200 g Nougatpaste
250 ml Obers
150 g Kakaobutter
300 g weiße Schokolade

Matchatee-Eis

125 g Zucker
100 g Eigelb
500 ml Milch
100 ml Obers
10 g Matchatee
in Pulverform

Bananenkompott

250 g Bananen
25 g brauner Zucker
Saft und Zesten von
1 Limette

Milchgelee

125 ml Milch
20 g Zucker
1 Blatt Gelatine

Zitronengelee

125 g neutrale Glasur
65 ml Zitronensaft
Zesten von 1 Limette

Haselnussdacquoise

Den Ofen auf 180 Grad vorheizen. Staubzucker und Haselnüsse fein vermixen. Eiweiß und Zucker aufschlagen. Die Haselnüssen unterheben und die Masse 3 Millimeter dick auf ein mit Backpapier ausgelegtes Backblech streichen. Im Ofen 10–12 Minuten backen, abkühlen lassen und in 9 x 3 Zentimeter große Stücke schneiden.

Nougatbarren

Milch aufkochen, die eingeweichte Gelatine darin auflösen, auf die Nougatpaste gießen und vermixen, bis die Masse auf 35 Grad abgekühlt ist. Das Obers schlagen, unterheben. In Flexipanformen füllen (9 x 3 Zentimeter), die Haselnussdacquoise auflegen und kalt stellen. Kakaobutter, weiße Schokolade vermengen, bei 40 Grad schmelzen lassen. In ein sauberes Airbrushsprühgerät einfüllen, den kalten Barren aus der Form nehmen und damit besprühen, anschließend erneut kalt stellen.

Matchatee-Eis

Zucker und Eigelb aufschlagen, bis die Masse hell und dicklich ist. Die Milch mit dem Obers aufkochen und über die Zucker-Ei-Masse gießen, in einen Topf geben und erneut aufkochen.
Das Matchateepulver in die Creme geben und vermixen. In Pacojetformen füllen und gefrieren. Vor Verwendung mit dem Pacojet aufrühren.

Bananenkompott

Bananen klein schneiden und mit den restlichen Zutaten in einen Topf geben und erhitzen. Mit einem Deckel verschließen und bei geringer Hitzezufuhr ziehen lassen, bis die Bananen weich gekocht sind. Mit einem Spachtel bearbeiten, bis eine feine Masse entsteht.

Milchgelee

Milch und Zucker aufkochen. Die eingeweichte Gelatine dazugeben und unter Rühren auflösen. Auf ein Blech circa 3 Millimeter hoch aufgießen und kalt stellen. Aus dem festen Gelee kleine Würfelchen ausschneiden (3 x 3 Millimeter).

Zitronengelee

Glasur mit den Limettenzesten und dem Zitronensaft aufkochen.

Anrichten

Das Zitronengelee dekorativ auf den Tellern verteilen, den Nougatbarren, das Milchgelee und das Eis darauf anrichten. Das Kompott mithilfe eines Dressiersacks auf den Nougatbarren auftragen.

Kirschentarte, Pfirsich und Pistazien

Zutaten für 10 Portionen ▮ Foto Seite 100

Bretonischer Mürbteig

75 g weiche Butter
75 g Zucker
2 g Salz
30 g Eigelb
100 g Mehl
3 ½ g Backpulver

Weinkirschen

100 g Rotwein
15 g Zucker
Gewürzmischung aus Vanille, Birne, Kardamom und Zimt
50 g Weichselmark (Sauerkirschmark)
60 Kirschen

Pfirsichmarmelade

100 g Pfirsich
150 g Zucker
1 EL Zitronensaft
½ Vanilleschote

Pistazien

25 g Zucker
15 g geriebene Pistazien
2 g Butter

Pfirsichsorbet

120 g Zucker
60 g Glukose
500 g Pfirsichmark
25 ml Zitronensaft

Pistazienmousse

125 g Milch
25 g Eigelb
25 g Zucker
15 g Puddingpulver
25 g Pistazienmark
1 Blatt Gelatine
75 g Crème légère

Hippen

12 ½ g Glukose
25 g Fondant
50 g Pistazienpulver

Kroketten

125 g Amarenakirschen in Sirup
125 g Weichselmark
2 g Agar-Agar
1 Ei
100 g Mehl
100 g Semmelbrösel
Öl zum Frittieren

Bretonischer Mürbteig

Den Ofen auf 160 Grad vorheizen. Butter, Zucker und Salz vermischen und mit den Eigelben cremig rühren. Mehl und Backpulver dazugeben und alles zu einem Teig verkneten. Den Teig zu einer Kugel formen, mit Klarsichtfolie einwickeln, 30 Minuten im Kühlschrank rasten lassen. Den Teig anschließend circa 1 Zentimeter dick ausrollen, mit Dessertringen (Durchmesser 6 Zentimeter) Kreise ausstechen und diese mit dem Ring auf ein mit Backpapier ausgelegtes Backblech geben. Im Ofen circa 8 Minuten backen. Sofort mithilfe eines Messers aus dem Ring entfernen.

Weinkirschen

Den Wein um die Hälfte reduzieren, den Zucker und die Gewürze nach Geschmack beigeben. Weichselmark beigeben und ziehen lassen. Durch ein feines Sieb streichen und die entsteinten Kirschen dazugeben. Etwas erhitzen, Kirschen bissfest garen, herausnehmen und kalt stellen. Den übrigen Sirup einreduzieren, bis er etwas dicker wird, und zum Dekorieren beiseitestellen.

Pfirsichmarmelade

Die Pfirsiche schälen, halbieren, entsteinen und mit der Hälfte des Zuckers und dem Zitronensaft vermischen. Die Vanilleschote auskratzen und sowohl das Mark als auch die Schote dazugeben. Alles zum Köcheln bringen, dann die zweite Hälfte Zucker unterrühren, die Vanilleschote herausnehmen und beiseitestellen.

Pistazien

Zucker und 7 Milliliter Wasser vermischen und auf 121 Grad erhitzen. Die Pistazien dazugeben und rühren, bis sie gut vom Zucker überzogen sind. Butter beigeben, verrühren und die Masse auf ein mit Backpapier belegtes Backblech streichen. Die Backofentemperatur auf 160 Grad erhöhen und die Masse leicht bräunen.

Pfirsichsorbet

Aus 240 Milliliter Wasser, Zucker und Glukose einen Sirup herstellen. Pfirsichmark und Zitronensaft in den heißen Sirup geben. Fein mixen, in eine Pacojetform füllen, abkühlen lassen und tiefkühlen. Vor Gebrauch mit dem Pacojet aufmixen.

Pistazienmousse

Milch aufkochen. Eigelb, Zucker und Puddingpulver aufschlagen, bis die Masse hell und dicklich ist. Milch daraufgießen und erneut aufkochen. Pistazienmark und aufgelöste Gelatine beimengen und abkühlen lassen. Dann die geschlagene Crème légère unterheben. In einen Dressiersack mit glatter Tülle füllen und kalt stellen.

Hippen

Den Ofen auf 190 Grad vorheizen. Die Glukose und das Fondant auf 155 Grad erhitzen und auf ein geöltes Backblech sehr fein aufstreichen. Erkalten lassen, in Stücke brechen und im Blender mit dem Pistazienpulver fein vermixen. Dieses Pulver durch ein feines Sieb auf Backpapier streuen, im Ofen circa 10 Minuten backen. Erkalten lassen, Hippen abbrechen.

Kroketten

Amarenakirschen und Weichselmark vermengen, einmal aufkochen und das Agar-Agar beigeben. In Flexipan-Halbkugeln füllen und gefrieren. Vor dem Anrichten die gefrorenen Halbkugeln nacheinander in verquirltem Ei, Mehl und Semmelbrösel panieren und frittieren.

Anrichten

Pfirsichmarmelade in der Mitte des Mürbteigs anrichten, die Kirschen rundherum setzen, kurz im Ofen erwärmen. Danach die Hippe auflegen und die Pistazienmousse dressieren. Mit den karamellisierten Pistazien garnieren, Pfirsichsorbet und Krokette danebenanrichten und mit dem Weinsirup dekorieren.

Schokoladenpralinen mit Nougatkrokant

Zutaten für 25 Stück | Foto Seite 102

Fülle

125 g Nougat
50 g Milchschokolade
125 g Pailleté feuilletine
(z. B. von Barry)

Glasur

300 g Zartbitterschokolade mit 66 % Kakaoanteil

Fülle

Nougat und Milchschokolade bei 32 Grad schmelzen, die Pailleté feuilletine beigeben. Gut vermischen und circa 1 Zentimeter hoch in einen Rahmen einfüllen. Bei Zimmertemperatur stocken lassen und in 2 Zentimeter große Würfel schneiden.

Glasur

Zartbitterschokolade auf 50 Grad erhitzen, anschließend auf 27 Grad runterkühlen und auf 32 Grad erwärmen. Sobald die richtige Temperatur erreicht ist, die Fülle in die Schokolade tauchen und auf speziellen Schokoladenfolien mindestens 12 Stunden bei Zimmertemperatur rasten lassen und dann servieren.

Cheesecaketörtchen mit Ananas und Kokos

Zutaten für 75 Minitörtchen | Foto Seite 102

Mürbteig

250 g Staubzucker
250 g Butter
4 Eigelb
500 g Mehl

Cheesecakemasse

600 g Frischkäse
2 Eier
1 Eigelb
125 g Zucker
40 ml Obers
50 g Mehl

Anrichten

1 Ananas
1 Päckchen Kokosraspel

Mürbteig

Staubzucker und Butter cremig rühren, die Eigelbe und das Mehl dazugeben und zu einem glatten Teig verrühren. In Folie einschlagen und ½ Stunde kalt stellen.
Den Ofen auf 170 Grad vorheizen. Den Teig ausrollen und im Ofen etwa 10 Minuten vorbacken, bis er leicht goldgelb ist.

Cheesecakemasse

Die Hitze im Ofen auf 120 Grad reduzieren. Alle Zutaten miteinander cremig verrühren. Auf den vorgebackenen Teig streichen und im Ofen in etwa 30 Minuten fertig backen.

Anrichten

Die Ananas schälen, in kleine Stäbchen schneiden und in den Kokosraspeln wälzen.
Den fertigen Cheesecake in kleine Würfel schneiden und mit Ananas-Kokos-Stäbchen dekorieren.

Macarons

Zutaten für 100 Küchlein **|** Foto Seite 102

Macarons

250 g Staubzucker
250 g Mandelpulver
300 g Zucker
200 g Eiweiß
Lebensmittelfarbe
 nach Geschmack
Aromen nach Geschmack
(z. B. Kokosraspel, flüssige
Vanille usw.)

Macarons

Den Ofen auf 160 Grad vorheizen. Staubzucker und Mandelpulver ganz fein vermixen und durch ein Sieb streichen. Zucker und 150 Milliliter Wasser auf 118 Grad erhitzen. Die Hälfte des Eiweißes aufschlagen und dabei das Zucker-Wasser-Gemisch dazugießen. So lange rühren, bis ein ganz fester, aber geschmeidiger Schnee entsteht. Das restliche Eiweiß mit dem Staubzucker-Mandel-Gemisch gut verrühren. Die beiden Eiweißmassen miteinander vermischen und gewünschte Farben und Aromen beigeben. In einen Dressiersack mit glatter Tülle füllen und kleine Kreise auf ein mit Backpapier ausgelegtes Backblech spritzen. Im Ofen circa 12 Minuten backen. Die Backzeit kann je nach verwendetem Ofen variieren.

Anrichten

Die Macarons können mit Marmelade oder geliertem Fruchtmark gefüllt werden.

Orangenküchlein

Zutaten für 50 Küchlein **|** Foto Seite 102

Küchlein

150 g Staubzucker
150 g Butter
Zesten von 1 Orange
3 Eier
190 g Mehl
5 g Backpulver
1 Prise Salz

Anrichten

Orangenmarmelade zum Füllen
Himbeeren, Erdbeeren,
dunkle Trauben
Staubzucker zum Bestreuen

Küchlein

Den Backofen auf 190 Grad vorheizen. Zucker und Butter schaumig schlagen und mit den restlichen Zutaten verrühren.
Den Teig in einen Spritzsack füllen und in Konfektschälchen (aus Papier) spritzen. Im Ofen circa 7 Minuten backen.

Anrichten

Küchlein auskühlen lassen, ein kleines Loch ausstechen und mithilfe eines Spritzbeutels mit Orangenmarmelade füllen. Mit den Früchten dekorieren und mit Staubzucker bestreuen.

Brioche mit Vanillecreme

Zutaten für 10 Portionen ❙ Foto Seite 102

Teig
250 g Mehl
35 g Zucker
5 g Salz
50 ml Milch
10 g frische Germ
3 Eier
80 g weiche Butter

Vanillecreme
50 g Zucker
30 g Vanillepuddingpulver
50 g Eigelb
250 ml Milch
75 g Butter

Teig
Mehl, Zucker und Salz vermengen. Milch, Germ und Eier ebenfalls miteinander vermengen und zum Mehl-Zucker-Gemisch gießen. Die Butter dazugeben und in der Küchenmaschine oder mit der Hand zu einem glatten Teig kneten. Rasten lassen, bis das Teigvolumen sich verdoppelt hat. Den Ofen auf 180 Grad vorheizen. Aus dem Teig 10 kleine Kugeln formen und auf ein mit Backpapier ausgelegtes Backblech geben. Im Ofen leicht bräunen lassen.

Vanillecreme
Zucker, Puddingpulver und Eigelb aufschlagen, bis die Masse hell und dicklich ist. Die Milch aufkochen, über die Masse gießen, in einem Topf erneut aufkochen. Vom Herd nehmen, Butter einrühren und kalt stellen.

Anrichten
Brioche halbieren, mit der Creme füllen, nach Belieben dekorieren.

Crevetten-Ricotta-Ravioli

Zutaten für 10 Personen ∎ Foto Seite 116

Ravioli

250 g Ricotta
125 g Crevetten
frische Kräuter
nach Geschmack (z. B. Petersil,
Schnittlauch, Basilikum)
2 Eier
200 g Nudelteig
(siehe Grundrezept Seite 335)
1 Eigelb
Salz, weißer Pfeffer

Sauce

Saft von 1 Limette
1/8 l Weißwein
125 g kalte Butter
1 Pfefferminzzweig
Salz, Pfeffer, Zucker

Anrichten

Zesten und Spalten von
1 Limette

Ravioli

Ricotta, Crevetten, fein gehackte Kräuter und Eier miteinander vermengen. Den Nudelteig dünn ausrollen, auf eine Hälfte die Fülle auftragen, mit Eigelb bestreichen, den Teig zusammenklappen, gut andrücken und Ravioli ausstechen. Die Ravioli in kochendem Salzwasser etwa 4 Minuten garen.

Sauce

Limettensaft und Weißwein kurz aufkochen lassen, mit der Butter montieren, mit Salz, Pfeffer und Zucker abschmecken und die gehackten Minzblättchen unterziehen.

Anrichten

Ravioli mit der Weißweinsauce beträufeln und vor dem Servieren mit Limettenzesten und -spalten garnieren.

Rieslingsbeuschel vom Kalb

Zutaten für 4 Personen ▎ Foto Seite 118

Rieslingsbeuschel

500 g Kalbsbeuschel (Lunge und Herz)
½ Zwiebel
1 Karotte
½ Lauchstange
¼ Sellerie
1 Lorbeerblatt
einige Pfefferkörner
1 KL scharfer Senf
Saft von 1 Zitrone
1 EL Weinessig
1 kleine Essiggurke
1 KL Kapern
1 EL Butter
¼ l Riesling
1/8 l Obers
1 Knoblauchzehe
1 Bund Petersil
Salz, weißer Pfeffer

Serviettenknödel

400 g Semmelwürfel
¼ l Milch
4 Eier
20 g gehackter Petersil
1 EL Butter
Salz, Pfeffer, Muskat

Anrichten

4 Eier

Rieslingsbeuschel

Die Vorbereitung des Beuschels bedarf der meisten Arbeit, wenn diese allerdings erledigt ist, geht alles schnell und ist einfach. Vom Beuschel Schlund, grobe Sehnen und Fett wegschneiden, mindestens 2 Stunden (ruhig auch länger) in kaltes Wasser einlegen, sodass alles Blut sauber ausgeschwemmt wird. Zwischendurch einige Male das Wasser wechseln und das Beuschel ein wenig hin und her bewegen.

Zwiebel, Karotte, Lauch und Sellerie putzen beziehungsweise schälen. Eine Hälfte davon in grobe Stücke schneiden, die andere Hälfte beiseitestellen. Das grob geschnittene Gemüse, ein Lorbeerblatt und einige angedrückte Pfefferkörner in einem ausreichend großen Topf mit circa 2 Litern Wasser aufkochen. Gewässertes Beuschel beigeben und etwa 40 Minuten zugedeckt kochen. Nach dieser Zeit könnte die Lunge schon weich sein. Das Herz braucht üblicherweise 10–15 Minuten länger. Weiche Beuschel aus dem Sud heben. Das Kochwasser abseihen und für das spätere Aufgießen beiseitestellen. Vom Beuschel die großen Blutgefäße entfernen, in einer großen Schüssel kalt stellen, mit einem Brett und Tellern beschweren und ein paar Stunden stehen lassen.

Beuschel in feine Streifen schneiden, dabei große Knorpel entfernen. Mit Senf, Zitrone, Essig, klein gehackter Essiggurke und Kapern vermischen. Mit Salz und Pfeffer abschmecken und etwa 2 Stunden, noch besser jedoch über Nacht, marinieren lassen.

Zur Fertigstellung des Beuschels das beiseitegestellte Gemüse in feine Streifen schneiden, in Salzwasser bissfest garen und kalt abschrecken. In einem geräumigen Geschirr die Butter erhitzen, Zwiebel anschwitzen, mit Weißwein ablöschen und Wein auf die Hälfte der ursprünglichen Menge einkochen. Die restlichen Gemüsestreifen und die Beuschelstreifen zugeben, mit dem Beuschelfond auffüllen und aufkochen. Obers zugießen und etwas einkochen lassen. Mit Salz, frisch geriebenem weißen Pfeffer und zerdrückten Knoblauch würzen. Gehackten Petersil einrühren.

Serviettenknödel

Die Semmelwürfel in Milch einweichen. Eier und Petersil unterrühren und mit Salz, Pfeffer und Muskat abschmecken. Knödelmasse in hitzebeständiger Klarsichtfolie straff einrollen und im Wasserbad bei 80 Grad 40 Minuten pochieren. Fertige Knödel aus dem Wasser nehmen und kalt stellen. Aus der Folie nehmen, in Scheiben schneiden und in Butter beidseitig braten.

Anrichten

Das Beuschel auf den Teller geben und mit den Serviettenknödeln dekorativ anrichten. Je ein in Form gebrachtes Spiegelei aufsetzen.

Punschkrapferl mit Nougatkrokant

Zutaten für circa 20 Stück ❙ Foto Seite 120

Biskuit

10 Eier
40 g Staubzucker
1 Prise Vanillezucker
1 Prise Salz
Zesten von 2 Zitronen
200 g Zucker
250 g Mehl

Punschfülle

200 g Marillenmarmelade
125 ml Rum
40 ml Läuterzucker
(siehe Grundrezept Seite 335)
50 g Zartbitterschokolade
Zesten von je 1 Zitrone
und Orange
1 Prise Zimt

Garnitur

ca. 50 g Marillenmarmelade
250 g Fondant, mit Lebensmittelfarbe rosa gefärbt
20 Amarenakirschen
20 Minzblätter
Blattgold zum Dekorieren

Biskuit

Den Backofen auf 200 Grad vorheizen. Eier trennen, Eigelb mit Staubzucker schaumig rühren, Vanillezucker, Salz und die Zesten unterrühren. Das Eiweiß mit dem Zucker zu Schnee schlagen. Beide Massen vorsichtig miteinander vermengen, das Mehl dazusieben und unterheben. Aus der Masse werden 2 Böden gebacken, dafür jeweils die Hälfte der Masse auf ein mit Backpapier ausgelegtes Blech streichen und im Backofen 10 Minuten backen. Aus beiden Böden je ein 20 x 25 Zentimeter großes Rechteck schneiden, die Reste für die Fülle beiseitestellen.

Punschfülle

Restlichen Biskuitteig für die Punschfülle zerkleinern und in einer Schüssel mit der Marillenmarmelade, dem Rum sowie Läuterzucker vermischen. Schokolade reiben, mit Orangen- und Zitronenzesten sowie Zimt zur Fülle geben. Die Masse durchkneten, bis sie gut zusammenhält.

Anrichten

Einen Biskuitboden mit Marillenmarmelade bestreichen, in einen Dessertrahmen geben und die Punschfülle aufstreichen. Mit dem zweiten Biskuitboden abdecken, beschweren und einige Stunden kalt stellen.
Biskuit aus der Form nehmen und in 20 Würfel zu 5 x 5 Zentimeter schneiden. Die Würfel seitlich und obenauf mit leicht erwärmter Marillenmarmelade bestreichen und abkühlen lassen. Danach mit erwärmtem Fondant glasieren. Mit Amarenakirschen, Minzblättern und Blattgold verzieren.

Schaumrollen

Zutaten für circa 15 Stück ❙ Foto Seite 120

Schaumrollen

500 g Blätterteig
4 Eiweiß
280 g Staubzucker
Staubzucker zum Bestreuen

Ofen auf 160 Grad vorheizen. Blätterteig circa 3 Milliliter dick ausrollen. Mit einem Teigrad 1 Zentimeter breite Streifen zuschneiden und diese um die Schaumrollenformen wickeln. Im Ofen 10–12 Minuten backen. Sofort von den Formen lösen und abkühlen lassen. Eiweiß und Staubzucker über einem Dampfbad zu einer sehr festen Masse schlagen, in einen Dressiersack füllen, in die Rollen spritzen und mit Staubzucker bestreuen.

Lauwarm marinierte Kalbszunge mit Wurzeln, Kren und Kernöl

Zutaten für 4 Personen | Foto Seite 134

Sauce
125 ml Obers
125 ml Rindsfond
100 g gehackte Kräuter
(Petersil, Estragon, Kerbel)
50 g Butter
Salz, Pfeffer

Wurzeln
2 Karotten
1 Gelbe Rübe
1 Lauchstange
6 cl Nussöl
3 cl Balsamico
Salz, Pfeffer

Anrichten
400 g gekochte Kalbszunge
½ Bund Schnittlauch
100 ml Kernöl
½ Krenwurzel

Sauce
Obers und Rindsfond einmal aufkochen, Kräuter und Butter einrühren und mit Salz und Pfeffer abschmecken. Durch ein feines Sieb passieren.

Wurzeln
Karotten, Gelbe Rübe und Lauch fein würfeln, in Salzwasser bissfest blanchieren, abschrecken, trocken tupfen, mit Nussöl, Balsamico, Salz und Pfeffer marinieren.

Anrichten
Kalbszunge in 2 Millimeter dünne Scheiben schneiden und flach auf gewärmten Tellern anrichten, Wurzeln darübergeben und mit der Sauce nappieren. Die angerichteten Teller mit fein geschnittenem Schnittlauch, Kernöl und frisch geriebenem Kren vollenden.

Bohnensalat mit Langostino und Weingartenpfirsich

Zutaten für 4 Personen | Foto Seite 136

Bohnensalat
je 50 g weiße, rote und
grüne Bohnen
1 Weingartenpfirsich
1 KL Senfkörner
1 EL Weißweinessig
3 EL Olivenöl
1 EL geschnittenen Schnittlauch
Salz, Pfeffer, Zucker

Langostino
8 frische Langostinos
Saft von ½ Limette
½ Bund Schnittlauch
Salz

Bohnensalat
Die Bohnen getrennt voneinander weich kochen. Pfirsich in dekorative Stücke schneiden.
Die Senfkörner dreimal in 125 Milliliter Wasser kochen, aus der Hälfte der Körner, Weißweinessig und 2 Esslöffeln Olivenöl ein Dressing erstellen. Die Bohnen und Pfirsichstücke damit marinieren, mit Salz, Pfeffer und etwas Zucker abschmecken.

Langostino
Die Langostinos aus der Schale brechen und den Darm entfernen. Mit Salz, Limettensaft, den restlichen gekochten Senfkörnern, 1 Esslöffel Olivenöl und frisch geschnittenem Schnittlauch roh marinieren.

Anrichten
Salat mit Langostinos und Weingartenpfirsichen anrichten.

Kastanienvelouté mit Zwetschken in Speck

Zutaten für 4 Personen ❙ Foto Seite 138

Velouté

13 Kastanien
3 EL kalte Butter
½ l Geflügelfond
125 ml Obers
50 g geschlagenes Obers
Salz, Pfeffer

Zwetschken

12 Dörrzwetschken
12 Scheiben Bauchspeck

Velouté

Den Backofen auf 200 Grad vorheizen. Die Kastanien mithilfe eines kleinen, scharfen Messers kreuzweise einschneiden und im Backofen auf einem Blech 10–15 Minuten backen. Nach der Hälfte der Backzeit mit kaltem Wasser bespritzen, so löst sich die Schale besser vom Fruchtfleisch. Die Kastanien schälen und in kleine Stücke schneiden.

In einer geräumigen Pfanne 2 Esslöffel der Butter nussbraun aufschäumen, die Kastanien hinzufügen und kurz anschwenken. Mit Geflügelfond ablöschen und 15 Minuten leicht köcheln lassen. Das Obers hinzufügen, nochmals kurz aufkochen lassen und mithilfe eines Stabmixers und unter Zugabe der restlichen kalten Butter pürieren. Mit Salz und Pfeffer abschmecken, geschlagenes Obers unterheben und servieren.

Zwetschken

Dörrzwetschken in den Speck einrollen und in einer beschichteten Pfanne knusprig braten.

Anrichten

Velouté in tiefe Teller geben, mit je 3 Dörrzwetschken anrichten und servieren.

Mariazeller Wildsaibling mit Petersilpappardelle und Rahmkohlrabi

Zutaten für 4 Personen | Foto Seite 140

Petersilnudelteig

100 g Petersil
1 Ei
1 Eigelb
½ KL Olivenöl
etwas Mineralwasser
200 g Mehl
1 Schuss Olivenöl
Salz

Wildsaibling

400 g Mariazeller Wildsaiblingsfilet
Saft von 1 Zitrone
1 EL Öl
1 KL Butter
Salz, Pfeffer

Rahmkohlrabi

200 g Kohlrabi
125 ml Obers
etwas glatten Petersil
40 g Butter

Petersilnudelteig

Petersil waschen und trocken tupfen, vom Stängel zupfen und mit Ei, Eigelb, Öl, Mineralwasser und Salz im Mixer fein pürieren. In eine Schüssel füllen; nach und nach das Mehl zugeben und so lange verkneten, bis sich der Teig vom Schüsselrand löst. Zu einer Kugel formen, in Klarsichtfolie einschlagen und 30 Minuten kühl stellen.
Den Teig mit der Nudelmaschine ausrollen und 2 Zentimeter breite Pappardelle zuschneiden.

Wildsaibling

Wildsaibling mit Salz, Pfeffer und Zitronensaft würzen. In einer Pfanne Öl erhitzen und die Wildsaiblingsfilet darin knusprig braten. Kurz vor dem Ende der Garzeit eine Butterflocke hinzugeben, den Saibling auf die Fleischseite drehen und kurz ziehen lassen.

Rahmkohlrabi

Den Kohlrabi schälen und raspeln, im Obers knackig garen und mit Salz, Pfeffer und Muskat würzen. Petersil in Streifen schneiden und mit der Butter unterrühren.

Anrichten

Die Pappardelle in Salzwasser bissfest kochen, abseihen, in den leeren Topf zurückgeben und mit einem Schuss Olivenöl vermischen. Pappardelle aufrollen und in je 3 Portionen auf den Teller setzen. Rahmkohlrabi dazwischen anrichten und das Saiblingfilet aufsetzen.

Kalbsvögerl in Senf-Kapern-Sauce mit Champignons und Basmatireis

Zutaten für 4 Personen | Foto Seite 142

Kalbsvögerl

100 g fetten Bauchspeck
3 EL Butterschmalz
1 kg Kalbsvögerl
1 Karotte
1 Gelbe Rübe
1 Zwiebel
¼ l Weißwein
¼ l Kalbsfond oder Rindsfond
2 Lorbeerblätter
Salz, Pfeffer

Champignons

200 g Champignons
2 EL Butter
125 ml Obers
1 EL Pommerysenf
1 EL Kapern
etwas Petersil
Salz

Anrichten

200 g Basmatireis
1 EL Butter
Salz

Kalbsvögerl

Den Bauchspeck in sehr dünne, ½ x 10 Zentimeter große Streifen schneiden und Vögerl damit spicken.

In einer Pfanne das Butterschmalz erhitzen, Kalbsvögerl rundherum anbraten, herausnehmen, salzen und pfeffern. Karotte, Gelbe Rübe und Zwiebel grob würfeln, im Bratenrückstand anbraten, die gesalzenen Kalbsvögerl wieder daraufsetzen, Weißwein und Kalbsfond aufgießen, kurz einreduzieren lassen und Lorbeerblatt dazugeben. Im Ofen circa 1 ½ Stunden weich dünsten, dabei die Vögerl immer wieder mit dem Sud übergießen. Kalbsvögerl aus dem Sud heben, Lorbeerblatt entfernen, den Bratensaft mit dem Gemüse durch ein Spitzsieb drücken.

Champignons

Champignons putzen, waschen und in nicht zu schmale Blätter schneiden. Champignons in schäumender Butter rasch sautieren, etwas salzen und zum Schmorsaft geben. Mit Obers auffüllen und circa 10 Minuten langsam köcheln lassen. Mit Pommerysenf und Kapern vollenden. Die Sauce kann mit frisch gehackter Petersil verfeinert werden.

Anrichten

Den Basmatireis unter fließendem Wasser abspülen. In Salzwasser bissfest kochen, abseihen und in Butter schwenken. Kalbsvögerl in die fertige Sauce einlegen, noch mal kurz erhitzen und auf Tellern mit etwas Sauce und dem Basmatireis anrichten.

Wildentenbrust und -keule auf süßsaurem Liebstöckelkraut

Zutaten für 4 Personen ❙ Foto Seite 144

Wildente
2 Wildenten
1 l Gemüsefond
Salz
Pfeffer

Liebstöckelkraut
1 Weißkraut (ca. 500 g)
1 EL Öl
2 EL Staubzucker
1 EL grob gehacktes Liebstöckel
3 EL Balsamico
¼ l Gemüsefond
Salz

Wildente
Den Ofen auf 120 Grad vorheizen. Die Wildenten in eine Bratpfanne setzen, circa 2 Fingerhoch Gemüsefond angießen und im Ofen circa 1 ½–2 Stunden garen. Brust und Keulen abtrennen. Die Knochen klein hacken und in dem Bratenrückstand auf dem Herd circa 15 Minuten auskochen. Anschließend den Fond abseihen, stark einreduzieren und abschmecken.
Brüste und Keulen mit der Hautseite nach oben auf ein Backblech legen. Bei mittlerer Oberhitze knusprig und braun fertig braten.

Liebstöckelkraut
Weißkraut vom Strunk befreien und in 4 x 4 Zentimeter große Fleckerl schneiden. In einer Pfanne in heißem Öl anbraten, salzen, mit den Staubzucker bestreuen und leicht karamellisieren lassen. Mit Balsamico ablöschen, Gemüsefond aufgießen, das Kraut weich schmoren und Liebstöckel unterrühren.

Anrichten
Je 1 Bruststück und 1 Keule der Wildente auf Tellern anrichten. Das Liebstöckelkraut dazugeben und mit dem reduzierten Fond servieren.

Soufflierte Topfenpalatschinken

Zutaten für 4 Personen, 8 Stück ▌ Foto Seite 146

Palatschinkenteig
100 g Mehl
200 g Milch
2 Eier
1 Prise Salz
Butter zum Braten

Fülle
125 g Topfen
75 g Sauerrahm
2 Eier
25 g Staubzucker
15 g Vanillezucker
20 g Vanillepuddingpulver
1 cl Amaretto
1 cl Kirschwasser
2 EL Rosinen
70 ml Obers

Anrichten
frische Früchte

Palatschinken
Aus Mehl, Milch, Eiern und einer Prise Salz einen glatten Teig herstellen. In etwas Butter 8 Palatschinken backen.

Fülle
Den Backofen auf 160 Grad vorheizen. Topfen passieren und mit allen Zutaten, außer dem Obers, verrühren. Nun das Obers schlagen und unterheben.
Die Fülle auf die Palatschinken streichen und die Palatschinken aufrollen. Auf einem gefetteten Backblech im Backofen circa 10 Minuten backen.

Anrichten
Je 2 Palatschinken mit frischen Früchten servieren.

Froschschenkel mit Zitronenconfit und Velouté von geräuchertem Kren

Zutaten für 4 Personen **I** Foto Seite 168

Zitronenconfit
1 Zitrone
30 cl Läuterzucker
(siehe Grundrezept Seite 335)

Velouté
2 Schalotten
2 EL Olivenöl
5 cl Weißwein
5 cl Fischfond
150 ml Obers
2 EL geräuchertes Krenpüree
2 KL Zitronensaft
Salz, Pfeffer

Gemüse
100 g Babylauch
1 Fenchel
100 g Babykarotten
4 Radieschen
6 Schalotten
1 EL Butter
200 ml Gemüsefond

Froschschenkel
24 Froschschenkel
1 EL Mehl
100 g Butter
1 EL Olivenöl
2 Knoblauchzehen
3 EL gehackte Kräuter
(z. B. Estragon, Schnittlauch,
Petersil, Kerbel, Pimpinelle)
Salz, Pfeffer

Anrichten
Kräuterspitzen (z. B. Dill,
Kerbel, Schnittlauch)

Zitronenconfit
Die Zitrone schälen und filetieren. Den Läuterzucker 2–3 Minuten aufkochen. Die Zitronenfilets dazugeben und über Nacht ziehen lassen.

Velouté
Die Schalotten in Brunoise schneiden und im Olivenöl 4–6 Minuten bei milder Hitze weich dünsten. Mit dem Wein deglacieren, reduzieren bis der Wein komplett verdunstet ist. Nun den Fischfond dazugeben und auf die Hälfte reduzieren. Obers und Kren dazugeben und die Sauce zu einer sämigen Konsistenz einkochen. Durch ein Spitzsieb passieren, mit Salz, Pfeffer und Zitronensaft abschmecken.

Gemüse
Babylauch in 3 Zentimeter lange Stücke schneiden, Fenchel in dünne Spalten schneiden, Babykarotten putzen, Radieschen und Schalotten vierteln. Die Butter bei mittlerer Hitze in einer Pfanne schmelzen, das Gemüse dazugeben und 2 Minuten schwenken. Mit dem Gemüsefond ablöschen, köcheln lassen und das Gemüse bissfest garen.

Froschschenkel
Froschschenkel ganz leicht mit sehr wenig Mehl bestäuben. Die Hälfte der Butter in einer Pfanne bei mäßiger Hitze zergehen lassen und mit Olivenöl vermischen. Die Froschschenkel hineinlegen und auf beiden Seiten goldgelb braten. Während des Bratens leicht pfeffern und salzen, Knoblauch in Brunoise schneiden, die frisch gehackten Kräuter und weitere 20 Gramm der Butter, in kleinen Stücken, dazugeben.
Froschschenkel herausnehmen und auf einer vorgewärmten Platte beiseitestellen. Die Bratbutter abgießen, den Bratensatz mit Weißwein ablöschen, die Hälfte der Kräuter dazugeben und einige Sekunden dünsten. Die restlichen 30 Gramm Butter dazurühren, über die Froschschenkel geben und mit den restlichen Kräutern bestreuen.

Anrichten
Die Zitronenfilets mit dem warmen Gemüse mischen und auf den Tellern anrichten, die Schenkel auf, neben oder rundherum platzieren. Die Velouté anlegen und mit Kräutern bestreut servieren.

Weinbergschnecken in Burgunderreduktion mit pochiertem Ei

Zutaten für 4 Personen ∎ Foto Seite 170

Weinbergschnecken
100 g Karotten
100 g Lauch
3 Lorbeerblätter
1 KL schwarze Pfefferkörner
1 unbehandelte Zitrone
500 ml Weißwein
(Sauvignon blanc)
24 Weinbergschnecken
25 g Schalottenwürfel
20 g Butter
1 EL gehackter Petersil und
Schnittlauch

Burgunderreduktion
60 g Schalottenwürfel
20 ml Olivenöl
5 g geschroteter
schwarzer Pfeffer
1 Thymianzweig
1 Lorbeerblatt
2 Flaschen Pinot Noir
200 ml Rindsjus
100 g Ochsenmark in feine
Würfel geschnitten

Schalotten
8 kleine runde Schalotten
oder 12 Perlzwiebeln
10 g Zucker
25 g Butter
Salz, Pfeffer

Pochiertes Ei
4 Eier
2 EL Tafelessig
Salz, Pfeffer

Anrichten
40 g Wurzelspeck

Weinbergschnecken
Karotten und Lauch dünn schneiden und in einem Topf mit 700 Millilitern Wasser, Lorbeerblättern und Pfefferkörnern zum Kochen bringen. Hitze reduzieren und köcheln lassen. Die Zitrone halbieren, den Saft auspressen und mit den Zitronenhälften und dem Wein in den Topf geben. Die Weinbergschnecken dazugeben und 5–6 Stunden köcheln lassen. Dann die Schnecken herausnehmen und mit den Schalottenwürfel und der Butter anschwitzen. Nach 5–6 Minuten, die Kräuter dazugeben, mit Salz und Pfeffer abschmecken.

Burgunderreduktion
Die Schalotten mit dem Olivenöl und 1 Kaffeelöffel des Pfeffers anschwitzen. Thymian und Lorbeerblatt dazugeben und mit der Hälfte einer Flasche Rotwein ablöschen. Reduzieren lassen, bis eine schöne Bindung erreicht ist. Rindsjus und das Ochsenmark in die Rotweinreduktion geben und ziehen lassen. Nebenbei die andere Hälfte der Rotweinflasche aufkochen, flambieren und zu einem sämigen Sirup reduzieren lassen. Die Hälfte des restlichen Rotweins dazugießen, wieder auf Sirupkonsistenz einkochen, mit dem restlichen Wein ebenso verfahren. Rotweinreduktion zum Ochsenmark geben und mit dem Rest des Pfeffers ziehen lassen.

Schalotten
Schalotten mit Zucker, 200 Milliliter Wasser, Butter, Salz und Pfeffer in einen Topf geben, abdecken und kochen lassen, bis die Schalotten karamellisieren.

Pochiertes Ei
Kurz vor Ende der Kochzeit die Eier pochieren. Dafür in einem weiteren Topf Wasser, Essig und Salz zum kochen bringen und die Eier über eine Kelle ins kochende Wasser gleiten lassen. Nach 3–4 Minuten ist das Eiweiß hart, das Eigelb aber noch flüssig.

Anrichten
Speck in dünne Scheiben schneiden und knusprig braten. Die warmen Schnecken in einem Kreis auf den Teller anrichten, das pochierte Ei in die Mitte setzen. Schalotten und Speck ansetzen und mit der Rotweinreduktion.

Hummer mit Pomelo-Honig-Reduktion, Blattspinat und Pommes Maxim

Zutaten für 4 Personen | Foto Seite 172

Hummer
2 Bretonische Hummer
à 800–1000 g
2 Thymianzweige
1 Knoblauchzehe
2 EL gesalzene Butter
Pfeffer

Pomelo-Honig-Reduktion
600 ml Pomelo-
oder Grapefruitsaft
2 EL Blütenhonig
oder Waldhonig
4 EL extra natives Olivenöl
Salz, Pfeffer

Blattspinat
1 Knoblauchzehe
30 g Butter
600 g frischer Blattspinat
Salz, Pfeffer, Muskat

Pommes Maxim
1 großer Erdapfel
125 ml flüssige Butter
Meersalz

Hummer
Dieses Rezept erfordert frische, das heißt lebende Hummer, die man beim Kauf am besten daran erkennt, dass sie sich lebhaft bewegen und ihr Schwanz gekrümmt ist. Jedes Tier muss einzeln gekocht werden, damit ein schneller Tod gewährleistet ist.

Den Hummer am Rücken festhalten und im kalten Wasser gründlich bürsten. Kopf und Schwanz bridieren, sodass der ganzer Hummer und der Schwanz gespannt bleiben. Die Gummiringe, mit denen die Scheren zusammengehalten werden, entfernen. Das Wasser zum Kochen bringen. Damit der Hummer möglichst schnell und schonend getötet wird, wird er mit dem Kopf zuerst in das kochende Wasser gedrückt. Noch einmal kurz wallend aufkochen lassen und dann 8–10 Minuten gar ziehen lassen (nicht mehr kochen). Der Panzer des Hummers verfärbt sich außen rot.

Die Hummer der Länge nach aufschneiden, die Sandbeutel (beige cremige Masse) entfernen und die Hummerhälften mit Thymian und Knoblauch in Butter anbraten.

Pomelo-Honig-Reduktion
Den Pomelosaft auf 100 Milliliter reduzieren. Mit Honig, Salz und Pfeffer abschmecken und mit dem Olivenöl montieren.

Blattspinat
Die gewürfelte Knoblauchzehe kurz in der Butter dünsten, den Blattspinat zugeben, heiß schwenken und mit Salz, Pfeffer und Muskat abschmecken.

Pommes Maxim
Den Ofen auf 150 Grad vorheizen. Erdapfel schälen und hauchdünne Scheiben hobeln. Die Scheiben mit der Butter vermischen und auf Backpapier oder am besten auf einer Silikonmatte auslegen. Mit Meersalz bestreuen. Die Erdäpfelscheiben circa 1 Stunde backen, bis sie goldbraun und knusprig sind.

Anrichten
Spinat gut abtropfen, zwei Drittel auf den Tellern anrichten, mit dem letzten Drittel den Hummer füllen. Je einen halben Hummer auf den Spinat geben, mit der Pomelo-Reduktion nappieren und den Pommes Maxim garniert servieren.

Kalbsniere mit Frühlingsspitzkraut, Eierschwammerl und Sauce Robert

Zutaten für 4 Personen | Foto Seite 174

Kalbsniere
2 Kalbsnieren
1 Thymianzweig
1 Rosmarinzweig
50 g Butter
200 ml Kalbsjus
Salz, Pfeffer

Spitzkraut
1 Kopf Spitzkraut
50 g Butter
100 ml Obers
Salz, Pfeffer

Eierschwammerl
30 g Schalotten
400 g Eierschwammerl
40 g Butter
1 EL fein geschnittener Schnittlauch
Salz, Pfeffer

Sauce Robert
50 g Schalotten
30 g Butter
100 ml Weißwein
250 ml Kalbsjus
3 EL Pommerysenf
15 g eiskalte Butter

Kalbsniere
Die Nieren mit Thymian und Rosmarin bei mittlerer Hitze in Butter braten, bis sie rosa sind. Den Kalbsfond reduzieren.

Spitzkraut
Spitzkraut ganz fein schneiden und in Butter dünsten. Mit Salz und Pfeffer abschmecken und mit Obers cremig binden.

Eierschwammerl
Schalotten in Brunoise schneiden und mit den Eierschwammerln in der Butter sautieren. Mit Salz und Pfeffer würzen und mit Schnittlauch abschmecken.

Sauce Robert
Schalotten fein schneiden und in Butter anschwitzen, mit Weißwein ablöschen und komplett verdunsten lassen. Den Kalbsjus dazugeben, 15 Minuten köcheln lassen. Den Senf zugeben. Mit der Butter montieren und durchpassieren.

Anrichten
Das Spitzkraut auf Tellern anrichten. Nieren in 1 Zentimeter dicke Scheiben schneiden, auf dem Spitzkraut platzieren, mit Salz und Pfeffer würzen und mit dem reduzierten Kalbsjus nappieren. Eierschwammerl anlegen und mit der Sauce Robert servieren.

Schweinsbauch mit Kaisergranat und Erbsensalat

Zutaten für 4 Personen | Foto Seite 176

Schweinsbauch

1 Schweinsbauch, ca. 2 kg
2 EL Öl
100 g Karotten
100 g Gelbe Rüben
100 g Zwiebeln
100 g Lauch
1 Knoblauchknolle
1 l Weißwein
2 l Kalbsjus
4 Lorbeerblätter
4 g Pfefferkörner
Salz, Pfeffer

Kaisergranat

16 Kaisergranatschwänze
30 g Butter
1 KL Limettenschalenbrunoise
Salz, Pfeffer

Erbsensalat

100 g blanchierte Erbsen
50 g Erbsenblätter
50 ml Marillenessig
100 ml Mandelöl
20 ml Honig
Salz, Pfeffer

Anrichten

50 ml zerlassene Butter

Schweinsbauch

Den Schweinsbauch beidseitig mit Salz und Pfeffer würzen, zu einer dicken Roulade rollen und verschnüren. Danach die Roulade im Öl auf allen Seiten schön knusprig braten.

Die Gemüse und den Knoblauch in kleine Stücke schneiden und goldbraun anrösten. Den Schweinsbauch darauflegen, mit Weißwein begießen und so lange auf mittlerer Hitze kochen lassen, bis der Wein verdunstet ist. Kalbsjus aufgießen, Gewürze dazugeben und ca. 2 Stunden schmoren lassen, bis das Fleisch weich ist. Zuletzt die Roulade herausnehmen, die Schnur entfernen und den Schweinsbauch zwischen zwei Backblechen flach auflegen. In der Zwischenzeit die Sauce passieren. Den Schweinsbauch über Nacht im Kühlschrank rasten lassen.

Kaisergranat

Kaisergranatschwänze putzen, in einer Pfanne mit Butter schwenken und zum Schluss mit Salz, Pfeffer und Limettenschale würzen.

Erbsensalat

Die Erbsen mit den Blättern in eine Schüssel geben. Die restlichen Zutaten mischen und damit die Erbsen nappieren.

Anrichten

Den Schweinsbauch in große Würfel schneiden und in zerlassener Butter auf allen Seiten anbraten. Die Sauce erhitzen. Kaisergranat und Schweinsbauch abwechselnd auf Tellern anrichten, mit der Sauce und dem Erbsensalat servieren.

Rindsbackerl, Schalotten, Kamptaler Wurzelspeck, Rucolajus und Powidl

Zutaten für 4 Personen ❙ Foto Seite 178

Rindsbackerl

4 Rindsbackerl à 180–200 g
100 g Karotten
100 g gelbe Rüben
100 g Zwiebeln
100 g Lauch
1 Knoblauchknolle
1 l Rotwein
4 g Pfefferkörner
4 Lorbeerblätter
200 g griffiges Mehl
500 ml Tafelöl
1 l Kalbsjus
Salz

Schalotten

24 Schalotten
25 g Butter
ca. 150 ml Rindssuppe oder Gemüsebouillon
Salz, Pfeffer

Rucolajus

20 g Butter
200 g Rucola
Salz, Pfeffer

Anrichten

8 dünne Scheiben vom Kamptaler Wurzelspeck
4 EL Powidl

Rindsbackerl

Die Rindsbackerl mit dem grob gehackten Gemüse, dem Rotwein, den Pfefferkörnern und Lorbeerblättern 48 Stunden marinieren.

Danach die Rindsbackerl mit einem Tuch abtupfen, salzen, pfeffern, mit griffigem Mehl panieren und knusprig braten.

Etwa 2 Esslöffel des Öls in einem Topf erhitzen und das abgetropfte Gemüse darin goldbraun braten. Mit dem Rotwein ablöschen, die Rindsbackerl dazugeben, mit Kalbjus übergießen und 2–3 Stunden schmoren lassen. Die weichen Rindsbackerln herausnehmen, warm halten und die Sauce passieren.

Schalotten

Geschälte Schalotten mit den restlichen Zutaten in einen Topf geben und kochen, bis die Suppe verdunstet ist. Erneut etwas Rindssuppe angießen, falls die Schalotten noch nicht weich sind.

Rucolajus

In einem Topf 75 Milliliter Wasser aufkochen, Butter und Rucola dazugeben, 1 Minute lang mit einem Stabmixer pürieren und dann durchpassieren. Mit Salz und Pfeffer abschmecken.

Anrichten

Den Backofen auf 150 Grad vorheizen. Die Speckscheiben nebeneinander flach auf das Backblech legen und im Ofen eine Stunde knusprig backen. Die Rindsbackerl auf der Tellermitte anrichten, die Bratensauce umgießen. Mit dem Rucolajus, 1 Esslöffel Powidl, den Schalotten und der Speckscheibe garniert servieren.

Limettensoufflé mit Himbeersorbet und Amarettosabayon

Zutaten für 4 Soufflés | Foto Seite 180

Himbeersorbet
125 g Zucker
125 g Wasser
500 g Himbeermark
Saft von 2 Zitronen

Amarettosabayon
3 Eigelb
40 g Zucker
40 g Wasser
20 g Amaretto

Soufflé
Butter zum Einfetten

Masse 1
4 Eigelb
30 g Zucker
60 g Sauerrahm
Zesten von 2 Limetten

Masse 2
120 g Eiweiß
80 g Zucker

Anrichten
Himbeeren und Hippen
(siehe Rezept Seite 297)
nach Wunsch

Sorbet
Zucker und Wasser aufkochen, Zucker lösen und eventuellen Schaum abschöpfen. Himbeermark und Zitronensaft dazugeben. In eine Pacojetform geben und gefrieren. Vor Gebrauch im Pacojet aufmixen.

Sabayon
Alle Zutaten in einer Schüssel über Dampf kräftig aufschlagen, bis eine schaumige, dickflüssige Creme entsteht.

Soufflé
Den Ofen auf 190 Grad vorheizen. Die 4 Souffléformen mit 8 Zentimeter Durchmesser buttern. Für die Masse 1 den Zucker und das Eigelb schlagen, bis die Masse weiß und dicklich ist. Den Sauerrahm und die Limettenzesten beigeben.
Für die Masse 2 Eiweiß und Zucker leicht aufschlagen. Die Masse 2 vorsichtig unter die Masse 1 heben und die vorbereiteten Formen zu drei Vierteln anfüllen. Im Ofen circa 8 Minuten backen.

Anrichten
Das Soufflé sofort mit Sorbet und Sabayon anrichten. Nach Geschmack mit Himbeeren und Hippen dekorieren.

Feine Zitronennudeln mit Ossietrakaviar

Zutaten für 4 Personen | Foto Seite 194

Nudeln
200 g frischen Nudelteig
(siehe Grundrezept Seite 335)
1 unbehandelte Zitrone
3 EL Butter
etwas Wasser oder
milder Rindsfond
2 EL eiskalte Butterwürfel
2 EL Sauerrahm
2 EL geschlagenes Obers
Salz, Pfeffer
4 EL Ossietrakaviar

Nudeln

Nudelteig mithilfe der Nudelmaschine dünn ausrollen und mit dem Aufsatz in feine Bandnudeln schneiden. Zitronen waschen, hauchdünne Zesten ziehen, die restliche Zitrone auspressen. Die Zesten in kochendem Wasser 1 Minute blanchieren, abseihen und gut abtropfen lassen. Nudeln in reichlich gesalzenem Wasser circa 15 Sekunden kochen, abseihen und kurz abschrecken.

In einer Pfanne die Butter aufschäumen, die Zitronenzesten dazugeben, kurz durchschwenken. Die Nudeln und etwas Wasser oder milden Rindsfond dazugeben, erwärmen und mit Salz und Pfeffer abschmecken. Unter ständigem Schwenken kalte Butter daruntermischen, sodass die Nudeln schön »mollig« werden. Sauerrahm und Zitronensaft dazugeben und zum Schluss das geschlagene Obers untermischen. In heißen tiefen Tellern anrichten und mit dem Kaviar krönen.

Maishendlbrust mit Eierschwammerlrisotto und schwarzem Ribiselessig

Zutaten für 4 Personen ❙ Foto Seite 196

Maishendl

4 Maishendlbrüste à 150 g
2 EL Sonnenblumenöl
1 Thymianzweig
Salz, Pfeffer

Risotto

2 Schalotten
50 g Butter
200 g Risottoreis
60 ml Weißwein
½ l Gemüsefond
150 g Eierschwammerl
40 g geriebenen Parmesan
Salz, Pfeffer

Anrichten

¼ l Geflügeljus
4 cl schwarzer Ribiselessig

Maishendl

Den Ofen auf 180 Grad vorheizen. Hendlbrüste mit Salz und Pfeffer würzen und auf beiden Seiten in einer Pfanne scharf anbraten. Den Thymian beigeben und im Ofen circa 5 Minuten braten.

Risotto

Schalotten fein hacken, in Butter andünsten, Risottoreis beigeben und 1 Minute mitschwitzen. Mit Weißwein ablöschen und vollständig einreduzieren. Unter Rühren etwas Gemüsefond angießen und einköcheln lassen. Nach und nach auf diese Weise mit dem gesamten Fond verfahren, bis der Reis eine cremige, aber bissfeste Konsistenz hat. Mit Salz und Pfeffer würzen. Die Eierschwammerl in Stücke schneiden und zum Risotto geben oder sautieren und separat servieren. Risotto mit Parmesan vollenden.

Anrichten

Den Geflügeljus mit dem Ribiselessig kurz aufkochen und mit dem Maishendl, dem Risotto und gegebenenfalls mit den sautierten Eierschwammerl anrichten.

Waldviertler Mohnbuchteln mit Apfelröster und Sauerrahmeis

Zutaten für circa 30 Minibuchteln | Foto Seite 198

Sauerrahmeis
180 g Zucker
Zesten von 2 Limetten
500 g Sauerrahm

Apfelröster
3 Äpfel
25 g Butter
2 EL Honig

Mohnfülle
125 g gemahlener Mohn
70 g Semmelbrösel
100 ml Milch
30 g Zucker
etwas Honig
1 Schuss Rum
Zesten von 1 Zitrone
1 Prise Zimt
50 g weiße Schokolade
1 Eigelb

Mohnbuchteln
500 g Mehl
75 g Zucker
10 g Salz
300 g Eier
1 Würfel frische Germ
300 g weiche Butter
75 g flüssige Butter

Sauerrahmeis
Zucker und 50 Milliliter Wasser zu einem Sirup aufkochen, die Zesten dazugeben, die Flüssigkeit erkalten lassen und durch ein Haarsieb abseihen. Den Sauerrahm beigeben, gut mixen und in eine Pacojetform geben. Gefrieren und vor Gebrauch im Pacojet aufmixen.

Apfelröster
Äpfel schälen, vierteln und entkernen, in feine Scheiben schneiden und in Butter bissfest braten. Dann den Honig beigeben und fertig braten.

Mohnfülle
Mohn und Semmelbrösel vermischen. Milch mit Zucker, etwas Honig, Rum, Zitronenzesten und Zimt aufkochen lassen, vom Herd nehmen und mit der Brösel-Mohn-Mischung vermengen. Schokolade schmelzen und gemeinsam mit dem Eigelb einrühren, einige Zeit kühl stellen.

Mohnbuchteln
Den Ofen auf 170 Grad vorheizen. Mehl, Zucker und Salz in eine Rührschüssel geben und vermengen. Unter Rühren nach und nach die Eier beigeben. Die Germ in die Schüssel bröseln und alles gut verkneten. Sobald ein homogener Teig entsteht, die weiche Butter nach und nach dazugeben und alles zu einem glatten Teig rühren. Die Masse in eine bemehlte Schüssel geben und gehen lassen, bis das Volumen verdoppelt ist. Auf einer bemehlten Fläche ausrollen und Kreise mit einem Durchmesser von 7 Zentimetern ausstechen. Auf jedes Stück einen Kaffeelöffel Mohnfülle geben, oben gut verschließen und eng nebeneinander in eine Backform setzen. Noch einmal gehen lassen, mit der flüssigen Butter gut bestreichen und im Ofen Grad circa 20 Minuten backen

Anrichten
Die Mohnbuchteln mit Apfelröster und Sauerrahmeis servieren.

Mariazeller Flusskrebserl mit Erdäpfelstroh auf Kalbskutteln

Zutaten für 4 Personen ❙ Foto Seite 222

Kutteln

1 Karotte
½ Selleriestange
400 g gekochte Kalbskutteln
2 Schalotten
100 g Butter
1 l Kalbsfond
½ l Obers

Flusskrebserl

8 Flusskrebserl
2 große Erdäpfel
1 Eiweiß
Öl zum Ausbacken

Anrichten

½ Bund Petersil
Öl zum Ausbacken
4 Bündel aus Gurkenstiften

Kutteln

Karotten und Sellerie in Brunoise schneiden. Die gekochten Kutteln fein schneiden und mit den gewürfelten Schalotten in der Butter anschwitzen. Den Kalbsfond zugeben und einreduzieren. Obers zugeben und leicht köcheln lassen. Zum Schluss die Karotten-Sellerie-Brunoise kurz mitköcheln lassen.

Flusskrebserl

Die Krebse kurz abkochen und schälen. Die Erdäpfel in feine dünne Julienne schneiden und mit dem Eiweiß vermengen. Die Krebse damit umhüllen und in heißem Öl ausbacken.

Anrichten

Den Petersil im Öl ausbacken. Kutteln in die Teller geben, darauf den Petersil geben, Flusskrebserl darüber anrichten, als Garnitur die Gurkenbündel anlegen.

Zanderroulade mit Petersilpüree und Gemüse-Beurre-blanc

Zutaten für 4 Personen | Foto Seite 224

Zander
400 g Zander
100 g Fischfarce
(Grundrezepte Seite 333)
80 g gebeizte Lachsforelle
4 Spinatblätter
150 g Semmelbrösel
10 g Sesam
1 l Öl

Gemüse-Beurre-blanc
1 l Weißwein
250 g Butter
etwas Fenchelkraut
und Koriander
100 g gemischte Gemüsebrunoise (Karotte, Stangensellerie, Lauch)
Salz, Cayennepfeffer

Petersilpüree
200 g Petersilwurzel
1 Erdapfel
100 g Petersil
1 EL Crème fraîche
Salz, Pfeffer

Anrichten
¼ Milch
Zesten von 1 Zitrone
4 KL Lachskaviar
(nach Wunsch)
etwas Fenchelgrün
Salz

Zander
Das Zanderfilet leicht plattieren, die Fischfarce aufstreichen. Die Lachsforelle in schöne Tranchen schneiden, mit den blanchierten Spinatblättern umwickeln, auf die Farce geben und den Zander stramm in Klarsichtfolie aufrollen. Die Stücke kurz anfrieren, die Folie entfernen, Semmelbrösel und Sesam mischen und den Zander mit dem Gemisch panieren. Im Fettbad ausbacken.

Gemüse-Beurre-blanc
Den Wein auf circa 125 Milliliter einreduzieren und mit der Butter aufmontieren, Kräuter, Gewürze und Gemüse dazugeben, kurz aufkochen lassen, abschmecken und vom Herd nehmen.

Petersilpüree
Petersilwurzel und Kartoffel schälen, grob würfeln, weich kochen und zerdrücken. Den fein gehackten Petersil zugeben, mit Salz und Pfeffer abschmecken und mit der Crème fraîche auflockern.

Anrichten
Die Milch mit dem Salz und den Zesten kurz aufkochen und mit dem Mixstab aufschäumen. Das Petersilpüree auf der Tellermitte anrichten, die Zanderroulade portionieren, daraufsetzen, die Beurre blanc anlegen, mit Kaviar und Fenchelgrün garnieren, mit der aufgeschäumten Milch dekorieren.

Rosa Kalbsleber mit Essigkirschen, Eierschwammerln und Erdäpfelpüree

Zutaten für 4 Personen | Foto Seite 226

Kalbsleber
500 g Kalbsleber
Mehl zum Mehlieren
Olivenöl zum Anbraten

Erdäpfelpüree
5 mittelgroße Erdäpfel
½ Knoblauchzehe
1 Rosmarinzweig
1 Thymianzweig
etwas Fleur de Sel
etwas Olivenöl

Essigkirschen
20 Kirschen
200 ml Kirschsaft
1 Thymianzweig
1 EL Honig
1 EL Balsamico
Butter zum Montieren

Eierschwammerl
300 g Eierschwammerl
1 KL Butter
1 KL gehackter Schnittlauch
Salz, Pfeffer

Anrichten
blanchierte Gemüsewürfel
nach Wunsch
10 g Petersilblätter
zum Garnieren

Kalbsleber
Den Ofen auf 180 Grad vorheizen. Die Kalbsleber zuputzen (Haut und Röhren entfernen) und in 8 gleichmäßige Portionen schneiden. Leicht in Mehl wenden und in etwas Öl langsam anrösten. Aus der Pfanne herausnehmen und im Ofen 3 Minuten garen. Bei lauer Hitze ruhen lassen, damit sich das Fleisch entspannen kann.

Erdäpfelpüree
Die Erdäpfel mit den Kräutern weich kochen, schälen und mit der Gabel zerstoßen, mit Fleur de Sel und Olivenöl abschmecken.

Essigkirschen
Die entsteinten Kirschen kurz im Saft schwenken, herausnehmen. Thymian und Honig in den Saft geben und einreduzieren lassen. Den Balsamico kurz vor Schluss zufügen, mit der Butter aufmontieren und die Kirschen schön im Fond lackieren.

Eierschwammerl
Die Eierschwammerln in der Butter sautieren und mit Schnittlauch, Salz und Pfeffer abschmecken.

Anrichten
Die Kalbsleber auf etwas Erdäpfelpüree anrichten, das restliche Püree anlegen, mit Eierschwammerln und Gemüsestücken garnieren. Lackierte Kirschen anlegen, Petersil darüberstreuen und mit dem reduzierten Sud nappieren.

Wachtelcrépinette mit Gänselebertrüffel und kleinem Wiesensalat

Zutaten für 4 Personen | Foto Seite 228

Wachtelcrépinette
2 Wachteln
100 g Geflügelfarce
(siehe Grundrezept Seite 334)
8 Scheiben schwarzer Trüffel
4 Spinatblätter
4 Scheiben Serranoschinken

Gänselebertrüffel
240 g marinierte Gänseleber
10 g geriebener
schwarzer Trüffel
20 g getrocknetes
gemahlenes Pumpernickel
20 g Semmelbrösel
10 g gehackte Pistazien
Öl zum Ausbacken

Wiesensalat
Kräuter nach Geschmack
(z. B. Schnittlauch, Basilikum,
Petersil, Kerbel, Lavendel,
Estragon, Waldklee)
1 kleiner Friséesalat
2 EL Walnussöl
Salz, Pfeffer

Anrichten
4 Wachteleier
4 tournierte Champignonköpfe
einige essbare Blüten

Wachtelcrépinette
Den Backofen auf 180 Grad vorheizen. Die Wachteln auslösen und leicht mit der Geflügelfarce einstreichen. Mit Trüffel und Spinatblättern belegen und im Serranoschinken einschlagen. Bei mäßiger Temperatur anrösten und 5 Minuten im Ofen backen. Anschließend ruhen lassen.

Gänselebertrüffel
Die marinierte Gänseleber mit dem geriebenen Trüffel gut verkneten und zu kleinen Knödeln formen, mit Pumpernickel, Semmelbrösel und Pistazien panieren und kurz im heißen Fettbad ausbacken.

Wiesensalat
Die Kräuter zupfen und waschen, mit dem Frisée vermengen und mit Öl, Salz und Pfeffer abschmecken.

Anrichten
Die Wachteleier 3 Minuten in kochendem Wasser garen, halbieren. Wachtelcrépinette, Gänselebertrüffel und den Wiesensalat auf Tellern anrichten und mit Wachteleiern, Champignons und essbaren Blüten garnieren.

Haustorte »Metternich«

Zutaten für 1 Torte ∎ Foto Seite 230

Boden

150 g weiche Butter
100 g Kristallzucker
6 Eigelb
6 Eiweiß
110 g Staubzucker
120 g Zartbitterschokolade
150 g Mehl

Creme

250 g weiche Butter
300 g Nougat, halbflüssig
150 g Staubzucker
4 Eigelb
2 EL Amaretto

Garnitur

200 g Pistazienmarzipan-
rohmasse
12 Dekor-Ganache
12 Hohlkugeln
100 g Krokant

Boden

Den Ofen auf 180 Grad Umluft vorheizen. Die Butter schaumig schlagen und nach und nach Zucker sowie Eigelb unterrühren.

Das Eiweiß steif schlagen, dabei langsam den Staubzucker zugeben. Die Schokolade schmelzen, mit der Zucker-Eigelb-Masse vermischen, langsam das Mehl einrieseln lassen und unterrühren. Zum Schluss den Eischnee sanft unterheben, den Teig in eine beschichtete Springform geben und im Ofen circa 30 Minuten backen.

Creme

Die Butter schaumig schlagen, den Staubzucker und das Nougat unterziehen. Das Eigelb langsam über Wasserdampf unter ständigem Rühren auf 72 Grad erhitzen. Von der Hitze nehmen, unter ständigem Schlagen den Amaretto und die Nougatmasse zugeben und kalt schlagen.

Garnitur

Den ausgekühlten Boden dritteln, jeweils mit einem Viertel der Creme bestreichen, aufeinandersetzen und mit der restlichen Creme die Torte rundum einstreichen. Für etwa 1 Stunde kühl stellen, dann die obere Cremeschicht dünn mit Marzipan verkleiden. Die Torte mit der Ganache, den Hohlkugeln und dem Krokant dekorieren.

Frischkäsebärlauchtascherl mit Spargel und Kerbelsabayon

Zutaten für 4 Personen | Foto Seite 240

Bärlauchtascherl

50 g Jungzwiebel
1 Knoblauchzehe
Butter zum Andünsten
200 g Bärlauch
150 g Frischkäse
1 gekochter mehliger Erdapfel
1 Schuss Milch
200 g Nudelteig
(siehe Grundrezept Seite 335)
1 Ei
Salz, Pfeffer, Muskat

Kerbelsabayon

2 Schalotten
2 mehlige Erdäpfel
40 g Butter
500 ml Geflügelfond
3 Eigelb
Kerbel nach Geschmack
Salz, Pfeffer
Cayennepfeffer
Muskat

Spargel

12 Stangen grüner Spargel
1 altbackene Semmel
Zucker, Butter
Salz, Pfeffer

Anrichten

braune Butter

Bärlauchtascherl

Jungzwiebel in Ringe schneiden, mit dem Bärlauch und dem gewürfelten Knoblauch in Butter andünsten. Herausnehmen und fein hacken. In eine Schüssel geben, mit dem Frischkäse, dem durchgedrückten Erdapfel und einem Schuss Milch gut verrühren. Mit Salz, Pfeffer und Muskat abschmecken.

Den Nudelteig dünn ausrollen, Kreise ausstechen, mit Ei bestreichen, die Bärlauchmasse teelöffelweise auf die Kreise geben, zu Halbkreisen zusammenklappen und die Ränder fest andrücken.

Kerbelsabayon

Die Schalotten fein schneiden, die Erdäpfel in dünne Scheiben schneiden, beides in Butter ohne Farbe andünsten. Mit Salz, Pfeffer, Cayennepfeffer und Muskatnuss würzen.

Geflügelfond aufgießen und circa 15 Minuten einkochen lassen. Mixen und durch ein Sieb passieren. Etwas abkühlen lassen.

Den Fond mit den Eigelben in einen Schneekessel geben und über dem heißen Wasserbad aufschlagen, bis die Masse dickschaumig ist. Kerbel hacken, einige Blätter zur Dekoration beiseitestellen. Die Sabayon pikant abschmecken und gehackten Kerbel untermischen.

Spargel

Die unteren Enden des Spargels entfernen, eventuell holzige Stellen schälen. Salzwasser aufkochen, Butter, Zucker und die Semmel zum Mitkochen dazugeben. Den Spargel bissfest garen, in Eiswasser abschrecken, auf einem Tuch abtropfen lassen.

Anrichten

Die Ravioli in Salzwasser circa 4 Minuten leicht kochend garen. Den Spargel im Spargelfond erwärmen. Die gekochten Tascherl in brauner Butter schwenken. Spargel auf Teller anrichten, Tascherl dazugeben und mit dem Kerbelsabayon überziehen. Mit den restlichen Kerbelblättchen ausgarnieren.

Gamspfeffer mit Preiselbeeren und Pilznudeln

Zutaten für 6 Personen | Foto Seite 242

Ragout

900 g Gamsschulter
4–5 Wacholderbeeren
1 Karotte
1 Gelbe Rübe
½ Sellerie
2 Lorbeerblätter
2 EL Sonnenblumenöl
1 EL Tomatenmark
4 cl Gin
½ l Rotwein
½ l Wildfond
½ l Obers
2 EL Preiselbeeren
Wacholder
Salz, weißer Pfeffer

Nudeln

200 g breite Nudeln
50 g Champignons
50 g Austernpilze
50 g Shiitakepilze
½ Zwiebel
1 EL Butter
1 Rosmarinzweig
etwas Petersil
Salz, Pfeffer

Ragout

Die Gamsschulter von groben Sehnen und Häuten befreien. In gleichmäßige Stücke schneiden, mit Salz und weißem Pfeffer würzen, mit den gestoßenen Wacholderbeeren einreiben und 1 Stunde im Kühlschrank ziehen lassen.

Karotte, Gelbe Rübe und Sellerie in 1 Zentimeter große Stücke schneiden und in einem Topf mit den Lorbeerblättern in heißem Öl hellbraun rösten. Das Tomatenmark beigeben, kurz mitrösten, mit Gin und Rotwein ablöschen, auf die Hälfte einreduzieren und mit Wildfond auffüllen. Die Gamsschulterstücke in den Ansatz geben und circa 1–2 Stunden bei kleiner Flamme kochen lassen.

Das Gamsfleisch ausstechen, Obers und Preiselbeeren zum Fond geben und nochmals auf die Hälfte reduzieren. Durch die Flotte Lotte passieren und das Gamsfleisch wieder beigeben. Aufkochen lassen und wenn nötig mit Salz, Pfeffer und Wacholder abschmecken.

Pilznudeln

Nudeln in Salzwasser bissfest kochen. Die Pilze klein schneiden, die Zwiebel fein würfeln. Butter in einer Pfanne erhitzen, Zwiebel und Pilze darin sautieren. Mit Salz und Pfeffer würzen, Rosmarin und Petersil fein hacken und durchschwenken.

Anrichten

Die Nudeln auf den Tellern anrichten, die Pilze auflegen und mit Sauce umgeben.

Grundrezepte

Artischockenchips
1–2 Artischocken
Öl zum Ausbacken

Die Artischocken putzen, mit einer Aufschnittmaschine in 1 Millimeter dünne Scheiben schneiden, anschließend blanchieren, trocken tupfen und in heißem Öl frittieren.

Champagner-Fisch-Nage
250 ml Fischfond
100 ml Champagner
300 ml Obers
100 g Butter
Salz

Den Fischfond mit Champagner und Obers aufkochen und auf die Hälfte reduzieren. Den Topf vom Herd nehmen und die Butter stückchenweise unterschlagen.
Die Sauce durch ein feines Spitzsieb passieren, mit Salz abschmecken und gut aufschäumen.

Cremespinat
300 g Blattspinat
125 ml Obers
Salz, Pfeffer, Muskat

Den Spinat putzen, in kochendem Salzwasser circa 2 Minuten blanchieren und in Eiswasser abschrecken. Abseihen und mit dem Mixstab fein pürieren. Mit dem Obers zu einer cremigen Konsistenz einkochen und mit Salz, Pfeffer und Muskat abschmecken.

Erbsenpüree
500 g Erbsen
250 ml Geflügel-
oder Gemüsefond
250 ml Obers
125 g braune Butter
Salz, Pfeffer

Die Erbsen blanchieren und in Eiswasser abschrecken. Mit den restlichen Zutaten fein vermixen und durch ein Haarsieb passieren.

Fischfarce

250 g Zander
1 Ei
250 ml Obers
Saft von ½ Zitrone
Salz, Piment d' Espelette
(französische Chili)

Das Zanderfilet häuten und die Gräten ziehen. Das Fleisch klein schneiden, in eine Pacojetform geben, mit Salz würzen. Das Obers über den Fisch geben und im Tiefkühlfach leicht anfrieren lassen, anschließend im Pacojet aufmixen. Die Farce durch ein feines Haarsieb streichen, mit Zitronensaft, Salz und Piment d' Espelette abschmecken.

Fischfond

500 g Fischgräten
(z. B. Steinbutt, Seeteufel)
2 Schalotten
2 Champignons
1 Staudensellerie
1 Lauchstange
2 EL Butter
5 Pfefferkörner
250 ml Weißwein
250 ml Noilly Prat
Salz

Fischgräten zerkleinern und in eine Schüssel geben. Unter kaltem fließendem Wasser wässern, bis das Wasser ganz klar abläuft. Schalotten schälen und vierteln, Champignons putzen und ebenfalls vierteln. Sellerie und Lauch waschen und würfeln. Schalotten in der erhitzten Butter glasig dünsten, Fischgräten, Gemüse und Gewürze zufügen, Wein, Noilly Prat und 1 Liter kaltes Wasser dazugeben. Bei milder Hitze im offenen Topf 15 Minuten köcheln lassen, falls nötig, zwischendurch abschäumen. Brühe durch ein sehr feines Haarsieb oder Tuch passieren.

Geflügelfarce

250 g Geflügelfleisch
1 Ei
250 ml Obers
Salz, weißer Pfeffer

Das Geflügelfleisch fein schneiden und in eine Pacojetform geben. Das Obers darübergeben und im Tiefkühlfach leicht anfrieren lassen. Anschließend das Ei dazugeben und im Pacojet aufmixen. Die Farce durch ein feines Haarsieb streichen, mit Salz und Pfeffer abschmecken.
Wichtig: Die Zutaten müssen gut durchgekühlt sind, sie werden sonst durch die hohe Drehzahl beim Mixen warm und die Farce verliert ihre Bindung.

Varianten

Das Geflügelfleisch kann durch Kalbsfleisch, Kaninchenfleisch oder Rehfleisch ersetzt werden und wie beschrieben zubereitet werden.

Kürbispüree

500 g Kürbis
Brunoise von
2 Schalotten
3 EL Olivenöl
3–4 zerdrückte
Knoblauchzehen
1 Thymianzweig
Salz, Pfeffer

Den Ofen auf 160–180 Grad vorheizen. Den Kürbis mit der Schale in grobe Stücke zerteilen, mit den restlichen Zutaten in Alufolie einschlagen und im Ofen 20–25 Minuten backen.
Den Kürbis aus der Folie nehmen, das Fruchtfleisch von der Schale kratzen und gut mixen. Im Passiertuch ausdrücken, bis die ganze Flüssigkeit entfernt ist.

Läuterzucker

150 g Zucker

Zucker mit 150 Milliliter Wasser in einen Topf füllen, unter Rühren zum Kochen bringen. Zucker so lange rühren, bis er sich vollständig im Wasser gelöst hat, gegebenenfalls entstehenden Schaum während des Kochens abschöpfen.

Nudelteig

2 Eier
200 g Mehl
Salz

Eier und Salz in eine Schüssel geben und mit dem Schneebesen gut verrühren. Das Mehl dazusieben, mit den Händen so lange verkneten, bis sich der Teig vom Schüsselrand und den Händen löst. Der Nudelteig muss schön glatt, aber noch fest und zäh sein, eventuell noch etwas Mehl dazugeben. Zur Kugel formen und 30 Minuten kühl stellen.

Petersilbutter

100 g Butter
100 g blanchierte Petersilblätter
Salz

Butter und Petersil in eine Pacojetform geben, mixen, mit Salz abschmecken, in Klarsichtfolie zu einer Rolle drehen und kalt stellen.

Wildnage

250 ml klarer Wildfond
250 ml Obers
100 g Butter
Salz

Den Wildfond mit Obers aufkochen und auf die Hälfte reduzieren. Den Topf vom Herd nehmen und die Butter stückchenweise unterschlagen. Die Sauce durch ein feines Spitzsieb passieren, mit Salz abschmecken und gut aufschäumen.

Wegbegleiter

TIEFE FREUNDSCHAFTEN UND KOLLEGIALES MITEINANDER

Wie Mörwald seine Welt bewegt
und seine Mitmenschen ihn bereichern

Toni Mörwald hat echte Entertainerqualitäten. Ob es dabei um seine Gäste geht oder er mit Freunden und Kollegen zusammentrifft – langweilig wird es mit ihm nie. Denn Toni macht den Genuss zu einer persönlichen Angelegenheit, »Essenszeit ist Lebenszeit«. Dieses Motto hat er sich auf die Fahne geschrieben und setzt es mit aller ihm zur Verfügung stehenden Konsequenz und Energie um. Anregung und konstruktive Kritik für seine Kreativität findet Mörwald nicht nur im trauten Familienleben, Zeit seines Lebens kommt er mit Freunden und Kollegen zusammen, mit denen ihn eins verbindet: Die Liebe zum Essen und zum Genuss.

Mit Dank und Verbundenheit erinnert Toni Mörwald sich an die Wegbegleiter der letzten 20 Jahre: Genießer aus allen Professionen, aus der eigenen Zunft, aus Kunst und Kultur, aus Wissenschaft und Forschung.

JEAN-CHRISTOPHE ANSANAY-ALEX

JUAN AMADOR

ARMIN AMREIN

MARTÍN BERASATEGUI

CHRISTOPHE M. BERGEN

RALF BERNHART

GEORGES BLANC

LEOPOLD BLAUENSTEINER

JONNIE BOER

RUDOLF BUCHBINDER

THOMAS BÜHNER

GISBERT BURGSTALLER

OSCAR DEL CAMPO

HANS DENK

LEO DOPPLER

339

| DORLI DRAXLER | GERHARD DRAXLER | FELIX DVORAK | FRANZ EHRENLEITNER | PETER ENGERT |

| ELISABETH ENGSTLER | BEATE ESPINOZA-MAYR | GERNOT FISCHER | KLAUS FLEISCHHAKER | HANS GASSER |

| ERWIN GEGENBAUER | KARL-HEINZ GRASSER | CHRISTIAN GRÜNWALD | MICHEL GUÉRAD | CHRISTIAN GUZY |

340

EDUARD HABSBURG

PER HALLUNDBAEK

HEINZ HANNER

MICHAEL HÄUPL

BALTHASAR HAUSER

DOMINIC HEINZL

ALEX. HESSE

FRANZ HIRTZBERGER

THOMAS HOPPE

KARIM JALLOUL

FRANZ JIRGAL

ALWIN, EDWIN, PAUL UND KARL JURTSCHITSCH

KELLY UND ANDY KAINZ

FRITZ KAUFMANN

GÜNTHER KIENPOINTNER RUDOLF KLINGOHR HARALD KNABL EDUARD KRANEBITTER SIEGFRIED KRÖPFL

PETER KUPER CHRISTOPH LEON FRANZ LETH FRED LOIMER HANS MAHR

KURT MANN SEPP MANTLER RÉGIS MARCON GUY MARTIN WERNER MATT

 WERNER MEISINGER
 MARC MENEAU
 NIKOLAUS MOSER
 SEPP MOSER
 DORLI MUHR

 ISAAF NAHAS
 BRIGITTE NEUMEISTER
 SILVIO NICKOL
 NORBERT NIEDERKOFLER
 PIERRE ORSI

 FRANZ PASCHINGER
 MICHAEL PECH
 HORST PETERMANN
 ANNE-SOPHIE PIC
 F.X. PICHLER

| JÜRGEN PICHLER | GEORG PÖLZL | ERICH PUCHER | RUTH UND ROLAND RABE | ALI RAHIMI |

PHILIPPE ROCHAT · WOLFGANG ROSAM · GERHARD SANDLER · RAKESH SARDANA · MICHAEL SCHILLINGER

WERNER SCHIMA · WOLFGANG SCHLÜTER · GABRIELA SCHNABEL · SISSY SONNLEITNER · ELISABETH STADLER

344

| GERHARD STRÖCK | FRANK STRONACH | JAUME TAPIES | FOLKE TEGETHOFF | HANS TOPF |

    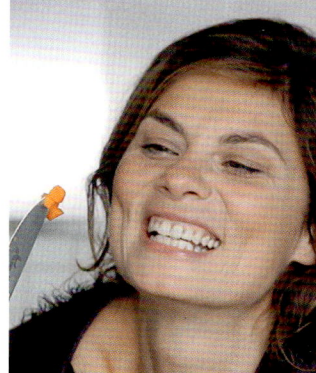

| GAETANO TROVATO | JOSEF VANICEK | URS WEBER | MARTIN WEILER | SARAH WIENER |

| HEINZ WINKLER | FRANZ WOHLFAHRT | HARALD WOHLFAHRT | SIEGFRIED WOLF | MINO ZACCARIA |

345

> *Für die freundliche Unterstützung bei der Realisierung unseres Buches möchten wir uns bei folgenden Partnern herzlich bedanken.*

HERING BERLIN
Königsweg 303
D-14109 Berlin

Tel.: 0049 - (0)30 - 810 541 - 0
Fax: 0049 - (0)30 - 810 541 - 29

www.hering-berlin.de

VILLEROY & BOCH AG
Hauptverwaltung
Postfach 1120
D-66688 Mettlach

Tel.: 0049 - (0)686 - 481 - 0

www.villeroy-boch.com

GOLLHAMMER KERAMIK GMBH
Aichergut
Kapellenweg 7
A-4863 Seewalchen am Attersee

Tel.: 0043 - (0)7662 - 22 466 - 80
Fax: 0043 - (0)7662 - 22 466 - 82

www.gollhammer.at

BERNDORF
BESTECK-TAFELGERÄTE GES.M.B.H.
Leobersdorfer Strasse 26
A-2560 Berndorf

Tel.: 0043 - (0)2672 - 83 610 - 43
Fax: 0043 - (0)2672 - 83 610 - 97

www.besteck.at

PORZELLANMANUFAKTUR FÜRSTENBERG GMBH
Meinbrexener Straße 2
D-37699 Fürstenberg

Tel.: 0049 - (0)5271 - 401 - 0
Fax: 0049 - (0)5271 - 401 - 100

www.fuerstenberg-porzellan.com

A.E. KÖCHERT JUWELIERE
Neuer Markt 15
A-1010 Wien

Tel.: 0043 - (0)1 - 512 - 58 28
Fax: 0043 - (0)1 - 513 - 40 22

www.koechert.com

MAJESTIC IMPERATOR TRAIN DE LUXE
WAGGON CHARTER GES.M.B.H.
Opernring 4/Top 8
A-1010 Wien

Tel.: 0043 - (0)1 - 513 - 28 81
Fax: 0043 - (0)1 - 513 - 28 83

www.imperialtrain.com

WEINGUT BERNHARD OTT
Neufang 36
A-3483 Feuersbrunn

Tel.: 0043 - (0)2738 - 2257
Fax: 0043 - (0)2738 - 2257 - 22

www.ott.at

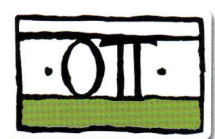

SCHLOSS GOBELSBURG
Schloßstrasse 16
A-3550 Langenlois

Tel.: 0043 - (0)2734 - 24 22
Fax: 0043 - (0)2734 - 24 22 - 20

www.schloss-gobelsburg.at

COCA-COLA HBC AUSTRIA GES.M.B.H
Triesterstrasse 91
A-1100 Wien

Tel.: 0043 - (0)1 - 610 - 60 - 0
Fax: 0043 - (0)1 - 610 - 60 - 329

www.roemerquelle.at

„Für ihr unermüdliches Engagement, ihre mitreißende Kreativität und ihre unglaubliche Begeisterung möchten wir uns bei allen Helfern aus dem Mörwaldschen Imperium bedanken."

DER DANK GEHT VOR ALLEM AN DIE FAMILIE MÖRWALD ▌

mit Frau Eva, den Töchtern Theresia, Antonia und Johanna, Vater Anton, dem Bruder Erhard Mörwald mit seiner Frau Angelika, der Schwester Andrea Schäffer, der Schwägerin Karin Pregesbauer und den Schwiegereltern Martha und Johann Pregesbauer.

AN DIE MITWIRKENDEN IM KLOSTER UND ▌

Erwin Windhaber, Thomas Serret und Erwin Riedrich

AN DEN KÜCHENCHEF DER TRAUBE ▌

François Laliberté

UND AN DEN KÜCHENCHEF IN SCHLOSS GRAFENEGG ▌

Thomas Törpel

AUSSERDEM GILT DER DANK ▌

Andrea Bierbaum, Nicolas Alandete, Ange Pacome Assori, Georg Bartsch, Evelyn Beeg, Astrid Bischel, Herta Brauner, Thomas Büttner, Tomas Cepo, Gabriel Christandl, Lisa Maria Daum, Konstantin Denk, Christian Diekmann, Daniel Ebner, Michael Fetter-Ilwof, Tamara Findenig, Marlene Flucher, Michaela Friedl, Angela Gosch, Paul Hartwig, Daniela Heiden, Peter Heneis, Simone Hofbauer, Simon Huber, Mohammad Iftikhar, Corina Ionescu, Andreas Jechsmayr, Teresa Karl, Daniel Kraschl, Manfred Kröll, Ingrid Lagsteiner, Ronny Laskosky, Magdalena Ludl, Michael Mair, Kathrin Miedler, Florian Mistelbauer, Klaus Müllauer, Nicole Neubauer, Axel Neuböck, Veronika Neudorfer, Maria Niederkofler, Philipp Oberleitner, Melanie Obritzberger, Wolfgang Poisinger, Stefan Prieler, Hartmuth Rameder, Kathinka Rauscher, Ahmed Sajjad, Julia Sattler, Bernd Schaludek, Dominik Scherz, Patrick Schimbäck, Stefan Schneider, Stefan Schragner, Martin Schreiner, Sabrina Sieger, Robert Simetzberger, Christoph Steinkellner, Irmgard Stepan, Jutta Stitz, Michael Stocker, Marion Süß, Franziska Thümmler, Mario Ulrich, Johannes Walch, Ramona Weißbach, Brigitta Winkler, Siegfried Wolfram, Rene Wutzl, Murat Özavsar, Ünal Bayrakdar, Gerald Diemt, Martina Kastl, Gabriele Sternecker, Andrea Unterburger

IMPRESSUM

© 2009 Neuer Umschau Buchverlag GmbH, Neustadt an der Weinstraße

Alle Rechte der Verbreitung in deutscher Sprache, auch durch Film, Funk, Fernsehen, fotomechanische Wiedergabe, Tonträger jeder Art, auszugsweisen Nachdruck oder Einspeicherung und Rückgewinnung in Datenverarbeitungsanlagen aller Art, sind vorbehalten.

PROJEKTLEITUNG I Hans-Jürgen Fug-Möller, Neustadt an der Weinstraße

KONZEPTION I Hans-Jürgen Fug-Möller, Ilka Grunenberg, Neustadt an der Weinstraße

TEXTE I Herbert Hacker, Wien

ENGLISCHE ÜBERSETZUNG I Andrew Cowin, Heidelberg

FRANZÖSISCHE ÜBERSETZUNG I
Rezepte: Virginie Güth für Linz Übersetzungen, Nürnberg
Texte: Anne-Marie Harnois, Gauties, Frankreich

REZEPTE I Toni Mörwald – mit herzlichem Dank an das ganze Team

FOTOS I Michael Eckstein, Fürth

FOTOS DER WEGBEGLEITER SEITE 339–345 I privat, außer: 339_Rudolf Buchbinder © Basta, 340_Gerhard Draxler © ORF, 340_Felix Dvorak © Hans Moser, 340_Elisabeth Engstler © ORF, 340_Klaus Fleischhaker © Helge Kirchberger, 340_Erwin Gegenbauer © Kristian Bissuti, 343_Nikolaus & Sepp Moser © Rita Newman, 343_Pierre Orsi © Jeff Nalin, 343_Anne-Sophie Pic © Jeff Nalin, 344_Rakesh Sardana © Fotostudio Schuster, 344_Gabriela Schnabel © Mani Hausler, 345_Folke Tegethoff © Christian Jungwirth

GESTALTUNG UND SATZ I Tina Defaux, Neustadt an der Weinstraße

LEKTORAT I Ilka Grunenberg, Neustadt an der Weinstraße

HERSTELLUNG I Hans-Jürgen Fug-Möller, Birgit Wucher, Neustadt an der Weinstraße

LITHOGRAFIE I posi.tiff GmbH, Frankfurt am Main

DRUCK I NINO Druck GmbH, Neustadt an der Weinstraße

Printed in Germany
ISBN: 978-3-86528-674-1

Die Ratschläge in diesem Buch sind von den Autoren und dem Verlag sorgfältig erwogen und geprüft, dennoch kann eine Garantie nicht übernommen werden. Eine Haftung der Autoren und des Verlags für Personen-, Sach- und Vermögensschäden ist ausgeschlossen.

STERNEKÜCHE
STAR-AWARDED CUISINE ★ HAUTE CUISINE

ENGLISH RECIPES
RECETTES FRANÇAISES

English Recipes

APPENDIX 4_A List of all Recipes

APPENDIX 7_Details of Preparation

For Starters

A VERY GIFTED CHEF AND HOST

How determination
and talent have helped
Toni Mörwald achieve his goals.

Dear Reader,

I'm always being asked what it takes to become a successful chef. A short and straightforward question that nonetheless can't be answered in a few – or even in a great many – words. Because being a chef nowadays doesn't merely demand creativity and commitment in the kitchen as such, but increasingly requires these qualities in a wide range of related areas. Consequently, in addition to talent and the necessary expertise, the following consideration is of crucial importance: only someone who pursues his or her aims with dogged determination, with unflagging commitment and with passionate creativity will manage to find and follow the professional pathway leading to a fulfilling and successful culinary career.

Toni Mörwald illustrates this point perfectly. He is a strikingly many-sided and talented representative of the culinary fraternity, who has built up a small business empire with undeviating and indomitable resolve.

He sometimes reminds me of Mozart's *Figaro*: wherever one goes, Toni Mörwald has already been there ...

Over the years, Toni Mörwald's and my paths have crossed a good many times. And, with time, this has led to a professional acquaintanceship marked by mutual rapport and empathy, and he can be entirely assured of the great respect I have for his achievements. Indeed, he has achieved a great deal that is remarkable as a chef, but also as a host. And, it is in these roles of which he is such a master that, in his new book, the interested reader will be able to enjoy Toni Mörwald in full flow.

With culinary collegiality,

A List of all Recipes

APPENDIX 6_KLOSTER UND

APPENDIX 7_Deep-Fried Cheese and Herb Balls

APPENDIX 7_Balik Salmon Served with Buttermilk Mousse, Blinis and Flying-Fish Green Caviar

APPENDIX 7_Roulade of Guinea Fowl with Creamy Celeriac and Potato Layer Cake

APPENDIX 7_Roulade Vert with Soured Cream and Vulcano Ham

APPENDIX 7_Rosemary Toast with Bell Pepper, Tomato and Green Asparagus

APPENDIX 7_Crostini with King Prawns, Melon and Cucumber

APPENDIX 8_Fried Black Bread with Baby Scallions and Bone-Marrow

APPENDIX 8_Crayfish Terrine with a Chervil Mousse

APPENDIX 8_Cannelloni with Duck Liver Served with Kohlrabi Puree and Madeira Jelly

APPENDIX 9_Raw Marinated Veal with a Vegetable Praline and Frisée-Lettuce Salad

APPENDIX 9_Tartar of Limousin Steak in Jellied Beef Consommé with a Wasabi Mousse and Beetroot

APPENDIX 9_Lobster Bisque with Green-Pea Soufflé and Ossetra Caviar

APPENDIX 9_Clear Consommé of Baby Venison and Tomatoes Served with Tomato and Game Roulade

APPENDIX 10_Consommé of Waldviertel Spotted Cattle with Hot Spleen Sandwiches

APPENDIX 10_Crayfish Ravioli with Quail's Eggs and Chanterelles

APPENDIX 10_Eggs à la Viennoise Served with Spinach, Smoked Bacon and Field Mushrooms

APPENDIX 10_Broccoli Tortellini with Tomato and Tarragon Butter

APPENDIX 11_Green-Pea Gnocchi with Poached Eggs and White Truffles

APPENDIX 11_Saffron Mussels off the Shell Cooked in White Wine and Served with Gnocchi

APPENDIX 11_Scallops à la St. Germain

APPENDIX 11_Sheatfish Medallions Served with Dijon Lentils and Rioja Butter

APPENDIX 11_Fillet of John Dory Served with Tomato Artichokes and Onions with Basil

APPENDIX 12_Fillet of Turbot with Pumpkin Gnocchi, Summer Truffles and Cinnamon

APPENDIX 12_Whole Sea Bass Cooked in a Salt Crust

APPENDIX 12_Calf's Sweetbreads with Field Mushrooms and Chervil

APPENDIX 12_Pigeon Galantine with Apple Chutney and Cornelian Cherries

APPENDIX 13_Breast of Bresse Chicken in a Crust of Olives and Tomatoes Served with Pine-Nut Couscous

APPENDIX 13_Fillet of Veal with a Bread Filling Served with Sautéed Artichokes

APPENDIX 13_Tender Veal Cutlet Served on Fine Noodles with Black Olives and Baby Leeks

APPENDIX 13_Saddle of Suckling Pig with Waldviertel Caraway, Pork Ravioli and Sautéed Pointed Cabbage

APPENDIX 14_Crown Rack of Veal with Veal-Sweetbread Ravioli, Parsnip Cream and Parsley Butter

APPENDIX 14_Roast Leg of Suckling Lamb Served with Potato Cakes Filled with Sautéed Red Swiss Chard

APPENDIX 14_Pink-Roasted Sirloin Steak with Whole Asparagus, Potato Patties and Béarnaise Sauce

APPENDIX 15_Fillet of Attergau Beef with Celeriac and Fried Goose Liver

APPENDIX 15_Fried Deer Liver Served with a Beetroot Carpaccio and Fresh Horseradish

APPENDIX 15_Saddle of Venison with Pumpkin-Seed Confit and Semolina Slices

APPENDIX 15_Pan-Fried Baby Venison Served on Potato Salad with Rocket Leaves

APPENDIX 15_Tender Fillet of Venison on Pyramid Cake Served with Chestnut-and-Prune Gnocchi

APPENDIX 16_Braised Leg of Wild Boar with Lentil and Bacon Sauce, Served with Parsnips and Palffy Brioche-Dumplings

APPENDIX 16_Millefeuille Slices with Yoghurt Mousse and Wild Berries

APPENDIX 16_Dessert with Apricots, Cardamom and Almonds

APPENDIX 17_Chocolate Petit Fours with Whisky Mousse and Coffee Parfait

APPENDIX 17_Nougat Mousse with Hazelnut Dacquoise Served with Matcha-Tea Ice Cream and Banana Compote

APPENDIX 18_Cherry Tartlets Served with Peach and Pistachio

APPENDIX 18_Chocolate Pralines with Crunchy Nougat

APPENDIX 18_Orange Cupcakes

APPENDIX 18_Macaroons

APPENDIX 19_Cheesecake Fancies with Pineapple and Coconut

APPENDIX 19_Brioches with Vanilla Cream

APPENDIX 20_CATERING

APPENDIX 21_Shrimp and Ricotta Ravioli

APPENDIX 21_Veal Lights Cooked in Riesling

APPENDIX 21_Punch Petit Fours

APPENDIX 21_Creamy Horns

APPENDIX 22_ZUR TRAUBE

APPENDIX 23_Warm Marinated Veal Tongue with Mixed Vegetables, Horseradish and Pumpkin-Seed Oil

APPENDIX 23_Mixed Bean Salad with Langoustines and White Peach

APPENDIX 23_Sweet-Chestnut Velouté with Prunes Wrapped in Bacon

APPENDIX 23_Wild Char with Parsley Pappardelle Served on Kohlrabi in Cream

APPENDIX 24_Larded Braised Veal Shank in a Mustard and Caper Sauce with Mushrooms, Served with Basmati Rice

APPENDIX 24_Breast and Leg of Wild Duck Served on Sweet-and-Sour Cabbage with Lovage

APPENDIX 24_Baked Austrian Pancakes with Curd-Cheese Filling

APPENDIX 25_VILLA KATHARINA

APPENDIX 26_TONI M.

APPENDIX 27_Frogs' Legs with Lemon Confit, Glazed Vegetables and a Velouté of Smoked Horseradish

APPENDIX 27_Snails in a Pinot Sauce with Poached Egg

APPENDIX 27_Aiguillettes of Breton Lobster Served with Honeyed Pomelo Juice, Spinach and Pommes Maxim

APPENDIX 28_Fried Veal Kidneys with Spring Pointed Cabbage, Chanterelles and Sauce Robert

APPENDIX 28_Pork Belly with Langoustines and Green-Pea Salad

APPENDIX 28_Braised Beef Cheeks with Tender Shallots, Kamptaler Wurzelspeck, Rocket-Leaf Jus and Damson Preserve

APPENDIX 28_Lime Soufflé with Raspberry Sorbet and Amaretto Sabayon

APPENDIX 29_CULINARY ACADEMY

APPENDIX 30_Fine Lemon Noodles with Ossetra Caviar

APPENDIX 30_Corn-Fed Chicken with Chanterelle Risotto and Blackcurrant Vinegar

APPENDIX 30_Waldviertel Poppy-Seed-Filled Sweet Rolls with Honeyed Apples and Soured Ice Cream

APPENDIX 31_VINTAGE MÖRWALD

APPENDIX 32_SCHLOSS GRAFENEGG

APPENDIX 33_Deep-Fried Crayfish Coated with Julienne Potatoes Served on Veal Tripe and Parsley

APPENDIX 33_Deep-Fried Roulade of Pike-Perch Served with Parsnip Puree and Vegetables in Beurre Blanc

APPENDIX 33_Fried Veal Liver with Braised Pickled Cherries, Sautéed Chanterelles and Potato Puree

APPENDIX 33_Quail Crépinette with Truffled Goose Liver and a Summer Country Salad

APPENDIX 34_Gâteau 'Metternich'

APPENDIX 35_M.KUNST.GENUSS

APPENDIX 36_Wild-Garlic Pasta Parcels Served with Asparagus and Chervil Sabayon

APPENDIX 36_Ragout of Chamois Venison with Cranberries and Mushroom Noodles

APPENDIX 37_THE MAN HIMSELF

APPENDIX 38_BASIC RECIPES

APPENDIX 39_CONVIVIAL COMPANIONS

Kloster Und

THE HAND OF DIVINE DESTINY AND A NURSERY OF BUDDING TALENT

Where Mörwald
nurtures young chefs, and gourmets devoutly tend
the garden of earthly delights.

In general, a monastery is considered to be a place characterised by renunciation and frugality. As to whether this is always the case is a matter of conjecture, but most people do tend to associate life in an abbey more with watery gruel and meditative interludes rather than with roast quail, refined wines and rare river fish. In Und Abbey by Krems, though, things are very different indeed, as this is a place where the delights of the bottle and table are savoured with gusto.

There's also another factor that makes Und Abbey so remarkable: this establishment is Mörwald's most successful nursery of budding culinary talent. In fact, in none of his other restaurants have the careers of up-and-coming chefs taken off as quickly as here. A prime example is Leonard Cernko, whose efforts, at a tender age, in the kitchen of Und Abbey led to his winning top awards in virtually every important restaurant guide in next to no time. As a result, Cernko – with the ongoing support of his mentor, Mörwald – soon received offers from all over the world. And Mörwald let him move on. Cernko is now working as a chef in Moscow where his culinary skills are in high demand and command a sizeable salary.

After Cernko's departure, the Abbey's kitchen passed into the hands of the 2-years-younger sous-chef, Erwin Windhaber. Much to the surprise of food critics, Windhaber was able to pull off what most had thought was hardly possible: he didn't only manage to maintain the standards set by his predecessor, but even succeeded in raising them. The promising commis de cuisine has meanwhile passed on the baton to Thomas Serret and Erwin Riedrich.

Mörwald has been the proprietor of the restaurant in Und Abbey since mid-2003. Its overall design was the work of the highly acclaimed Viennese duo of architects, »Eichinger oder Knechtl«. Some may see the hand of divine destiny in the fact that, after a chequered history, this ecclesiastical gem has found a new secular function in which pleasure and joie de vivre are written large. Where monks once battled against the temptations of the flesh, heavenly ambrosial delights can now be enjoyed to the full.

Such is the fickleness of history. During the mid-17th century, a fire seriously damaged the Abbey. It was rebuilt in 1656 under the supervision of the architect, Domenico Sciassia, but was eventually secularised in 1796 in accordance with the wishes of the citizens of Krems. After this, it fell into disuse for many years, eventually serving – rather inappropriately, perhaps – at various times as a military hospital and as a residential building. Since 1987, the building has housed a wine college.

Today, the Relais & Châteaux-Kloster Und has a Michelin star as well as three Gault Millau toques (chef's hats), thus making it one of the top-ranked restaurants of Mörwald's culinary empire – and obviously also one of the best restaurants in Austria.

In addition to its exquisite courtyard garden with impressive arcading, the ensemble of monastic buildings includes a fine ceiling fresco in the nave of the church dating from 1756. The space beneath this attractive cupola serves as the regular venue for gala dinners, conferences and culinary events.

Here, Toni Mörwald has succeeded in breathing new life into a long-forgotten architectural jewel. An achievement that has won the undying enthusiasm of Hans Denk, the Lower Austrian »wine priest«, who is well-known figure among epicures. »I'm convinced«, says this Reverend partaker of earthly pleasures, »that my boss on high is extremely well-pleased with the development of this divine terrestrial base.«

Deep-Fried Cheese and Herb Balls
Makes about 45 balls **|** Photo Page 24

45 g soft butter **|** 2 egg yolks **|** 1 whole egg **|** 125 g breadcrumbs **|** 400 g curd cheese **|** 70 g chopped mixed fresh herbs according to taste (e.g. parsley, chives, tarragon, chervil) **|** 150 g breadcrumbs for coating **|** oil for deep frying **|** salt, pepper, nutmeg

Beat the butter until it is light and creamy, and then stir in the egg yolks and whole egg a little at a time. Add the breadcrumbs and curd cheese, mix well, and stir in a mixture of fresh herbs of your own choice. Roll the mixture into small balls (each weighing about 15 grams), turn in breadcrumbs until coated all over, and deep fry in hot oil.

Balik Salmon
Served with Buttermilk Mousse, Blinis and Flying-Fish Green Caviar
Makes about 30 tidbit appetizers **|** Photo Page 24

Blinis | 40 g flour **|** 20 g rye flour **|** 50 ml lukewarm milk **|** 1 egg **|** pinch sugar **|** generous pinch salt **|** 5 g fresh yeast **|** 2 tbsp oil for frying
Buttermilk mousse | 200 ml buttermilk **|** 50 g crème fraîche **|** juice of ½ lemon **|** 3 leaves gelatine **|** 125 ml cream **|** salt, pepper, cayenne pepper
For serving | 300 g smoked Balik salmon **|** 30 g green caviar from flying fish **|** a little red cress

Blinis | Stir together all of the ingredients thoroughly before leaving to prove for about 30 minutes at 35° C. Heat the oil in a non-stick frying pan, pour in the batter to a thickness of about ½ cm, and fry on both sides until golden brown. Continue until all of the batter has been used up. Allow to cool before cutting out rounds.
Buttermilk mousse | Stir together the buttermilk and crème fraîche, add the lemon juice, and season with salt, cayenne pepper and pepper. Soak the gelatine, press out carefully, and warm gently until melted before stirring into the buttermilk mixture. Fold in the whipped cream, and then leave the mousse in the fridge to cool.
To serve | Slice the salmon finely, sandwich the slices between sheets of cling film, and then flatten them until very thin. Cover each with a thin layer of buttermilk mousse before rolling them up. The roulades should have the same diameter as the blinis. Wrap in cling film, and place in the fridge. Just before serving, slice the fish roulades, and place on the blinis. Decorate with flying-fish green caviar and cress.

Roulade of Guinea Fowl with Creamy Celeriac and Potato Layer Cake
Makes about 30 small roulades **|** Photo Page 24

Potato layer cake | 100 g floury potatoes **|** 35 g soft butter **|** 3 egg yolks **|** 3 egg whites **|** 10 g sugar **|** 20 g flour **|** 50 g corn starch **|** salt, pepper, nutmeg
Roulade of guinea fowl | 150 ml cream **|** 150 g chicken **|** 35 g tramezzini bread **|** 2 eggs **|** 25 g parsley (blanched and pureed) **|** 2 guinea-fowl breasts **|** salt, pepper
Creamy celeriac | ½ celeriac **|** 250 ml cream **|** salt, pepper
For serving | a little garden cress

Potato layer cake | Boil the potatoes in their skins until cooked, peel, and press through a fine sieve. Beat the butter until it is fluffy before adding it, along with the egg yolks, to the potatoes and stirring well. Mix the egg whites and sugar, and beat until the mixture forms peaks before folding it into the potatoes. Now carefully mix in the flour and corn starch. Spread some of the mixture thinly (about 1 mm thick) on a baking tray covered with greaseproof paper. Toast under the grill (or directly under the top heating element of the oven) until pale brown in colour. Now spread another layer of the same thickness on top, and toast the same way until light brown. Repeat this procedure until the layered mix is about 5 mm thick.
Roulade of guinea fowl | Put the cream, chicken, tramezzini bread, eggs and parsley into a food cutter, season with salt and pepper, and puree until smooth. Place the guinea-fowl breasts between sheets of cling film, and flatten until very thin using a meat mallet. Spread the filling on top of each piece of meat, roll up tightly, wrap in tinfoil, and poach for 20 minutes at 75° C.
Creamy celeriac | Chop the celeriac into pieces and cook for 10 minutes in salted water. Then transfer the celeriac with the other ingredients in a food cutter, process until the mixture is very smooth, and press through a fine sieve. Transfer to a piping bag, and place in the fridge to cool.
To serve | Cut the rolled-up meat into 30 small roulades. Cut out rounds of the layered potato cake with the same diameter as that of the roulades (about 3 cm). Place a potato round on each roulade, add some creamy celeriac, and decorate with cress.

Roulade Vert with Soured Cream and Vulcano Ham
Makes about 30 small roulades **|** Photo Page 24

Soured-cream mousse | 60 g soured cream **|** juice and zest of ¼ lime **|** 1 leaf gelatine **|** 50 g whipped cream **|** salt, pepper
Crêpes | 90 ml milk **|** 40 g flour **|** 1 egg **|** 5 g mixed herbs, blanched and pureed **|** a little oil
For serving | 12 slices Vulcano ham **|** a little cress

Soured-cream mousse | Put the soured cream, lime juice and zest, and salt and pepper in a bowl, and stir well. Squeeze all excess water from the soaked gelatine before warming it a little until melted and then mixing it into the soured-cream mixture. Fold in the whipped cream, and season to taste with salt and pepper.
Crêpes | Mix all of the ingredients to make a smooth pancake batter. Heat a little oil in a frying pan, pour in some of the mixture, spread thinly, and fry on both sides. The mixture should be enough for 6 crêpes.
To serve | Cut each crêpe in half before spreading with the soured-cream mixture. Now place a slice of ham on each half before spreading on another layer of cream. Roll up the halved crêpes tightly, carefully wrap in cling film, and put aside in the fridge. Before serving, cut into very thin slices, and decorate with a little cress.

Rosemary Toast with Bell Pepper, Tomato and Green Asparagus
Serves 4 **|** Photo Page 26

1 yellow bell pepper **|** 2 tomatoes **|** 2 tbsp olive oil **|** 2 dashes balsamic vinegar **|** 1 clove garlic **|** 2 tsp chopped parsley **|** 4 stalks green asparagus (tips only) **|** 4 slices sliced bread **|** 1 tbsp butter **|** 1 sprig of rosemary **|** salt, pepper

Rosemary toast | Dice the pepper and tomatoes, sauté very gently in olive oil until cooked, and deglaze with a couple of dashes of balsamic vinegar. Remove from the heat, add the crushed garlic, chopped rosemary leaves and chopped parsley. Cook the asparagus tips in salted water until they are tender but not soft.
Halve the slices of bread. Warm the butter in a frying pan, and fry the bread on both sides until golden brown. Allow excess oil to drain off on kitchen-roll paper.
To serve | Put the pepper and tomatoes on the slices of toast while they are still warm, garnish with the asparagus tips, and serve at once.

Crostini with King Prawns, Melon and Cucumber
Serves 4 **|** Photo Page 26

Crostini | ¼ honeydew melon **|** ½ cucumber **|** 1 tbsp white balsamic vinegar **|** 2 tbsp yoghurt **|** 4 tbsp olive oil **|** juice of 1 lemon **|** 4 slices Tuscan bread or 8 slices French stick **|** 8 king prawns **|** salt, cayenne pepper, pepper
For serving | 8 mint leaves

Crostini | Peel the honeydew melon and cucumber, remove the seeds, slice thinly, and place in a bowl. Now add the white balsamic vinegar, yoghurt, 2 tbsp of the olive oil, salt and pepper, and stir well. Add cayenne pepper and lemon juice according to taste, and leave to marinate for a few minutes.

Fry the slices of bread in olive oil until golden brown on both sides, remove from the pan, and place on kitchen paper to absorb the excess oil.

Peel and clean the prawns, taking particular care when removing the stomach sac. Season with salt and pepper, and fry in the remaining olive oil for about 4 minutes on both sides.

To serve ▍ Put the melon and cucumber salad on the slices of bread while they are still warm, and garnish with the prawns. Sprinkle with thinly sliced mint leaves to decorate.

Fried Black Bread with Baby Scallions and Bone-Marrow
Serves 4 ▍ Photo Page 26

2 slices black bread ▍ 60 g bone-marrow ▍ 2 bunches scallions ▍ Maldon sea salt ▍ a little coarsely ground black pepper

Black bread ▍ Cut the black bread into 4 rectangles, and heat in a dry pan until crispy. Poach the bone-marrow in salted water, plunge into cold water for a few moments, and slice while still lukewarm. Scrub the scallions before chopping them into very thin rings.

To serve ▍ Put slices of marrow on the pieces of black bread, arrange the onion rings on top, and round off by sprinkling with Maldon sea salt and pepper.

Crayfish Terrine with a Chervil Mousse
Enough for 1 terrine dish (40 cm long, 5 cm deep) ▍ Photo Page 28

Aspic jelly ▍ 300 g root vegetables ▍ 2 shallots ▍ 2 tomatoes ▍ ¼ l fish stock ▍ 2 egg whites ▍ 1 bay leaf ▍ 5 white peppercorns ▍ 2 juniper berries ▍ 700 ml Noilly Prat ▍ 14 leaves gelatine ▍ salt, cayenne pepper

Crayfish ▍ 10 large crayfish ▍ 200 g spinach ▍ caraway seeds, dill ▍ salt

Chervil mousse ▍ 100 g chervil ▍ 50 g soured cream ▍ 100 g crème légère ▍ salt, cayenne pepper, Pernod

Soured-cream mousse ▍ 1 lemon ▍ 250 g soured cream ▍ 3 leaves gelatine ▍ 200 g crème légère ▍ salt, cayenne pepper, Noilly Prat

For serving ▍ a small mixed salad ▍ a few 'Deep-Fried Cheese and Herb Balls' (see page 7)

Aspic jelly ▍ Mince together the root vegetables, shallots and tomatoes before putting them in a saucepan with the fish stock, ¼ l water and the egg whites. Mix thoroughly, and then add the bay leaf, peppercorns and juniper berries, slowly bring to the boil over a very low heat, and then leave to simmer as gently as possible for about 2 hours. In another saucepan, reduce the Noilly Prat until only about one-quarter of the original volume remains, and put aside for later use. While it is still hot, strain the stock through a piece of muslin. Soak the gelatine in cold water, remove from the water, strain well, and dissolve in the stock. Season to taste with salt, cayenne pepper and a little of the reduced Noilly Prat. About one-half of the mixture should be kept warm (so that it doesn't set) and ready for use, while the rest should be allowed to cool.

Cover a flat baking tray with cling film as smoothly as possible, so that none of the liquid can run off. The size of the covered tray will depend on the size of the terrine dish you are using; it should measure at least 50 x 50 cm, so that there is enough to line the terrine dish twice with the aspic jelly and also to cover the dish once.

Pour the cooled aspic mixture (about 3 mm thick) onto the tray, and place in the fridge.

Crayfish ▍ Cook the crayfish in boiling salted water containing a few caraway seeds and some dill. Break off their tails and claws, and put aside separately.

After the crayfish tails have dried off somewhat, place them in a triangular terrine dish (this should fit inside the terrine dish that you will be using later). After it has been allowed to cool a little, pour all of the warm aspic jelly – except for about 2–3 tbsp that should be reserved and kept warm – over the crayfish tails until they are just covered. Allow to cool thoroughly.

Wash the spinach leaves well, blanch them in boiling salted water, and then plunge them in iced water. Having reserved a few leaves, lay the other leaves in a roof-tile pattern on a cloth. The resulting thick mat of leaves should be dabbed dry with a cloth and then brushed with the reserved warm aspic jelly. By now, the crayfish in aspic should have set, and this should now be wrapped in the dry spinach mat. Cover with cling film, and return to the fridge.

Chervil mousse ▍ Chop the chervil finely, puree with the soured cream until very smooth (adding a little water if necessary), and press through a fine sieve. A small amount of this puree (about 2–3 tbsp) should now be warmed through. Soak the gelatine in water until soft, strain well, and dissolve in the warmed puree, which should then be stirred into the rest of the puree. Beat the crème légère (a low-fat version of crème fraîche) until it is quite thick before folding it into the chervil puree. Season to taste with salt, cayenne pepper and a dash of Pernod.

While it is still sticky, cut the aspic spread on the baking tray into three pieces; two should be of the same size as the inside of the terrine dish, while the third piece should be of the right size to serve as a top layer on the terrine.

Spread the chervil mousse thinly and evenly on one of the two lining sheets of aspic, and allow to set firmly. (If the mousse isn't completely used up, some rounds can be later cut out for decoration.) Now place the reserved spinach leaves on the mousse before placing the second lining sheet of aspic on top.

Soured-cream mousse ▍ Warm the juice of the lemon before adding the soaked and strained gelatine, and stirring until dissolved. Beat the soured cream until it is smooth and creamy, and then mix it with the gelatine and lemon juice. Beat the crème légère until it is quite thick, and then fold it into the soured-cream mixture. Season to taste with salt, cayenne pepper and the reduced Noilly Prat.

Making the terrine ▍ Brush the inside of a suitably sized terrine dish with oil. Carefully place the aspic coated with chervil mousse on a sheet of cling film, and then put it into the dish with the cling film at the bottom. Put the terrine dish in a bowl containing iced water. Pour in half of the soured-cream mousse. Now press the triangular crayfish jelly wrapped in spinach into the mousse. Pour in the remaining soured-cream mousse, and cover with the last sheet of aspic jelly. Allow the terrine to cool well.

To serve ▍ Turn the terrine out of the dish, remove the cling film, and cut the crayfish terrine into slices about 2 cm thick. Put some of the salad on each plate, along with some rounds of chervil mousse (if any is left over), before arranging the pieces of terrine and crayfish claws.

Cannelloni with Duck Liver
Served with Kohlrabi Puree and Madeira Jelly
Serves 4 ▍ Photo Page 30

Duck-liver parfait ▍ 600 g duck liver ▍ about 1 l milk ▍ 10 g curing salt ▍ 12 g fleur de sel ▍ 3 tsp white port, reduced ▍ 1 tsp reduced Noilly Prat ▍ 1 tsp Madeira ▍ 2 cl Cognac ▍ green bacon (Pastetenspeck) ▍ pepper

Kohlrabi puree ▍ 125 ml Noilly Prat ▍ 1 kohlrabi ▍ 70 ml cream ▍ 1 leaf gelatine ▍ 1 egg ▍ 2 tbsp flour ▍ 1 slice tramezzini bread ▍ oil for frying ▍ salt, pepper

Madeira jelly ▍ 300 ml beef consommé ▍ 5 leaves gelatine ▍ 2 tbsp reduced Madeira ▍ 1 tbsp truffle jus ▍ salt, pepper

Duck-liver cannelloni ▍ 200 g duck-liver parfait (see above) ▍ 20 g summer truffles

Duck-liver parfait ▍ Remove all skin from the duck liver before cutting it into bite-sized pieces and cutting away any veins. Put the cleaned liver into a high-sided bowl, cover with milk, and leave to stand in a cold place for 24 hours. Now place the liver in a narrow and tall container, and allow it to marinate for a further 24 hours in a mixture of curing salt, fleur de sel, pepper, port, Noilly Prat, Madeira and Cognac, after sealing well.

Line a terrine dish (15 x 4 x 4 cm) with bacon (preferably Pastetenspeck) before adding the duck liver with its marinade. Cover with bacon and then a sheet of tinfoil before putting on the lid and cooking in a bain-marie at 85° C, so that the temperature inside the parfait is 42° C. Squeeze the parfait to press out all of the excess fat before allowing to cool, and then leave to stand for 24 hours.

Kohlrabi puree ▍ Reduce the Noilly Prat until only about one-quarter of the original volume is left. Peel the kohlrabi, cook in boiling water until soft, and puree before adding the cream and seasoning with salt, pepper and reduced Noilly Prat. Press the puree through a fine sieve. Soak the gelatine until it is soft, and then stir it into 60 g of the puree until it has dissolved completely. Allow the puree to set a little before shaping it into four balls of the same size. Coat the balls by rolling them successively in flour, egg and finely crumbled tramezzini bread. Chill them for 10 minutes in the freezing compartment before deep frying.

Madeira jelly | Warm the consommé before dissolving the soaked gelatine in it. Season to taste with salt, pepper, Madeira and truffle jus, pour onto a baking tray covered with cling film to a thickness of about 1.5 mm, and allow to set firmly.

Duck-liver cannelloni | Using cling film, roll up the duck-liver into four rolls each weighing about 50 g. Sprinkle with grated truffle before rolling up in the Madeira jelly.

To serve | Place some of the remaining kohlrabi puree in the centre of each plate, and arrange one of the cannelloni and a deep-fried kohlrabi ball on the puree.

Raw Marinated Veal
with Vegetable Pralines and Frisée-Lettuce Salad
Serves 10 | Photo Page 32

Veal | 1 kg veal tenderloin | kohlrabi in cream (see page 23)
Vegetable pralines | 1 kohlrabi | 1 carrot | 100 ml cream | gelatine | 2 eggs | 100 g flour | 50 g dry sliced bread | oil for deep frying
Salad | 1 frisée lettuce | salt, pepper | sugar | 1 tbsp red-wine vinegar | 2 tbsp nut oil

Veal | Remove all fat and skin from the veal tenderloin, which should then be cut into strips about 10 cm long. Using a sharp knife, roll up the individual strips as tightly as possible. Flatten evenly with a meat mallet, before spreading on a thin layer of kohlrabi cream and rolling up tightly like a snail's shell. Wrap in cling film and tinfoil before placing in the freezing compartment.

Vegetable pralines | Peel the kohlrabi and carrot, finely grate away the rounded edges, and leave to soak in water. Dice the vegetables into very small cubes (2 x 2 mm), and blanch in boiling salted water.

Put the diced, blanched vegetables and the remaining watered vegetables in a saucepan, pour in the cream, bring up to the boil once, and then season with salt and pepper.

Now pour the vegetables and cream into a measuring jug. For each 100 ml, place 1 gelatine leaf in cold water to soak and, when soft, dissolve these in the hot cream mixture. Keep one-third of the mixture warm and ready for use, and place the rest in the fridge. When the latter has set well, it can be shaped into small balls.

Roll these balls twice successively in flour and egg before turning in crumbled pieces (about 5 x 5 mm) of dried bread (the crusts should be cut off first). Immediately before serving, the pralines should be deep fried in hot oil.

Salad | Wash the frisée lettuce well, and then dry it using a salad spinner. Now add the dressing made with salt, pepper, sugar, red-wine vinegar and nut oil.

To serve | Allow the veal to defrost slightly before cutting it into thin slices using a sharp knife or a meat-slicer. Arrange on individual plates, and season with salt and pepper.

Place a little of the lettuce on the meat, and top with deep-fried vegetable pralines.

Tartar of Limousin Steak in Jellied Beef Consommé
with a Wasabi Mousse and Beetroot
Serves 4 | Photo Page 34 | 4 ring forms (diameter, 7.5 cm; depth, 3 cm)

Tartar | ¼ l strong beef consommé | 4 leaves gelatine | 1 shallot | 200 g fillet steak | 2 small pickled gherkins | 3 capers | 1 tsp Dijon mustard | 5 tsp tomato ketchup | 2 tbsp olive oil | dash Worcester sauce | Tabasco sauce (to taste) | dash lemon juice | 2 tbsp chopped parsley | salt, pepper
Wasabi mousse | 20 g wasabi | ½ leaf gelatine | 100 ml cream
Beetroot | 1 beetroot | 2 tbsp raspberry vinegar | 1 tbsp nut oil | sugar, caraway seeds, salt, pepper

Tartar | Heat the consommé, dissolve the soaked (in cold water) gelatine in this stock, check the seasoning, and then pass through a fine sieve. Stretch cling film across the bottom of the ring forms, so that no liquid can escape from them.

Pour the jellied stock into each form until it is about 5 mm below the rim, and allow to set firmly. When this is solid enough, turn it out of the forms, and use a smaller ring to cut out a round from the centre of each piece. Warm up the remaining jelly again a little until it melts, and use this to coat thinly the bases of the ring forms. As soon as this coating has become a little more firm yet is still sticky to the touch, place the cut-out jelly rounds on top. Reserve the rest of the jelly as a topping for the ring forms.

Finely dice the shallot before blanching. Mince the fillet steak, gherkins and capers very finely. Add the diced shallot, Dijon mustard, tomato ketchup, olive oil, Tabasco sauce, lemon juice and chopped parsley. Stir thoroughly before adjusting the seasoning with salt, pepper and Tabasco sauce. Put the tartar mixture onto the jellied bases in the ring forms, smooth evenly, cover with a layer of the remaining cooled jelly, and leave in a cold place.

Wasabi mousse | Soak the gelatine in cold water until soft, and strain well. Mix with the wasabi paste, warm until the gelatine has dissolved, and then press through a fine sieve. Just before the wasabi begins to set, fold in the whipped cream, and season with a little salt before placing the mousse in the fridge.

Beetroot | Boil the beetroot until tender in water containing an appropriate amount of vinegar, salt, sugar and caraway seeds. Next, cut the beetroot into small cubes of the same size, and dress with a mixture of raspberry vinegar, nut oil, salt, pepper and sugar.

To serve | Put some tartar in the centre of each plate, and top this with a ball of wasabi mousse before arranging the beetroot cubes around the meat.

Lobster Bisque with Green-Pea Soufflé and Ossetra Caviar
Serves 4 | Photo Page 36

Soup | shell(s) of 1–2 lobsters | 1 tbsp butter | 1 tbsp olive oil | ½ small celeriac | 2 cl Cognac | 2 cl Pernod | ¼ l Sauvignon Blanc white wine | ½ l lobster stock | ½ l cream | 2–3 knobs butter | salt, white pepper
Soufflé | 100 g pureed peas (see Basic Recipe on page 38) | 50 ml milk | 50 ml cream | 2 eggs | salt, pepper | a little butter
For serving | 40 g Ossetra caviar

Soup | Break the lobster shells into small pieces, and sauté them in a saucepan with the butter and olive oil. Peel the celeriac, dice finely, add to the lobster shells, and continue cooking. Pour in the Cognac and Pernod, and flambé before adding the white wine and simmering until only about half of the liquid is left. Now add the lobster stock, and again reduce by half before adding the cream and seasoning to taste with salt and white pepper. Pass the soup through a very fine sieve before binding with the knobs of butter or lobster butter.

Soufflé | Mix together all of the ingredients, and season to taste. Grease small soufflé moulds with butter, pour in the mixture to a depth of about 4 cm, cover with heatproof cling film, and cook in a bain-marie for about 30 minutes.

To serve | Turn a green-pea soufflé onto each plate, garnish with caviar, and pour the soup around the soufflé.

Clear Consommé of Baby Venison and Tomatoes
Served with Tomato and Game Roulade
Serves 6 | Photo Page 38

Consommé | 1 kg bones from a young deer | 200 g root vegetables | 1 tbsp tomato puree | ½ l red wine | 125 ml sherry | 5 juniper berries | 1 bay leaf | 6 egg whites | 400 g very lean venison suitable for making a stock | salt, freshly ground white pepper
Baby venison filling | 150 g tender venison shoulder, minced | 150 g cream | 35 g sliced bread (without crusts) | 1 egg | 1 tbsp tomato puree | salt, pepper
Roulade | 50 g flour | 50 ml milk | 1 egg | pinch salt | 100 g venison filling (see above)

Consommé | Brown the bones and vegetables well, add the tomato puree, and continue cooking briefly before deglazing with red wine and sherry. Reduce the liquid somewhat, and then pour in 2 litres of water to cover the bones. Simmer for 2–3 hours, adding the juniper berries and bay leaf halfway through the cooking time. When the stock has cooled, skim off the excess fat, and add the lean venison and egg whites to the stock. Return to the stove, and heat gently, stirring all the time and taking care not to let the stock come to the boil. When the broth has cleared, sieve carefully, and then use a paper towel to remove any remaining fat floating on the soup. Season to taste with salt and pepper.

Baby venison filling | Mince all of the ingredients finely in a food cutter, and then season with salt and pepper.

Roulade | Make a smooth batter from the flour, milk, egg and salt. Fry the pancakes on both sides, and spread some venison filling on the top side. Roll up very tightly, wrap in tinfoil, and place in a bain-marie for 10 minutes at 90° C. Remove the tinfoil, and cut the rolled pancakes into slices.

To serve | Serve the consommé containing pieces of roulade in soup bowls or coffee cups.

Consommé of Waldviertel Spotted Cattle with Hot Spleen Sandwiches
Serves 4 | Photo Page 40

Consommé | 2 carrots | ½ leek | 1 swede | 1 stick celery | 1 onion | about 1–2 kg Tafelspitz (bottom sirloin primal cut, preferably from the Waldviertel region of Austria) | 5 l water | 1 bunch lovage | ½ bunch parsley | 1 bunch chives | 5 peppercorns | 1 bay leaf
To clear the broth | 500 g ground beef | 1 carrot | 1 swede | ½ celeriac | 5 egg whites
Hot spleen sandwiches | 160 g finely ground beef spleen | 3 eggs | pinch marjoram | 1 tbsp chopped parsley | 1 tsp finely chopped garlic | 4 slices bread | 2 tbsp oil | 4 tbsp flour | salt, pepper

Consommé | Clean and coarsely chop the carrots, leek, swede and celery. Halve the onion, and brown the cut surfaces in a hot frying pan.
Bring the water to the boil in a large saucepan, and add the Tafelspitz with all of the other ingredients except the peppercorns and bay leaf. Bring to the boil once more, and simmer over a very low heat for 2–3 hours, adding the bay leaf and peppercorns halfway through the cooking time. Remove any grey foam that gathers on the surface using a flat skimming spoon. Leave the soup in a cold place overnight.
To clear the broth | Coarsely grind the minced meat and the other ingredients using a food cutter, and then add these to the cold soup. Bring to the boil very slowly, stirring all the time so that the meat does not stick to the bottom of the saucepan. Leave to simmer very gently for about 2 hours before passing through a very fine sieve.
Hot spleen sandwiches | Mix together the minced spleen, two of the eggs, the herbs and the garlic before seasoning with salt and pepper. Spread the mixture about ½ cm thick on a slice of bread. Place a second slice on top and spread again some of the mixture on top. Repeat with a third slice of bread and finish with the fourth.
Heat the oil in a large frying pan, turn the 'sandwiches' first in flour and then in the remaining egg, and fry them in the oil until golden brown. Remove from the pan, allow the excess oil to drain off, and cut into pieces of the desired size.
To serve | Pass the beef consommé first through a fine sieve and then through fine muslin, season to taste, and serve with the fried spleen sandwiches.

Crayfish Ravioli with Quail's Eggs and Chanterelles
Serves 4 | Photo Page 42

Ravioli | 100 g pasta dough (see Basic Recipe on page 38) | 1 egg (to brush over the pasta) | 16 tsp creamed spinach (see Basic Recipe on page 38) | yolks from 16 quail's eggs | 8 crayfish | a little butter
Sauce | 500 ml fish stock (see Basic Recipe on page 38) | 250 ml cream | 1 tbsp cold butter | salt, pepper
Chanterelles | 100 g fresh chanterelles
For serving | 1 potato | a little fat

Ravioli | Roll out the pasta dough thinly either by hand or using a pasta machine. Brush with egg before distributing 16 portions of the creamed spinach over the sheet of dough. Make a small depression in each spinach portion, and add a quail's egg yolk to each of these. Place the crayfish in boiling water for a few moments, and break open the shells. Remove and halve the tails, and place one piece on each of the spoonfuls of spinach topped with a tiny egg yolk. Very carefully place a second sheet of pasta dough on top of the first sheet with its 16 fillings, and press down firmly. Cut out the ravioli, and place them (with the egg yolks upwards) in boiling salted water until just cooked through. Melt a little butter in a pan, and toss the cooked ravioli in the butter for a few moments.
Sauce | Reduce the fish stock for a little while before adding the cream. Bring back to the boil gently, add the cold butter, and stir in carefully until well mixed.
Chanterelles | Clean the chanterelles thoroughly before sautéing them.
To serve | Arrange the chanterelles on individual plates, pour over the sauce, and top with the ravioli. Use deep-fried diced potato to garnish.

Eggs à la Viennoise
Served with Spinach, Smoked Bacon and Field Mushrooms
Serves 4 | Photo Page 44

Eggs | 4 eggs | 1 dash vinegar | 1 egg | 50 g flour | 50 g white breadcrumbs | oil for frying | salt, pepper
Side dishes | 200 g spinach | 1 tsp butter | 80 g Austrian smoked bacon (Wurzelspeck) | 120 g field mushrooms

Eggs | Put the eggs in boiling water containing a dash of vinegar for 4 minutes. Remove the eggs, plunge into cold water, and peel. Season the peeled eggs with salt and pepper, dust with flour, turn in beaten egg, and coat with breadcrumbs. Heat enough oil, so that the eggs can float in it while frying until golden brown in colour.
Side dishes | Wash the spinach thoroughly, heat the butter in a frying pan, and gently sauté the spinach. Season to taste with salt and pepper. Cut the bacon into strips, and cook in a non-stick pan until browned. Make wedge-shaped incisions in the caps of the mushrooms before adding them to the bacon and frying until done.
To serve | Put some spinach onto each plate, place an egg in the centre of the spinach, and arrange bacon and mushrooms around it. Put a mushroom on top of each egg.

Broccoli Tortellini with Tomato and Tarragon Butter
Serves 4 | Photo Page 46

Tortellini | 350 g broccoli | 200 g pasta dough (see Basic Recipe on page 38) | 2 tbsp béchamel sauce | 1 egg | 1 egg yolk | 40 ml cream | 25 g melted butter
Tomato and tarragon butter | 100 ml white wine | 2 cl sherry | 1 shallot | ½ l chicken stock | 200 ml cream | 30 g butter | tarragon (according to taste) | 2 tbsp diced tomato | salt
For serving | tarragon | brown butter | Grana Padano or a strong, hard cheese like Cheddar or Gruyère

Tortellini | Clean and blanch the broccoli. Using a blender, puree the remaining ingredients to make a smooth filling. Season to taste with salt and pepper.
Roll out the pasta dough thinly either by hand or using a pasta machine, and then brush with the lightly beaten egg. Place florets of the cooled broccoli on a rolled-out sheet of pasta, place a similarly sized sheet of pasta dough on top, and press down firmly. Cut out individual ravioli, and cook these for about 4 minutes in gently simmering salted water.
Tomato and tarragon butter | Add the finely chopped shallot to the white wine and sherry, bring to the boil, add the chicken stock, and reduce until only about one-quarter of the liquid is left. Add the cream and butter, simmer very gently for 10 minutes, and press through a fine sieve. Work in a blender until very smooth before testing the flavour and seasoning with tarragon and salt. Stir in the chopped tomatoes just before serving.
To serve | Toss the cooked ravioli in brown butter. Pour some of the béarnaise sauce on individual plates, and sprinkle some tarragon leaves and diced tomato on top before arranging the pasta parcels on the butter. Finally, dredge with some roughly grated cheese

Green-Pea Gnocchi with Poached Eggs and White Truffles
Serves 6 I Photo Page 48

Poached eggs I 6 eggs I 2 tbsp vinegar
Green-pea gnocchi I 500 g peas I 2 leaves gelatine I 1 tsp truffle butter I 100 g boiled potatoes (floury) I 50 g potato starch I 20 g melted butter I 1 egg yolk I 50 ml cream I salt
For serving I 1 small white truffle I 100 ml truffle sauce

Poached eggs I Crack the eggs, and place each one separately on a plate or in a small bowl, taking care not to break the yolk. Warm some water to a temperature of 80° C, add the vinegar, and stir rapidly with a whisk to create a circular vortex. Slide 2 or 3 eggs carefully into the saucepan, as close to the edge as possible, and allow them to poach for about 2 minutes. Cook the rest of the eggs in the same way. Cool quickly by plunging into iced water, rinse off, and put aside.
Green-pea gnocchi I Cook the peas in boiling salted water until tender. Plunge into iced water, puree until smooth, and press through a fine sieve.
Soak the gelatine in cold water until soft. Gently warm 100 g of the pureed peas, add truffle butter and salt to taste, and then stir in the gelatine. Cover a small baking tray or a large plate with cling film. Spread with puree (about 5 mm thick), and allow to set.
Place 200 g of the puree in a piece of cloth suitable for straining, and press until almost all of the liquid has been squeezed out. Make a smooth pasta dough by mixing together the strained puree of peas, the finely pureed potatoes, starch, butter, egg yolks and salt. Use this to make 42 gnocchi. Cut the gelatinised pea puree into small cubes (5 x 5 mm), which can then be used to fill the gnocchi.
To serve I Mix the remaining pea puree with the cream, warm gently, season to taste, and pour into deep plates. Cook the gnocchi by placing them in hot water for 2 minutes, before briefly turning them in melted butter and arranging them around the creamy puree. Warm the poached eggs in the truffle sauce before placing one on each plate in the centre of the puree. Beat the truffle sauce until frothy, and pour it over the eggs before grating a little white truffle on top.

Saffron Mussels off the Shell
Cooked in White Wine and Served with Gnocchi
Serves 4 I Photo Page 50

Mussels I 1 kg mussels I 3–4 shallots I 2 tbsp olive oil I 10 saffron strands I ½ l white wine I ½ l fish stock or mildly flavoured fish broth I 100 g cold butter I salt, white pepper
Gnocchi I 100 g pureed potatoes I 20 g potato starch I 1 egg yolk I 1 tbsp melted butter I salt, nutmeg
For serving I 6 baby leeks I a little butter

Mussels I Clean the mussels well, using a knife to remove any beard-like filaments. Discard any mussels that are not tightly closed or have damaged shells.
Finely chop the shallots. Warm the olive oil in a saucepan, add the mussels, shallots and saffron strands, cover, and cook for a while, shaking the saucepan occasionally. Deglaze with a little white wine, bring to the boil, and remove the mussels. Discard any mussels whose shells have failed to open. Add the remaining white wine to the saucepan, and reduce completely before adding the fish stock. Bring to the boil, season with salt and pepper, and bind with the cold butter. Remove the mussel flesh from the shells, and put this back into the sauce.
Gnocchi I Mix all of the ingredients to make a smooth pasta dough, shape into round gnocchi, and cook in hot salted water for 2 minutes, before draining well and briefly turning in the melted butter.
To serve I Chop the baby leeks coarsely, and sauté them in butter. Arrange the gnocchi on individual plates, and put some mussels in saffron sauce on top. Garnish with the sautéed baby leeks.

Scallops à la St. Germain
Serves 4 I Photo Page 52

Cream sauce I 100 g soured cream I juice and zest of ½ lime I salt, pepper
Shortcrust pastry I 1 egg yolk I 45 g butter I 25 g Parmesan I 60 g flour I salt, pepper
Scallops I 8 scallops I 2 tbsp olive oil I sea salt I a little cress and lime zest for decoration

Cream sauce I Mix all of the ingredients to make a smooth and creamy sauce, and put aside in a cold place.
Shortcrust pastry I Cream together the egg yolk and butter, stir in the Parmesan, salt, pepper and flour, and work until the pastry is smooth. Wrap in cling film, and leave in the fridge for at least 1 hour. After this, roll out the pastry between two sheets of greaseproof paper, and return to the fridge. When the pastry is quite hard, cut out rounds with a diameter of about 10 cm, and place these on a baking tray covered with greaseproof paper. Bake for about 10 minutes at 160° C, and allow to cool before carefully removing from the paper.
Scallops I Cut each portion of two scallops into a total of 8 slices, and marinate in olive oil seasoned with sea salt.
To serve I Warm the scallops a little just before serving them. Put some cream sauce on each plate, place a pastry round on the sauce, and arrange the scallopslices in a fan pattern on top. Garnish with cress and lime zest.

Sheatfish Medallions Served with Dijon Lentils and Rioja Butter
Serves 4 I Photo Page 54

Dijon lentils I 100 g beluga lentils I 3 shallots I 2 slices streaky bacon I 1 tsp olive oil I ¼ l poultry stock I ¼ l cream I 2 tsp Dijon mustard I balsamic vinegar I 1 tbsp chopped parsley I salt, pepper
Rioja butter I 4 shallots I 1 sprig of rosemary I 1 tbsp butter I 1 tbsp granulated sugar I ½ l Rioja red wine I cold butter
Sheatfish I 12 sheatfish medallions each weighing about 50 g (The sheatfish resembles a catfish and is native to the Danube and some of its tributaries.) I a little corn oil I salt, pepper

Dijon lentils I Soak the lentils in cold water. Dice the shallots and bacon finely, and gently fry for a while in a little olive oil. Blanch the lentils in boiling salted water for 2 minutes, drain, rinse with cold water, and add to the bacon and shallots. Pour in the stock, bring to the boil, and reduce somewhat before adding the cream and then reducing a little more until thickened. Add Dijon mustard, balsamic vinegar, salt and pepper to the lentils according to taste. Immediately before serving, stir in the chopped parsley.
Rioja butter I Dice the shallots finely, and sauté gently in butter with the sprig of rosemary. Add the sugar, and continue cooking until it is lightly caramelised. Pour in the Rioja, reduce over a low heat until only about one-third of the liquid remains, and then pass through a fine sieve. Just before serving, bind by stirring in the cold butter using a whisk.
Sheatfish I Season the fish medallions with salt and pepper. Heat some corn oil in a non-stick frying pan, and put the pieces of fish in the pan with the skin side downwards. Fry until the underside becomes quite crispy, and then turn the medallions over, reduce the heat, and allow the fish to cook for a little longer until it has a glassy appearance.
To serve I Place some lentils in the centre of each plate, top with three sheatfish medallions, and put some of the Rioja butter next to the lentils.

Fillet of John Dory
Served with Tomato Artichokes and Onions with Basil
Serves 4 I Photo Page 56

Tomato artichokes I 2 tomatoes I 4 artichoke hearts I 2 tbsp olive oil I bay leaf and thyme, according to taste I 1 clove garlic I 25 g cold butter I salt, pepper
Onions with basil I 2 white onions I 2 tbsp olive oil I 1 stalk basil I 60 ml white wine I salt, pepper
John dory I 400 g filleted john dory I 1 tbsp butter I salt
For serving I potato roses I basil pesto

Tomato artichokes | Blanch the tomatoes in boiling water before transferring to cold water. Peel and dice. Cut the artichoke hearts into thin strips. Heat the olive oil in a pan, and sauté the sliced artichoke hearts for 2 minutes before adding the diced tomatoes, herbs and finely chopped garlic. Cover the pan with tinfoil, put in the oven, and cook gently for 15 minutes at 150° C before binding with the cold butter.
Onions with basil | Halve the onions, and cut them into very thin strips. Sauté very gently in olive oil until soft. Add a little salt, pepper and white wine to taste before stirring in the chopped basil leaves.
John dory | Cut the fish fillet into 4 pieces of the same size, sprinkle with salt, and fry in butter for 4–5 minutes until just cooked through.
To serve | Put the tomato and artichoke mixture in the middle of each plate, place a slice of fish on top, and arrange the onion with basil on the fillet. Garnish with potato roses and basil pesto before serving.

Fillet of Turbot
with Pumpkin Gnocchi, Summer Truffles and Cinnamon
Serves 6 | Photo Page 58

Gnocchi | 200 g boiled potatoes (floury type) | 100 g pumpkin puree (see Basic Recipe on page 38) | 4 tbsp potato starch | 2 eggs | melted butter to toss the gnocchi in | salt
Sauce | 10 tbsp diced pumpkin | 1 tbsp butter | 40 g black truffles | 2 tbsp raisins | 1 dash truffle jus | 100 ml Madeira | 100 ml truffle jus | 100 ml cream | 100 ml veal stock | nutmeg, cinnamon, pepper
Turbot | 600 g turbot fillet | 1 tbsp butter | salt
For serving | champagne-fish nage (see Basic Recipe on page 38) | a little grated truffle, if desired

Gnocchi | Mash the potatoes using a potato press before mixing them with the pumpkin puree, starch, eggs and a little salt, and working the mixture until it forms a smooth dough. Having allowed the dough to rest for a while, break off small pieces and shape them into round gnocchi. Cook in well-salted boiling water before tossing the gnocchi in melted butter.
Sauce | Sauté the diced pumpkin in butter for a while before adding the grated truffles, cinnamon and raisins. Deglaze with a little truffle jus, boil down until all of the liquid has evaporated, and adjust the seasoning if necessary.
Place the Madeira, veal stock and truffle jus in a saucepan, bring to the boil, and reduce until about 100 ml liquid is left. Season with salt and pepper, and pour over the pumpkin mixture.
Turbot | Fry the turbot in butter, and then sprinkle it with a little salt.
To serve | Place some gnocchi and sauce next to one another on each plate. Now put the fillet of turbot and frothed-up champagne-fish nage on the plate before, if you wish, adding a little grated truffle.

Whole Sea Bass Cooked in a Salt Crust
Serves 4 | Photo Page 60

1 sea bass weighing about 1.2 kg | 2 kg coarse sea-salt | 4 egg whites | 1 bunch thyme | 2 cloves garlic

Sea bass | Wash and dry the fish. Fill the abdominal cavity with thyme and the whole garlic cloves. Pre-heat the oven to 220° C. Meanwhile, mix the salt and egg whites, adding a little water if the resulting mixture is too hard and dry. Cover a baking tray with cooking foil, and place the fish on top. Cover the fish completely with the salt mixture, which should be pressed down firmly by hand, the aim being that the salt-covered fish should still have a recognisable fish shape. Roll up the edges of the aluminium foil, and bake the fish for 20 minutes.
To serve | Break open and remove the salt crust. Bone and fillet the fish, and serve with suitable accompaniments and side dishes.

Calf's Sweetbreads with Field Mushrooms and Chervil
Serves 4 | Photo Page 62

Potato noodles | 50 g potatoes (floury) | 200 g flour | 100 ml cold water | 1 egg (if required) | 2 tbsp semolina | salt
Sweetbreads | 200 g calf's sweetbreads (cleaned, soaked and with the skin and fibres removed) | 2 tbsp flour | 1 tbsp oil | 1 tbsp butter | salt, pepper
Field mushrooms | 300 g field mushrooms | 1 tbsp butter | 2 cloves garlic | 100 ml veal stock | 1 tbsp chopped chervil | salt, pepper

Potato noodles | Boil the potatoes in their skins, allow to cool briefly, peel, and mash using a potato press while still hot. Add the flour and some water before mixing well to make a firm and smooth dough. If you prefer, mix in an egg. Use a pasta machine (without flour) to roll out thinly (1–2 mm thick) several portions of pasta, which should then be cut into strips about 1 cm wide. Roll these strips between your hands to make rounded tapered noodles (so-called Schupfnudeln), which should then be dipped in semolina and left on a baking tray to dry for a while. Cook the noodles in boiling salted water until 'al dente'.
Sweetbreads | Dip the sweetbreads in flour, and season well. In a frying pan, sauté them in oil until golden brown. Remove from the pan and keep warm.
Field mushrooms | Clean the mushrooms. Heat the butter in a pan, and sweat the mushrooms with the finely chopped garlic. Season with salt and pepper, pour in the veal stock, and stir in the chervil. Put the sweetbreads into the stock, and allow to stand for a few minutes.
To serve | Put the potato noodles on deep plates, and then arrange the sweetbreads and mushrooms on top. Garnish with fresh chervil.

Pigeon Galantine with Apple Chutney and Cornelian Cherries
Serves 6 | Photo Page 64

Pigeon galantine | 2 pigeons | 200 g poultry farce (see Basic Recipe on page 38) | 1 tbsp diced carrot | 1 tbsp diced swede | 1 tbsp diced celeriac | 2 pigeon fillets | 2 tbsp chanterelles or morels | 1–2 tbsp cream | 1 l strong poultry stock | salt, pepper | 1 clean, soaked cloth | kitchen twine
Apple chutney | 1 apple | 1 tbsp honey | dash white-wine vinegar | salt, pepper
For serving | 24 marinated cornelian cherries (preferably from the Wagram region of Austria) | lettuce of the season

Pigeon galantine | Bone the pigeons, place the meat between two sheets of cling film, and flatten using a meat mallet. Mix the poultry farce with the diced vegetables, the finely chopped pigeon fillets and the wild mushrooms, and add a little cream to make the mixture easier to spread. Season to taste with salt and pepper. Spread the filling mixture over the pigeon meat, roll up tightly, wrap in a cloth, and sew up using kitchen twine. Place the pigeon galantine in strong poultry stock, and poach it for about 30 minutes at 80° C.
After cooking, leave the galantine in the stock while cooling, as this improves its flavour.
Apple chutney | Peel the apple and remove its pips before dicing it into small pieces. Caramelise the honey in a frying pan before adding the diced apple. Toss until covered with the honey (taking care that it doesn't stick), and deglaze by adding a dash of white-wine vinegar. Continue cooking gently over a medium heat before seasoning to taste with salt and pepper.
To serve | Arrange the cornelian cherries and lettuce leaves on each plate, and then add small scoops of apple chutney and slices of the galantine.

Breast of Bresse Chicken
in a Crust of Olives and Tomatoes Served with Pine-Nut Couscous
Serves 4 I Photo Page 66

Bresse chicken I 4 breast fillets (about 150 g each) of Bresse chicken (preferably the black-feathered variety) I 1 tbsp oil I 150 g tomatoes I 2 tbsp olive oil I 60 g olives I 1 sprig of thyme I 60 g sun-dried tomatoes I 80 g breadcrumbs I garlic I salt, pepper
Pine-nut couscous I 80 g couscous I ½ bunch basil I 2 tbsp olive oil I 2 tbsp water I 2 tbsp grated Parmesan I 40 g toasted pine nuts I salt, pepper
For serving I poultry jus

Bresse chicken I Season the chicken breasts with salt and pepper before browning them on both sides in a very hot frying pan. Cook in the oven for about 5 minutes at 180° C.
Peel and dice the tomatoes, sauté them gently in olive oil, season with salt and pepper, and leave to cool.
Finely chop the olives, thyme leaves and sun-dried tomatoes, and mix these with the cooled sautéed tomatoes. Stir in enough breadcrumbs to make a mixture that is smooth and easy to spread. Season to taste.
Spread this mixture over the chicken breasts, and bake at the top of the oven at 220° C (or under the grill) until the crust is golden brown.
Pine-nut couscous I Soak the couscous in cold water until it softens. Mix the basil with the olive oil, water and Parmesan to make a smooth pesto. Drain the couscous, cook in a large shallow saucepan with the pine nuts and pesto, and then season with salt and pepper.
To serve I Put some of the couscous on each plate, place a chicken breast on top with the crust facing upwards, and serve with poultry jus.

Fillet of Veal with a Bread Filling Served with Sautéed Artichokes
Serves 4 I Photo Page 68

Fillet of veal I 600 g fillet of veal I 150 g tramezzini bread I 50 g veal farce I oil for roasting I 100 ml veal sauce I salt, pepper
Artichokes I 2 tomatoes I 2 tbsp olive oil I 2 artichoke hearts I bay leaf and thyme, according to taste I 1 clove garlic I 12 g cold butter I salt, pepper
For serving I parsley butter I artichoke crisps (for both see Basic Recipe on page 38)

Fillet of veal I Clean the meat, divide it into 4 portions, and season. Use a rolling pin to roll out the tramezzini bread very thinly, and then spread the bread with the veal farce before placing the veal fillet on top. Roll up tightly, place in a roasting tin containing plenty of oil, and roast for 5 minutes at 180° C. Allow to rest for a further 5 minutes at 80° C.
Artichokes I Blanch the tomatoes in boiling water, and plunge them into cold water before removing the skins and dicing finely. Heat the olive oil in a pan, and sauté the diced artichoke hearts for a while before adding the tomatoes, herbs and finely chopped garlic. Cover with tinfoil, and continue cooking for 15 minutes in the oven at 150° C. Remove from the oven, and bind with the cold butter.
To serve I Put a portion of the rolled veal in the centre of each plate, and arrange the artichoke and tomato mixture around the meat. Add some parsley butter and the artichoke crisps before serving.

Tender Veal Cutlet
Served on Fine Noodles with Black Olives and Baby Leeks
Serves 4 I Photo Page 70

Saddle of veal I 1 kg saddle of veal (on the bone) I 1 sprig of rosemary I a little pork dripping I 1 tbsp butter I salt, white pepper
Noodle dough I 200 g sieved flour I 1 tbsp olive oil I 1 egg I 3 egg yolks I salt
Olive glace I 12 baby leeks I ½ tbsp butter I 65 ml vegetable stock I 60 g black olives (stoned) I ¼ l veal glace I 40 g cold butter

Saddle of veal I Remove any tendons from the meat, and then season it with salt and pepper. Brown the meat by frying it in hot dripping with the sprig of rosemary, before transferring it to the oven to roast in the butter for 25 minutes at 180° C. After this, reduce the oven temperature to 85° C, and allow the meat to rest for a further 10 minutes.
Noodle dough I Work all of the ingredients together to make a smooth dough, and leave this in the fridge for 1 hour. Using a pasta machine, roll out the dough thinly, and cut out long, thin, spaghetti-like noodles. Cook the noodles in boiling salted water until al dente.
Olive glace I Clean the baby leeks before chopping them into medium-sized pieces and sautéing them gently in butter. Deglaze with a little stock. Slice the olives thinly. Bring the veal glace to the boil, and bind with the cold butter before adding the olives.
To serve I Use a meat fork to twist the noodles into whorls. Cut the saddle of veal into 4 portions, and put one on each plate. Top with baby leeks, and arrange some of the olive glace around the meat.

Saddle of Suckling Pig
with Waldviertel Caraway, Pork Ravioli and Sautéed Pointed Cabbage
Serves 4 I Photo Page 72

Saddle of suckling pig I 800 g saddle of suckling pig (boned but with its rind) I 1 sprig of rosemary I 1 sprig of thyme I 1 bay leaf I 2 cloves garlic I olive oil I caraway seeds (preferably from the Waldviertel region of Austria) I salt, pepper
Pork ravioli I 2 pork knuckles I 8 peppercorns I 2 bay leaves I 200 g root vegetables (carrot, swede, celeriac) I 1 onion I 2 tbsp sunflower oil I ½ l white wine I 50 g cold butter I 200 g pasta dough (see Basic Recipe on page 38) I salt, caraway seeds
Pointed cabbage I 400 g pointed cabbage I 80 g butter I salt, pepper

Saddle of suckling pig I Using a sharp knife, make deep incisions into the rind before seasoning the meat all over with salt and pepper. Sprinkle some caraway seeds on the meat side, rub in the crushed garlic, sprinkle with olive oil, and add the rosemary, thyme and bay leaf.
Now carefully put the seasoned saddle of suckling pig into a vacuum pouch, vacuumise the pouch at the highest setting, and cook the meat in a bain-marie for 3.5–4 hours at a temperature not exceeding 75° C. If you don't have a vacuum machine at home, ask your butcher to put the meat and other ingredients into a vacuumised pouch.
After cooking, remove the meat from the vacuum pouch, dab dry, and either grill or fry (in a large frying pan) the rind side until the crackling becomes crispy. Put aside in a warm place ready for serving.
Pork ravioli I Put the pork knuckles in a saucepan, add enough water to cover them, and simmer with the peppercorns, bay leaves, caraway seeds and salt for about 1 hour. In a sautéing pan, fry the diced root vegetables and onion in sunflower oil until they begin to brown. Remove the pork from its cooking water, dab dry, add to the fried vegetables, and continue frying for a while. Deglaze with white wine, before transferring to the oven and roasting for about 40 minutes at 200° C.
Remove the knuckles from the roasting tray, and use a small knife to cut off the jelly-like skin, which should then be chopped finely. Remove the meat from the bone, and cut into small pieces. Put half of the cooked vegetable mixture into a bowl, and mash with a fork until smooth. Mix together the meat, pork skin and mashed vegetables, and season to taste with salt and pepper. To make a sauce, brown the rest of the cooked vegetables and the knuckle bones in a hot pan before pouring in 2 l water and simmering for 20 minutes. Pass the resulting stock through a fine sieve, and then reduce it until only about ¼ l is left. Adjust the seasoning with salt and pepper before binding with the cold butter.
Using a pasta machine, roll out the noodle dough as thinly as possible. Brush half of the rolled-out dough with a little water, place small blobs of the pork filling over this half of the sheet, and then cover with the other half of the sheet of dough. Press down firmly, and cut out individual ravioli that should be cooked in boiling salted water for about 2 minutes and then tossed briefly in butter in a frying pan.
Pointed cabbage I If you can't obtain pointed cabbage, normal white cabbage could also be used, although its flavour and texture are not quite as good. Separate the cabbage into individual leaves, remove the hard stems, and cut the leaves into small squares (about 3 x 3 cm).

Heat half of the butter in a large frying pan, add the cabbage squares, and fry a little until the leaves soften slightly. Pour in about 60 ml water before adding the remaining butter and continuing to cook until the mixture has a creamy consistency. Season to taste with salt and pepper.
To serve I Arrange the cabbage squares on each plate, cut the wild boar into equally sized portions, and put the meat on top of the cabbage. Place the ravioli and sauce next to the meat and cabbage.

Crown Rack of Veal
with Veal-Sweetbread Ravioli, Parsnip Cream and Parsley Butter
Serves 4 I Photo Page 74

Crown rack of veal I 1.5 kg crown rack of veal (on the bone) I 2 tbsp oil I 1 sprig of sage I 2 tbsp butter I salt, pepper
Ravioli I 160 g flour (type 550) I 160 g durum-wheat flour I 2 eggs I 2 egg yolks I 15 ml olive oil I durum-wheat flour for rolling out the dough I 1 egg for brushing the dough I 20 small rosettes veal sweetbreads I 2 tbsp butter
Parsnip cream I 300 g parsnips I 50 g brown butter I 100 ml cream I salt
Parsley butter I 100 g parsley I 75 g butter I 20 ml water I salt
For serving I chanterelles I scallions I a little butter

Crown rack of veal I Season the meat all over with salt and pepper. Heat the oil in a frying pan, and quickly brown the meat on all sides. Roast for about 40 minutes at 200° C until the veal is a delicate pink in colour, and then leave to rest in the oven for a further 10–15 minutes at 60° C. Brown the butter in a frying pan, and fry the roast rack of veal in it for a few moments.
Ravioli I Make a smooth dough from the two types of flour, eggs, egg yolks and olive oil, adding a little water if necessary. Cover, and place in the fridge for about 1 hour. Using a pasta machine, roll out the dough thinly, occasionally sprinkling with a little durum-wheat flour to prevent it sticking.
Poach the veal sweetbreads for a few minutes, remove them from the saucepan, and drain well. Place the small pieces of meat about 4 cm apart on half of the sheet of pasta dough. Brush the parts between with egg, cover with the other half of the rolled-out dough, cut out the ravioli, and press the edges down firmly. Cook the ravioli in a large saucepan containing boiling salted water for about 2 minutes, drain well, and then toss in a frying pan containing a little butter.
Parsnip cream I Peel the parsnips, chop them into medium-sized pieces, cook in lightly salted boiling water until soft, and then drain thoroughly. Add the brown butter and cream to the parsnips, puree until smooth, add salt to taste, and press through a fine sieve.
Parsley butter I Wash the parsley, and pluck the leaves into small pieces before blanching for a few moments and then plunging into cold water. Using a liquidiser, puree the parsley and the remaining ingredients to make a paste, which should then be pressed through a fine sieve. Warm the paste gently, and use a whisk or hand-blender to emulsify it.
To serve I Slice the chanterelles and scallions, and sauté them briefly in butter. Divide the crown rack of veal into 4 portions, and place these on individual plates surrounded with some of the parsley butter. Now arrange the ravioli and parsley cream on each plate before adding the chanterelles with scallions.

Roast Leg of Suckling Lamb
Served with Potato Cakes Filled with Sautéed Red Swiss Chard
Serves 6 I Photo Page 76

Leg of suckling lamb I 1 leg of suckling lamb I 1 tbsp Pommery mustard I 1 sprig of rosemary I 1 sprig of thyme I 1 tbsp olive oil I 1 tbsp butter I 1 tbsp sunflower oil I salt, pepper I 1 vacuum pouch
Potato cakes I 5 potatoes I 1 bunch red Swiss chard I 1 shallot I 1 clove garlic I 2 tbsp butter I 4 tbsp mashed and sieved potatoes I 1 egg I salt, pepper, nutmeg I 1 egg yolk for brushing
For serving I ¼ l lamb sauce

Leg of suckling lamb I Season the meat all over with salt and pepper, and then rub in the chopped herbs, mustard and olive oil. Place in a vacuum pouch and vacuumise (or ask your butcher to do this for you) before cooking in a bain-marie for 3 hours with a water temperature of 72° C. Remove from the pouch, and fry briefly in butter and oil.
Potato cakes I Using the slicing part of a grater, cut 12 round slices of potato (2 for each small ring form). Cut the remaining potatoes into thin julienne strips, which should be cooked in boiling salted water and then plunged into cold water.
Cut the chard into thin strips. Chop the shallot and garlic finely, and sauté gently in butter. Add the chard, season to taste, and continue sautéing over a very low heat until the chard is tender and almost no liquid remains. Reserve a little of the chard for decoration.
Add the rest of the chard mixture to the smooth pureed potatoes, mix well, add the egg, and then season to taste.
Put one thin round slice of potato on the base of a ring form, and line the sides of the form with standing julienne strips of potato before pouring in the chard mixture, which should then be topped with a second round slice of potato. Brush with egg yolk, and bake for 15 minutes at 200° C in a convection oven.
To serve I Put a little of the reserved chard mixture on each plate, carve the leg of lamb, and place slices on the chard mixture. Put a potato cake on each plate, and add the lamb sauce.

Pink-Roasted Sirloin Steak
with Whole Asparagus, Potato Patties and Béarnaise Sauce
Serves 6 I Photo Page 78

Sirloin steak I about 800 g sirloin steak (single piece) I a little Dijon mustard I 1 sprig of thyme I salt, freshly ground white pepper
Asparagus I 18 stalks white asparagus I juice of ½ lemon I 1 bread roll I salt, sugar
Potato patties I 4 medium-sized potatoes I 4 egg yolks I 1 tbsp soft butter I oil for frying I salt, pepper
Béarnaise sauce I 4 egg yolks I 1 tbsp white wine I 2 tbsp beef broth I 1 tbsp cream I juice of ½ lemon I 300 g clarified butter (slightly warmed) I 2–3 tbsp chopped tarragon I generous pinch cayenne pepper I salt, pepper

Sirloin steak I Season the meat with salt and freshly ground white pepper, brush with mustard, and brown all over in a hot frying pan containing a little oil and the sprig of thyme, before transferring to an oven pre-heated to 160° C for about 1 hour.
Asparagus I Peel the asparagus stalks, taking care to remove all of the tough outer skin. Put them in a saucepan with the lemon juice, bread roll and a little salt and sugar, cook for 1 minute, remove from the heat, and allow to stand for 2 hours.
Potato patties I Boil the potatoes before peeling them and pureeing them using a potato press. Mix the mashed potatoes with the egg yolks, salt and pepper until smooth before stirring in the butter. Fry in hot oil to make round, golden-brown potato patties.
Hollandaise sauce I Mix the egg yolks with the white wine, beef broth, cream and lemon juice, and then beat the mixture over steaming water until light and frothy. Slowly add the butter, beating all the time before seasoning to taste with salt and cayenne pepper and then adding the chopped tarragon.
To serve I Cut the meat into 6 portions, and place the beef on each plate next to three asparagus stalks, over which some hollandaise sauce should be poured. Serve with the potato patties.

Fillet of Attergau Beef with Celeriac and Fried Goose Liver
Serves 4 I Photo Page 80

Beef fillet I 600 g fillet of beef (preferably from the Attergau region of Upper Austria) I 1 tbsp butter I salt, pepper
Celeriac I 1 celeriac I 1 stick celery I 250 ml veal stock I 150 ml cream I salt, pepper, nutmeg
Goose liver I 4 goose livers (each weighing about 50 g) I a little flour I a little sunflower oil I salt, pepper
For serving I 60 ml veal glace

Fillet of beef I Clean and trim the fillet of beef, cut into 4 portions, and season well, before gently frying on both sides in butter until the steak is medium rare. Allow to rest for 1–2 minutes.
Celeriac I Peel the celeriac, and trim the ends of the stick of celery. Cut both into small, bite-sized chunks, reserving the irregularly shaped pieces of celeriac left over. Cook the celeriac in the veal stock until it is about half done; add the celery and continue cooking until both are soft. Remove the vegetables from the stock, puree them with the cream, and season with salt, pepper and nutmeg.
Goose liver I Season each goose liver before turning it in flour and then frying it in a little oil in a non-stick frying pan for about 1 ½ minutes on each side.
To serve I Warm the veal glace in a saucepan. Put some of the celeriac puree on each plate, place the fillet of beef in the centre of the plate, and surround it with vegetables. Top with a fried goose liver before drizzling some of the veal glace around the meat.

Fried Deer Liver
Served with a Beetroot Carpaccio and Fresh Horseradish
Serves 4 I Photo Page 82

Carpaccio I 4 beetroots (of the same size) I 2 tbsp Dijon mustard I balsamic vinegar I olive oil I generous pinch of caraway seeds I salt, pepper
Deer liver I 400 g deer liver I 100 g flour I 1 egg I 100 g breadcrumbs I concentrated butter for deep frying
For serving I potato puree (see page 33) I freshly lifted horseradish root, according to taste

Carpaccio I Peel the beetroots, and boil in water containing a generous sprinkling of caraway seeds until tender. Allow to cool before using a slicer to cut into slices about 1 mm thick. Quickly blend 100 g beetroot ends with 200 ml cooking stock and the Dijon mustard, a couple of shakes of balsamic vinegar and olive oil until smooth and creamy.
Deer liver I Remove all the skin and veins from the deer liver before cutting into slices about 3 cm thick. Sprinkle with pepper, and then coat all over, first with flour, followed by egg and finally with breadcrumbs. Deep fry until golden in colour, and allow to drain on kitchen paper.
To serve I Arrange slices of beetroot, so that they look like red 'scales'. Drizzle over the creamy sauce, and then sprinkle with grated horseradish according to taste. Now put some potato puree on each plate, and top with sliced liver.

Saddle of Venison with Pumpkin-Seed Confit and Semolina Slices
Serves 4 I Photo Page 84

Saddle of venison I 4 pieces saddle of venison (each about 140 g) I 2 tbsp chopped parsley I 5 juniper berries I 1 tbsp oil I 300 ml game stock I 50 g cranberries I 1 tsp butter I salt, pepper
Pumpkin-seed confit I 200 g pumpkin (only the fleshy part) I ½ onion I 2 tbsp olive oil I 50 g honey I 50 g pumpkin seeds I salt, pepper
Semolina slices I ¼ l milk I 125 ml cream I 125 ml vegetable stock I 150 g semolina I 10 g cold butter I 10 g grated Parmesan I 1 tbsp olive oil I salt, pepper, nutmeg

Saddle of venison I Season the pieces of venison with salt and pepper, and rub them with the chopped parsley and crushed juniper berries. Brown the meat briskly on both sides in a pan containing hot oil. Transfer for about 5 minutes to an oven at 180° C, remove from the pan, and keep warm. Add the game stock and the cranberries to the juices left in the pan, sieve, and reduce before binding with a little butter.
Pumpkin-seed confit I Dice the pumpkin before sautéing it with the chopped onion in hot olive oil. Season with salt and pepper, add the honey, and reduce a little before gently stirring in the toasted, chopped pumpkin seeds.
Semolina slices I Stir together the milk, cream and vegetable stock, and season with salt, pepper and nutmeg. Bring to the boil, add the semolina, and continue cooking gently until the mixture thickens. Remove from the stove, stir in the butter and grated Parmesan, and spread (about 1.5 cm thick) on a baking tray. Leave for 2–3 hours until completely cooled. Cut out either rounds or diamond shapes of the semolina mixture. Brush a sheet of tinfoil with olive oil, put it on a grill tray, and toast the semolina slices on both sides until pale brown in colour.
To serve I Arrange semolina slices on each plate, place a piece of venison on top, and serve with the pumpkin-seed confit and a little sauce.

Pan-Fried Baby Venison Served on Potato Salad with Rocket Leaves
Serves 4 I Photo Page 86

Potato salad I 400 g potatoes I 2 tbsp white-wine vinegar I 3 tbsp sunflower oil I 1 onion I a little sugar I salt, white pepper
Venison I 400 g venison from a very young deer (leg or part of the saddle) I 1 egg I 100 g each, white breadcrumbs and flour (to coat the meat) I freshly chopped parsley leaves I lard for deep frying I salt, pepper
For serving I 200 g rocket leaves

Potato salad I Wash the potatoes, and boil them in their skins until cooked. Allow to cool a little before peeling and slicing. Make a vinaigrette out of vinegar, oil, salt, pepper and sugar. Chop the onion very finely, and add this and the vinaigrette to the potatoes. Stir well, and leave to stand (not in the refrigerator) for 30 minutes before checking the seasoning – because potatoes tend to absorb a lot of flavour – and adjusting as required.
Venison I Cut the venison into 4 portions, and flatten using a meat mallet before seasoning with salt, pepper and parsley. Coat on all sides first in flour, then with beaten egg and finally with breadcrumbs. Deep fry in hot lard until golden brown.
To serve I Place some potato salad on each plate, put the venison on top, and garnish with rocket leaves.

Braised Leg of Wild Boar with Lentil and Bacon Sauce,
Served with Parsnips and Palfy Brioche-Dumplings
Serves 8–10 I Photo Page 88

Wild boar I 1 leg of wild boar I 1 tbsp juniper berries I 2 tbsp oil I 2 onions I 4 carrots I 3 parsnips I 2 sprigs of thyme I 1 bay leaf I 2 tbsp sherry I 1 tbsp honey I 1 l game stock I salt, pepper
Lentil and bacon sauce I 100 g smoked streaky bacon I 3 shallots I 1 clove garlic I 4 cl balsamic vinegar I 90 g red lentils I ¼ l vegetable stock I ¼ l cream I 20 g butter I salt, pepper, parsley
Parsnips I 4 parsnips I 2 tbsp olive oil I 1 cl white-wine vinegar I 6 cl beef stock I 50 g parsley I salt, pepper
Palfy brioche-dumplings I 250 g old (dry) brioche I 150 ml milk I 100 ml cream I ½ onion I 40 g butter I 4 eggs I 15 g whipped cream I salt, pepper, nutmeg

Wild boar I Rub the meat with salt, pepper and chopped juniper berries. Heat the oil in a frying pan, and briskly brown the meat on both sides. Roast for 30 minutes in a hot oven at 220° C. Wash and peel the onions, carrots and parsnips, chop into large pieces, and arrange around the meat. Pour in a little game stock, add the bay leaf, and reduce the oven temperature to 180° C. Roast for about 1 hour until cooked, basting often with the meat juices. If necessary, pour in a little more game stock to prevent the meat becoming dry.
Remove the meat from the oven, and allow to rest for 10 minutes in a warm place. Meanwhile, raise the oven temperature to 250° C. Skim the fat off the meat juices in the roasting tray, add a little water, and then boil vigorously. Pour the resulting stock through a fine sieve before

adding sherry to taste. Brush the piece of meat with honey, put it back in the roasting tray, and return to the oven for a few minutes to glaze. Finally, sprinkle with freshly ground pepper.

Lentil and bacon sauce I Dice the bacon, shallots and garlic. Fry the bacon for a few moments before adding the shallots and garlic, and then sauté very gently until the shallots are transparent. Add the balsamic vinegar, and continue cooking to reduce the liquid. Pour in the vegetable stock and cream, and season with salt and pepper. Bring to the boil again, and reduce somewhat before stirring in the butter with a whisk. Soak the lentils until softened, and drain well. Gently stir the lentils and parsley into the sauce just before serving.

Parsnips I Peel the parsnips, and chop into medium-sized strips. Heat the olive oil, and sauté the parsnips for a while before pouring in the white-wine vinegar and then seasoning with salt and pepper. Add the beef stock, bring to the boil, and simmer gently. Stir in the chopped parsley just before serving.

Palfy brioche-dumplings I Break the brioche into small pieces, add the milk and cream, and mix well. Sweat the finely chopped onion in butter until transparent. Beat the eggs lightly in a bowl, and then fold these, along with the whipped cream, into the brioche mixture. Season to taste with salt, pepper and nutmeg. Mix thoroughly, and leave to rest for 30 minutes. Now shape the mixture into small dumplings, and cook these for 12 minutes over a low heat in boiling water.

To serve I Put a portion of the roast meat on each plate, along with one dumpling and some of the parsnip. Arrange some of the lentil and bacon sauce next to the meat.

Tender Fillet of Venison on Pyramid Cake Served with Chestnut-and-Prune Gnocchi
Serves 4 I Photo Page 90

Fillet of venison I 600 g best fillet of venison I 150 g pyramid cake I 50 g veal farce I 4 sheets strudel pastry I 2 tbsp oil I salt, pepper, juniper berries
Chestnut-and-prune gnocchi I 100 g potatoes I 100 g chestnut puree I 20 g potato starch I 1 tbsp butter I 1 egg yolk I 25 g prunes I salt, pepper
For serving I sugared quince I game nage (see Basic Recipe on page 38) I 250 ml venison sauce

Fillet of venison I Clean the meat, divide into 4 pieces, and season well. Cut the strudel pastry into 4 pieces of the same size (15 x 15 cm). Cut the pyramid cake horizontally into 4 very thin slices, and place one slice on each layers of pastry, thinly brushing the farce on top. Place a piece of meat on top. Roll up the meat, cake and pastry, and brown on all sides in oil before cooking in the oven for 5 minutes at 180° C and then allowing to rest for a further 5 minutes at 80° C.

Chestnut-and-prune gnocchi I Boil the potatoes in their skins, allow to cool briefly, peel, then mash using a potato press while still hot. Mix with the chestnut puree before adding the starch, butter and egg yolk, and mixing to make a firm dough. Chop the prunes into small pieces, form the pieces into small balls, and chill. As soon as these are hard, make gnocchi from the dough, and fill each one with a small prune ball. Place for a few minutes in hot salted water until cooked.

To serve I Arrange the gnocchi and meat on individual plates along with the sugared quince, game nage and venison sauce.

Millefeuille Slices with Yoghurt Mousse and Wild Berries
Serves 10 I Photo Page 92

Vanilla cream I 125 g sugar I 60 g custard powder I 100 g egg yolk I 500 ml milk I 250 ml whipped cream
Wild-berry jelly I 250 g wild-berry puree I 25 g sugar I 2 leaves gelatine
Crème-brûlée ice cream I 375 ml cream I 375 ml milk I 2 vanilla pods I 7 egg yolks I 60 g sugar I 50 g brown sugar
Yoghurt mousse I 250 g yoghurt I 25 g sugar I 2 leaves gelatine I 125 ml cream
Wild-berry sauce I 200 g wild berries I 25 g sugar I juice of 1 lemon
Pastry I 500 g puff pastry I a little sugar I a little icing sugar **For serving I** fresh berries

Vanilla cream I Beat the egg yolk with the sugar and custard powder until the mixture is pale in colour and quite thick. Bring the milk to the boil, and pour it over the beaten egg yolks. Place the milk and egg mixture in a saucepan, and then bring up to the boil again. Remove from the heat, and leave to cool before folding in the whipped cream. Put the mixture into a piping bag with a smooth-rimmed nozzle, and leave to cool completely.

Wild-berry jelly I Boil up the fruit puree and sugar, add the soaked gelatine, and stir well. Pour onto a baking tray covered with greaseproof paper, and leave to cool. Use a small biscuit cutter to cut out 50 rounds of jelly.

Crème-brûlée ice cream I Put the cream, milk, scraped-out flesh of the vanilla pods and the pods themselves in a saucepan. Bring to the boil. Meanwhile, beat the egg yolks with the sugar until very pale before adding to the vanilla mixture. Remove the vanilla pods, and pour the custard-like mixture into a sufficiently deep baking tray. Cook in the oven for about 1 hour at 90° C. Remove from the oven, sprinkle with brown sugar, and caramelise using a kitchen blowtorch or brazing torch. Place the crème brûlée in a bowl, and blend thoroughly. Place in Pacojet containers, and deep freeze. Before serving, beat using the Pacojet.

Yoghurt mousse I Stir the sugar into the yoghurt, add the gelatine (soaked, drained, and disolved), and mix well. Fold in the whipped cream, and use the resulting mousse to half-fill cocktail glasses, which should then be put aside in a cold place.

Bilberry sauce I Put the fruit and sugar in a saucepan, cover, bring to the boil, and simmer until soft. Puree until smooth before adding the lemon juice and pressing through a fine sieve.

Pastry I Roll out the puff pastry to a thickness of about 3 mm, transfer it to a baking tray covered with greaseproof paper, and sprinkle with a little sugar. Bake for about 20–25 minutes at 175° C. Halfway through baking, place a baking tray on top of the pastry to flatten it. After removing from the oven, leave to cool completely before cutting into squares (4.5 x 4.5 cm). Separate the individual squares, sprinkle each with a little icing sugar, and then caramelise them using a kitchen blowtorch or brazing torch. Allow about 10 squares per portion.

To serve I Before serving, marinate the wild berries in some of the wild-berry sauce. Layer the squares of puff pastry, adding a filling of vanilla cream between each layer. Also add a round of wild-berry jam between every second pastry layer. Decorate the individual plates with wild-berry sauce, and place some ice cream on top of each millefeuille. Make an attractive arrangement of berries on the mousse.

Dessert with Apricots, Cardamom and Almonds
Serves 10 I Photo Page 94

Cardamom crust I 100 g brown sugar I 250 g flour I 125 g butter I 1 egg yolk I ground cardamom
Curled cookies I 30 g butter I 100 g brown sugar I 50 g egg whites I 75 g flour
Apricots in caramel I 20 fresh sweet apricots I 25 g sugar I 25 g butter I 1 tsp honey I a little ground cardamom
Brioche I 1 brioche I 25 g butter I pinch sugar
Almond mousse I 200 ml milk I 100 g marzipan I 50 g Calisson (a Provençal sweetmeat) I 2 leaves gelatine I 2 drops bitter-almond essence I 125 ml cream
Apricot sorbet I 500 g ripe sweet apricots I 160 g sugar I 50 g glucose I juice of 1 lemon
Almond ice cream I 500 ml milk I 185 g sugar I 6 egg yolks I 150 g roasted ground almonds I 100 ml cream
Apricot-cardamom delight I 200 g apricot puree I 100 g crème légère (low-fat crème fraîche) I 25 g sugar I 1 leaf gelatine I pinch cardamom

Cardamom crust I Put all of the ingredients into a blender with a non-serrated blade, and work until the mixture has the texture of very fine breadcrumbs. Spread over a baking tray covered with greaseproof paper, and leave in a cold place.

Curled cookies I Melt the butter, and heat until it begins to go brown. Mix the sugar, egg whites and flour into the melted butter. Use a kitchen spatula to spread the mixture thinly on a baking tray covered with greaseproof paper (3 x 18 cm). Sprinkle with ground cardamom, and bake at 180° C until the cookies are light brown. While they are still warm, roll up the cookies on a rolling pin to give them a curved shape.

Apricots in caramel I Stone the apricots, and chop each one into eight pieces. Melt the butter in a frying pan, add the sugar and honey, and heat until lightly caramelised. Put the apricots into the pan, sprinkle with cardamom, and stew gently until the fruit is tender. Remove from the heat, and allow to cool.

Brioche ▍ Cut the brioche into slices about 5 mm thick before cutting out rounds with the same diameter as that of your rolling pin. Fry gently in butter mixed with a little sugar until lightly browned.

Almond mousse ▍ Heat the milk before adding the marzipan and Calisson. Soak the gelatine, drain off excess water, and stir into the milk mixture. Add the almond essence, mix thoroughly, and leave to cool until the mousse is just starting to set. Now fold in the whipped cream before it sets properly.

Pour the mixture into a rectangular form (8 x 20 cm), and leave in the refrigerator until it has set. Cut out rounds of the same diameter as the brioche circles.

Apricot sorbet ▍ Stone the apricots before putting them in a saucepan and adding the sugar and glucose. Cook until the fruit is soft, add the lemon juice, blend until smooth, and press through a fine sieve. Place in a Pacojet container. Allow to cool before placing in the freezer. Before serving, blend again using the Pacojet.

Almond ice cream ▍ Dissolve the sugar in the milk, bring to the boil, and stir in the egg yolks. Put the mixture in a bain-marie at 84° C, and stir constantly to make a crème anglaise. Add the ground almonds and cream, stir well, and place in a Pacojet container. Allow to cool before placing in the freezer. Before serving, blend again using the Pacojet.

Apricot-cardamom delight ▍ Heat the apricot puree, and add the sugar, cardamom and soaked gelatine. Stir thoroughly before leaving to cool. Fold in the crème légère, and transfer to an iSi siphon.

To serve ▍ Place a brioche round in each curled cookie, add some of the apricots in caramel, and top with the apricot-cardamom delight. Put the almond mousse in very small separate serving bowls, and arrange the ice cream and sorbet appropriately.

Chocolate Petit Fours with Whisky Mousse and Coffee Parfait
Serves 10 ▍ Photo Page 96

Chocolate sponge cake ▍ 150 g butter ▍ 100 g dark chocolate (66% cocoa) ▍ 120 g eggs ▍ 180 g sugar ▍ 80 g flour
Chocolate ganache ▍ 250 ml cream ▍ 175 g chocolate 'Pure Caraibe'
Caramelised filo pastry ▍ 3 sheets filo pastry ▍ 50 g butter ▍ 20 g icing sugar ▍ 10 g cocoa powder
Chocolate cream ▍ 25 g sugar ▍ 50 g egg yolks ▍ 125 ml milk ▍ 125 ml cream ▍ 140 g Jivara milk chocolate
Whisky mousse ▍ 25 g sugar ▍ 25 g egg yolks ▍ 125 ml milk ▍ 1 leaf gelatine ▍ 65 ml cream ▍ 15 ml whisky
Coffee parfait ▍ 150 g white-chocolate glaze ▍ 20 g sugar ▍ 40 g egg yolks ▍ 100 ml milk ▍ 100 ml cream ▍ 1 leaf gelatine ▍ 5 g Nescafé coffee powder
Fondant cookies ▍ 75 g fondant ▍ 75 g glucose ▍ 75 g Isomalt (sugar substitute) ▍ 1 tonka bean

Chocolate sponge cake ▍ Melt the butter and chocolate in a microwave oven. Mix the eggs and sugar, and beat lightly. Beat together the butter and egg mixtures, fold in the flour, and spread onto a greased and floured baking tray, so that the cake mixture is about 2 cm thick. Bake for about 12 minutes at 180° C, leave to cool, and cut into small squares (6 x 6 cm).

Chocolate ganache ▍ Gently bring the cream to the boil, and then pour it over the chocolate. Stir thoroughly, until the mixture is smooth and creamy. Allow to cool before transferring to a piping bag with a smooth-rimmed nozzle.

Caramelised filo pastry ▍ Cut the sheets of pastry into 20 squares (8 x 8 cm). Melt the butter, stir in the icing sugar and cocoa powder, and then brush the mixture onto the pastry squares. Transfer these to a baking tray covered with greaseproof paper, cover with a second sheet of greaseproof paper, and weigh this down by placing another baking tray on top. Bake in the oven at 160° C until the pastry squares have become caramelised.

Chocolate cream ▍ Beat the sugar and egg yolks until pale in colour and quite thick. Bring the milk and cream to the boil, and then pour the mixture over the beaten yolks. Stir well, and then put the mixture in a saucepan, reheat to just below boiling point (86° C), and then add the chocolate, and mix thoroughly. Leave to cool completely, and then put in a piping bag with a star-shaped nozzle.

Whisky mousse ▍ Melt the white-chocolate glaze. Beat the sugar and egg yolks until pale in colour and quite thick. Bring the milk and cream to the boil, and pour over the beaten yolks. Stir well, and put the mixture in a saucepan, reheat to just below boiling point (86° C), and then add the soaked gelatine, cream and whisky. Stir thoroughly before transferring to an iSi siphon.

Coffee parfait ▍ Beat the sugar and egg yolks until pale in colour and quite thick. Bring the milk and cream to the boil, and then pour the mixture over the beaten yolks. Stir well, and put the mixture in a saucepan, reheat to just below boiling point (86° C), and stir in the soaked gelatine and chocolate. Add the Nescafé powder, and mix thoroughly. Line a cylinder (3 cm in diameter, 5 cm high) with greaseproof paper, and pour the mixture in. Place the cylinder in the freezing compartment of the refrigerator.

Fondant cookies ▍ Put the fondant, glucose and Isomalt in a saucepan, and heat to 165° C. Spread the hot syrup onto a silicone pastry mat, and leave to cool. Break the cooled sheet into chunks, and work in a blender until the resulting powder is very fine. Spread again over a silicone pastry mat. Now grate the tonka bean over the powder using a small, fine grater. Bake in the oven at 190° C until the sugar has melted completely. Allow to harden before cutting into pieces of the desired size.

To serve ▍ Spread the ganache over each chocolate sponge base. Place a square of caramelised filo pastry on top, followed by a layer of piped chocolate cream. Add a further filo square and another layer of chocolate cream. Now top with the parfait, decorate with fondant cookies, and finally pipe on some whisky mousse to decorate.

Nougat Mousse with Hazelnut Dacquoise
Served with Matcha-Tea Ice Cream and Banana Compote
Serves 10 ▍ Photo Page 98

Hazelnut dacquoise ▍ 85 g icing sugar ▍ 85 g ground hazelnuts ▍ 100 g egg whites ▍ 30 g sugar
Nougat mousse ▍ 100 ml milk ▍ 2 leaves gelatine ▍ 200 g nougat cream ▍ 250 ml cream ▍ 150 g cocoa butter ▍ 300 g white chocolate
Matcha-tea ice cream ▍ 125 g sugar ▍ 100 g egg yolks ▍ 500 ml milk ▍ 100 ml cream ▍ 10 g matcha tea (powder)
Banana compote ▍ 250 g bananas ▍ 25 g brown sugar ▍ juice and zest of 1 lime
Milk jelly ▍ 125 ml milk ▍ 20 g sugar ▍ 1 leaf gelatine
Lemon glaze ▍ 125 g unflavoured cake glaze ▍ 65 ml lemon juice ▍ zest of 1 lime

Hazelnut dacquoise ▍ Mix together well the icing sugar and finely grated hazelnuts. Beat the egg white mixed with sugar until it forms stiff peaks. Fold in the nut and sugar mixture, and then spread over a baking tray covered with greaseproof paper to a thickness of about 3 mm. Bake for 10–12 minutes at 180° C, and allow to cool before cutting into strips (9 x 3 cm).

Nougat mousse ▍ Bring the milk to the boil, stir in the soaked gelatine until completely dissolved, and then pour over the nougat cream. Continue stirring vigorously until the mixture has cooled to 35° C. Whip the cream, and fold it into the mixture carefully. Transfer to small Flexipan baking moulds (9 x 3 cm), place a strip of hazelnut dacquoise on top, and place in the refrigerator.

Melt the cocoa butter and white chocolate at 40° C, and mix well. Pour into a clean airbrush container, and spray the mixture onto the cooled mousse. Return the mousse to the refrigerator.

Matcha-tea ice cream ▍ Beat the mixture of sugar and egg yolks until it is pale in colour and quite thick. Bring the milk and cream to the boil, pour over the yolk mixture, and stir. Put the resulting mixture in a saucepan, and bring to the boil again.

Add the powdered matcha tea to the cream, and mix thoroughly. Place in Pacojet moulds. Allow to cool before placing in the freezer. Before serving, beat again using the Pacojet.

Banana compote ▍ Chop the bananas thinly before placing them in a saucepan with all of the other ingredients. Warm carefully, cover, and allow to cook over a very low heat until the bananas are soft. Using a kitchen spatula, work the mixture until it is very smooth.

Milk jelly ▍ Bring the milk and sugar to the boil. Add the soaked gelatine, and stir until completely dissolved. Pour onto a shallow tray, so that the warm jelly mixture is about 3 mm thick. Leave to cool, and then cut into very small cubes (3 x 3 mm).

Lemon glaze ▍ Mix the glaze with the lime zest and lemon juice, and bring to the boil.

To serve ▍ Arrange the glaze, mousse, jelly and ice cream on individual plates. Pipe the banana compote onto the bars of nougat.

Cherry Tartlets Served with Peach and Pistachio
Serves 10 ∎ Photo Page 100

Breton shortcrust pastry ∎ 75 g soft butter ∎ 75 g sugar ∎ 2 g salt ∎ 30 g egg yolks ∎ 100 g flour ∎ 3.5 g baking powder
Peach conserve ∎ 100 g peaches ∎ 150 g sugar ∎ a little lemon juice ∎ ½ vanilla pod
Cherries in wine ∎ 100 ml red wine ∎ 15 g sugar ∎ spice mixture containing vanilla, pear, cardamom and cinnamon ∎ 50 g morello cherry puree ∎ 60 cherries
Pistachios ∎ 25 g sugar ∎ 7 g water ∎ 15 g ground pistachios ∎ 2 g butter
Pistachio mousse ∎ 125 ml milk ∎ 25 g egg yolk ∎ 25 g sugar ∎ 15 g custard powder ∎ 25 g pistachio essence ∎ 1 leaf gelatine ∎ 75 g crème légère (a low-fat version of crème fraîche)
Peach sorbet ∎ 240 ml water ∎ 120 g sugar ∎ 500 g peach puree ∎ 60 g glucose ∎ 25 ml lemon juice
Fondant cookies ∎ 12.5 g glucose ∎ 25 g fondant ∎ 50 g finely ground pistachios
Croquettes ∎ 125 g amareno cherries in syrup ∎ 125 g morello cherry puree ∎ 2 g agar-agar ∎ 1 egg ∎ 100 g flour ∎ 100 g breadcrumbs ∎ oil for deep frying

Breton shortcrust pastry ∎ Mix the butter, sugar and salt, add the egg yolks, and beat until smooth and creamy. Add the flour and baking powder, and mix thoroughly to make a pastry dough. Roll into a ball, wrap in cling film, and put in the refrigerator for 30 minutes. After this, roll out the pastry to a thickness of about 1 mm, cut out rounds using small cake rings (diameter, 6 cm), and place these on a baking tray covered with greaseproof paper. Bake for about 8 minutes at 160° C, and then remove from the rings immediately using a knife.
Peach conserve ∎ Peel, halve, and stone the peaches, place in a saucepan, and stir in half of the sugar and all of the lemon juice. Scrape out the contents of the vanilla pod, and add the flesh and pod to the sugared peaches. Bring to the boil before stirring in the rest of the sugar. Remove the vanilla pod, and set aside.
Cherries in wine ∎ Heat the wine, and reduce until only about half of the liquid is left. Add the sugar along with the spices according to taste. Finally, add the cherry puree, and allow to stand for a while before pressing through a fine sieve and adding the stoned fresh cherries. Return to the heat, and simmer until the cherries have softened somewhat. Now remove the cherries, and put these in the refrigerator. Reduce the remaining syrup until it becomes quite thick, and reserve for decoration.
Pistachios ∎ Dissolve the sugar in the water, and heat to 121° C. Add the pistachios, and stir well until the nuts are covered all over with sugar. Stir in the butter, and spread the mixture over a baking tray covered with greaseproof paper. Put in a low oven at 160° C until lightly browned.
Pistachio mousse ∎ Bring the milk to the boil. Beat the egg yolk, sugar and custard powder until pale and thick. Pour the milk into the mixture, stir well, and bring to the boil again. Stir in the pistachio essence and gelatine (soaked and drained) before leaving to cool, after which the whipped crème légère should be folded in gently. Transfer the mixture to a piping bag with a smooth-rimmed nozzle, and leave in the refrigerator to keep cool.
Peach sorbet ∎ Combine the water, sugar and glucose, and heat to make a syrup. Add the peach puree and lemon juice to the hot syrup, mix until very smooth, and place in a Pacojet container. Allow to cool before placing in the freezer. Before serving, beat again using the Pacojet.
Fondant cookies ∎ Heat the glucose and fondant to 155° C, and then spread the mixture very thinly over a greased baking tray. After it has cooled, break into chunks, and put these in a blender with the ground pistachios to make a very fine powder. Finely sieve the powder onto greaseproof paper, and place in the oven for about 10 minutes at 190° C. Allow to cool before breaking into cookies.
Croquettes ∎ Mix the amareno cherries and cherry puree, bring to the boil, and stir in the agar-agar. Put into small Flexipan rounded cake moulds, and deep freeze. The hemispherical croquettes should be coated with breadcrumbs and briefly deep fried immediately before serving.
To serve ∎ Put some of the peach conserve in the centre of each round of pastry, surround with cherries, and warm for a few moments in the oven. After this, place fondant cookies on top, and pipe on some of the pistachio mousse. Garnish with caramelised pistachios, arrange the peach sorbet and croquettes around the tart, and finally decorate with the wine syrup.

Chocolate Pralines with Crunchy Nougat
Makes 25 chocolates ∎ Photo Page 102

Filling ∎ 125 g nougat ∎ 50 g milk chocolate ∎ 125 g pailleté feuilletine (crunch made from crushed crêpes dentelles from Brittany)
To glaze ∎ 300 g dark chocolate (66% cocoa)

Filling ∎ Melt the nougat and milk chocolate at 32° C, and then add the pailleté feuilletine. Mix thoroughly before pouring into a suitable frame to a depth of about 1 cm. Allow to set at room temperature before cutting out small squares (2 x 2 cm).
Glaze ∎ Warm the dark chocolate to 50° C, allow to cool to 27° C, and then warm slightly to 32° C. As soon as this last temperature has been reached, dip the squares of nougat filling into the molten chocolate, and then leave the chocolates to stand on special chocolate foil for at least 12 hours at room temperature before serving.

Cheesecake Fancies with Pineapple and Coconut
Makes 75 tiny cheesecakes ∎ Photo Page 102

Shortcrust pastry ∎ 250 g icing sugar ∎ 250 g butter ∎ 4 egg yolks ∎ 500 g flour
Cheesecake filling ∎ 600 g cream cheese ∎ 2 eggs ∎ 1 egg yolk ∎ 125 g sugar ∎ 40 ml cream ∎ 50 g flour
For serving ∎ 1 pineapple ∎ 1 small packet desiccated coconut

Shortcrust pastry ∎ Beat the icing sugar and butter until light and creamy, add the egg yolks and flour, and mix well to make a pastry dough. Wrap in cling film, and leave in a cold place for 30 minutes.
Roll out the pastry, and bake blind at 170° C for about 10 minutes until pale golden in colour.
Cheesecake filling ∎ Stir together all of the ingredients until smooth and creamy. Spread over the pre-baked pastry, and then bake for a further 30 minutes at 120° C.
To serve ∎ Peel the pineapple, and cut into thin sticks that should then be dipped into desiccated coconut.
Cut the cooled cheesecake into small cubes, and decorate with the little sticks of coconut-coated pineapple.

Macaroons
Makes 100 macaroons ∎ Photo Page 102

250 g icing sugar ∎ 250 g ground almonds ∎ 300 g sugar ∎ 150 ml water ∎ 200 g egg whites ∎ food colouring ∎ flavouring/colouring, as preferred, e.g. desiccated coconut, vanilla essence, etc.

Finely grind the mixture of icing sugar and almonds before sieving. Dissolve the sugar in the water, and heat to 118° C. Beat half of the egg whites, adding the sugared water a little at a time. Continue beating until the mixture forms firm (but not very stiff) peaks. Stir the mixture of icing sugar and almonds into the remaining egg whites, and mix thoroughly. Now combine the two egg-white mixtures, and add the preferred food colouring/flavouring. Place the mixture in a piping bag with a smooth-rimmed nozzle, and press out small rounds onto a baking tray covered with greaseproof paper. Bake for about 12 minutes at 160° C. The exact baking time may vary depending on your oven. These macaroons may be filled with jam or thickened fruit puree.

Orange Cupcakes
Makes 50 small cupcakes ▌ Photo Page 102

Sponge cake ▌ 150 g icing sugar ▌ 150 g butter ▌ zest of 1 orange ▌ 3 eggs ▌ 190 g flour ▌ 5 g baking powder ▌ a little salt
For serving ▌ marmalade for the filling ▌ raspberries, strawberries, black grapes ▌ icing sugar

Sponge cake ▌ Beat the sugar and butter until pale and creamy, and then mix with the rest of the ingredients.
Transfer the sponge mix to a piping bag, and press the mixture into individual cupcake paper bases. Bake in the oven for about 7 minutes at 190° C.
To serve ▌ Allow the cakes to cool. Cut out a small round hole in the centre of each cupcake, and pipe in a little marmalade filling. Decorate with the fruit, and sprinkle with icing sugar just before serving.

Brioches with Vanilla Cream
Makes 10 brioches ▌ Photo Page 102

Brioche dough ▌ 250 g flour ▌ 35 g sugar ▌ 5 g salt ▌ 50 ml milk ▌ 10 g fresh yeast ▌ 3 eggs ▌ 80 g soft butter
Vanilla cream ▌ 50 g sugar ▌ 30 g custard powder ▌ 50 g egg yolks ▌ 250 ml milk ▌ 75 g butter

Dough ▌ Mix together the flour, sugar and salt. Combine the milk, yeast and eggs before adding to the flour mixture. Now add the butter. Either using a dough mixer or by hand, knead the mixture to make a smooth dough.
Leave to rest until the dough has doubled in volume. Divide the dough into 10 equal portions, and roll these into balls. Put them on a baking tray covered with greaseproof paper, and bake in the oven at 180° C until lightly browned.
Vanilla cream ▌ Beat the sugar, custard powder and egg yolks until pale in colour and quite thick. Bring the milk to the boil, and pour it over the mixture. Now transfer the milk mixture to a saucepan, and bring to the boil once more. Remove from the heat, and stir in the butter.
To serve ▌ Halve the small round brioches as you would a breakfast roll, garnish with the cream, and decorate as the fancy takes you.

Catering

LOGISTICS AND LOBSTERS

How Mörwald, in his role as manager,
chef and caterer, has long been delighting a large
and growing regular clientele
with his extramural culinary artistry.

All of the guests have arrived, champagne is being served. After a while, the host announces that dinner will now be served before asking for a few moments' attention. He wants to introduce the man who he has engaged specially for this occasion: it is none other than Toni Mörwald, who will be cooking this evening for this 'at home' gathering of illustrious bon vivants. The menu is what one would otherwise only expect in a top-class gourmet restaurant: a light, frothy lobster soup with crayfish, glazed pâté de foie gras à la Provence, poached halibut with fennel vegetables and, as the main course, fillet of duck à l'orange. The dessert is a nougat mousse with mint and fresh strawberries.

The brief announcement has not been without its effect. The guests' mouths have begun watering in anticipation, while the hosts are also evidently totally at ease. Instead of having to dash about in the kitchen themselves, they can give their guests their undivided attention all evening. Even the serving of the food is in the hands of one of Mörwald's staff. As midnight approaches, the cooking and serving wizards again make their appearance and enjoy the enthusiastic applause of the delighted company.

»Rent a Cook« is the name of this service that allows connoisseurs of the good things of life to enjoy the pleasure of being cooked for by a master chef within their own four walls – without having to don an apron themselves and in the surety of culinary standards normally only to be found at the finest gourmet addresses.

Rent a Cook is currently a booming business. Extramural cooking commissions for prominent virtuosos of the kitchen are very much in fashion, and the demand for such services is increasing rapidly. »Our order-books are full«, says Mörwald. »In the past few years, this area of our work has become a roaring success.«

Many years ago, Mörwald made this service into a separate branch of his culinary empire, complete with an official price list and set rates and costs. For such work, the innovative and ever-active gastronomist even has specially adapted transport vehicles. All of the shopping is part of the service, and if requested, he will bring along the necessary crockery, cutlery, glasses and any cooking utensils that might be needed. »We take a look at the kitchen well in advance and then bring with us anything that might be missing«, Mörwald adds. »If the worst comes to the worst, we even have a fully equipped kitchen in our vehicle.«

Rent a Cook, though, is only one of the catering services offered by Mörwald. Along with assignments in private households, this type of service is also available for events of every sort. Whether it be receptions, cocktail parties or gala dinners, Mörwald's team is ready and able to deliver, prepare and serve just about anything that might possibly be required. From the food to the necessary utensils, from the wine to the décor, from the kitchen equipment to the serviettes, nothing is left to chance.

Recent years have seen major changes not only in the type of dishes served in top-rated restaurants; the expectations with respect to modern catering services are also very different these days as compared to the past. For some time now, no-one offering run-of-the-mill quality has any chance of surviving in this hotly contested market segment.

Toni Mörwald is well aware of this and was quick to realise that there is much more to catering than merely feeding and watering as many people as possible at some party or celebration. As a chef awarded stars by the Guide Michelin, his name alone is a sure-fire guarantee of exceptional quality, of a culinary artistry certain to delight even the most demanding of connoisseurs rather than merely staving off the pangs of hunger.

Shrimp and Ricotta Ravioli
Serves 10 ▮ Photo Page 116

Ravioli ▮ 250 g ricotta ▮ 125 g shrimps ▮ mixed fresh herbs (parsley, chives, basil, etc.), according to taste ▮ 2 eggs ▮ 200 g pasta dough (see Basic Recipe on page 38) ▮ 1 egg yolk ▮ salt, white pepper
Sauce ▮ juice of 1 lime ▮ 125 ml white wine ▮ 125 g cold butter ▮ a few peppermint leaves ▮ salt, pepper, sugar
For serving ▮ zest of 1 lime cut into wedges

Ravioli ▮ Mix together the ricotta cheese, shrimps, finely chopped herbs and whole eggs. Roll out the pasta dough thinly, spread the shrimp and ricotta filling over half of the sheet, brush the other half with egg yolk, fold this half over the other one, press down firmly, and cut out the ravioli. These should now be cooked in boiling salted water for about 4 minutes.
Sauce ▮ Combine the lime juice and white wine, bring to the boil briefly, and bind with the cold butter. After seasoning with salt, pepper and sugar, fold in the chopped mint leaves.
To serve ▮ Arrange the ravioli on plates, sprinkle with a little white wine sauce, and garnish with lime zest and wedges just before serving.

Veal Lights Cooked in Riesling
Serves 4 ▮ Photo Page 118

Veal lights in Riesling ▮ 500 g veal lights (lung, heart) ▮ ½ onion ▮ 1 carrot ▮ ½ leek ▮ ¼ celeriac ▮ 1 bay leaf ▮ a few peppercorns ▮ 1 tsp hot mustard ▮ juice of 1 lemon ▮ 1 tbsp wine vinegar ▮ 1 small pickled gherkin ▮ 1 tsp capers ▮ 1 tbsp butter ▮ ¼ l Riesling white wine ▮ 125 ml cream ▮ 1 clove garlic ▮ 1 bunch parsley ▮ salt, white pepper
Dumplings ▮ 400 g dry bread rolls, cut into small cubes ▮ ¼ l milk ▮ 4 eggs ▮ 20 g chopped parsley ▮ 1 tbsp butter ▮ salt, pepper, nutmeg
For serving ▮ 4 eggs

Veal lights ▮ The most time-consuming part of this recipe is preparing the lights: when this has been done, everything goes very quickly and easily. Separate the windpipe and gullet from the lungs, and remove any thick tendons and fatty parts. Leave to soak in cold water for no less than 2 hours (longer if possible), so that any blood is completely flushed out. Change the soaking water several times, and move the lights around in it occasionally.
Peel the onion, carrot, leek and celeriac. Half of these vegetables should be chopped into medium-sized pieces, and the rest put to one side for the time being. Put the chopped vegetables along with the bay leaf and a few lightly crushed peppercorns into a large saucepan containing about 2 l water. Bring to the boil, and then add the soaked lights. Cover, and simmer for about 40 minutes. This should be enough to cook the lung, but the heart will probably need a further 10–15 minutes. When cooked, remove all of the lights from the cooking stock, which should now be strained and reserved for later use. Remove any large blood vessels from the lights, before placing these to cool in a large bowl. Now put a cutting-board on top, weigh this down with a few plates, and leave the lights to stand for a couple of hours. After this, cut the lights into very thin strips, carefully removing any gristle. Add mustard, lemon, vinegar, the finely chopped gherkin and capers to the lights before seasoning with salt and pepper. Leave to marinate for about 2 hours or, even better, overnight if possible.
To complete the preparation of the lights, cut the reserved vegetables into julienne strips, and cook these in boiling salted water until tender but not soft, before plunging them into cold water. Heat the butter in a large saucepan, sauté the onion strips gently, deglaze with the white wine, and reduce until only about half of the liquid is left. Add the vegetables cut into julienne strips along with the sliced lights, pour in the strained cooking stock of the lights, and bring to the boil. Now add the cream, and continue cooking for a while to reduce the sauce a little. Add salt, freshly ground white pepper and the crushed garlic clove to taste, before stirring in the chopped parsley.
Dumplings ▮ Soak the dried bread in milk before stirring in the eggs and parsley, and then seasoning with salt, pepper and nutmeg. Tightly wrap the dumpling dough in heat-proof foil, and cook for 40 minutes in a bain-marie at 80° C. Now remove the cooked dumpling from the water, and place in the fridge. When cold, remove from the foil, cut into thick slices, and fry each slice in butter on both sides.
To serve ▮ Place some of the lights mixture on each plate, and then arrange the dumpling slices decoratively around meat. Top with a fried egg 'sunny side up' cooked in a ring so that it is perfectly round.

Punch Petit Fours
Makes about 20 cakes ▮ Photo Page 120

Sponge mix ▮ 10 egg yolks ▮ 40 g icing sugar ▮ pinch vanilla sugar ▮ pinch salt ▮ zest of 2 lemons ▮ 10 egg whites ▮ 200 g sugar ▮ 250 g flour
Punch filling ▮ 200 g apricot jam ▮ 125 ml rum ▮ 40 ml sugar syrup ▮ 50 g dark chocolate ▮ zest of 1 lemon and 1 orange ▮ pinch cinnamon
Decoration ▮ about 50 g apricot jam ▮ 250 g fondant (turned pink using food colouring) ▮ 20 amareno cherries ▮ 20 mint leaves ▮ a little gold leaf

Sponge mix ▮ Beat the egg yolks and icing sugar until the mixture is light and creamy. Stir in the vanilla sugar, salt and the lemon zest. Beat the egg whites and the sugar until the mixture forms stiff peaks. Fold carefully into the beaten egg yolks. Add the sieved flour, and fold this in gently. Divide the mixture in half, and place each half in a baking tin lined with greaseproof paper. Bake for 10 minutes in an oven pre-heated to 200° C. Cut a rectangle measuring 20 x 25 cm out of each cooled sponge cake, reserving what is left for the filling.
Punch filling ▮ Crumble the remaining sponge cake into a bowl containing the apricot jam, rum and syrup. Mix well before adding the grated chocolate, orange and lemon zest and cinnamon. Mix well with your hands until the mixture forms a firm ball.
Decoration and serving ▮ Spread apricot jam on one of the sponge bases, which should then be put in a rectangular dessert mould and topped with punch filling. Place the other sponge on top, weigh down with a heavy plate, and leave in the refrigerator for several hours.
Remove the sponge cake from the mould, and cut into 20 small cubes (5 x 5 cm each). Brush the sides and tops with warm apricot jam, and allow to cool. Now glaze with the warmed fondant. Decorate with amareno cherries, mint leaves and gold leaf.

Creamy Horns
Enough to make about 15 cakes ▮ Photo Page 120

500 g puff pastry ▮ 4 egg whites ▮ 280 g icing sugar (plus a little more for sprinkling over the rolls)

Roll out the puff pastry until it is about 3 mm thick. Using a wheel pastry cutter, cut the pastry into strips 1.5 cm wide, and wrap these around forms for making cream horns. Bake in the oven for 10–12 minutes at about 160° C. Remove from the oven and, while still hot, carefully separate the pastry horns from the forms, and allow to cool.
In a bowl suspended over steaming water, whisk the egg whites and icing sugar until the mixture is very thick and creamy. Transfer to a piping bag, and pipe the mixture into the horns.
To serve ▮ Cover the creamy horns with a sprinkling of icing sugar.

Zur Traube

ROOTS AND TRADITION

Where Mörwald's career began,
and where, even today,
tradition is still his source of inspiration.

If it weren't for the name, Mörwald, Feuersbrunn would still be little more than an idyllic tiny village in Lower Austria. Nowadays, though, this small settlement with a population of about 700 people is a place of pilgrimage for gourmets not only from Austria, but also from much further afield. Culinary connoisseurs from just about everywhere make the journey here to enjoy a mixture of rustic idyll and gastronomic pyrotechnics. Thanks to Mörwald's name, Feuersbrunn has acquired a new and distinctive identity; for the people who live here, Toni Mörwald is the maestro of delectation, in whose realms there is an endless supply of delightful dainties.

It was right here in Feuersbrunn that Mörwald's career began; it was from here that he succeeded in building up, in record time, a gastronomic empire that includes several top-ranked restaurants, a flourishing college for chefs and a profitable catering service. His gourmet restaurants have brought Mörwald no less than a total of seven toques (chef's hats) from Gault Millau and two stars in the Guide Michelin. His determination and fixity of purpose in realising his ideas have earned him much-coveted titles like »Restaurant Proprietor of the Year«, »Gastronomer of the Year« and »Grande Chef de Cuisine Europe«.

Actually, his aunt, Rikki, is to blame for all of this. For a long time, she ran a simple village tavern in Feuersbrunn, until a farmer from the Waldviertel area appeared on the scene, made her his wife and carried her off into the less-temperate climes of his home region. Suddenly, Feuersbrunn was a village without a pub – a desperate situation indeed.

The villagers now began to put pressure on the renegade landlady's brother-in-law, who just happened to be Toni Mörwald's father. He was told that he had better take over the abandoned hostelry with all due haste, because a village without an inn is simply unthinkable.

After several attempts to persuade them, the Mörwald Family did then actually leap into the breach. Under the supervision of Mörwald senior, the tavern underwent extensive renovation and conversion, while his wife, Erika, took charge of the kitchen, and grandmother took up position behind the bar during the daytime.

It was in such surroundings that young Toni Mörwald grew up, and his fascination with his mother's cooking skills began in the early years of childhood. It was a world of tempting aromas and flavours, whose inevitable outcome was that there no question about which profession he would later take up: Toni was resolved to become a chef.

Mörwald learned the finer points of his trade from, among others, Austria's highly renowned chef, Reinhard Gerer, while also gathering valuable experience in France, Monaco, Italy, Spain and China. Finally, in 1989, he took over the tavern, Zur Traube, from his parents. Soon after, he was awarded his first toque by Gault Millau, at that time the youngest-ever Austrian cook to enjoy this distinction.

The outstanding achievements of this upwardly mobile chef rapidly led to the fully booked Traube having a waiting list of several weeks. Everybody in Feuersbrunn began to wonder where all the people were suddenly coming from.

Several phases of extensive rebuilding mean that, although somewhat ramified, the present-day restaurant complex offers visitors a pleasantly contemporary ambience. In addition to the classic tavern-like section, the imposing gourmet restaurant, »Toni M«, a herb room, a garden hall, three garden rooms, a conservatory and a ballroom, the restaurant also has a wine bar with an inexhaustible selection of vintages, as well as a state-of-the-art kitchen that serves as the venue for cooking seminars every Wednesday and Thursday. Nonetheless, many rooms of the Traube have retained the cosy and congenial atmosphere of a traditional old country inn. For its 'landlord', this is a matter of great importance, because the Traube also serves to ensure that Mörwald never loses sight of his own culinary roots. Here, where everything began, today Françoise Laliberté serves his guests exclusive Austrian dishes – a perfect foil to the international gourmet cuisine to be found elsewhere in his culinary empire.

Warm Marinated Veal Tongue
with Mixed Vegetables, Horseradish and Pumpkin-Seed Oil
Serves 4 I Photo Page 134

Sauce I 125 ml cream I 125 ml beef broth I 100 g chopped mixed herbs (parsley, tarragon, chervil) I 50 g butter I salt, pepper

Mixed vegetables I 2 carrots I 1 swede I 1 leek I 6 cl nut oil I 3 cl balsamic vinegar I salt, pepper
For serving I 400 g cooked veal tongue I ½ bunch chives I 100 ml pumpkin-seed oil I ½ root horseradish

Sauce I Mix together the cream and beef broth, and bring to the boil before adding the butter and herbs, pureeing, seasoning with salt and pepper, and passing through a fine sieve.
Mixed vegetables I Finely dice the carrots, swede and leek, blanch in boiling salted water until tender but not soft, plunge into cold water, and dab dry. Marinate in a mixture of nut oil, balsamic vinegar, salt and pepper.
To serve I Cut the veal tongue into slices 2 mm thick, which should then be placed flat on warmed plates. Put some of the mixed vegetables on top before drizzling over some of the sauce. Now arrange the finely chopped chives, some pumpkin-seed oil and freshly grated horseradish on the other parts of the plate.

Mixed Bean Salad with Langoustines and White Peach
Serves 4 I Photo Page 136

Mixed bean salad I 50 g white haricot beans I 50 g red kidney beans I 50 g French beans I 1 white peach (preferably one grown in the Wachau region of Austria) I 1 tsp mustard seeds I 1 tbsp white-wine vinegar I 3 tbsp olive oil I 1 tbsp chopped chives I salt, pepper, sugar
Langoustines I 8 fresh langoustines I juice of ½ lime I ½ bunch chives I salt

Mixed bean salad I Cook the different types of beans separately until tender. Cut the peach into attractively shaped pieces.
Boil the mustard seeds in three times in 125 ml water, and use half of the seeds with the white-wine vinegar and 2 tbsp olive oil to make a dressing. Separately turn in the cooked beans and peach pieces, and season to taste with salt, pepper and a little sugar.
Langoustines I Break open the shells of the langoustines, and remove the stomach sac. Marinate the raw flesh of the langoustines in a mixture made with salt, lime juice, the remaining cooked mustard seeds, 1 tbsp olive oil and the freshly chopped chives.
To serve I Place some of the salad on each plate, and add the marinated langoustines.

Sweet-Chestnut Velouté with Prunes Wrapped in Bacon
Serves 4 I Photo Page 138

Velouté I 13 sweet chestnuts I 3 tbsp cold butter I ½ l poultry stock I 125 ml cream I 50 g whipped cream I salt, pepper
Prunes I 12 prunes I 12 rashers streaky bacon
Velouté I Using a sharp knife, make cross-like incisions in the chestnut shells before placing the chestnuts on a baking tray and putting them into an oven preheated to 200° C for 10–15 minutes. Halfway through, spray the chestnuts with some cold water, as this makes the shells easier to remove afterwards. After the chestnuts have cooled a little, remove their shells, and chop the chestnuts into small pieces.
In a large frying pan, heat 2 tbsp butter until it bubbles and turns brown in colour; now add the chopped chestnuts, and turn them in the butter for a few moments. Deglaze with the poultry stock, return to the boil, and simmer gently for a further 15 minutes. Add the cream, and bring back to the boil. Now add the remaining cold butter by working the mixture with a hand-blender to make a smooth puree. Season with salt and pepper, fold in the whipped cream, and serve at once.
Damsons I Wrap each of the damsons with a rasher of streaky bacon, and fry them in a non-stick pan until the bacon is crisp.
To serve I Pour the velouté into deep plates, adding three bacon-wrapped prunes to each plate before serving.

Wild Char with Parsley Pappardelle Served on Kohlrabi in Cream
Serves 4 I Photo Page 140

Parsley pasta I 100 g parsley I 1 egg I 1 egg yolk I ½ tsp olive oil I a little sparkling mineral water I 200 g flour I dash olive oil I salt
Wild char I 400 g filleted char (preferably from Mariazell in Lower Austria) I juice of 1 lemon I 1 tbsp oil I knob butter I salt, pepper
Kohlrabi in cream I 200 g kohlrabi I 125 ml cream I salt, pepper, nutmeg I a little flat-leaf parsley I 40 g butter

Parsley pasta I Wash the parsley well, dab dry, and pluck the leaves from the stalks. Blend the parsley leaves, egg, egg yolk, olive oil, mineral water and salt until the mixture is very smooth. Transfer to a bowl. Add the flour a little at a time, and continue mixing until the dough stops adhering to the sides of the bowl. Roll into a ball, cover with cling film, and leave for 30 minutes in the refrigerator.
Using a pasta machine, roll out the pasta dough thinly, and then cut it into pappardelle (long strips about 2 cm wide).
Wild char I Season the fish fillets with salt, pepper and lemon juice. Heat oil in a frying pan, and fry the fish until the underside is quite brown and crispy. Just before the fish is cooked though, add a knob of butter, turn over the fillets, and allow the upper side to cook for a few moments.
Kohlrabi in cream I Peel the kohlrabi before grating coarsely. Cook in the cream until al dente, and then season with salt, pepper and nutmeg. Cut the parsley leaves into strips. Stir the parsley and butter into the creamy sauce.
To serve I Cook the pappardelle in boiling salted water until al dente, drain well, return to the empty saucepan, and toss in a dash of olive oil. Roll up each of the pappardelle, and place them in threes on each plate. Arrange the kohlrabi in cream between the pasta rolls, and place a char fillet on top.

Larded Braised Veal Shank in a Mustard and Caper Sauce with Mushrooms, Served with Basmati Rice
Serves 4 I Photo Page 142

Veal shank I 1 kg veal shank I 100 g very fat streaky bacon I 3 tbsp butter oil I 1 carrot I 1 swede I 1 onion I ¼ l white wine I ¼ l veal stock or beef broth I 2 bay leaves I salt, pepper
Mushrooms I 200 g mushrooms I 2 tbsp butter I 125 ml cream I 1 tbsp Pommery mustard I 1 tbsp capers I a little parsley I salt
For serving I 200 g basmati rice I 1 tbsp butter I salt

Veal shank I Cut the streaky bacon into very thin, long strips (0.5 x 10 cm), and use these to lard the veal shank.
Heat the butter oil in a pan, brown the larded veal shank on all sides, remove from the pan, and season with salt and pepper. Chop the carrot, swede and onion into medium-sized chunks, put these into the oil and juices remaining in the pan, and fry for a while before returning the seasoned meat to the pan. Pour the white wine and stock over the meat, reduce for a couple of minutes, and add the bay leaves. Transfer to the oven, and slowly braise the meat for about 1½ hours until tender, frequently basting it with its own juices. Remove the meat and the bay leaves, and pass the remaining meat juices through a pointed sieve.
Mushrooms I Wipe the mushrooms with a damp cloth, and slice them not too thinly. Heat some butter until it begins to bubble, and sauté the mushrooms briskly. Season the mushrooms before transferring them to the sieved meat juices. Add the cream, and simmer very gently for about 10 minutes. Finally, stir in the Pommery mustard and capers. If you wish, you can add chopped fresh parsley to the sauce.
To serve I Wash the basmati rice under cold running water. Cook in boiling salted water until tender but not soft, drain well, and briefly toss in butter. Put the meat in the prepared sauce, warm through again briefly, cut the meat into 4 portions, and put it on individual plates with a little sauce and some of the basmati rice.

Breast and Leg of Wild Duck Served on Sweet-and-Sour Cabbage with Lovage
Serves 4 I Photo Page 144

Wild duck I 2 whole wild ducks I 1 l vegetable stock I salt, pepper
Cabbage with lovage I 1 white cabbage (about 500 g) I 1 tbsp oil I 2 tbsp icing sugar I 1 tbsp coarsely chopped lovage I 3 tbsp balsamic vinegar I ¼ l vegetable stock I salt

Wild duck I Put the wild ducks in a large, deep roasting pan, pour in the vegetable stock to a depth of about 4 cm, and gently braise the meat in the oven at 120° C for about 1.5–2 hours. Put aside the breasts and legs after separating them from the carcases. Chop the remaining bones into small pieces, return them to the meat juices in a saucepan, and boil briskly for about 15 minutes on the stove. Strain the resulting stock, reduce until only a little of the liquid remains, and check the seasoning.
Put the duck breasts and legs on a grill tray with the skin side facing upwards, and put them under a moderately hot grill until the skin is brown and crisp.
Cabbage with lovage I Remove the hard stems from the cabbage, and cut the leaves into smallish squares (4 x 4 cm). Fry these in hot oil in a pan, season with salt, sprinkle with the icing sugar, and continue cooking until the leaves become slightly caramelised. Deglaze with balsamic vinegar, pour in the vegetable stock, and continue cooking until the cabbage is tender before stirring in the chopped lovage.
To serve I Place one half of the breast and a leg on each plate. Put some of the cabbage with lovage next to the meat, and add a little of the reduced poultry stock.

Baked Austrian Pancakes with Curd-Cheese Filling
Serves 4 (2 pancakes each) I Photo Page 146

Pancake batter I 100 g flour I 200 ml milk I 2 eggs I pinch salt I a little butter
Filling I 125 g curd cheese I 75 g soured cream I 2 eggs I 25 g icing sugar I 15 g vanilla sugar I 20 g custard powder I 1 cl amaretto I 1 cl kirsch I 2 tbsp raisins I 70 g whipped cream
For serving I mixed fresh fruit

Pancakes I Mix together the flour, milk, eggs and a pinch of salt to make a smooth pancake batter. Use this to make 8 pancakes, each fried in a little butter.
Filling I Pass the curd cheese through a fine sieve before stirring it together with all of the other ingredients except the cream until thoroughly mixed. Finally, fold in the whipped cream. Spread the filling on the pancakes, and roll them up. Place the pancakes on a greased baking tray, and bake in the oven for about 10 minutes at 160° C.
To serve I Arrange 2 pancakes with some fresh fruit on each plate.

Villa Katharina

DELIGHTFUL DOMICILE FOR EPICURES

Where Mörwald offers
his guests a fine hotel characterised
by traditional rustic hospitality.

The Villa Katharina, a hotel for true connoisseurs of the best things of life, is located directly opposite Mörwald's home base, the Zur Traube restaurant in Feuersbrunn. This means that the location of this hostelry for lovers of epicurean pleasures makes it the ideal point of departure for a wide range of culinary campaigns and expeditions. Needless to say, the top address for such delights is the neighbouring Traube with its many facets – from the rustic rooms of its country-style tavern to the tiptop gourmet ambience of Toni M. – as it were, a restaurant within a restaurant distinguished by an overall design and character that is both upbeat and remarkable.

The Villa Katharina is also the perfect base from which to explore every corner of the Wagram wine-growing region, with its many romantic wine cellars located in quaint lanes and where numerous top wine-growers have recently won widespread acclaim for their excellent vintages. For this reason if no other, Toni Mörwald has named each of the hotel's ten rooms after a particular variety of grape, i.e. the types that are of outstanding importance in the region, from Grüner Veltliner to Riesling to Chardonnay.

Feuersbrunn is quite close to the better-known Wachau, too, which is why many guests take the opportunity to make an excursion to the unique cultural landscape of this charming region flanking the Danube. The Wachau is not merely a UNESCO World Heritage Site but is one of the loveliest and most fascinating parts of Austria. It can boast a remarkable density of culinary hotspots thanks to its numerous top-grade restaurants as well as its wine-producers of international stature. Indeed, many wine-growers here are known throughout the world and, as not a few of these are good friends of Toni Mörwald, he often organises special trips for his guests under the motto, »Wagram meets Wachau«.

Obviously, whoever books in for a weekend of rare delights at the Villa Katharina can rest assured that even the highest culinary and vinicultural expectations will be fulfilled if not exceeded. A broad range of other activities are also on offer, usually kicking off with some morning exercise or sport in Feuersbrunn, for example, some jogging along charming alleys and through the local vineyards. Such exertions are followed by a gourmet breakfast in the Traube that includes Chardonnay sparkling wine and tasty local sausage specialities. During the day, guests may opt to visit a vineyard and drop in on a wine-grower, before settling down to a plentiful lunch in the Traube's rustic inn with simple yet delicious home-style cooking.

Finally, when evening comes round, Toni Mörwald's guests can look forward to a memorable 'freestyle cuisine' surprise menu served in the Korab Dining Room in the Traube. The day is then usually rounded off in the candlelit surroundings of the Vinothek wine bar to the accompaniment of exquisite vintages, as one might easily imagine.

Toni M.

A GOURMET HEAVEN LIT BY CULINARY STARS

Where Mörwald has created
a restaurant within a restaurant
that just keeps on winning award after award.

Salad of wild carrots, celeriac and fillet of Limousin beef. Scrambled eggs with black truffles. Bouillon of pheasant with ravioli of goose-liver pâté. The local speciality, Beuscherl (calf's lung), cooked in Riesling with quail eggs. Breast of wild duck served with roast wild boar on tender beluga lentils with diced Wurzelspeck (an Austrian bacon speciality with garlic and herbs). Soufflé of sweet chestnuts and walnuts with Schaffenburger chocolate served on a sabayon made with Eiswein (a very expensive sweet wine, whose grapes are harvested while frozen).

These are just a few of the dishes that are typical features on the menu of the restaurant, Toni M., in Feuersbrunn. Toni M. stands for a totally independent and self-contained culinary approach, for epicurean delights of the highest-possible order. Whoever sits down to dine in the elegant surroundings of Toni M. can rest assured that every single dish is a product of the creative imagination of the master himself, who is only content with the very best quality. The interior design and décor of the restaurant alone provide an ambience that is unique and memorable. An elegant, state-of-the-art gourmet restaurant situated within the walls of a country inn, a restaurant within a restaurant. That's the underlying concept – unusual perhaps, yet remarkably successful. For years now, it has earned Toni Mörwald the highest accolades of culinary journalists and connoisseurs.

Specifically for Toni M., Mörwald has developed his very own style of fusion cuisine, a term that might easily give rise to misunderstandings. Because the aim here is not to lump together the most diverse cooking styles from every corner of the world as the mood takes one. In fact, the very opposite is the case: Mörwald confines his creativity exclusively to the established canon of Austrian cuisine, combining the basic concepts of classic dishes with a contemporary approach to their preparation. His principal aim is to infuse such recipes with a new lightness, refinement and elegance, to achieve a modern cooking style based on regional basic products of outstanding quality.

One of Toni Mörwald's most striking talents is his ability to sniff out new suppliers of regional delicacies. These include such idealists as Alexander Quester with his wild char from Mariazell and the specialist for Lower Austrian cheeses, Robert Paget. For snails, Mörwald buys from a supplier located south of Vienna, while even the pasta he uses like spaghetti and tagliolini no longer comes from Italy but is obtained from a producer in the nearby Waldviertel region. For his suppliers, Mörwald is much more than just a business partner. By turning local produce and specialities into exquisite dishes in his restaurant, Toni M., the chef ensures that the names and products of these suppliers are continually on the tips of his guests' tongues – in every sense.

Frogs' Legs with Lemon Confit, Glazed Vegetables and a Velouté of Smoked Horseradish
Serves 4 ❙ Photo Page 168

Lemon confit ❙ 1 lemon ❙ 30 cl sugar syrup (see Basic Recipe on page 38)
Velouté ❙ 2 shallots ❙ 2 tbsp olive oil ❙ 50 ml white wine ❙ 50 ml fish stock ❙ 150 ml cream ❙ 2 tbsp smoked horseradish puree ❙ 2 tsp lemon juice ❙ salt, pepper
Vegetables ❙ 100 g baby leeks ❙ 1 bulb fennel ❙ 100 g baby carrots ❙ 4 radishes ❙ 6 shallots ❙ 1 tbsp butter ❙ 200 ml vegetable stock
Frogs' legs ❙ 24 frogs' legs ❙ 1 tbsp flour ❙ 100 g butter ❙ 1 tbsp olive oil ❙ 2 cloves garlic ❙ 3 tbsp chopped herbs (e.g. tarragon, chives, parsley, chervil, salad burnet) ❙ salt, pepper
For serving ❙ tips of the leaves of various herbs (e.g. dill, chervil, chives)

Lemon confit ❙ Peel the lemons, and 'fillet' them by carefully cutting away the pith and all of the tough parts inside. Boil the sugar syrup for 2–3 minutes before adding the lemon pieces. Leave to stand overnight.
Velouté ❙ Cut the shallots to make a fine brunoise, which should then be sautéed in olive oil over a very moderate heat for 4–6 minutes until soft. Deglaze by adding the wine, and then reduce until all of the liquid has evaporated. Now add the fish stock, and reduce until only about half of the liquid is left. Add the cream and horseradish, and simmer until the sauce has a smooth, creamy consistency. Press through a pointed sieve, and season to taste with salt, pepper and lemon juice.
Vegetables ❙ Cut the baby leeks into pieces about 3 cm long and the fennel into thin strips. Clean the baby carrots well, and quarter the radishes and shallots. Melt the butter in a frying pan over a moderate heat, and toss the prepared vegetables in the butter for about 2 minutes. Add the vegetable stock, bring to the boil, and simmer until the vegetables are tender but not soft.
Frogs' legs ❙ Dust the frogs' legs with very little flour. Melt half of the butter in a frying pan over a very moderate heat, pour in the olive oil, and mix well. Put the frogs' legs in the pan, and fry on both sides until pale golden brown. Season them with salt and pepper while frying. Meanwhile, finely dice the garlic, and stir in the freshly chopped herbs along with 20 g of the remaining butter, which should also have been cut into very small pieces. Remove the frogs' legs from the pan, and place on a warmed platter until required. Pour away the butter used for frying, add the white wine, and stir to release and dissolve the remnants in the pan. Now add half of the chopped herbs, and sauté for a few moments. Stir in the remaining butter (30 g), and pour the resulting sauce over the frogs' legs before sprinkling the rest of the chopped herbs over them.
To serve ❙ Mix the pieces of lemon into the warm vegetables, and put some of this mixture on each plate before arranging frogs' legs on, next to and around the vegetable mixture. Having put the velouté on the plates, sprinkle with leaf tips of various herbs.

Snails in a Pinot Sauce with Poached Egg
Serves 4 ❙ Photo Page 170

Snails ❙ 100 g finely sliced carrots ❙ 100 g finely sliced leek ❙ 3 bay leaves ❙ 1 tsp black peppercorns ❙ 1 untreated lemon ❙ 500 ml white wine (Sauvignon Blanc) ❙ 24 edible snails ❙ 25 g diced shallots ❙ 20 g butter ❙ 1 tbsp each chopped parsley and chives
Pinot sauce ❙ 60 g diced shallots ❙ 20 ml olive oil ❙ 5 g coarsely ground black pepper ❙ 1 sprig thyme ❙ 1 bay leaf ❙ 2 bottles red wine (Pinot Noir) ❙ 200 ml beef jus ❙ 100 g beef bone-marrow, finely diced
Shallots ❙ 8 small, round shallots or 12 pearl onions ❙ 10 g sugar ❙ 25 g butter ❙ salt, pepper
Poached eggs ❙ 4 eggs ❙ 2 tbsp vinegar ❙ salt, pepper
For serving ❙ 40 g Wurzelspeck (dried smoked bacon – an Austrian speciality)

Snails ❙ Put the carrots, leek, bay leaves and peppercorns in a saucepan containing 700 ml water, and bring to the boil. Reduce the heat, and allow to simmer for a while. Halve the lemon, press out the juice, and put this along with the peel and white wine into the saucepan.
Now add the snails, and leave to simmer very gently for 5–6 hours. Remove the snails, and sauté these with the diced shallots in butter. After 5–6 minutes, add the chopped herbs, and season with salt and pepper.
Pinot sauce ❙ Sweat the shallots (along with 1 tsp pepper) in the olive oil. Add the thyme and bay leaf before deglazing with half a bottle of red wine. Reduce until the sauce has a pleasantly thick and creamy consistency, at which point the beef jus and bone-marrow should be added, and the sauce left to stand for a while. Meanwhile, bring the other half of the bottle of red wine to the boil and, after flambéing, reduce it to a thickish syrup. Add half of the remaining red wine, continue boiling until it again has a syrupy consistency, and repeat the process after adding the last half-bottle of wine. Add the reduced wine sauce to the bone-marrow mixture, stir in the rest of the pepper, and allow to stand for a while.
Shallots ❙ Put the shallots in a saucepan with the sugar, 200 ml water, butter, salt and pepper, cover, bring to the boil, and continue cooking until the shallots have caramelised.
Poached eggs ❙ Poach the eggs shortly before serving. To do this, bring salted water containing vinegar to the boil in a saucepan, and then allow the whole eggs to slide gently into the water using a ladle. After 3–4 minutes, the white is firm while the yolk is still soft.
To serve ❙ Cut the bacon into thin slices, and fry until crisp. Place six warm snails in a circle on each plate, and then position a poached egg in the centre of the snails. Arrange some of the shallots and bacon on the plate before adding a little of the Pinot sauce.

Aiguillettes of Breton Lobster Served with Honeyed Pomelo Juice, Spinach and Pommes Maxim
Serves 4 ❙ Photo Page 172

Lobster ❙ 2 Breton lobsters (800–1000 g each) ❙ 2 sprigs thyme ❙ 1 garlic clove ❙ 2 tbsp salted butter ❙ pepper
Honeyed pomelo juice ❙ 600 ml pomelo (shaddock) or grapefruit juice ❙ 2 tbsp honey (flower or woodland) ❙ 4 tbsp extra-virgin olive oil ❙ salt, pepper
Spinach ❙ 1 garlic clove ❙ 30 g butter ❙ 600 g fresh spinach ❙ salt, pepper, nutmeg
Pommes Maxim ❙ 1 large potato ❙ 125 ml melted butter ❙ sea salt

Lobster ❙ For this recipe, you will need fresh lobsters, which means that you will have to buy live ones. When purchasing, make sure that the lobsters have lively reflexes and that their tails are still curved. Each lobster has to be cooked separately to ensure that it dies almost instantly when dropped into the boiling water.
Hold the back of each lobster firmly, and scrub it well in cold water. Use kitchen twine to tie the head and tail, so that the whole lobster and its tail are stretched out. Remove the rubber rings used to tie the claws together. Bring a large saucepan full of water to the boil. To ensure that the lobster dies as quickly as possible, push it head first into the boiling water. Now turn up the heat until the water is again boiling vigorously before removing from the heat and leaving for 8–10 minutes until the lobster is cooked through. The shell of the lobster will now have turned a characteristic red.
Halve the lobsters lengthways, remove and discard the gravel pocket (the beige-coloured soft part), and sauté each half in butter with the thyme and chopped garlic.
Honeyed pomelo juice ❙ Reduce the pomelo juice until only 100 ml remains. Add the honey and salt and pepper to taste before binding with the olive oil.
Spinach ❙ Briefly sauté the finely diced clove of garlic in butter before adding the spinach to the pan. Toss for a few moments in the hot butter, and season to taste with salt, pepper and nutmeg.
Pommes Maxim ❙ Pre-heat the oven to 150° C. Peel the potato, and cut it into paper-thin slices using a slicing machine. Turn the slices in the melted butter until covered all over before laying them on a sheet of greaseproof paper or (even better) on a silicone baking mat. Sprinkle with sea salt.
Place the potato slices in the oven, and bake for about 1 hour until they are crisp and golden.
To serve ❙ Drain the spinach very well before placing about two-thirds of it on individual plates. Use the remaining third to fill the lobster halves. Place a lobster half on each plate, pour on a little of the honeyed pomelo juice, and garnish with the Pommes Maxim.

Fried Veal Kidneys
with Spring Pointed Cabbage, Chanterelles and Sauce Robert
Serves 4 I Photo Page 174

Veal kidneys I 2 veal kidneys I 1 sprig thyme I 1 sprig rosemary I 50 g butter I 200 ml veal jus I salt, pepper
Pointed cabbage I 1 head pointed cabbage I 50 g butter I 100 ml cream I salt, pepper
Chanterelles I 30 g shallots I 400 g chanterelles I 40 g butter I 1 tbsp finely chopped chives I salt, pepper
Sauce Robert I 50 g shallots I 30 g butter I 100 ml white wine I 250 ml veal jus I 3 tbsp Pommery mustard I 15 g ice-cold butter

Veal kidneys I Fry the kidneys (along with the sprigs of thyme and rosemary) in butter over a moderate heat until they are pale pink. Reduce the veal stock until only a little liquid is left.
Pointed cabbage I Chop the pointed cabbage very finely before sautéing it in butter. Season to taste with salt and pepper before mixing in the cream to make a smooth sauce.
Chanterelles I Chop the shallots very finely à la brunoise, and then sauté them with the chanterelles in butter. Season with salt and pepper, and add the chopped chives according to taste.
Sauce Robert I Chop the shallots finely, sweat in butter until almost transparent, and deglaze with white wine, which should then be reduced until all of the liquid has evaporated. Add the veal jus, and simmer gently for 15 minutes. Stir in the mustard, bind with the chilled butter, and strain through a fine sieve.
To serve I Arrange some of the pointed cabbage on each plate. Cut the kidneys into slices about 1 cm thick, and place these on top of the creamy cabbage. Season with salt and pepper before pouring over a little of the reduced veal jus. Place some chanterelles next to the cabbage, and serve with the Sauce Robert.

Pork Belly with Langoustines and Green-Pea Salad
Serves 4 I Photo Page 176

Pork belly I 1 pork belly (about 2 kg) I 2 tbsp oil I 100 g carrots I 100 g swede I 100 g onions I 100 g leek I 1 bulb garlic I 1 l white wine I 2 l veal jus I 4 bay leaves I 4 g peppercorns I salt, pepper
Langoustines I 16 langoustine tails I 30 g butter I 1 tsp very finely diced (à la brunoise) lime peel I salt, pepper
Green-pea salad I 100 g blanched peas I 50 g pea leaves I 50 ml apricot vinegar I 100 ml almond oil I 20 ml honey I salt, pepper
For serving I 50 ml melted butter

Pork belly I Season both sides of the pork belly with salt and pepper before rolling up tightly to make a roulade, which should then be tied up securely with kitchen twine. Fry the roulade in oil until brown and crispy all over.
Chop the vegetables and garlic into small pieces, and sauté until golden brown. Now place the meat on top of the vegetables, pour over the white wine, and simmer over a medium heat until all of the wine has evaporated. Now pour the veal jus over the meat, and add the bay leaves and peppercorns. Braise for about 2 hours until the meat is tender. Take the roulade out of the stock, remove the kitchen twine, and unroll the meat, which should then be pressed flat between two baking trays. Meanwhile, pass the gravy through a very fine sieve.
Leave the pork belly to rest overnight in the fridge.
Langoustines I Clean the langoustine tails before tossing them in a pan in butter and seasoning with salt, pepper and finely diced lime peel.
Green-pea salad I Put the blanched peas and leaves in a bowl. Mix together the remaining ingredients, and pour the resulting vinaigrette over the peas.
To serve I Chop the pork belly into bite-sized cubes, and fry these on all sides in melted butter. Warm the sauce. Arrange the langoustine tails and meat cubes alternately on each plate, and serve with the sauce and green-pea salad.

Braised Beef Cheeks with Tender Shallots,
Kamptaler Wurzelspeck, Rocket-Leaf Jus and Damson Preserve
Serves 4 I Photo Page 178

Beef cheeks I 4 beef cheeks (180–200 g each) I 100 g carrots I 100 g swede I 100 g onions I 100 g leek I 1 bulb garlic I 1 l red wine I 4 g peppercorns I 4 bay leaves I 200 g strong flour I 500 ml oil I 1 l veal jus I salt
Shallots I 24 shallots I 25 g butter I about 150 ml beef broth or vegetable bouillon I salt, pepper
Rocket-leaf jus I 20 g butter I 200 g rocket leaves I salt, pepper
For serving I 8 thin slices Kamptaler Wurzelspeck (dried smoked bacon – an Austrian speciality)
4 tbsp Powidl (a damson preserve that is very popular in Austria)

Beef cheeks I Marinate the beef cheeks and coarsely chopped vegetables for 48 hours in the red wine containing the peppercorns and bay leaves.
Remove the meat from the marinade, dab dry, and season with salt and pepper. Now dip the beef cheeks into the flour until coated all over, and fry in oil until crispy.
Heat about 2 tbsp oil in a saucepan, and sauté the well-drained vegetables until golden brown. Deglaze with the red wine before adding the beef cheeks and pouring in the veal jus. Braise gently for 2–3 hours. Remove the tender meat, and keep warm while passing the sauce through a very fine sieve.
Shallots I Place the peeled shallots with all of the other ingredients in a saucepan, and simmer until all of the broth has evaporated. If the shallots are not quite soft enough, add a little more broth, and continue cooking for a little while.
Rocket-leaf jus I Place 75 ml water in a saucepan, and bring to the boil before adding the butter and rocket leaves. Puree for 1 minute using a hand-blender before pressing through a very fine sieve. Season to taste with salt and pepper.
To serve I Pre-heat the oven to 150° C. Place the slices of smoked bacon next to each other on a baking tray, and bake in the oven for about 1 hour until crisp. Put a beef cheek in the centre of each plate, and drizzle some of the sauce around the meat. Garnish with the rocket-leaf jus, shallots, 1 tbsp damson preserve and two slices of crispy bacon.

Lime Soufflé with Raspberry Sorbet and Amaretto Sabayon
Makes 4 small soufflés I Photo Page 180

Raspberry sorbet I 125 g sugar I 125 g water I 500 g raspberry puree I juice of 2 lemons
Amaretto sabayon I 3 egg yolks I 40 g sugar I 40 g water I 20 ml amaretto
Lime soufflé I butter for greasing the soufflé dishes
Mixture 1 I 4 egg yolks I 30 g sugar I 60 g soured cream I zest of 2 limes
Mixture 2 I 120 g egg whites I 80 g sugar
To serve I Raspberries and curled cookies (see page 16) at will I 4 soufflé dishes with a diameter of 8 cm

Raspberry sorbet I Bring the sugar and water to the boil, stirring until the sugar has dissolved completely. Skim off any froth if necessary. Add the raspberry puree and lemon juice. Place in a Pacojet container, and deep freeze. Before serving, puree using the Pacojet.
Amaretto sabayon I In a bowl warmed over steam, beat all of the ingredients together vigorously until they form a frothy but rather thick cream.
Lime soufflé I Grease the soufflé dishes with butter, and preheat the oven to 190° C.
To make *mixture 1*, whisk the sugar and egg yolks until very pale and quite thick. Add the soured cream and lime zest.
To make *mixture 2*, lightly whisk the egg whites and the sugar. Gently fold *mixture 2* into *mixture 1*, and then pour the soufflé mixture into the greased dishes (they should be three-quarters full). Bake in the oven for about 8 minutes at 190° C.
To serve I As soon as they come out of the oven, put the soufflés on individual plates, along with portions of the sorbet and sabayon. Decorate as you fancy with raspberries and curled cookies.

Culinary Academy

SCHOOLMASTER OF EPICUREAN MASTERY

Where Mörwald turns the kitchen into a classroom,
and enterprising hobby cooks imbibe true culinary mastery

The rustic restaurant, Zur Traube, in Feuersbrunn: proprietor Toni Mörwald turns up at 5 p.m. on the dot. A group of about ten people are already waiting for the well-known chef with an air of tense expectation.

Every Wednesday at this time, hobby cooks gather here to find out how to make soups, how to prepare a game stock, how to create a sauce, how to fillet fish or how to cut and carve a quail or chicken correctly – all things that Mörwald covers in his regular cooking seminars. For precisely this purpose, the Traube is equipped with a gleaming, ultra-modern kitchen. As Mörwald puts it, »we've got everything here that we need, so that everybody can do their own thing to their heart's content.«

Cookery courses like this are all the go at the moment. The demand is tremendous. Whether it be women or men, students, bank employees, managers or high-flying executives, they are all eager to get their pans sizzling and stewing. Indeed, taking part in such courses has now become as much a matter of course as booking a weekend in a hotel with wellness facilities.

In Austria, Toni Mörwald is very much at the forefront of this development. He gives by far the most seminars: for over 20 years, he's been offering weekly courses about different subjects, whose broad spectrum ranges from Mediterranean cuisine to typical Viennese cooking, and might focus on anything from sea fish and shellfish to cuisine naturelle or how to broil, fry, stuff and roast a free-range chicken à point.

This time, sushi and Japanese cuisine are on the agenda. Before things get serious, though, everybody expectantly dons aprons while taking the occasional, slightly nervous sip from their champagne glasses. One last »cheers«, and then it's time to get started.

The first dish is »tuna sushi with chilli sauce and green pepper«: Mörwald demonstrates everything step by step: how to slice the fish properly, how to make a chilli sauce and how to cook the right sort of rice. After this, he lays out a whole organic salmon for the preparation of »wild-salmon sashimi with wasabi«. After being admired by all present, the splendid fish is immediately cut into thin fillets.

Mörwald's cookery courses are extremely popular. Many participants come back over and over again, and some have attended 20 or 30 seminars. »What's important for me«, says Mörwald, »is that people have fun cooking and learn techniques suitable for hands-on applications.«

With several thousand courses under its belt, Mörwald's cooking academy enjoys a reputation second to none when it comes to passing on culinary fundamentals, along with all of those tips and tricks that make life at the stove a little easier for hobby cooks, while also sharpening the participants' ambitions to 'cook up a storm.'

When the teaching is over, the participants themselves sit down to enjoy all of the dishes that have been prepared, with Mörwald serving up a fitting selection of wines. Finally, each of the culinary novices is presented with a folder of recipes, an apron and a certificate to take home – an award that has since become almost as coveted among hobby cooks as toques and stars among professional virtuosos of the stove and saucepans.

Fine Lemon Noodles with Ossetra Caviar
Serves 4 I Photo Page 194

Noodles I 200 g freshly made pasta dough (see Basic Recipe on page 38) I 1 lemon I 3 tbsp butter I a little water or mild beef stock I 2 tbsp ice-cold butter (in small cubes) I 2 tbsp soured cream I 2 tbsp whipped cream I salt, pepper
For serving I 4 tbsp Ossetra caviar

Noodles I Using a pasta machine, roll out the pasta dough very thinly, and then use the appropriate attachment to cut into ribbon noodles. Wash the lemon, and use a zester to remove the fine upper layer of peel before squeezing out its juice. Blanch the lemon zest in boiling water for 1 minute, strain well, and briefly plunge into very cold water. Cook the noodles in well-salted boiling water for about 15 seconds, drain, and plunge into very cold water for a few moments.

In a frying pan, froth up the butter before adding the lemon zest and tossing this in the butter for a few seconds. Add the noodles along with a little water or mild beef stock, warm through, and season to taste with salt and pepper. Add the cold butter, stirring gently all the time: this gives the noodles a particularly appetising, glossy appearance. Pour in the soured cream and lemon juice before finally folding in the whipped cream.

To serve I Put the noodles in warmed deep plates, and top with the caviar.

Corn-Fed Chicken
with Chanterelle Risotto and Blackcurrant Vinegar
Serves 4 I Photo Page 196

Corn-fed chicken I 4 breasts (150 g each) from corn-fed chickens I 2 tbsp sunflower oil I 1 sprig thyme I salt, pepper
Risotto I 2 shallots I 50 g butter I 200 g risotto rice I 60 ml white wine I ½ l vegetable stock I 150 g chanterelles I 40 g grated Parmesan I salt, pepper
For serving I ¼ l poultry jus I 40 ml blackcurrant vinegar

Corn-fed chicken I Season the chicken breasts with salt and pepper before browning them on both sides in a hot pan. Add the sprig of thyme, transfer to the oven, and roast for about 5 minutes at 180° C.

Risotto I Chop the shallots finely, and sauté them gently in butter before adding the risotto rice and cooking for a further minute or so. Add the white wine, and cook slowly until all of the liquid has been absorbed. Stirring all the time, pour in a little of the vegetable stock, and continue cooking until it has been absorbed. Add more stock, and repeat the process until all of the stock has been used up, and the rice mixture has a creamy consistency. The individual grains of rice should still be al dente, though. Season with salt and pepper. Slice the chanterelles, and either add them to the risotto or sauté them and serve separately. Finally, stir the grated Parmesan into the risotto.

To serve I Bring the vegetable jus and blackcurrant vinegar briefly to the boil. Arrange a chicken breast and some risotto (and separately sautéed chanterelles, if you prefer) on each plate, before pouring on a little of the jus and vinegar mixture.

Waldviertel Poppy-Seed-Filled Sweet Rolls
with Honeyed Apples and Soured Ice Cream
Makes about 30 small sweet rolls I Photo Page 198

Ice cream I 50 ml water I 180 g sugar I zest of 2 limes I 500 g soured cream
Honeyed apples I 3 apples I 25 g butter I 2 tbsp honey
Poppy-seed filling I 125 g ground poppy seeds I 70 g breadcrumbs I 100 ml milk I 30 g sugar I a little honey I dash rum I zest of 1 lemon I pinch cinnamon I 50 g white chocolate I 1 egg yolk
Dough I 500 g flour I 75 g sugar I 10 g salt I 300 g whole eggs I 1 cube (40 g) fresh yeast I 300 g soft butter I 75 g melted butter

Ice cream I Boil up the water and sugar until a syrup is formed, add the lime zest, and allow to cool before passing through a hair sieve. Stir in the soured cream until well mixed, and place in a container. Deep freeze, and before serving, puree using the Pacojet.

Caramelised apples I Peel, quarter, and seed the apples, before cutting the pieces into thin slices and frying gently in butter until tender but not soft. Add the honey, and cook for a little longer until done.

Poppy-seed filling I Mix together the ground poppy seeds and breadcrumbs. Put the milk, sugar, a little honey, rum, lemon zest and cinnamon in a saucepan, bring to the boil, and remove from the heat before stirring in the poppy-seed mixture. Melt the chocolate, and stir it with the egg yolk into the mixture, which should then be put in a cold place for a while.

Sweet filled rolls I Put the flour, sugar and salt in a mixing bowl, and stir well. Continue to stir while adding the eggs a little bit at a time. Now crumble the fresh yeast into the bowl, and stir vigorously until the ingredients are evenly mixed. Add the melted butter to the dough a little at a time, stirring constantly, and continue mixing until the dough is smooth. Put the dough into a floured bowl, and leave to rise until its volume has roughly doubled. Roll the dough out on a floured surface, and then cut out rounds with a diameter of 7 cm. Place a teaspoon of poppy-seed filling in the centre of each round, fold up the edges, and press them together firmly. Put these round rolls close together in a baking dish, and allow the dough to rise again. Brush the rolls with melted butter, and bake for about 20 minutes in the oven at 170° C.

To serve I On each plate, arrange a few sweet rolls, along with some of the honeyed apple and soured ice cream.

Vintage Mörwald

WINE-GROWING TRADITIONS IN THE WAGRAM REGION

Where Mörwald's family makes wine
using traditional methods.

The Wagram is an Austrian wine-growing region in which the people who live there have managed to preserve a certain imperturbable serenity. There's nothing they dread more than the type of tourism that might be a threat to their identity. And that's why this enchanting stretch of countryside is still such an oasis of peace and tranquillity. Thanks to the favourable climate, the area also yields excellent wines. Although these might not be quite as well-known abroad as the vintages of the nearby Wachau, the region's steep, south-facing slopes of loamy soil containing large amounts of loess now account for some of Austria's very best Grüner Veltliner white wines.

Wine-growing here has a tradition extending back over centuries, and many of the ancient cellars have been preserved. In this green and pleasant land, the Mörwald family has been making wines for generations, or to be more precise, since 1860. Today, their vineyards are in the hands of a brother and his wife, Erhard and Angelika Mörwald. The family-run estate has about 35 acres of vineyards along with nearly 100 acres of farmland, part of which contains orchards whose fruit is used to make a broad variety of schnapps and other local firewaters.

The range of wines offered by the Mörwalds is anything but narrow: for their white wines, the grape varieties they cultivate include Grüner Veltliner, Frühroter Veltliner, Sauvignon Blanc, Weissburgunder (Pinot Blanc), Riesling and Gelber Muskateller, while their reds are made from Blauer Zweigelt, Cabernet Sauvignon, Merlot and Blauburgunder (Pinot Noir) grapes.

Toni's brother, Erhard Mörwald, is a shrewd and subtle wine-grower whose highly developed intuition enables him to strike the right balance between traditional methods and modern cellar techniques. As a result, all of his wines have very pronounced and personal character.

Like all wines, those produced in the Wagram owe a great of their character to the geology of the terrain. In particular, Grüner Veltliner grapes thrive in the loamy, loess-containing soil found here, while Roter Veltliner is another of the region's specialities. In contrast, Riesling grapes prefer the stonier, more gravelly soil found higher up the hillsides, and this terrain expands the flavour palette of these grapes. Last but not least, the Wagram enjoys wide renown for its red wines notable for their delicacy and elegance.

In addition to its wines, the Mörwald estate offers a selection of fine brandies and traditional schnapps. The variety is quite bewildering, ranging from apricot to Williams pear, apple and rowan berry to raspberry and cherry. Several of these premium distilled products are constantly winning prizes in their respective categories, for example the outstanding Veltliner grape schnapps that matures in wooden kegs.

And because, in everything the Mörwalds do, innovation never means neglecting tradition, Erhard Mörwald has not turned his back on his good old, homemade schnapps varieties. Just as well, because if his legendary nut schnapps – either as a powerful brandy or as a liqueur – should ever suddenly vanish from the scene, a good many of the Mörwalds' regular customers would be literally up in arms about it.

Schloss Grafenegg

CULTURAL DELIGHTS IN A PRINCELY IDYLL

Where Mörwald runs
a distinguished Castle Restaurant
for visitors of an internationally acclaimed music festival.

It was a truly kingly inspiration of a prince. In the early 1990s, though, when Prince Franz Albrecht Metternich Sandor was on the lookout for a proven and prominent culinary maestro for his Castle Restaurant Grafenegg in Lower Austria, his initial approach to Toni Mörwald met with a refusal. However, the chef's initial scepticism soon gave way to growing enthusiasm for what, in the final analysis, looked to be an exceptionally attractive adventure. After all, Grafenegg Castle in Lower Austria is not just somewhere or other. On closer inspection, it was evident that what the prince had to offer was highly impressive, to put it mildly. Set in a vast, sweeping park, the splendid and palatial Castle is rather reminiscent of a French château. Directly opposite, the elegant restaurant with its lovely garden. A delightful gem of a place in the very heart of Lower Austria. An ensemble that one might normally only expect to find in France, where such places are not infrequently dedicated to the joys of the table.

The upshot was that Mörwald changed his mind. Today, Grafenegg Castle is not merely a rendezvous for discerning gourmets, because it has since become the venue of a music festival whose renown attracts visitors from far beyond Austria's borders. Located directly next to Mörwald's Schlosstaverne, the »Auditorium« is a state-of-the-art concert hall, while the adjacent »Wolkenturm« is a futuristic open-air stage. Every year, well-known ensembles and internationally acclaimed soloists perform here. In an amazingly short time, the Grafenegg International Music Festival has emerged as an innovative cultural event showcasing truly outstanding artists.

Its very location means that this restaurant enjoys a context that is very special and attractive. Steeped in aristocratic charms, the Schlosstaverne is also remarkable in another respect, though. Toni Mörwald's team headed by head chef, Thomas Törpel, offers refreshingly straightforward, unpretentious regional cuisine using basic ingredients purchased exclusively within Austria: thus, instead of turbot from the Atlantic, visitors can enjoy Mariazell char fresh from the river, or Limousin beef from the rustic Waldviertel rather than Argentinian steak. Even the caviar comes from a sturgeon farm near Salzburg instead of from Russia or Iran.

Food critics have continually shown their appreciation of this strict culinary approach and thus, in 2009, the Schlosstaverne in Grafenegg was again awarded a toque (chef's hat) by Gault Millau, as well as receiving 80 out of a possible 100 points in the Austrian Falstaff Restaurant Guide.

In the meantime, a hotel with modern and comfortably appointed rooms has been added, thereby giving concert visitors and restaurant guests the opportunity to extend their stay over a complete weekend. And those who are fortunate enough to be staying in Grafenegg when the weather is at its best can also book an open-air picnic in the beautifully tended Castle Park, where delicious culinary specialities can be enjoyed in a setting that one is unlikely to forget in a hurry.

Grafenegg Castle: an incomparable combination of cultural and culinary delights, and quite evidently, a truly kingly inspiration of a prince.

Deep-Fried Crayfish
Coated with Julienne Potatoes Served on Veal Tripe and Parsley
Serves 4 I Photo Page 222

Veal tripe I 1 carrot I ½ stalk celery I 400 g cooked veal tripe I 2 shallots I 100 g butter I 1 l veal stock I ½ l cream
Crayfish I 8 crayfish (preferably from Mariazell in Austria) I 2 large potatoes I 1 egg white I oil for deep frying
For serving I ½ bunch parsley I oil for deep frying I 4 bundles of cucumber strips

Veal tripe I Dice the carrot and celery very finely (à la brunoise). Slice the cooked tripe very thinly, and sauté gently in butter with the chopped shallots. Add the veal stock, and reduce for a while before adding the cream and allowing to simmer gently. Now add the brunoise of carrot and celery, and continue simmering for a little while until cooked.
Crayfish I Boil the crayfish for a few moments before peeling and cleaning them. Cut the potatoes into very thin julienne strips, and then mix them with the egg white. Cover the crayfish with the potato mixture, and deep fry in hot oil.
To serve I Deep fry the parsley in oil. Place some of the tripe mixture on each plate, put some parsley on top, and then top with 2 crayfish. Garnish with the cucumber bundles.

Deep-Fried Roulade of Pike-Perch
Served with Parsnip Puree and Vegetables in Beurre Blanc
Serves 4 I Photo Page 224

Pike-perch I 400 g pike-perch I 80 g graved salmon trout I 100 g fish farce (see Basic Recipe on page 38) I 4 spinach leaves I 150 g breadcrumbs I 10 g sesame seeds I 1 l oil
Vegetables in beurre blanc I 1 l white wine I 250 g butter I a few fennel and coriander leaves I 100 g brunoise of mixed vegetables (finely diced carrot, celery, leek) I salt, cayenne pepper
Parsnip puree I 200 g parsnips I 1 potato I 100 g parsley I 1 tbsp crème fraîche I salt, pepper
For serving I ¼ l milk I zest of 1 lemon I 4 tsp salmon caviar (optional) I a few fennel leaves I salt

Pike-perch I Flatten out the fillet of pike-perch a little, and then spread the fish farce on top. Cut the salmon trout into attractive slices, coat with the blanched parsley, place on top of the layer of fish farce, and then tightly roll up the pike-perch before covering in a sheet of cling film. Put the fish in the freezer until slightly frozen, and remove the cling film. Roll the fish in the mixture of breadcrumbs and sesame seeds until coated all over. Deep fry in the oil.
Vegetables in beurre blanc I Reduce the wine until its volume has decreased to just 125 ml, and then bind with the butter. Add the fresh herbs and finely diced vegetables, bring to the boil for a few moments, season to taste, and remove from the heat.
Parsnip puree I Peel and coarsely chop the parsnips and potato before cooking until soft. Mash to make a smooth puree before adding the chopped parsley. Season to taste with salt and pepper, and fold in the crème fraîche.
To serve I Boil up the milk with the salt and lemon zest, and then puree with a hand-blender until frothy. Put some of the parsnip puree in the middle of each plate, cut the roulade into 4 portions, place a pike-perch roulade on top, and then put some of the beurre blanc next to the fish. Garnish with caviar and finely chopped fennel leaves before decorating with a little of the frothed-up milk.

Fried Veal Liver
with Braised Pickled Cherries, Sautéed Chanterelles and Potato Puree
Serves 4 I Photo Page 226

Veal liver I 500 g veal liver I a little flour I a little olive oil
Potato puree I 5 medium-sized potatoes I ½ clove garlic I 1 sprig rosemary I 1 sprig thyme I a little fleur de sel I a little olive oil
Pickled cherries I 20 cherries I 200 ml cherry juice I 1 tbsp balsamic vinegar I 1 sprig thyme I 1 tbsp honey I a little butter
Chanterelles I 300 g chanterelles I 1 tsp butter I 1 tsp chives (chopped) I pinch paprika I salt, pepper
For serving I 10 g parsley for garnish I blanched diced vegetables, according to taste

Veal liver I Clean and trim (skin, vein ducts) the veal liver, and cut into 8 portions of the same size. Turn in flour until lightly coated, and fry very gently in a little oil until browned. Remove from the frying pan, and place in the oven for 3 minutes at 180° C. Leave to rest in the warm for a few minutes, so that the meat relaxes.
Potato puree I In water containing the garlic, rosemary and thyme, boil the potatoes in their skins until soft. Peel, and mash with a fork before adding fleur de sel and olive oil to taste.
Pickled cherries I Having removed their stones, dip the cherries briefly in the cherry juice, remove, and put aside. Now add the thyme and honey to the juice, and reduce the mixture. Just before it dries up, add the balsamic vinegar, bind with butter, and dip the cherries in again to give them a glossy coating.
Chanterelles I Sauté the chanterelles in butter, and season to taste with chives, salt and pepper.
To serve I Place 2 slices of veal liver on each plate, add some of the potato puree, and garnish with the chanterelles and diced vegetables. Now add the coated cherries, and pour a little of the vinegar sauce over them.

Quail Crépinette
with Truffled Goose Liver and a Summer Country Salad
Serves 4 I Photo Page 228

Quail crépinette I 2 quails I 100 g poultry farce (see Basic Recipe on page 38) I 8 slices black truffle I 4 spinach leaves I 4 slices Serrano ham
Truffled goose liver I 240 g marinated goose liver I 10 g grated black truffle I 20 g fine breadcrumbs made from dry pumpernickel black bread I 20 g breadcrumbs I 10 g chopped pistachios I oil for deep frying
Summer country salad I mixed fresh herbs, such as chives, basil, parsley, chervil, lavender, tarragon, wood sorrel I 1 small frisée lettuce I 2 tbsp walnut oil I salt, pepper
For serving I 4 quail's eggs I 4 mushroom heads I a few edible flower petals

Quail crépinette I Bone the quails, and brush the 4 meat portions thinly with the poultry farce. Put the truffle slices and spinach leaves on top, and wrap each portion in a slice of Serrano ham. Brown slightly over a low heat before cooking in the oven for 5 minutes at 180° C. After cooking, allow to rest for a few minutes.
Truffled goose liver I Mix the marinated goose liver and grated truffle thoroughly, and then form the meat into small balls. These should then be rolled in the crushed dry pumpernickel, breadcrumbs and pistachios until coated all over, and then briefly deep fried in hot oil.
Summer country salad I Pluck the herb leaves into small pieces before washing them and mixing them with the lettuce leaves. Dress with a mixture of oil, salt and pepper.
To serve I Cook the quail's eggs for 3 minutes in boiling water, remove the shells, and halve. Place a quail crépinette, deep-fried balls of truffled goose liver and some of the salad on each plate, and garnish with a halved quail's egg, a mushroom head and a few flower petals.

Gâteau 'Metternich'
Makes 1 cake **I** Photo Page 230

Sponge base I 150 g soft butter **I** 100 g granulated sugar **I** 6 egg yolks **I** 6 egg whites **I** 110 g icing sugar **I** 120 g dark chocolate **I** 150 g flour

Cream filling I 250 g soft butter **I** 300 g very soft nougat **I** 150 g icing sugar **I** 4 egg yolks **I** 2 tbsp amaretto

Decoration I 200 g pistachio marzipan **I** a little ganache cream **I** 12 hollow chocolate spheres **I** 100 g brittle (croquante)

Sponge base I Beat the butter until light and creamy. Add the sugar and egg yolks a little at a time, stirring all the while.

Beat the egg whites until they form stiff peaks, adding the icing sugar little by little. Melt the chocolate before mixing it into the egg-yolk mixture. Sprinkle the flour, a little at a time, into this mixture, stirring continuously, until all of the flour has been mixed in well. Finally, fold in the beaten egg whites very carefully. Place the sponge mixture into a non-stick spring-form cake tin, and bake in a convection oven at 180° C for about 30 minutes.

Cream filling I Beat the butter until light and creamy before adding the icing sugar and nougat. Gently warm the egg yolks over boiling water to 72° C, stirring all the time. Remove from the heat and, beating continuously, add the amaretto and soft nougat, continuing to stir until the mixture has cooled.

Decoration I After it has cooled, cut the sponge base lengthways into three. Spread a quarter of the cream filling on each of these before making a sandwich cake. Spread the remaining cream around the outside of the cake. Place in the refrigerator for about 1 hour, and then spread a thin layer of marzipan on top. Decorate with dots of granache cream, the hollow chocolate spheres and the brittle.

m.kunst.genuss

CULINARY REFINEMENT AND FINE ART

How Mörwald with his 'm.-Linie'
provides brisk service
and contemporary cuisine for museum visitors and radio staff.

In his Michelin- and Gault-Millau-acclaimed restaurants, Zur Traube, Schloss Grafenegg and Kloster Und, Toni Mörwald principally caters for a clientele of gourmets and connoisseurs with very elevated culinary expectations.

However, the enjoyment of excellent food is by no means exclusively confined to such epicurean sanctuaries. After all, it doesn't have to be lobster and caviar every day of the week. And this is why Mörwald has come up with his slim-line 'm.-Linie' (i.e. 'm.-line'), whose target clientele are companies and organisations that require cuisine that can be served without delay, is good value for money and yet is of high quality.

The café-restaurant in the Kunsthalle (Art Gallery) in Krems is a perfect example of this concept in action. Under the aegis of Michael Mayr, the 'm.kunst.genuss' ('m.art.enjoyment') offers much more than one might expect in the cafeteria of a museum. Not only does the overall ambience blend in perfectly with the architecture of the museum, but the food provided here is fully in accordance with the requirements and wishes of exhibition visitors. Breakfast, snacks, reasonably priced menus of several courses, a range of Mediterranean dishes, along with coffee and various cakes: the selection is broad without making the slightest compromise with respect to quality.

Since 2003, Mörwald's staff cafeteria, m.hitradio.genuss, has been responsible for the culinary well-being of those who work for Austria's best-known radio station, Ö3. This also necessitated an innovative approach from the culinary point of view. Because a restaurant on the premises of a radio station makes even higher demands with respect to pace, creativity and gastronomic innovation. As Mörwald explains, »what certain airlines have managed to achieve in terms of in-flight service is what we want to attain when catering for the staff of an organisation. This is an area of gastronomy that has attracted far too little interest and attention up to now«.

The third branch of Mörwald's 'm.-Linie' is the most down-to-earth: the tavern, 'm.wirts.haus', in his home restaurant in Feuersbrunn. Here, Mörwald has set out to demonstrate that traditional no-frills tavern fare using regional products can, at the same time, be marketed according to present-day criteria. Thus, guests can enjoy country cooking with excellent local produce that is reasonably priced but can also, if necessary, be prepared and served very quickly.

Those who have more time on their hands, though, can savour at their leisure the cosy country-pub atmosphere, lingering over their meal just as long as they like.

Wild-Garlic Pasta Parcels Served with Asparagus and Chervil Sabayon
Serves 4 I Photo Page 240

Wild-garlic pasta parcels I 50 g scallions, cut into rings I 1 clove garlic I butter I 200 g wild garlic (ramsons) I 150 g cream cheese I 1 boiled potato (floury) I a little milk I 200 g pasta dough (see Basic Recipe on page 38) I 1 egg I salt, pepper, nutmeg
Chervil sabayon I 2 shallots I 40 g butter I 2 floury potatoes I 500 ml poultry stock I 3 egg yolks I chervil, according to taste I salt, pepper, cayenne pepper, nutmeg
Asparagus I 12 stalks green asparagus I 1 dry bread roll (to be added during cooking) I salt, pepper, sugar, butter
For serving I brown butter

Wild-garlic pasta parcels I Chop the scallions into rings, and sauté them gently in butter with the wild garlic and chopped garlic clove. Remove the scallion and garlic mixture from the pan, chop finely, and transfer to a bowl. Mash the potato using a potato press, add it to the garlic mixture with a little milk, and stir with a fork until well mixed. Season to taste with salt, pepper and nutmeg.

Roll out the pasta dough thinly, cut out rounds, brush these with egg, and put a teaspoon of garlic mixture on each round. Fold each round in half, and firmly press together the edges of the resulting semicircular parcels.

Chervil sabayon I Chop the shallots finely, cut the potatoes into thin slices, and sauté them both in butter very gently until they look almost transparent. Season with salt, pepper, cayenne pepper and nutmeg. Pour in the poultry stock, and simmer for about 15 minutes. Puree the stock mixture, and pass through a fine sieve. Allow to cool a little before transferring to a mixing bowl and adding the egg yolks. The mixture should now be beaten over a hot bain-marie until it is thick and creamy. Chop the chervil, reserving a few leaves for decoration. When seasoning the sabayon, add enough cayenne pepper to give it a noticeable 'bite'. Finally, stir in the chopped chervil.

Asparagus I Remove the lower parts of the asparagus stalks, and peel any parts where the skin seems tough. Put in salted water, bring to the boil, and add the butter, sugar and dry bread roll. Continue cooking until the asparagus is tender but not soft, plunge into iced water, and leave to dry on a cloth.

To serve I Cook the ravioli in gently simmering salted water for about 4 minutes. Warm the asparagus stalks in a little of their cooking water. Toss the cooked pasta parcels briefly in brown butter. Arrange 3 asparagus stalks on each plate, then add some of the pasta parcels, over which the chervil sabayon should be poured. Garnish with the reserved chervil leaves.

Ragout of Chamois Venison with Cranberries and Mushroom Noodles
Serves 6 I Photo Page 242

Ragout I 900 g shoulder of chamois I 4–5 juniper berries I 1 carrot I 1 swede I ½ celeriac I 2 bay leaves I 2 tbsp sunflower oil I 1 tbsp tomato puree I 40 ml gin I ½ l game stock I ½ l cream 2 tbsp cranberries I salt, white pepper
Noodles I 200 g broad noodles I 50 g mushrooms I 50 g oyster mushrooms I 50 g shiitake mushrooms I ½ onion I 1 tbsp butter I 1 sprig rosemary I a little parsley I salt, pepper

Ragout I Remove any large sinews and areas of skin on the shoulder of venison, before cutting the meat into bite-sized pieces. Season with salt and white pepper, rub with the crushed juniper berries, and leave to stand in the fridge for about 1 hour to allow the meat to absorb the seasoning.

Chop the carrot, swede and celeriac into cubes (sides about 1 cm long), add the bay leaves, and fry in a saucepan containing the hot oil until the vegetables begin to brown. Add the tomato puree, and cook for a little longer before deglazing with the gin and red wine. Reduce until only about half of the liquid is left before adding the game stock. Put the pieces of meat in the stock mixture, and simmer very gently over a low heat for 1–2 hours. When it is tender, remove the venison, and then add the cream and cranberries to the stock, which should then be reduced by half. Now pass the stock through a food mill before returning the meat to the resulting smooth sauce. Bring to the boil, and if necessary, adjust the seasoning with salt, pepper and crushed juniper berries.

Mushroom noodles I Cook the noodles in boiling salted water until they are al dente. Chop the mushrooms into small pieces, and dice the onion finely. Heat the butter in a frying pan, and sauté the onion and mushrooms until cooked. Season with salt and pepper. Chop the rosemary and parsley finely, and stir the herbs into the mushroom mixture.

To serve I Put noodles on each plate, and spoon some of the mushroom mixture on top. Place the venison by the noodles, and drizzle some sauce around the meat.

The man himself

CALLING AND COOKING

How Toni Mörwald, as an internationally acclaimed chef
and the manager of a culinary empire,
finds the energy to continue reaching for the stars.

Toni Mörwald's favourite pastime is making telephone calls. There's hardly a moment when you'll see him without a mobile phone pressed against his ear. However, in most cases, he is not content to have just one mobile in operation; often enough, he'll also be holding a second phone against the other ear, so that he can talk with two people at the same time. Mörwald is a master of synchronised telephoning and, over the years, has become a veritable virtuoso in this discipline. His motto is that if you don't do something that needs doing immediately, you probably won't ever get round to doing it. So, he tends to have one telephone permanently in use, with a second one also in action as often as not.

Mörwald's attitude towards cars and driving is just as extreme. Being at the head of a culinary empire whose diverse branches requiring constant supervision include several restaurants and taverns in Lower Austria and Vienna, a school for chefs and a catering company, he has no choice but to spend considerable amounts of time in his car. He might drive up to 300 miles in a day, and one wouldn't be far wrong in supposing that he makes considerable use of the blessings of mobile telecommunication while on the road.

He is not an advocate of slow, staid driving. When Toni Mörwald is at the wheel, passengers can't help feeling that the car isn't so much being driven as being flown. Certainly, Mörwald makes every effort to ensure that the time that elapses between take-off and landing is kept to an absolute minimum. At such times, the sophisticated star chef is transformed into a fearless pilot, and his car becomes a fighter-jet on the verge of breaking the sound barrier.

For Toni Mörwald, though, this is all part of a normal day's work. He is not the sort of person to hesitate or dither, not someone who does things by halves. Mörwald is a man in a hurry with a mission, someone bursting with an unusual amount of energy. But how does a person like him keep up this sort of pace, where does he replenish his energy reserves, and how does he manage to compensate for the constant high level of stress? One of his main sources of strength and energy is definitely his family. His wife, Eva, and his three daughters, Antonia, Johanna and Theresia, are the main focus of Toni Mörwald's life. »An intact family life is more important to me than anything else«, says Mörwald, »that's the solid basis that I need, my inner centre of gravity«.

Mörwald's profession is itself also a source of refreshment and inspiration. It might, at first glance, seem rather odd that someone who spends most of his time rushing from one appointment to another is always telling his guests »to take time to enjoy your food, because time spent at the dining table is the best time of your life«. Yet it is precisely this apparent contradiction that encapsulates the Mörwald phenomenon. The never-ending realising of ideas itself creates an ongoing motivation – and all this in a service branch in which relaxed enjoyment is the most important commodity on offer. As a result, there is no clear dividing line between Toni Mörwald's private and professional life. Even on days when his programme is particularly hectic, he may actually find time for a full-blown, leisurely lunch. For professional just as much as for private reasons. Even within his own four walls not far from Feuersbrunn, he himself enjoys that very lifestyle that he markets with such success. At home, he delights in celebrating the good things of life with his family and friends. And yet his house is also often used as the set for film shoots for various television shows.

Toni Mörwald is a man with a very pronounced taste for the best things of life. In contrast to many others, though, he is not someone who has to strain and struggle to obtain such pleasures; rather, he is able to live from them, as a manager, chef and private person.

Basic Recipes

Artichoke Crisps
1–2 globe artichokes ▌oil for deep frying

Wash the artichokes well before using a slicing machine to cut them into 1-mm-thick slices, which should then be blanched, dabbed dry and deep fried in oil.

Champagne-Fish Nage
250 ml fish stock ▌100 ml champagne ▌300 ml cream ▌100 g butter ▌salt

Add the champagne and cream to the stock, bring to the boil, and reduce until half of the liquid has evaporated. Remove the saucepan from the heat, and beat in the butter a little at a time. Strain the sauce through a fine pointed sieve, season with salt, and whisk until light and frothy.

Creamed Spinach
300 g spinach ▌125 ml cream ▌salt, pepper, nutmeg

Wash the spinach well before blanching it in boiling salted water for about 2 minutes and then plunging it into ice-cold water. Strain the spinach carefully, and then puree until smooth using a hand-blender. Mix with the cream, and simmer gently until it has a creamy consistency. Finally, season to taste with salt, pepper and nutmeg.

Fish Farce
250 g fillet of pike-perch ▌1 egg ▌250 ml cream ▌juice of ½ lemon ▌salt, piment d'Espelette (a peppery spice from the Basque region)

Skin and bone the fillet of pike-perch, chop the fish into small pieces, and place in a Pacojet container. Season with salt before pouring the cream over the fish and placing in the freezing compartment until slightly frozen. Now add the egg, and puree in the Pacojet before pressing the farce through a hair sieve and then adding lemon juice, salt and piment d'Espelette to taste.

Fish Stock
500 g fish bones (e.g. turbot, monkfish, angler-fish) ▌2 shallots ▌2 mushrooms ▌1 stick celery ▌1 leek ▌2 tbsp butter ▌5 peppercorns ▌250 ml white wine ▌250 ml Noilly Prat ▌salt

Break up the fish bones into small pieces. Put them in a bowl, and rinse under cold running water until the water draining off is completely clear. Peel and quarter the shallots; wipe and quarter the mushrooms, too. Wash and dice the celery and leek. Heat the butter, and sauté the shallots until they are almost transparent before adding the fish bones, vegetables and peppercorns, followed by the wine, Noilly Prat and 1 l cold water. Bring to the boil, and simmer uncovered over a moderate heat for 15 minutes, skimming off any foam or froth whenever necessary. Pass the stock through a very fine hair sieve or a straining cloth.

Game Nage
250 ml clear game stock ▌250 ml cream ▌100 g butter ▌salt

Add the cream to the stock, bring to the boil, and reduce until half of the liquid has evaporated. Remove the saucepan from the heat, and beat in the butter a little at a time. Strain the sauce through a fine pointed sieve, season with salt, and whisk until light and frothy.

Green-Pea Puree
500 g peas ▌250 ml poultry or vegetable stock ▌250 ml cream ▌125 g brown butter ▌salt, pepper

Blanch the peas in boiling salted water before plunging them into ice-cold water. Puree the cooked peas with the remaining ingredients until smooth, and then press through a hair sieve.

Parsley Butter
100 g butter ▌100 g blanched parsley leaves ▌salt

Put the butter and parsley in a Pacojet container, puree until smooth, and season with salt. Transfer to a sheet of cling film, and roll up into a sausage before placing in the fridge to keep cold.

Pasta Dough
200 g flour ▌2 eggs ▌salt

Mix all of the ingredients thoroughly to make a smooth dough, roll into a ball, wrap in cling film, and leave to rest for 30 minutes.

Poultry Farce
250 g lean poultry meat ▌1 egg ▌250 ml cream ▌salt, white pepper

Chop the meat into small pieces, and place in a Pacojet container. Pour the cream over the meat, and place in the freezing compartment until slightly frozen. Now add the egg, and puree in the Pacojet before pressing the farce through a hair sieve and seasoning with salt and pepper.

Pumpkin Puree
500 g pumpkin ▌brunoise of 2 very finely diced shallots ▌3 tbsp olive oil ▌3-4 crushed garlic cloves ▌1 sprig thyme ▌salt, pepper

Pre-heat the oven to 160°–180° C. Chop the pumpkin (with its skin) into quite large chunks, wrap them, along with the remaining ingredients, in tinfoil, and bake in the oven for 20–25 minutes.
Remove the pieces of pumpkin from the tinfoil, and scrape the flesh from the hard skin. Put the soft pumpkin into a straining cloth, and squeeze hard until all of the liquid has been pressed out.

Sugar Syrup
150 g sugar

Put the sugar in a saucepan with 150 ml water, and bring to the boil, stirring constantly. Continue stirring until the sugar has dissolved completely, skimming off any foam or froth whenever necessary.

Convivial Companions

CORDIAL FRIENDSHIPS AND COLLEGIAL CO-OPERATION

How Mörwald
keeps his world on the move,
and how he benefits
from his acquaintances.

Toni Mörwald has got all it takes to be a genuine entertainer. Whether it's in his dealings with guests or when he meets friends and people working in the same field, one thing's sure: there's never a dull moment when you're in his company. Because, for Toni, enjoyment is a serious personal concern: »the time you eat is the time you're alive«. This saying has become his guiding motto that he puts into practice with all of the determination and energy at his disposal.

To hone his creativity, Mörwald also looks for stimuli and creative criticism beyond the bosom of his family, and so, for all of his life, he has been keen to meet friends and colleagues who share one particular characteristic: a love of fine food and the good things of life.

It is with feelings of gratitude and solidarity that Toni Mörwald recalls those who have accompanied him over the past 20 years or so: connoisseurs from every imaginable profession, from his own field, from artistic and cultural circles, and from science and research.

STERNEKÜCHE

STAR-AWARDED CUISINE ★ HAUTE CUISINE

ENGLISH RECIPES
RECETTES FRANÇAISES

Recettes françaises

APPENDICE 42_Une vue d'ensemble

APPENDICE 47_La preparation

Avant-propos

UN CUISINIER INSPIRE DOUBLE D'UN HOTE MERVEILLEUX

Comment Toni Mörwald atteint
ses objectifs en alliant ténacité et talent.

Cher lecteur,

on me pose souvent la question suivante: Comment devient-on un grand cuisinier ? Si concise que soit la question, une réponse explicite ne se résume pas en quelques phrases. Car être cuisinier aujourd'hui c'est exercer une profession dans laquelle, outre la scène principale qui est la cuisine, la créativité et l'engagement doivent de plus en plus souvent s'exercer sur des scènes secondaires. Il faut donc posséder d'autres qualités en plus du talent et du métier: on ne peut parvenir à l'aboutissement et au succès qu'en poursuivant son objectif obstinément, avec un engagement à toute épreuve et une créativité enthousiaste.

Toni Mörwald est exemplaire en cela. C'est un confrère véritablement polyvalent et doué qui a érigé un petit empire en faisant preuve d'une obstination à toute épreuve.

Il me rappelle parfois le «Figaro» de Mozart : quoi que l'on fasse, où que l'on aille, Toni Mörwald a toujours une longueur d'avance ...

Nos chemins se sont souvent croisés. Au fil des ans, Toni Mörwald et moi avons tissé une relation collégiale empreinte de beaucoup de sympathie; mon grand respect pour ses réalisations lui est absolument acquis. Ses performances de cuisinier mais aussi de maître de maison sont remarquables à plus d'un titre. C'est dans ces deux rôles de prédilection que le lecteur de ces pages découvrira Toni Mörwald.

Avec mes salutations gastronomiques

Eckart Witzigmann

Une vue d'ensemble

APPENDICE 46_KLOSTER UND

APPENDICE 47_Boulettes frites au fromage blanc et aux herbes

APPENDICE 47_Saumon Balik à la mousse de babeurre, avec blini et caviar vert de poisson volant

APPENDICE 47_Paupiette de pintade à la crème de céleri et gâteau de pommes de terre à la broche

APPENDICE 47_Rouleaux verts à la crème aigre et au jambon cru Vulcano

APPENDICE 47_Toasts au romarin avec poivron, tomates et asperges vertes

APPENDICE 47_Crostinis aux gambas, melon et concombre

APPENDICE 48_Pain noir grillé aux jeunes oignons et à la moelle de boeuf

APPENDICE 48_Terrine d'écrevisses à la mousse de cerfeuil

APPENDICE 48_Cannellonis au foie de canard avec purée de chou-rave et gelée au Madère

APPENDICE 49_Veau cru mariné aux pralines de légumes et salade frisée

APPENDICE 49_Tartare de bœuf limousin du Waldviertel dans un consommé de bœuf gélifié avec mousse de Wasabi et betterave rouge

APPENDICE 49_Velouté de homard avec soufflé aux petits pois et caviar Ossietra

APPENDICE 49_Essence de faon et tomate avec rouleaux de tomates

APPENDICE 50_Consommé de bœuf du Waldviertel avec petits sandwichs à la rate

APPENDICE 50_Raviolis d'écrevisses aux œufs de caille et girolles

APPENDICE 50_Œuf «à la viennoise» aux épinards, au lard à l'ail et aux champignons des prés

APPENDICE 50_Tortellini aux brocolis avec beurre à la tomate et à l'estragon

APPENDICE 51_Gnocchis de petits pois à l'œuf poché et à la truffe blanche

APPENDICE 51_Moules au safran décoquillées au vin blanc et gnocchis

APPENDICE 51_Saint-Jacques à la Saint-Germain

APPENDICE 51_Médaillons de poisson-chat aux lentilles de Dijon et beurre au vin de Rioja

APPENDICE 52_Saint-Pierre avec artichauts à la tomate et oignons au basilic

APPENDICE 52_Tranches de turbot avec gnocchis au potiron, truffes d'été et cannelle

APPENDICE 52_Bar entier en croûte de sel

APPENDICE 52_Ris de veau aux champignons des prés et cerfeuil

APPENDICE 53_Galantine de pigeon au chutney de pomme et Dirndln de Wagram

APPENDICE 53_Blancs de poulet fermier noir dans une croûte aux olives et tomates avec couscous aux pignons

APPENDICE 53_Filet de veau en croûte et artichauts à l'étouffée

APPENDICE 53_Tendre côtelette de veau sur pâtes fines aux olives noires et jeunes poireaux

APPENDICE 53_Carré de cochon de lait au cumin du Waldviertel, raviolis de jarret de porc et chou pointu sauté

APPENDICE 54_Couronne de veau avec raviolis aux ris de veau, crème de persil racine et beurre persillé

APPENDICE 54_Gigot d'agneau de lait sur blettes à l'étouffée et gâteau de pommes de terre

APPENDICE 54_Faux-filet rosé de bœuf aux asperges blanches, crêpes de pommes de terre et sauce béarnaise

APPENDICE 55_Filet de bœuf d'Attergau au céleri et foie d'oie rôti

APPENDICE 55_Foie de chevreuil poêlé au carpaccio de betteraves rouges et vinaigrette au raifort

APPENDICE 55_Râble de chevreuil au confit de graines de courge et aux tranches de semoule

APPENDICE 55_Faon sur lit de salade de pommes de terre et roquette

APPENDICE 56_Rôti de mou de cerf dans un gâteau à la broche avec gnocchis aux marrons et pruneaux

APPENDICE 56_Gigot de sanglier braisé à la sauce lard-lentilles, avec Knödel de brioche Palfy au persil-racine

APPENDICE 56_Millefeuille à la mousse de yogourt et myrtilles

APPENDICE 57_Dessert aux abricots, cardamome et amandes

APPENDICE 57_Dessert au chocolat, whisky et café

APPENDICE 58_Barre de nougat, glace au thé matcha et banane

APPENDICE 58_Tarte aux cerises, aux pêches et aux pistaches

APPENDICE 59_Chocolats pralinés à la nougatine

APPENDICE 59_Tartelettes de cheesecake à l'ananas et à la noix de coco

APPENDICE 59_Macarons

APPENDICE 59_Nonnettes à l'orange

APPENDICE 59_Brioches fourrées de crème à la vanille

APPENDICE 60_CATERING

APPENDICE 61_Raviolis aux crevettes et à la ricotta

APPENDICE 61_Mou de veau au Riesling

APPENDICE 61_Beignets au punch

APPENDICE 61_Rouleaux de neige

APPENDICE 62_ZUR TRAUBE

APPENDICE 63_Langue de veau tiède marinée aux légumes racines, raifort et huile de pépins

APPENDICE 63_Salade de haricots avec langoustines et pêches de vigne

APPENDICE 63_Velouté de châtaignes avec pruneaux lardés

APPENDICE 63_Truite rouge sauvage de Mariazell rôtie avec pappardelle au persil
      et chou-rave à la crème

APPENDICE 63_Jarret de veau lardé dans une sauce à la moutarde et aux câpres
      avec champignons de Paris et riz Basmati

APPENDICE 64_Suprême et cuisse de canard sauvage sur chou aigre-doux à la livèche

APPENDICE 64_Crêpes soufflées au fromage blanc

APPENDICE 65_VILLA KATHARINA

APPENDICE 66_TONI M.

APPENDICE 67_Cuisses de grenouilles au confit de citron, légumes glacés et velouté
      de raifort fumé

APPENDICE 67_Escargots des vignes dans une réduction de Bourgogne avec œufs pochés

APPENDICE 67_Aiguillettes de homard breton, dans une réduction de pomélo et miel,
      épinards et pommes Maxim's

APPENDICE 68_Rognons de veau rôtis au chou pointu de printemps, girolles et sauce Robert

APPENDICE 68_Panse de porc aux langoustines et salade de petits pois

APPENDICE 68_Joues de bœuf braisées, échalotes fondues, lard à l'ail de Kamptal,
      jus de roquette et Powidl

APPENDICE 68_Soufflé aux limettes avec sorbet de framboises & sabayon à l'Amaretto

APPENDICE 69_ECOLE DE CUISINE

APPENDICE 70_Pâtes fines au citron et caviar Ossietra

APPENDICE 70_Blanc de poulet jaune fermier au risotto de girolles et vinaigre
      de groseilles noir

APPENDICE 70_Brioches au pavot du Waldviertel avec pommes poêlées et crème glacée

APPENDICE 71_VITICULTURE MÖRWALD

APPENDICE 72_SCHLOSS GRAFENEGG

APPENDICE 73_Ecrevisses de Mariazell frites avec pommes pailles sur tripes de veau et persil

APPENDICE 73_Rouleau de sandre frite à la purée persillée et au beurre blanc de légumes

APPENDICE 73_Foie de veau rosé rôti aux cerises cuites au vinaigre, girolles sautées
      et purée de pommes de terre

APPENDICE 73_Cailles lardées au foie gras d'oie truffé et petite salade des prés

APPENDICE 74_Gâteau maison «Metternich»

APPENDICE 75_M.KUNST.GENUSS

APPENDICE 76_Raviolis au fromage frais et à l'ail des ours avec asperges
      et sabayon de cerfeuil

APPENDICE 76_Ragoût de chamois aux airelles rouges et pâtes aux champignons

APPENDICE 77_MÖRWALD EN PRIVE

APPENDICE 78_RECETTES DE BASE

APPENDICE 79_LE COMPAGNON

Kloster Und

PROVIDENCE DIVINE ET PEPINIERE DE TALENTS

Où Mörwald forme de futurs cuisiniers
et où les gourmets s'adonnent
avec recueillement aux délices d'ici-bas.

Un monastère est habituellement un lieu de renoncement et de vie spartiate. Et même si les exceptions sont nombreuses, chez la plupart des gens ce mot évoque plutôt les bouillons maigres et la vie méditative que la dégustation de cailles et de délicieux poissons, le tout arrosé de vins fins. Le monastère de Krems Und est différent: ici l'on boit sans restriction et la chère y est exquise. Cela se comprend aisément, puisque le seigneur de l'endroit (outre le Bon Dieu) n'est autre que Toni Mörwald.

Und est un monastère incomparable à plus d'un titre. C'est la pépinière de talents la plus prolifique de Mörwald, et les jeunes cuisiniers y font carrière plus rapidement que dans ses autres restaurants. Le meilleur exemple en est Leonard Cernko qui a fait ses débuts dans la cuisine du monastère de Und et qui, très rapidement, s'est vu décerner les plus hautes distinctions de la part de presque tous les grands guides gastrono-miques. Toujours encouragé par son mentor, Cernko reçut des propositions venant du monde entier et Mörwald sut alors que le moment de la séparation était arrivé. Cernko est aujourd'hui un chef de cuisine recherché et bien rémunéré à Moscou.

Il a confié la direction de la cuisine à son sous-chef Erwin Windhaber, de deux ans son cadet. A la surprise de tous les critiques, Windhaber a réussi ce que personne n'aurait osé envisager: non seulement il a su maintenir le niveau de la cuisine, mais il l'a porté encore plus haut. Nourrissant maintenant de grands espoirs, le jeune chef Windhaber a confié la direction de la cuisine au duo Thomas Serret et Erwin Riedrich.

C'est au cours de l'année 2003 que Mörwald a pris en main les rênes du restaurant du monastère de Und. Ce restaurant a été décoré par le duo d'architectes viennois «Eichinger oder Knechtl». Après avoir connu une histoire mouvementée, ce paradis religieux est maintenant voué à une utilisation laïque sous le signe des plaisirs des sens et de la joie de vivre; certains verront là une intervention divine. Des mets divins d'une qualité supra-terrestre sont servis à l'endroit même où, jadis, les moines s'efforçaient de pratiquer l'abstinence.

Ce sont là des surprises telles que l'Histoire nous en réserve parfois. Au milieu du XVIIe siècle, le monastère fut détruit par les flammes. En 1656, il fut reconstruit sous la houlette de l'architecte Domenico Sciassia puis sécularisé comme le souhaitaient les citoyens de Krems. Il resta longtemps à l'abandon, désaffecté, servant d'hôpital pour les troupes ou bien de lieu d'habitation. A partir de 1987, les bâtiments abritèrent un «Weinkolleg», un centre d'œnologie.

Avec une étoile Michelin et trois toques dans le Gault-Millau, le monastère Relais & Châteaux Kloster Und compte parmi les restaurants les plus récompensés de tout l'empire de Mörwald.

A côté de la cour intérieure entourée d'arcades, transformée en un magnifique jardin, l'ensemble s'enorgueillit aussi d'une fresque datant de 1756 qui orne le plafond de la nef de l'église. C'est sous cette coupole pittoresque qu'ont lieu régulièrement des banquets, des conférences et des événements culinaires.

Toni Mörwald a ainsi réussi à insuffler une nouvelle vie à un bijou architectural tombé en désuétude. Le Père Hans Denk, éminent œnologue, bien connu dans les cercles gastronomiques, n'en finit pas de s'extasier: «Je suis persuadé» affirme ce révérend amateur de bonne chère, «que mon Chef là-haut éprouve une grande satisfaction face à la tournure que prennent les événements pour cette céleste station au sol.»

Boulettes frites au fromage blanc et aux herbes
Ingrédients pour 45 boulettes environ ❙ Photo Page 24

45 g de beurre mou ❙ 2 jaunes d'œufs ❙ 1 œuf entier ❙ 125 g de chapelure ❙ 400 g de fromage blanc ❙ 70 g d'herbes fines hachées, selon les goûts (par ex. persil, ciboulette, estragon, cerfeuil) ❙ 150 g de chapelure ❙ Huile pour friture ❙ Sel, poivre, muscade

Battre le beurre en mousse, ajouter un à un les jaunes d'œufs et l'œuf entier. Incorporer la chapelure et le fromage blanc, assaisonner avec les épices et les herbes. Former des boulettes de 15 grammes environ, les rouler dans la chapelure et les faire frire dans de l'huile chaude.

Saumon Balik à la mousse de babeurre, avec blini et caviar vert de poisson volant
Ingrédients pour 30 bouchées environ ❙ Photo Page 24

Blinis ❙ 40 g de farine de blé ❙ 20 g de farine de seigle ❙ 50 ml de lait tiède ❙ 1 œuf ❙ 1 pincée de sucre ❙ 1 pincée de sel ❙ 5 g de levure fraîche ❙ 2 cuillères à soupe d'huile
Mousse de babeurre ❙ 200 ml de babeurre ❙ 50 g de crème aigre ❙ Jus d'½ citron ❙ 3 feuilles de gélatine ❙ 125 g de crème ❙ Sel, poivre, piment de Cayenne
Présentation ❙ 300 g de saumon Balik fumé ❙ 30 g de caviar vert de poisson volant ❙ Cresson rouge pour la décoration

Blinis ❙ Bien mélanger tous les ingrédients et laisser lever la pâte à 35 degrés pendant 30 minutes environ. Verser la pâte dans une poêle chaude sur une hauteur de ½ centimètre environ et faire dorer des deux côtés. Renouveler l'opération avec la totalité de la pâte. Laisser refroidir et découper des cercles à l'aide d'un emporte-pièces.
Mousse ❙ Mélanger le babeurre avec la crème aigre, ajouter le jus de citron puis assaisonner avec le sel, le poivre et le piment de Cayenne. Ramollir la gélatine, bien la presser, la faire fondre et la mélanger au babeurre. Incorporer la crème fouettée et mettre la mousse au frais.
Présentation ❙ Couper le saumon en tranches fines et aplatir les tranches une par une, entre deux feuilles de film transparent. Vaporiser la mousse de babeurre et enrouler, afin de former des rouleaux du même diamètre que celui des blinis. Envelopper dans un film alimentaire et mettre au frais. Avant de dresser sur le plat, couper en tranches et disposer sur le blini. Décorer avec le caviar vert de poisson volant et le cresson.

Paupiette de pintade à la crème de céleri et gâteau de pommes de terre à la broche
Ingrédients pour 30 paupiettes environ ❙ Photo Page 24

Gâteau de pommes de terre à la broche ❙ 100 g de pommes de terre farineuses ❙ 35 g de beurre mou ❙ 3 jaunes d'œufs ❙ 3 blancs d'œufs ❙ 10 g de sucre ❙ 20 g de farine ❙ 50 g de fécule de maïs ❙ Sel, poivre, muscade
Paupiettes de pintade ❙ 150 g de crème ❙ 150 g de poulet ❙ 35 g de pain tramezzini ❙ 2 œufs ❙ 25 g de persil (blanchi et haché) ❙ 2 blancs de pintade ❙ Sel, poivre
Crème de céleri ❙ ½ céleri-rave ❙ 250 ml de crème ❙ Sel, poivre
Présentation ❙ Un peu de cresson de jardin

Gâteau de pommes de terre à la broche ❙ Faire cuire les pommes de terre avec la peau, les peler et les passer à travers une passoire à trous fins. Battre le beurre en mousse, l'ajouter avec le jaune d'œuf à la préparation de pommes de terre et bien mélanger. Battre les blancs d'œufs en neige avec le sucre et les incorporer à la préparation de pommes de terre. Incorporer délicatement la farine et la fécule de maïs. Préchauffer le four à 10°C. Etaler une partie du mélange sur une plaque à pâtisserie recouverte de papier sulfurisé sur une hauteur de 1 millimètre environ et cuire au four jusqu'à coloration. Etaler ensuite une deuxième couche par-dessus et cuire de nouveau jusqu'à coloration. Répéter l'opération jusqu'à ce que la pâte ait 5 mm de hauteur.
Paupiette de pintade ❙ Mettre la crème, le poulet, le pain tramezzini, les œufs et le persil dans un Cutter, saler, poivrer et mixer finement.

Aplatir très finement les blancs de pintade entre deux feuilles de film transparent. Les recouvrir de farce, les rouler et les entourer de film transparent, puis les envelopper dans une feuille d'aluminium. Faire pocher 20 minutes à 75 degrés.
Crème de céleri ❙ Mettre tous les ingrédients dans un Cutter, mixer très finement et passer à travers une passoire à trous fins. Remplir une poche à douille et mettre au frais.
Présentation ❙ Couper env. 30 cercles de la taille de la paupiette dans le gâteau à la broche (3 centimètres de diamètre environ), déposer la paupiette dessus, garnir avec la crème de céleri et décorer avec le cresson.

Rouleaux verts à la crème aigre et au jambon cru Vulcano
Ingrédients pour 30 rouleaux environ ❙ Photo Page 24

Mousse de crème aigre ❙ 60 g de crème aigre ❙ Jus et zestes d'¼ de limette ❙ 1 feuille de gélatine ❙ 50 g de crème fouettée ❙ Sel, poivre
Crêpe ❙ 90 g de lait ❙ 40 g de farine ❙ 1 œuf ❙ 5 g de fines herbes blanchies et ciselées selon les goûts ❙ Un peu d'huile
Présentation ❙ 12 tranches de jambon cru Vulcano ❙ Un peu de cresson pour la décoration

Mousse de crème aigre ❙ Mélanger la crème aigre, le jus et les zestes de limette, le sel et le poivre, puis bien presser la gélatine ramollie et la chauffer jusqu'à ce qu'elle fonde avant de la mélanger avec la préparation à base de crème aigre. Incorporer la crème fouettée et assaisonner le mélange.
Crêpe ❙ Mélanger tous les ingrédients jusqu'à obtenir une pâte lisse. Faire chauffer un peu d'huile dans la poêle, étaler régulièrement une petite quantité de pâte et cuire la crêpe des deux côtés. Faire six crêpes en tout.
Présentation ❙ Couper les crêpes en deux, les recouvrir de mousse de crème aigre, garnir de jambon cru Vulcano et d'une nouvelle couche de mousse. Enrouler, envelopper précautionneusement dans un film transparent et mettre au frais. Couper en tranches fines, dresser le plat et décorer avec un peu de cresson.

Toasts au romarin avec poivron, tomates et asperges vertes
Ingrédients pour 4 personnes ❙ Photo Page 26

1 poivron jaune ❙ 2 tomates ❙ 2 cuillères à soupe d'huile d'olive ❙ 2 filets de vinaigre balsamique ❙ 1 gousse d'ail ❙ 2 cuillères à café de persil haché ❙ 1 branche de romarin ❙ 4 pointes d'asperges vertes ❙ 4 tranches de pain de mie ❙ 1 cuillère à soupe de beurre ❙ Sel, poivre

Toast au romarin ❙ Couper le poivron et les tomates en dés, les faire suer dans l'huile d'olive, assaisonner et mouiller avec le vinaigre balsamique. Retirer du feu, y presser l'ail et ajouter le persil et le romarin haché. Cuire les pointes d'asperges «al dente» dans de l'eau salée. Couper le pain de mie en carrés, hacher finement le romarin. Chauffer le beurre dans une poêle et faire dorer les toasts des deux côtés. Laisser égoutter sur un papier absorbant.
Présentation ❙ Dresser des petits tas de légumes sur les tranches de pain encore chaudes, garnir avec les pointes d'asperges et servir.

Crostinis aux gambas, melon et concombre
Ingrédients pour 4 personnes ❙ Photo Page 26

Crostinis ❙ ¼ de melon ❙ ½ concombre ❙ 1 cuillère à soupe de vinaigre balsamique blanc ❙ 2 cuillères à soupe de yogourt ❙ 4 cuillères à soupe d'huile d'olive ❙ Jus d'un citron ❙ 4 tranches de pain de Toscane ou 8 tranches de baguette ❙ 8 crevettes ❙ Sel, piment de Cayenne, poivre
Présentation ❙ 8 feuilles de menthe

Crostinis ❙ Eplucher le melon et le concombre, enlever les pépins, les couper en petites tranches et les mettre dans un saladier. Y ajouter le vinaigre balsamique blanc, le yogourt, les 2 cuillères à soupe d'huile d'olive, le sel et le poivre puis mélanger. Assaisonner avec le piment de Cayenne et le jus de citron et laisser mariner quelques minutes. Faire dorer les tranches de pain des deux côtés dans un peu d'huile d'olive et égoutter sur un papier absorbant.

Décortiquer les crevettes, enlever l'intestin, saler et poivrer et faire dorer 4 minutes de chaque côté dans l'huile d'olive restante.

Présentation ❙ Déposer la salade de concombre-melon sur les tranches de pain encore chaudes et garnir avec les crevettes. Ciseler la menthe et la répartir dessus.

Pain noir grillé aux jeunes oignons et à la moelle de boeuf
Ingrédients pour 4 personnes ❙ Photo Page 26

2 tranches de pain noir ❙ 60 g de moelle de boeuf ❙ 2 oignons frais ❙ Sel de Maldon ❙ Poivre noir, concassé

Pain noir ❙ Couper le pain noir en 4 carrés et le faire griller dans une poêle sans matière grasse. Pocher la moelle de boeuf dans de l'eau salée, la refroidir quelque peu et la couper en tranches alors qu'elle est encore tiède. Nettoyer les jeunes oignons et les couper en fines rondelles.
Présentation ❙ Poser des tranches de moelle sur la pain, couvrir avec les rondelles de jeunes oignons et terminer de dresser avec le sel de Maldon et le poivre.

Terrine d'écrevisses à la mousse de cerfeuil
Ingrédients pour un moule à terrine (longueur 40 cm, hauteur 5 cm) ❙ Photo Page 28

Gelée ❙ 300 g de légumes-racines ❙ 2 échalotes ❙ 2 tomates ❙ ¼ l de fumet de poisson ❙ 2 blancs d'œufs ❙ 1 feuille de laurier ❙ 5 grains de poivre blanc ❙ 2 baies de genévrier ❙ 0,7 l de Noilly Prat ❙ 14 feuilles de gélatine ❙ Sel, piment de Cayenne
Aspic d'écrevisses ❙ 10 grosses écrevisses ❙ 200 g de feuilles d'épinard ❙ Cumin, aneth ❙ Sel
Mousse de cerfeuil ❙ 100 g de cerfeuil ❙ 50 g de crème aigre ❙ 1 ½ feuille de gélatine ❙ 100 g de crème légère ❙ Sel, piment de Cayenne, Pernod
Mousse de crème aigre ❙ 1 citron ❙ 250 g de crème aigre ❙ 3 feuilles de gélatine ❙ 200 g de crème légère ❙ Sel, piment de Cayenne ❙ Noilly Prat réduit
Présentation ❙ Feuilles de salades variées ❙ Quelques petites boules de fromage blanc aux fines herbes (voir page 47)

Gelée ❙ Hacher les légumes-racines, les échalotes et les tomates, bien mélanger dans une casserole avec le fumet de poisson, ¼ de litre d'eau et le blanc d'œuf. Ajouter la feuille de laurier, les grains de poivre et les baies de genévrier, laisser bouillir lentement à feu moyen puis faire mijoter pendant 2 heures environ à tout petit feu. Réduire le Noilly Prat au ¼ dans une casserole, et le réserver pour l'assaisonnement ultérieur. Passer le fond encore chaud à travers une étamine. Ramollir la gélatine dans de l'eau froide, la retirer de l'eau, la presser et la dissoudre dans le fond. Assaisonner avec le sel, le piment de Cayenne et un peu de Noilly Prat réduit. Réserver environ la moitié du mélange, le tenir au chaud (afin qu'il reste liquide) et laisser refroidir l'autre moitié. Recouvrir une plaque lisse de film alimentaire, avec le moins de plis possibles et de telle sorte qu'aucun liquide ne puisse s'écouler. La taille de la plaque dépend des dimensions du moule, elle devrait au moins mesurer 50 x 50 centimètres, pour revêtir 2 fois la terrine et pour la recouvrir une fois. Verser le mélange refroidi sur la plaque, sur une hauteur de 3 millimètres environ, et mettre au réfrigérateur.

Aspic d'écrevisses ❙ Faire cuire les écrevisses dans l'eau bouillante avec du sel, un peu de cumin et de l'aneth. Retirer les queues et les pinces et les réserver séparément.
Sécher les queues d'écrevisses décortiquées et les déposer dans un moule à terrine triangulaire (de plus petite taille que le plat ultérieur). Maintenir au chaud 2 à 3 cuillères à soupe de la gelée chaude réservée, laisser refroidir le reste et en recouvrir les queues d'écrevisses se trouvant dans le moule. Bien laisser refroidir.
Nettoyer les feuilles d'épinard, bien les laver, les faire blanchir dans de l'eau bouillante salée et les refroidir dans de l'eau glacée.
Réserver quelques feuilles et déposer le reste sur un tissu en les faisant se chevaucher de façon à former un lit d'épinard dense. Le sécher avec un tissu puis, pour terminer, badigeonner avec la gelée mise en réserve.

Envelopper l'aspic triangulaire figé dans le lit séché d'épinards et de gelée, enrouler de film alimentaire et remettre au frais.

Mousse de cerfeuil ❙ Émincer le cerfeuil et le réduire finement en purée avec la crème aigre (ajouter un peu d'eau si besoin), puis passer à travers une passoire à trous fins.
En réchauffer une petite partie (2 à 3 cuillères à soupe environ). Ramollir la gélatine dans de l'eau, la presser, la dissoudre dans le mélange chaud et l'incorporer au reste du mélange. Battre la crème légère en Chantilly semi-ferme et l'incorporer au mélange de cerfeuil. Assaisonner avec le sel, le piment de Cayenne et un doigt de Pernod.
Couper la gelée encore collante (de la plaque) en 3 morceaux : deux de la même taille pour habiller le moule et un pour le recouvrir au final.
Etaler finement et de façon régulière la mousse de cerfeuil sur l'un des deux morceaux de gelée de même taille et laisser figer (s'il reste de la mousse, la réserver pour éventuellement confectionner des quenelles pour le décor). Disposer dessus les feuilles d'épinards réservées et recouvrir avec le deuxième lit de gelée.

Mousse de crème aigre ❙ Faire chauffer le jus d'un citron et y dissoudre la gélatine ramollie dans l'eau froide puis pressée. Battre la crème aigre et la mélanger rapidement à la gélatine. Battre la crème légère jusqu'à ce qu'elle soit semi-ferme et l'incorporer à la crème aigre. Assaisonner avec le sel, le piment de Cayenne et le Noilly Prat réduit.

Terminer la terrine ❙ Badigeonner d'huile un moule à terrine. Déposer délicatement le lit de gelée recouvert de mousse de cerfeuil sur un film alimentaire et le poser au fond du moule. Mettre le moule dans un récipient avec de l'eau glacée. Verser la moitié de la mousse de crème aigre. Presser l'aspic d'écrevisses dans le manteau d'épinards. Remplir avec le reste de la mousse de crème aigre et couvrir avec le dernier morceau de gelée. Bien laisser refroidir la terrine.

Présentation ❙ Démouler la terrine d'écrevisses, retirer le film alimentaire et couper des tranches de 2 centimètres d'épaisseur. Répartir un peu de salade sur les assiettes, confectionner éventuellement quelques quenelles de mousse de cerfeuil, puis dresser les tranches de terrine, la mousse de crème aigre et les pinces d'écrevisses.

Cannellonis au foie de canard
avec purée de chou-rave et gelée au Madère
Ingrédients pour 4 personnes ❙ Photo Page 30

Parfait de foie de canard ❙ 600 g de foie de canard ❙ 1 l de lait environ ❙ 10 g de sel pour salaison ❙ 12 g de fleur de sel ❙ 3 cuillères à café de Porto blanc réduit ❙ 1 cuillère à café de Noilly Prat réduit ❙ 1 cuillère à café de Madère réduit ❙ 2 cl de Cognac ❙ Lard gras frais ❙ Poivre
Purée de chou-rave ❙ 1 chou-rave ❙ 70 ml de crème ❙ 125 ml de Noilly Prat ❙ 1 feuille de gélatine ❙ 1 œuf ❙ 2 cuillères à soupe de farine ❙ 1 tranche de pain tramezzini ❙ Huile pour friture ❙ Sel, poivre
Gelée au Madère ❙ 300 ml de consommé de bœuf ❙ 5 feuilles de gélatine ❙ 2 cuillères à soupe de Madère réduit ❙ 1 cuillère à soupe de jus de truffe ❙ Sel, poivre
Cannellonis au foie de canard ❙ 200 g de parfait de foie de canard ❙ 20 g de truffes d'été

Parfait de foie de canard ❙ Retirer la peau du foie de canard, le couper en morceaux de la taille d'une noix et le déveiner. Mettre le foie nettoyé dans un récipient à bord hauts, le recouvrir de lait et le mettre au frais pendant 24 heures. Puis le laisser mariner 24 heures dans la saumure, la fleur de sel, le poivre, le Porto, le Noilly Prat, le Madère et le Cognac dans un récipient haut, étroit et bien fermé. Barder de lard gras un plat à terrine (15 x 4 x 4 centimètres) et y verser le foie de canard avec la marinade, recouvrir à nouveau de lard, sceller avec un film transparent et fermer avec le couvercle. Faire pocher à 85 degrés, pour une température à cœur de 42 degrés. Presser le parfait afin de faire sortir toute la graisse. Laisser au frais pendant 24 heures.

Purée de chou-rave ❙ Réduire le Noilly Prat à 30 millimètres. Eplucher le chou-rave, le faire cuire, le mixer finement, y ajouter la crème et assaisonner avec le sel, le poivre et le Noilly Prat réduit. Passer la purée à travers une passoire à trous fins. Ramollir la gélatine, la dissoudre et la mélanger à 60 grammes de purée. Laisser durcir un peu et former 4 boules de la même grosseur. Paner ensuite les boules de purée avec la farine, l'œuf et le pain tramezzini coupé en dés fins, les mettre 10 minutes au congélateur puis les faire frire.

Gelée au Madère ❙ Réchauffer le consommé et y dissoudre la gélatine ramollie. Assaisonner avec le sel, le poivre, le Madère et le jus de truffes, verser la préparation sur une plaque recouverte de film transparent sur une hauteur de 1 ½ millimètres environ et laisser gélifier.

Cannellonis au foie de canard ▮ A l'aide d'un film transparent, former 4 rouleaux de parfait de foie de canard de 50 grammes chacun. Garnir ces rouleaux de truffes râpées et les rouler dans la gelée de Madère.
Présentation ▮ Dresser la purée de chou-rave au centre de l'assiette, puis disposer les cannellonis et les boules de chou-rave.

Veau cru mariné aux pralines de légumes et salade frisée
Ingrédients pour 10 personnes ▮ Photo Page 32

Filet de veau ▮ 1 kg de filet de veau
Pralines de légumes ▮ 1 chou-rave ▮ 1 carotte ▮ 100 ml de crème ▮ 1–2 feuilles de gélatine ▮ 2 œufs ▮ 100 g de farine ▮ 50 g de toast rassis ▮ Huile pour friture
Salade ▮ 1 salade frisée ▮ Sel, poivre ▮ 1 pincée de sucre ▮ 1 cuillère à soupe de vinaigre de Zweigelt ▮ 2 cuillères à soupe d'huile de noix

Pralines de légumes ▮ Eplucher le chou-rave et la carotte, retirer les arrondis à l'aide d'une râpe fine et les mettre dans l'eau. Couper les légumes en dés de 2 x 2 millimètres et les faire blanchir dans l'eau salée.
Mettre les morceaux de légumes retirés et les légumes blanchis dans une poêle, y verser la crème, porter à ébullition puis saler et poivrer.
Verser le mélange dans un verre mesureur, ramollir une feuille de gélatine pour 100 millilitres de mélange et la dissoudre dans le mélange chaud. Réserver un tiers du mélange, mettre l'autre partie au frais. Dès que le mélange est bien gélifié, il est alors possible d'en former de petites boules.
Paner doublement les boules dans la farine et dans l'œuf, puis les rouler dans les petits dés de toasts sans croûte (de 5 x 5 millimètres grosseur). Faire frire les pralines dans de l'huile chaude avant de dresser les plats.
Filet de veau ▮ Retirer le gras et la peau du filet de veau. Le découper en tranches de 10 centimètres de long environ. Dérouler aussi finement que possible chacune des tranches à l'aide d'un couteau tranchant. Les aplatir de façon égale, répartir dessus une fine couche de crème de chou-rave et les enrouler fermement comme un escargot. Les envelopper dans un film alimentaire et dans une feuille de papier aluminium, puis les congeler.
Salade ▮ Laver la salade frisée puis l'essorer. La faire mariner ensuite avec le sel, le poivre, le sucre, le vinaigre de Zweigelt et l'huile de noix.
Présentation ▮ A l'aide d'un couteau tranchant ou d'une machine à découper, couper le veau décongelé en tranches fines, les placer sur une assiette. Saler et poivrer.
Dresser la salade sur les tranches de veau et poser dessus les pralines de chou-rave frites.

Tartare de bœuf limousin du Waldviertel dans unconsommé de bœuf gélifié avec mousse de Wasabi et betterave rouge
Ingrédients pour 4 personnes ▮ Photo Page 34

Tatare et consommé de bœuf ▮ ¼ l de consommé de bœuf ▮ 4 feuilles de gélatine ▮ 1 échalote 200 g de filet de bœuf ▮ 2 petits cornichons ▮ 3 câpres ▮ 1 cuillère à café de moutarde de Dijon ▮ 5 cuillères à café de ketchup ▮ 2 cuillères à soupe d'huile d'olive ▮ 1 filet de sauce Worcester ▮ Tabasco selon les goûts ▮ 1 filet de jus de citron ▮ 2 cuillères à soupe de persil haché ▮ Sel, poivre
Mousse de Wasabi ▮ 20 g de Wasabi ▮ ½ feuille de gélatine ▮ 100 ml de crème
Betterave rouge ▮ 1 betterave rouge ▮ 2 cuillères à soupe de vinaigre de framboise ▮ 1 cuillère à soupe d'huile de noix ▮ Sucre, cumin, sel, poivre

Tatare ▮ Faire chauffer la soupe, y dissoudre la gélatine ramollie dans de l'eau froide, assaisonner et passer à travers une passoire à trous fins. Tapisser hermétiquement les moules circulaires (Ø 7 ½ cm, 3 cm de hauteur) d'un film transparent.
Remplir les moules de gelée jusqu'à environ 5 millimètres du bord et laisser figer. Dès que la gelée est ferme, la démouler et la découper au centre avec un emporte-pièces de taille plus petite. Réchauffer de nouveau légèrement la partie centrale découpée, jusqu'à ce qu'elle soit liquide, en napper le fond des moules. Dès qu'elle devient un peu ferme, mais encore collante, déposer dessus les anneaux de gelée. Réserver la gelée restante pour couvrir les moules. Couper l'échalote en dés fins et la blanchir. Hacher finement le filet de bœuf, les petits cornichons et les câpres. Y ajouter les dés d'échalotes, la moutarde de Dijon, le ketchup, l'huile d'olive, le Tabasco, le jus de citron et le persil haché, puis mélanger vigoureusement. Assaisonner avec le sel, le poivre et le Tabasco. Remplir de tartare les moules gélifiés, lisser, couvrir avec le reste de gelée refroidie et mettre au frais.
Mousse de Wasabi ▮ Faire chauffer légèrement le Wasabi et la gélatine (après l'avoir ramollie dans de l'eau froide et pressée) jusqu'à ce qu'elle soit dissoute, puis passer à travers une passoire à trous fins. Incorporer la crème fouettée juste avant que le mélange ne se fige et assaisonner avec un peu de sel. Mettre la mousse au frais.
Betterave rouge ▮ Cuire la betterave «al dente» dans une eau bien assaisonnée avec le vinaigre, le sel, le sucre et le cumin. La couper en dés réguliers et assaisonner avec le vinaigre de framboises, l'huile de noix, le sel, le poivre et le sucre.
Présentation ▮ Dresser le tartare au centre de l'assiette, coiffer d'une quenelle de mousse de Wasabi et décorer le tartare avec les dés de betterave.

Velouté de homard avec soufflé aux petits pois et caviar Ossietra
Ingrédients pour 4 personnes ▮ Photo Page 36

Velouté ▮ 1 à 2 carcasses de homard ▮ 1 cuillère à soupe de beurre ▮ 1 cuillère à soupe d'huile d'olive ▮ ½ bulbe de céleri ▮ 2 cl de Cognac ▮ 2 cl de Pernod ▮ ¼ l de Sauvignon Blanc ▮ ½ l de fumet de homard ▮ ½ l de crème ▮ 2 à 3 noix de beurre ▮ Sel, poivre blanc
Soufflé ▮ 100 g de purée de petits pois (voir recette de base page 78) ▮ 50 g de lait ▮ 50 ml de crème ▮ 2 œufs ▮ Sel, poivre ▮ Beurre pour le moule
Présentation ▮ 40 g de caviar Ossietra

Velouté ▮ Casser les carcasses de homards en petits morceaux, les faire griller dans une casserole avec du beurre et de l'huile d'olive. Eplucher le céleri, le couper en dés fins, ajouter les dés dans la casserole et leur faire prendre couleur. Ajouter le Cognac, le Pernod et flamber. Ajouter le vin blanc, laisser réduire de moitié, ajouter le fumet de homard, laisser réduire à nouveau de moitié, ajouter la crème, assaisonner avec le sel et le poivre blanc. Verser à travers une passoire à trous fins et monter avec le beurre ou du beurre de homard.
Soufflé ▮ Mélanger tous les ingrédients et assaisonner. Beurrer un petit moule à soufflé, remplir avec le mélange sur une hauteur de 4 centimètres environ, couvrir avec un film transparent résistant à la chaleur et pocher au bain-marie pendant 30 minutes environ.
Présentation ▮ Démouler le soufflé dans l'assiette, garnir avec le caviar et arroser avec le velouté.

Essence de faon et tomate avec rouleaux de tomates
Ingrédients pour 6 personnes ▮ Photo Page 38

Essence de faon ▮ 1 kg d'os de faon ▮ 200 g de légumes-racines ▮ 1 cuillère à soupe de concentré de tomates ▮ ½ l de vin rouge ▮ 125 ml de Xérès ▮ 5 baies de genévrier ▮ 1 feuille de laurier ▮ 6 blancs d'œufs ▮ 400 g de viande maigre de faon pour la clarification ▮ Sel, poivre blanc fraîchement moulu
Farce de faon ▮ 150 g d'épaule de faon hachée ▮ 150 g de crème ▮ 35 g de pain de mie sans croûte ▮ 1 œuf ▮ 1 cuillère à soupe de concentré de tomates ▮ Sel, poivre
Rouleaux de crêpes ▮ 50 g de farine ▮ 50 ml de lait ▮ 1 œuf ▮ 1 pincée de sel ▮ 100 g de farce de faon (voir la recette ci-dessus)

Essence de faon ▮ Faire rissoler les os et les légumes-racines, y ajouter le concentré de tomates et mouiller avec le vin rouge et le Xérès. Laisser réduire et rajouter 2 litres d'eau froide. Laisser mijoter 2 à 3 heures ; à mi-cuisson ajouter les baies de genévrier et la feuille de laurier. Filtrer après la fin de la cuisson et mettre à refroidir. Dégraisser le fond lorsqu'il est froid, puis y ajouter la viande et le blanc d'œuf pour la clarification. Remettre sur le feu et faire mijoter lentement en mélangeant constamment, ne pas faire bouillir! Lorsque la soupe est claire, la passer lentement à travers une passoire. Retirer le reste de gras avec un papier absorbant, puis saler et poivrer.

Farce de faon I Mixer finement tous les ingrédients de la farce dans un Cutter et assaisonner avec le sel et le poivre.

Rouleaux de crêpes I Former une pâte homogène à partir de la farine, du lait, de l'œuf et du sel. Faire des crêpes et les recouvrir de farce. Les rouler de façon bien serrée, les envelopper dans une feuille d'aluminium et les faire cuire 10 minutes au bain-marie à 90 degrés. Retirer la feuille d'aluminium et couper en tranches.

Présentation I Servir la soupe avec les rouleaux dans des assiettes ou dans de petites tasses.

Consommé de bœuf du Waldviertel avec petits sandwichs à la rate
Ingrédients pour 4 personnes I Photo Page 40

Consommé 2 carottes I ½ poireau I 1 rave jaune I 1 céleri-branche I 1 oignon I 1 culotte de bœuf Fleckvieh du Waldviertel (1 à 2 kg environ) I 5 l d'eau I 1 bouquet de livèche I ½ bouquet de persil I 1 bouquet de ciboulette I 5 grains de poivre I 1 feuille de laurier

Clarification I ½ kg de bœuf haché I 1 carotte I 1 rave jaune I ½ céleri-rave I 5 blancs d'œufs

Petits sandwichs à la rate I 160 g de rate finement hachée I 3 œufs I 1 pincée de marjolaine I 1 cuillère à soupe de persil haché I 1 cuillère à café d'ail finement haché I 4 toasts ou tranches de pain blanc I 2 cuillères à soupe d'huile I 4 cuillères à soupe de farine I Sel, poivre

Consommé I Nettoyer et couper en gros morceaux les carottes, le poireau, la rave et le céleri. Couper l'oignon en deux et faire brunir la surface coupée dans une poêle brûlante. Faire chauffer l'eau dans une grande casserole, ajouter dans l'eau bouillante la culotte de Fleckvieh et le reste des ingrédients (en réservant le poivre et la feuille de laurier). Après le premier bouillon, laisser cuire à très petit feu pendant 2 à 3 heures. A mi-cuisson, ajouter la feuille de laurier et les grains de poivre. Entre-temps écumer la mousse grise se formant à la surface à l'aide d'une écumoire. Mettre la soupe au frais toute la nuit.

Clarification I Mixer grossièrement la viande hachée et le reste des ingrédients dans un Cutter et y ajouter la soupe froide. Porter lentement à ébullition tout en mélangeant, car la viande ne doit pas attacher. Laisser bouillir pendant 2 heures environ, puis passer à travers une passoire à trous fins.

Petits sandwichs à la rate I Mélanger la rate, 2 œufs, les herbes et l'ail, saler et poivrer. Etaler un doigt de mélange sur 2 tranches de pain et recouvrir avec les tranches restantes. Chauffer l'huile dans une poêle suffisamment grande. Enduire le sandwich de farine, le passer dans l'œuf battu restant et le faire dorer des deux côtés dans de la matière grasse chaude. Le retirer de la poêle, le laisser égoutter et le couper au nombre de morceaux souhaités.

Présentation I Verser le consommé de bœuf à travers une passoire puis à travers une étamine, assaisonner et servir avec l'accompagnement.

Raviolis d'écrevisses aux œufs de caille et girolles
Ingrédients pour 4 personnes I Photo Page 42

Raviolis I 100 g de pâte à pâtes fraîches (voir recette de base page 78) I 1 œuf pour badigeonner I 16 cuillères à café d'épinards à la crème (voir recette de base page 78) I 16 jaunes d'œufs de caille I 8 écrevisses I Un peu de beurre

Sauce I 500 ml de fumet de poisson (voir recette de base page 78) I 250 ml de crème I 1 cuillère à soupe de beurre froid I Sel, poivre

Girolles I 100 g de girolles

Présentation I 1 pomme de terre I Un peu de matière grasse

Raviolis I Nettoyer les épinards, les cuire dans de l'eau salée 2 minutes environ et les refroidir dans de l'eau glacée. Les verser dans une passoire et les réduire finement en purée avec le mixeur. Faire épaissir avec la crème jusqu'à obtenir une consistance crémeuse et assaisonner avec le sel, le poivre et la muscade.

Abaisser finement la pâte à la main ou avec la machine à pâtes, la badigeonner avec l'œuf et répartir dessus les épinards à la crème, faire un petit creux et y poser chaque fois un jaune d'œuf de caille. Cuire les écrevisses dans l'eau bouillante, les ouvrir et couper les queues en deux, les ajouter également à l'épinard et à l'œuf de caille. Mettre le plus précautionneusement possible une autre couche de pâte par dessus et bien appuyer.

Cuire à point les raviolis dans de l'eau bouillante salée, avec le jaune d'œuf vers le haut. Faire fondre du beurre dans une poêle et y faire revenir les raviolis.

Sauce I Réduire un peu le fumet de poisson. Ajouter la crème, faire légèrement bouillir, ajouter le beurre froid et mélanger.

Girolles I Nettoyer et faire sauter les girolles.

Présentation I Dresser les girolles, napper avec la sauce, déposer les raviolis. En guise de garniture, ajouter par-dessus des dés de pommes de terre frits

Œuf « à la viennoise » aux épinards, au lard à l'ail et aux champignons des prés
Ingrédients pour 4 parts I Photo Page 44

Œufs I 4 œufs I 1 filet de vinaigre I 50 g de farine I 50 g de chapelure I Huile pour la cuisson I Sel, poivre

Accompagnement I 200 g d'épinards I 1 cuillère à café de beurre I 80 g de lard à l'ail autrichien I 120 g de champignons des prés

Œufs I Cuire les œufs 4 minutes dans de l'eau vinaigrée, les sortir de l'eau, les refroidir et les écaler. Saler et poivrer, les rouler légèrement dans la farine, les faire passer dans l'œuf battu et les paner avec la chapelure. Chauffer l'huile et y frire les œufs, jusqu'à ce qu'ils soient dorés.

Accompagnement I Laver les épinards, chauffer le beurre dans une poêle et y faire suer les épinards, asaler et poivrer. Couper le lard en lamelles et le faire griller dans une poêle à revêtement antiadhésif. Couper les champignons en biseau et les faire griller avec le lard.

Présentation I Dresser les épinards et poser un œuf dessus. Les entourer du mélange lardons-champignons et coiffer chaque œuf d'un champignon.

Tortellini aux brocolis avec beurre à la tomate et à l'estragon
Ingrédients pour 4 personnes I Photo Page 46

Tortellini I 350 g de brocolis I 200 g de pâte à pâtes fraîches (voir recette de base page 78) I 2 cuillères à soupe de sauce Béchamel I 1 œuf I 1 jaune d'œuf I 40 ml de crème I 25 g de beurre fondu

Beurre à la tomate et à l'estragon I 100 ml de vin blanc I 2 cl de Xérès I 1 échalote I ½ l de fond de volaille I 200 ml de crème I 30 g de beurre I 2 cuillères à soupe de dés de tomates I Estragon I Sel

Présentation I Beurre brun I Grana Padano ou fromage de montagne

Tortellinis I Nettoyer les brocolis et les faire blanchir. Les passer au mixeur avec le reste des ingrédients jusqu'à obtenir une farce fine ouréduire en purée. Saler et poivrer.

Abaisser finement la pâte à pâtes à la main ou avec la machine et la badigeonner avec l'œuf battu. Mettre une petite quantité de mélange refroidi de brocolis sur une couche de pâte. Recouvrir avec une deuxième couche, bien appuyer et découper des raviolis. Laisser cuire les raviolis préparés dans de l'eau salée frémissante pendant 4 minutes environ.

Beurre à la tomate et à l'estragon I Porter à ébullition le vin blanc, le Xérès et les échalotes finement coupées en dés, y ajouter le fond de volaille et laisser réduire au quart. Ajouter la crème et le beurre, laisser mijoter légèrement pendant 10 minutes, passer à travers une passoire fine, puis battre au mixeur, goûter et rectifier l'assaisonnement si nécessaire. Peu avant de servir, ajouter l'estragon et les dés de tomates et bien mélanger.

Présentation I Faire revenir les petits raviolis cuits dans le beurre brun. Mettre le beurre à la tomate et à l'estragon sur l'assiette et dresser les petits raviolis dessus. Parsemer de Grana Padano ou de fromage de montagne grossièrement râpé.

Gnocchis de petits pois à l'œuf poché et à la truffe blanche
Ingrédients pour 6 personnes I Photo Page 48

Œufs pochés I 6 œufs I 2 cuillères à soupe de vinaigre
Gnocchis de petits pois I 500 g de petits pois I 2 feuilles de gélatine I 1 cuillère à café de beurre de truffes I 100 g de pommes de terre à chair farineuse I 50 g de fécule de pommes de terre I 20 g de beurre liquide I 1 jaune d'œuf I 50 ml de crème I Sel
Présentation I 1 petit tubercule de truffe blanche I 100 ml de sauce aux truffes

Œufs pochés I Casser les œufs un par un et les mettre précautionneusement sur une assiette ou dans un saladier. Chauffer l'eau à environ 80 degrés. Ajouter le vinaigre et mélanger avec un fouet jusqu'à ce qu'un tourbillon apparaisse. Laisser glisser successivement dans une casserole 2–3 œufs à partir du bord de la casserole et les pocher pendant environ 2 minutes. Procéder de la même façon avec le reste des œufs. Les refroidir dans de l'eau glacée, les nettoyer et les réserver.
Gnocchis de petits pois I Cuire les petits pois dans de l'eau salée, les refroidir dans de l'eau glacée, les réduire en purée et les faire passer à travers une passoire fine.
Ramollir la gélatine dans de l'eau froide. Réchauffer 100 grammes de cette purée, assaisonner avec le sel et le beurre de truffes et y délayer la gélatine. Recouvrir une petite plaque ou une grosse assiette avec du film transparent. Y étaler la purée sur environ 5 millimètres d'épaisseur et la laisser se figer. Presser 200 grammes de cettepurée à l'aide d'une étamine, jusqu'à ce qu'elle ne contienne quasiment plus de liquide. Confectionner une pâte lisse à partir de cette purée asséchée, des pommes de terre moulinées, du fécule, du beurre, du jaune d'œuf et du sel. Former 42 gnocchis à partir de cette pâte. Couper la purée gélifiée en petits dés (5 x 5 millimètres) et en remplir les gnocchis.
Présentation I Chauffer le reste de la purée de petits pois avec la crème, rectifier l'assaisonnement et dresser dans des assiettes creuses. Cuire les gnocchis de petits pois dans de l'eau chaude pendant 2 minutes, les faire revenir dans du beurre et les disposer autour de la purée. Réchauffer les œufs pochés dans la sauce aux truffes et les déposer au centre de la purée. Ecumer la sauce aux truffes, napper l'œuf avec et râper la truffe blanche au-dessus.

Moules au safran décoquillées au vin blanc et gnocchis
Ingrédients pour 4 personnes I Photo Page 50

Moules I 1 kg de moules I 3 ou 4 échalotes I 2 cuillères à soupe d'huile d'olive I 10 pistils de safran I ½ l de vin blanc I ½ l de fumet de poisson ou de consommé léger I 100 g de beurre froid I Sel, poivre blanc
Gnocchis I 100 g de pommes de terre moulinées I 20 g de fécule de pommes de terre I 1 jaune d'œuf I 1 cuillère à soupe de beurre liquide I Sel, muscade
Présentation I 6 jeunes poireaux I Un peu de beurre
Moules I Nettoyer les moules, retirer la barbe à l'aide d'un couteau et jeter les moules ouvertes ou celles dont la coquille est endommagée.
Couper les échalotes en dés fins. Chauffer l'huile d'olive dans une casserole, y ajouter les moules, les échalotes et le safran, couvrir et faire revenir rapidement. Mouiller avec un peu de vin blanc, faire bouillir, retirer les moules et jeter celles qui sont fermées. Mettre le vin blanc restant dans une casserole et le réduire complètement, y ajouter le fumet de poisson, faire bouillir, saler, poivrer et monter avec le beurre froid. Sortir les moules de leur coquille et les remettre dans la casserole.
Gnocchis I Malaxer tous les ingrédients en une pâte homogène, former des gnocchis, les faire cuire 2 minutes dans de l'eau chaude salée, puis les faire revenir dans du beurre.
Présentation I Couper grossièrement les jeunes poireaux et les faire cuire doucement dans le beurre. Disposer les gnocchis sur les assiettes, dresser dessus les moules avec le bouillon de safran. Garnir avec les jeunes poireaux.

Saint-Jacques à la Saint-Germain
Ingrédients pour 4 personnes I Photo Page 52

Saint-Jacques I 8 noix de Saint-Jacques I 2 cuillères à soupe d'huile d'olive I Sel marin
Sauce à la crème I 100 g de crème fraîche I Jus et zestes d'une ½ limette I Sel, poivre
Pâte brisée I 1 jaune d'œuf I 45 g de beurre I 25 g de parmesan I 60 g de farine I Sel, poivre
Présentation I Un peu de cresson et quelques zestes de limette pour la décoration

Sauce à la crème I Mélanger tous les ingrédients jusqu'à obtenir un mélange homogène et mettre au frais.
Pâte brisée I Préchauffer le four à 160 degrés. Mélanger le beurre et le jaune d'œuf, incorporer le parmesan, le sel, le poivre et la farine et travailler jusqu'à obtenir une pâte souple. Envelopper dans un film transparent et laisser reposer au moins 1 heure au réfrigérateur. Rouler entre deux feuilles de papier sulfurisé et mettre au frais. Lorsque le mélange est dur, découper des cercles (de 10 centimètres de diamètre environ) et les déposer sur une plaque recouverte de papier sulfurisé. Cuire environ 10 minutes au four. Laisser refroidir et empiler précautionneusement.
Saint-Jacques I Par portion, découper 2 noix de Saint-Jacques en 8 tranches et les faire mariner dans l'huile d'olive et le sel marin.
Présentation I Avant de dresser les plats, laisser les noix de Saint-Jacques à température ambiante. Répartir la sauce à la crème sur les assiettes, déposer un cercle de pâte et dresser dessus les noix de Saint-Jacques en éventail. Garnir avec le cresson et les zestes de limette.

Médaillons de poisson-chat aux lentilles de Dijon et beurre au vin de Rioja
Ingrédients pour 4 personnes I Photo Page 54

Lentilles de Dijon I 100 g de lentilles beluga I 3 échalotes I 2 tranches de poitrine fumée I 1 cuillère à café d'huile d'olive I ¼ l de fond de volaille I ¼ l de crème I 2 cuillères à café de moutarde de Dijon I Vinaigre balsamique I 1 cuillère à soupe de persil haché I Sel, poivre
Beurre au vin de Rioja I 4 échalotes I 1 branche de romarin I 1 cuillères à soupe de beurre I 1 cuillère à soupe de sucre en poudre I ½ l de Rioja I Beurre froid
Poisson-chat I 12 médaillons de poisson-chat de 50 g I Un peu d'huile de germe de maïs I Sel, poivre

Lentilles de Dijon I Faire tremper les lentilles dans de l'eau. Couper les échalotes et la poitrine fumée en dés fins et les faire rissoler légèrement dans un peu d'huile d'olive. Faire blanchir les lentilles 2 minutes dans de l'eau salée, les égoutter, les refroidir et les ajouter à la poitrine fumée. Verser le fond de volaille et laisser réduire. Ajouter la crème et laisser réduire également. Assaisonner les lentilles avec la moutarde de Dijon, le vinaigre balsamique, le sel et le poivre. Incorporer du persil au dernier moment.
Beurre au vin de Rioja I Couper les échalotes en dés fins et les faire suer avec du romarin dans un peu de beurre. Ajouter le sucre en poudre et laisser caraméliser légèrement. Ajouter le Rioja, laisser réduire au tiers et passer à travers une passoire. Au dernier moment, battre le beurre froid avec un fouet jusqu'à ce que la réduction attache légèrement.
Poisson-chat I Saler et poivrer les médaillons de poisson-chat. Chauffer l'huile de germe de maïs dans une poêle avec revêtement antiadhésif, y déposer les médaillons côté peau et les faire frire jusqu'à ce qu'ils soient croustillants. Puis les retourner, réduire la chaleur et laisser le poisson mijoter jusqu'à ce qu'il soit transparent.
Présentation I Dresser les lentilles au centre des assiettes, déposer dans chaque assiette trois médaillons de poisson-chat et avec, à côté, le beurre au vin de Rioja.

Saint-Pierre avec artichauts à la tomate et oignons au basilic
Ingrédients pour 4 personnes I Photo Page 56

Artichauts à la tomate I 2 tomates I 4 cœurs d'artichauts I 2 cuillères à soupe d'huile d'olive I Feuille de laurier et thym selon les goûts I 1 gousse d'ail I 25 g de beurre froid I Sel, poivre
Oignons au basilic I 2 oignons blancs I 2 cuillères à soupe d'huile d'olive I 1 bouquet de basilic I 6 cl de vin blanc I Sel, poivre
Saint-Pierre I 400 g de filets de Saint-Pierre I 1 cuillère à soupe de beurre I Sel
Présentation I 4 rosettes de pommes de terre I Pistou au basilic

Artichauts à la tomate I Préchauffer le four à 150 degrés. Blanchir les tomates dans de l'eau bouillante, les refroidir, retirer la peau et les couper en dés. Couper les cœurs d'artichauts en lamelles. Chauffer l'huile d'olive dans une poêle et y faire suer les artichauts. Après 2 minutes, ajouter les tomates, les épices et l'ail coupé en dés fins, recouvrir d'une feuille d'aluminium et faire cuire à l'étouffée au four pendant 15 minutes. Pour terminer, lier avec le beurre.
Oignons au basilic I Couper les oignons en deux et les trancher en fines lamelles. Les faire suer très doucement dans l'huile d'olive. Saler, poivrer, ajouter le vin blanc. Pour terminer, incorporer le basilic ciselé.
Saint-Pierre I Diviser le Saint-Pierre en 4 parts égales, saler et faire suer dans le beurre 4 à 5 minutes.
Présentation I Disposer les artichauts à la tomate au centre de l'assiette, mettre le poisson dessus et recouvrir d'oignons au basilic. Servir, garni de rosettes de pomme de terre et d'un peu de pistou.

Tranches de turbot avec gnocchis au potiron, truffes d'été et cannelle
Ingrédients pour 6 personnes I Photo Page 58

Gnocchis I 200 g de pommes de terre farineuses I 100 g de purée de potiron (voir recette de base page 78) I 4 cuillères à soupe de fécule de pommes de terre I 2 œufs I Un peu de beurre I Sel
Sauce I 10 cuillères à soupe de dés de potiron I 1 cuillère à soupe de beurre I 40 g de truffes noires I 2 cuillères à soupe de raisins secs I 1 trait de jus de truffes I 100 ml de Madère I 100 ml de jus de truffes I 100 ml de crème I 100 ml de fond de veau I Poivre, muscade, cannelle
Turbot I 600 g de filet de turbot I 1 cuillère à soupe de beurre I Sel
Présentation I Nage de poisson au Champagne (voir recette de base page 78)
Un peu de truffes, selon les envies

Gnocchis I Mouliner les pommes de terre, les travailler avec la purée de potiron, la fécule de pommes de terre, les œufs et un peu de sel jusqu'à obtenir une pâte lisse puis laisser reposer. Former des gnocchis à partir de la pâte de pommes de terre et potiron, les cuire dans de l'eau bien salée puis les faire revenir dans le beurre.
Sauce I Faire mijoter les dés de potiron dans le beurre, ajouter les truffes hachées, la cannelle et les raisins secs, mouiller avec un peu de jus de truffes, laisser réduire puis assaisonner.
Réduire le Madère, le fond de veau et le jus de truffes à 100 millimètres, ajouter la crème, saler et poivrer puis ajouter cette sauce aux dés de potiron.
Turbot I Faire frire le turbot dans le beurre et le saler légèrement.
Présentation I Dresser côte à côte les gnocchis et la sauce, déposer le turbot, ajouter un peu de mousse de lait et râper un peu de truffes dessus, selon les envies.

Bar entier en croûte de sel
Ingrédients pour 4 personnes I Photo Page 60

1 bar d'environ 1,2 kg I 2 kg de gros sel de mer I 4 blancs d'œufs I 1 bouquet de thym I 2 gousses d'ail
Présentation I épinard blanchi (si nécessaire)

Bar I Laver le poisson et le sécher. Recouvrir la cavité abdominale avec le thym et les gousses d'ail entières. Préchauffer le four à 220 degrés et mélanger le sel de mer avec les blancs d'oeufs. Si le mélange est trop dur, ajouter un peu d'eau. Recouvrir une plaque de cuisson d'une feuille d'aluminium et y déposer le poisson. Recouvrir le poisson avec le mélange à base de sel et appuyer fermement avec les mains, pour lui donner la forme d'un poisson. Entourer avec la feuille d'aluminium et faire cuire au four pendant 20 minutes.
Présentation I Casser la croûte de sel et la retirer, découper le poisson en filets et servir avec un accompagnement approprié (par ex. des épinards blanchis).

Ris de veau aux champignons des prés et cerfeuil
Ingrédients pour 4 personnes I Photo Page 62

Pâtes aux pommes de terre I 50 g pommes de terre à chair farineuse I 200 g de farine I 100 ml d'eau froide I evtl. 1 œuf I 2 cuillères à soupe de semoule de blé I Sel
Ris de veau I 200 g de ris de veau nettoyé, égoutté et épluché I 2 cuillères à soupe de farine I 1 cuillère à soupe d'huile I 1 cuillère à soupe de beurre I Sel, poivre
Champignons des prés I 300 g de champignons des prés I 1 cuillère à soupe de beurre I 2 gousses d'ail I 100 ml de fond de veau I 1 cuillère à soupe de cerfeuil haché I Sel, poivre

Pâtes aux pommes de terre I Cuire les pommes de terre dans leur peau, les laisser sécher quelques instants, les peler, les passer encore chaudes au presse-purée. Ajouter la farine et malaxer le tout avec de l'eau jusqu'à obtenir une pâte ferme et lisse. Rajouter éventuellement un œuf et continuer à travailler la pâte.
Avec la machine à pâtes, abaisser la pâte (sans farine) en portions de 1 à 2 millimètres d'épaisseur puis couper des bandes d'1 centimètre de large environ. Les rouler entre les mains afin d'obtenir des petites quenelles, les passer dans la semoule de blé et les laisser un peu sécher sur une plaque. Cuire les pâtes dans de l'eau salée bouillante jusqu'à ce qu'elles soient al dente.
Ris de veau I Fariner et assaisonner les morceaux de ris de veau. Les rissoler à la poêle dans de l'huile et du beurre, les retirer de la poêle et les réserver au chaud.
Champignons des prés
Nettoyer les champignons, mettre du beurre dans la poêle et les faire suer avec l'ail finement haché. Saler et poivrer, verser le fond de veau et incorporer le cerfeuil. Ajouter le ris de veau et laisser mariner un instant.
Présentation I Mettre les pâtes aux pommes de terre dans des assiettes creuses. Répartir dessus le ris de veau et les champignons des prés. Garnir avec le cerfeuil frais.

Galantine de pigeon au chutney de pomme et Dirndln de Wagram
Ingrédients pour 6 personnes I Photo Page 64

Galantine de pigeon I 2 pigeons I 200 g de farce de volaille (voir recette de base page 78) I cuillère à soupe de dés de carottes I 1 cuillère à soupe de dés de rave jaune I 1 cuillère à soupe de dés de céleri I 2 filets de pigeon I 2 cuillères à soupe de girolles ou morilles I 1 à 2 cuillères à soupe de crème I 1 l de fond de volaille corsé I Sel, poivre I 1 tissu propre et mouillé I Fil de cuisine
Chutney de pomme I 1 pomme I 1 cuillère à soupe de miel I 1 filet de vinaigre de vin blanc I Sel, poivre
Présentation I 24 morceaux de Dirndln de Wagram confit I Feuilles de salade de saison

Galantine de pigeon I Désosser les pigeons et les aplatir entre deux films transparents humidifiés. Mélanger la farce de volaille avec les dés de légumes, les filets de pigeon coupés en petits morceaux et les girolles, puis allonger avec un peu de crème. Saler et poivrer.
Etaler le mélange sur le pigeon, enrouler en prenant soin de bien serrer, envelopper dans un tissu et fermer avec le fil de cuisine. Pocher la galantine de pigeon dans fond de volaille corsé à 80 degrés pendant 30 minutes environ.
Il est essentiel de mettre la galantine au frais immédiatement après cuisson, afin qu'elle développe une saveur encore plus intense.
Chutney de pomme I Peler la pomme, l'épépiner et la couper en dés fins. Caraméliser le miel dans une poêle, y ajouter les dés de pomme, les faire revenir et mouiller avec le vinaigre de vin blanc. Laisser cuire à feu moyen, saler et poivrer.
Présentation I Disposer le Dirndln de Wagram et la salade sur l'assiette. Confectionner des quenelles de chutney et dresser les tranches de galantine.

Blancs de poulet fermier noir
dans une croûte aux olives et tomates avec couscous aux pignons
Ingrédients pour 4 parts I Photo Page 66

Poulet fermier noir I 4 filets de blanc de poulet fermier noir de 150 g I 1 cuillère à soupe d'huile I 150 g de tomates I 2 cuillères à soupe d'huile d'olive I 60 g d'olives I 1 bouquet de thym I 60 g de tomates séchées I 80 g de chapelure I Ail I Sel, poivre

Couscous aux pignons I 80 g de graines de couscous I ½ bouquet de basilic I 2 cuillères à soupe d'huile d'olive I 2 cuillères à soupe d'eau I 2 cuillères à soupe de parmesan râpé I 40 g de pignons grillés I Sel, poivre
Présentation I Jus de poulet

Poulet fermier noir I Saler et poivrer les blancs de poulet et bien les saisir des deux côtés dans une poêle. Les faire rôtir au four à 180 degrés pendant 5 minutes environ.
Peler les tomates, les couper en dés, les faire cuire dans l'huile d'olive, saler et poivrer, puis mettre au frais.
Préchauffer le four à 220 degrés (voûte). Couper les olives, hacher fin les feuilles de thym et faire des dés de tomates séchées, incorporer le tout aux dés de tomates refroidis. Ajouter autant de chapelure que nécessaire pour obtenir un mélange souple à étaler et rectifier l'assaisonnement.
Etaler cette croûte sur les blancs de poulet et faire dorer au four.
Couscous aux pignons I Faire tremper les graines de couscous dans de l'eau froide. Mixer le basilic avec l'huile d'olive, l'eau et le parmesan en un fin pesto. Egoutter les graines de couscous, les faire cuire dans une large casserole avec les pignons et le pesto, saler et poivrer.
Présentation I Servir le couscous dans les assiettes et dresser les blancs de poulet noir dessus. Garnir avec le jus de poulet.

Filet de veau en croûte et artichauts à l'étouffée
Ingrédients pour 4 personnes I Photo Page 68

Filet de veau I 600g de filet de veau I 150 g de pain tramezzini I 50 g de farce de veau I Huile pour saisir I 100 ml de sauce de veau I Sel, poivre
Artichauts I 2 tomates I 2 cuillères à soupe d'huile d'olive I 2 coeurs d'artichauts I Feuille de laurier et thym selon les goûts I 1 gousse d'ail I 12 g de beurre froid I Sel, poivre
Présentation I Beurre persillé (voir recette de base page 78) I Chips d'artichauts (voir recette de base page 78)
Filet de veau I Préchauffer le four à 180 degrés. I Nettoyer le filet de veau, le découper en plusieurs morceaux et l'assaisonner. Abaisser finement le pain tramezzini à l'aide d'un rouleau à pâtisserie, le recouvrir de farce et poser le filet de veau dessus. Rouler le tout en serrant bien et saisir de tous les côtés dans l'huile, faire cuire 5 minutes au four et laisser reposer 5 minutes supplémentaires à 80 degrés.
Artichauts I Blanchir les tomates dans de l'eau bouillante, les peler et les découper en petits dés. Faire chauffer l'huile d'olive dans une poêle et y faire suer les dés d'artichauts, ajouter les tomates, les épices et l'ail coupé en dés fins, couvrir avec une feuille d'aluminium et laisser cuire au four à l'étouffée à 150 degrés pendant 15 minutes. Retirer du four, lier avec le beurre.
Présentation I Partager le filet en croûte en 4 parts, dresser au centre des assiettes, ajouter un peu de beurre persillé et servir avec les chips d'artichauts.

Tendre côtelette de veau
sur pâtes fines aux olives noires et jeunes poireaux
Ingrédients pour 4 personnes I Photo Page 70

Longe de veau I 1 kg de longe de veau avec os I 1 branche de romarin frais I Un peu de saindoux I 1 cuillère à soupe de beurre I Sel, poivre blanc
Pâte à pâtes fraîches I 200 g de farine fluide I 1 cuillère à soupe d'huile d'olive I 1 œuf I 3 jaunes d'œufs I Sel
Glace aux olives I 2 jeunes poireaux I ½ cuillère à soupe de beurre I 60 ml de fond de légumes I 60 g d'olives noires dénoyautées I ¼ l de glace de veau I 40 g de beurre froid

Longe de veau I Préchauffer le four à 180 degrés. Retirer les tendons de la longe de veau, saler et poivrer. Saisir à la poêle dans le saindoux chaud avec la branche de romarin frais, mettre au four avec le beurre pendant 25 minutes. Terminer la cuisson à 85 degrés pendant 10 minutes.
Pâtes fraîches I Pétrir tous les ingrédients jusqu'à obtenir une pâte lisse puis mettre 1 heure au frais. Abaisser finement la pâte à l'aide de la machine à pâtes et confectionner des pâtes fines (par exemple des spaghettis). Cuire les pâtes «al dente» dans de l'eau salée.
Glace aux olives I Nettoyer les jeunes poireaux et les couper en gros morceaux. Faire cuire dans la poêle avec le beurre et mouiller avec un peu de fond. Couper les olives en fines lamelles. Faire bouillir la glace de veau, la monter avec le beurre froid et affiner avec les olives.
Présentation I Enrouler les pâtes à l'aide d'une fourchette à viande, découper la viande en 4 morceaux, les dresser, déposer les jeunes poireaux et arroser de glace aux olives.

Carré de cochon de lait au cumin du Waldviertel,
raviolis de jarret de porc et chou pointu sauté
Ingrédients pour 4 personnes I Photo Page 72

Carré de cochon de lait I 800 g de carré de cochon de lait, désossé, avec couenne I 1 branche de romarin I 1 branche de thym I 1 feuille de laurier I 2 gousses d'ail I Huile d'olive I Cumin du Waldviertel, sel, poivre
Raviolis au jarret de porc I 2 jarrets de porc I 8 grains de poivre I 2 feuilles de laurier I 200 g de légumes-racines (carottes, rave jaune, céleri) I 1 oignon I 2 cuillères à soupe d'huile de tournesol I ½ l de vin blanc I 50 g de beurre froid I 200 g de pâte à pâtes fraîches (voir recette de base page 78) I Sel, graines de cumin I Beurre pour la poêle

Carré de cochon de lait I Entailler la couenne avec un couteau aiguisé, saler et poivrer de tous les côtés. Frotter la viande avec un peu de cumin, la recouvrir de romarin, thym, laurier et ail pressé, puis l'enduire d'huile d'olive. Mettre précautionneusement le carré de cochon de lait dans un sac sous vide, faire le vide au maximum et cuire au bain-marie 3 heures et demie à 4 heures, à 75 degrés maximum. Si vous ne possédez pas de dispositif sous vide chez vous, vous pouvez le demander à votre boucher. Sortir le carré de cochon de lait du sac sous vide, le tamponner pour le sécher et le faire griller, la couenne tournée vers le bas, sur une plaque à griller ou dans une grosse poêle, jusqu'à ce qu'il soit croustillant. Réserver au chaud.

Raviolis au jarret de porc I Préchauffer le four à 200 degrés. Couvrir le jarret d'eau, laisser mijoter 1 heure environ avec les grains de poivre, les feuilles de laurier, le cumin et le sel. Faire dorer dans une sauteuse les légumes-racines coupés en gros morceaux et les oignons coupés en dés dans l'huile d'olive. Retirer le jarret du bouillon, le tamponner pour le sécher, le mettre dans la sauteuse et le faire griller rapidement avec les légumes. Mouiller avec le vin blanc et faire cuire au four pendant 40 minutes environ.

Retirer le jarret de la sauteuse, racler la peau gélatineuse avec un petit couteau et la hacher finement. Détacher la chair du jarret et la hacher elle aussi finement. Ecraser dans un saladier la moitié des légumes cuits à l'aide d'une fourchette. Mélanger la chair du jarret, la peau et les légumes, assaisonner avec le sel et le poivre.

Bien faire griller le reste des légumes-racines avec les os, verser 2 litres d'eau et laisser mijoter 20 minutes, afin de préparer une sauce. Passer le fond à travers une passoire à trous fins et réduire à ¼ de litre. Saler et poivrer, puis monter avec le beurre.

Abaisser aussi finement que possible la pâte à l'aide de la machine à pâtes. Badigeonner la moitié de la pâte avec un peu d'eau, y répartir la farce en petits tas, recouvrir avec la deuxième moitié, bien appuyer sur les bords et découper des raviolis. Cuire 2 minutes environ dans l'eau salée et faire revenir dans une poêle avec le beurre.

Chou pointu I Vous pouvez utiliser du chou blanc à la place de chou pointu, mais il n'est pas aussi fin en goût et en texture. Séparer le chou en feuilles, enlever les trognons et couper les feuilles en fins copeaux de 3 x 3 centimètres environ. Faire chauffer la moitié du beurre dans une large poêle, y ajouter les lanières de chou et les faire rissoler légèrement. Mouiller avec 60 ml d'eau, ajouter le reste de beurre et réduire jusqu'à obtenir une consistance onctueuse. Saler et poivrer.

Présentation I Dresser le chou pointu sur les assiettes et disposer des parts de cochon de lait dessus. Ajouter les raviolis et la sauce.

Couronne de veau avec
raviolis aux ris de veau, crème de persil racine et beurre persillé
Pour 4 personnes I Photo Page 74

Couronne de veau I 1 ½ kg de couronne de veau avec os I 2 cuillères à soupe d'huile I 1 branche de sauge I 2 cuillères à soupe de beurre I Sel, poivre

Raviolis I 160 g de farine de blé (type 550) I 160 g de semoule de blé dur I 2 œufs I 2 jaunes d'œufs I 15 ml d'huile d'olive I Semoule de blé dur pour abaisser la pâte I 1 œuf pour badigeonner I 20 petits morceaux de ris de veau I 2 cuillères à soupe de beurre

Crème de persil racine I 300 g de persil racine I 50 g de beurre bruni I 100 g de crème I Sel

Beurre persillé I 100 g de feuilles de persil I 75 g de beurre I 20 g d'eau I Sel

Présentation I Girolles I Jeunes oignons I Un peu de beurre

Couronne de veau I Préchauffer le four (sole et dôme) à 200 degrés. Saler et poivrer la couronne de veau. Faire chauffer l'huile dans une poêle et bien saisir la viande de tous les côtés. Cuire au four pendant 40 minutes environ de sorte que la viande soit rosée. Faire brunir le beurre dans une poêle, y ajouter la sauge et poêler rapidement la couronne de veau.

Raviolis I Pétrir la farine, la semoule, les œufs, les jaunes d'œufs et l'huile d'olive, ajouter de l'eau si besoin pour obtenir une pâte souple. Laisser reposer à couvert pendant 1 heure environ au réfrigérateur. Abaisser finement la pâte à l'aide d'une machine à pâtes, en saupoudrant régulièrement avec un peu de semoule.

Pocher les morceaux de ris de veau pendant quelques minutes et les égoutter. Disposer les morceaux espacés de 4 centimètres sur la moitié de la pâte, badigeonner les bords avec le jaune d'œuf. Recouvrir avec la deuxième moitié de la pâte, découper les raviolis et bien appuyer sur les bords. Faire cuire les raviolis dans une grosse casserole pendant 2 minutes environ, les égoutter et les faire revenir dans une poêle avec un peu de beurre.

Crème de persil racine I Eplucher le persil racine, le couper en gros morceaux, le faire cuire dans de l'eau légèrement salée et égoutter. Ajouter au persil racine cuit le beurre bruni avec la crème, mixer, saler et passer à travers une passoire à trous fins.

Beurre persillé I Laver le persil, l'équeuter et le blanchir rapidement. Le refroidir, le travailler en une pâte dans un robot avec le reste des ingrédients. Réchauffer doucement la pâte et émulsionner à l'aide d'un fouet ou d'un mixeur à main, puis passer à travers une passoire à trous fins.

Présentation I Faire sauter rapidement les girolles et les jeunes oignons coupés en tranches. Découper la couronne de veau en parts, les disposer sur les assiettes et les entourer de beurre persillé. Dresser les raviolis et la crème de persil racine, servir avec les girolles.

Gigot d'agneau de lait sur blettes
à l'étouffée et gâteau de pommes de terre
Ingrédients pour 6 personnes I Photo Page 76

Gigot d'agneau de lait I 1 gigot d'agneau de lait I 1 cuillère à soupe de moutarde de Pommery I 1 branche de romarin I 1 branche de thym I 1 cuillère à soupe d'huile d'olive I 1 cuillère à soupe de beurre I 1 cuillère à soupe d'huile de tournesol I Sel, poivre I 1 sac sous vide

Gâteau de pommes de terre I 5 pommes de terre I 1 bouquet de blettes rouges I 1 échalote I 1 gousse d'ail I 2 cuillères à soupe de beurre I 4 cuillères à soupe de pommes de terre moulinées I 1 œuf I 1 jaune d'œuf pour badigeonner I Sel, poivre, muscade

Présentation I ¼ l de sauce d'agneau

Gigot d'agneau de lait I Saler et poivrer le gigot, l'enduire de moutarde, de fines herbes hachées et d'huile d'olive. Le mettre dans un sac sous vide, faire le vide (le boucher peut également s'en charger) et laisser mariner dans de l'eau à 72 degrés pendant 3 heures. Le sortir et le faire rôtir dans l'huile et le beurre.

Gâteau de pommes de terre I Râper les pommes de terre en 12 rondelles, les réserver pour les moules à savarin. Couper le reste des pommes de terre en allumettes. Les faire bouillir dans l'eau salée, puis les refroidir dans de la glace. Couper les blettes en fines lamelles. Couper l'échalote et l'ail en dés fins et les faire suer dans le beurre. Y ajouter les blettes, assaisonner et les faire cuire à l'étouffée à petit feu, jusqu'à ce qu'elles soient tendres et que l'eau se soit presque toute évaporée. Réserver quelques blettes pour le dressage.

Lier le reste du mélange avec les pommes de terre moulinées, y ajouter l'œuf et assaisonner. Mettre une couche de rondelles de pommes de terre au fond du moule à savarin, tapisser les parois du moule avec les allumettes, remplir avec le mélange de blettes et refermer avec une autre couche de rondelles de pommes de terre. Badigeonner avec le jaune d'œuf et cuire dans le four à air chaud à 200 degrés pendant 15 minutes.

Présentation I Dresser sur les assiettes le mélange de blettes réservé, découper le gigot d'agneau, le placer sur les blettes et servir avec le gâteau de pommes de terre et la sauce d'agneau.

Faux-filet rosé de bœuf aux asperges blanches,
crêpes de pommes de terre et sauce béarnaise
Ingrédients pour 6 personnes I Photo Page 78

Faux-filet de bœuf I Un morceau entier de faux-filet de bœuf de 800 g environ I Un peu de moutarde de Dijon I 1 branche de thym I Sel, poivre blanc fraîchement moulu

Asperges blanches I 18 grosses asperges blanches I Jus d'½ citron I 1 petit pain I Sel, sucre

Crêpes de pommes de terre I 4 pommes de terre de taille moyenne I 4 jaunes d'œufs I 1 cuillère à soupe de beurre mou I Huile pour friture I Sel, poivre

Sauce béarnaise I 4 jaunes d'œufs I 1 cuillère à soupe de vin blanc I 2 cuillères à soupe de bouillon de bœuf I 1 cuillère à soupe de crème I Jus d'½ citron I 300 g de beurre clarifié tiède 2–3 cuillère à soupe de estragon haché I 1 pincée de piment de Cayenne I Sel, poivre

Faux-filet de bœuf I Assaisonner le faux-filet avec le sel et le poivre blanc fraîchement moulu, le badigeonner de moutarde et le saisir de tous les côtés avec la branche de thym dans une poêle très chaude. Le mettre dans le four préchauffé à 160 degrés pendant 1 heure environ.

Asperges blanches ▌ Peler soigneusement les asperges et les faire bouillir 1 minute avec le jus de citron, le petit pain et un peu de sel, les retirer du feu et les laisser infuser pendant 2 heures.

Crêpes de pommes de terre ▌ Faire bouillir les pommes de terre, les éplucher et les passer dans un presse-purée. Les mélanger avec les jaunes d'œufs, le sel et le poivre jusqu'à obtenir une pâte lisse. Incorporer le beurre former des médaillons et poêler dans l'huile brûlante pour les faire dorer.

Sauce béarnaise ▌ Mélanger les jaunes d'œufs avec le vin blanc, le bouillon de bœuf, la crème, le jus de citron et battre en mousse au-dessus de la vapeur d'eau. Ajouter le beurre tout en continuant de battre. Pour terminer, assaisonner avec le sel et le piment de Cayenne, puis ajouter l'estragon haché menu.

Présentation ▌ Découper le faux-filet en parts, les disposer sur l'assiette, dresser les asperges, napper de sauce hollandaise et servir avec les médaillons.

Filet de bœuf d'Attergau au céleri et foie d'oie rôti
Ingrédients pour 4 personnes ▌ Photo Page 80

Filet ▌ 600 g de filet de bœuf ▌ 1 cuillère à soupe de beurre ▌ Sel, poivre
Céleri ▌ 1 céleri-rave ▌ 1 branche de céleri ▌ 250 ml de fond de veau ▌ 150 ml de crème ▌ Sel, poivre, muscade
Foie d'oie ▌ 4 foies d'oie de 50 g chacun ▌ Un peu de farine ▌ Un peu d'huile d'olive ▌ Sel, poivre
Présentation ▌ 6 cl de glace de veau

Filet ▌ Nettoyer le filet de bœuf, le diviser en 4 morceaux et assaisonner, faire lentement rôtir les morceaux de chaque côté dans du beurre jusqu'à ce que la viande soit cuite à point. Laisser reposer 1 à 2 minutes.

Céleri ▌ Eplucher le rave et la branche de céleri. Les couper tous les deux en morceaux réguliers de la taille d'une noix et réserver les morceaux restants irréguliers du céleri-rave. Faire cuire dans un premier temps « al dente » dans le fond de veau les noix de céleri-rave, puis y ajouter le céleri-branche, laisser bouillir doucement et les retirer de l'eau. Faire cuire alors les morceaux restants du céleri-rave, les mixer finement avec la crème et assaisonner avec le sel, le poivre et la muscade.

Foie d'oie ▌ Assaisonner les foies d'oie, les passer dans la farine et les faire revenir de chaque côté pendant 1 ½ minute environ, dans une poêle avec revêtement antiadhésif.

Présentation ▌ Chauffer la glace de veau dans une casserole. Etaler la purée de céleri sur les assiettes, placer le filet au centre et l'encercler de légumes. Couronner avec le foie d'oie et arroser de glace de veau.

Foie de chevreuil poêlé au carpaccio de betteraves rouges et vinaigrette au raifort
Ingrédients pour 4 personnes ▌ Photo Page 82

Carpaccio ▌ 4 betteraves rouges (de même taille) ▌ 2 cuillères à soupe de moutarde de Dijon ▌ Vinaigre balsamique ▌ Huile d'olive ▌ Cumin, en quantité ▌ Sel, poivre
Foie de chevreuil ▌ 400 g de foie de chevreuil ▌ 100 g de farine ▌ 1 œuf ▌ 100 g de chapelure ▌ Beurre fondu pour frire le foie
Présentation ▌ Purée de pommes de terre (voir recette page 73) ▌ Raifort fraîchement râpé, selon les goûts

Carpaccio ▌ Eplucher les betteraves rouges et les cuire dans de l'eau avec beaucoup de cumin. Laisser refroidir et les couper en tranches fines d'1 millimètre environ à l'aide d'une machine à trancher. Mélanger rapidement 100 grammes de restes de betteraves à 200 millilitres de fond de cuisson, la moutarde de Dijon, quelques filets d'huile d'olive et de vinaigre balsamique, jusqu'à obtenir une consistance onctueuse.

Foie de chevreuil ▌ Retirer la peau et déveiner le foie de chevreuil, le couper en tranches de 3 centimètres d'épaisseur, poivrer uniquement. Le paner dans la farine, l'œuf et la chapelure et le faire dorer. Bien le laisser égoutter sur un papier absorbant.

Présentation ▌ Disposer les betteraves rouges en écailles sur l'assiette, arroser avec la sauce onctueuse et saupoudrer de raifort selon les goûts.

Râble de chevreuil au confit de graines de courge et aux tranches de semoule
Ingrédients pour 4 personnes ▌ Photo Page 84

Dos de chevreuil ▌ 4 faux-filets de chevreuil de 140 g ▌ 2 cuillères à soupe de persil haché ▌ 5 baies de genévrier ▌ 1 cuillère à soupe d'huile ▌ 300 ml de fond de gibier ▌ 50 g d'airelles rouges ▌ 1 cuillère à café de beurre ▌ Sel, poivre
Confit de graines de courge ▌ 200 g de chair de courge ▌ ½ oignon ▌ 2 cuillères à soupe d'huile d'olive ▌ 50 g de miel ▌ 50 g de graines de courge ▌ Sel, poivre
Tranches de semoule ▌ ¼ l de lait ▌ 125 ml de crème ▌ 125 ml de fond de légumes ▌ 150 g de semoule de blé ▌ 10 g de beurre froid ▌ 10 g de parmesan râpé ▌ 1 cuillère à soupe d'huile d'olive Sel, poivre, muscade

Râble de chevreuil ▌ Assaisonner le râble de chevreuil avec le sel, le poivre, le persil et les baies de genévrier écrasées. Bien saisir des deux côtés dans de l'huile chaude. Cuire à point au four à 180 degrés pendant 5 minutes environ, puis retirer de la poêle et garder au chaud. Mouiller avec le fond de gibier, passer, ajouter airelles rouges, laisser épaissir et lier avec un peu de beurre.

Confit de graines de courge ▌ Couper la chair de courge en dés et faire suer avec l'oignon haché dans l'huile d'olive chaude. Saler et poivrer, ajouter le miel, laisser mijoter un peu puis incorporer les graines de courge hachées et grillées.

Tranches de semoule ▌ Assaisonner le lait, la crème et le fond de légumes avec le sel, le poivre et la muscade, porter à ébullition, ajouter la semoule et laisser épaissir. Retirer du feu, incorporer le beurre et le parmesan, étaler sur une plaque à pâtisserie sur une hauteur de 1 ½ centimètres environ et bien laisser refroidir pendant 2 à 3 heures.

Découper des tranches de semoule en cercles ou en losanges. Badigeonner une feuille d'aluminium d'huile d'olive, la mettre sur le gril, déposer les tranches de semoule et les faire griller des deux côtés.

Présentation ▌ Placer les tranches de semoule sur les assiettes, dresser le râble de chevreuil dessus et servir avec le confit de graines de courge et un peu de sauce.

Faon sur lit de salade de pommes de terre et roquette
Ingrédients pour 4 personnes ▌ Photo Page 86

Salade de pommes de terre ▌ 400 g de pommes de terre ▌ 2 cuillères à soupe de vinaigre de vin blanc ▌ 3 cuillères à soupe d'huile de tournesol ▌ 1 oignon ▌ Un peu de sucre ▌ Sel, poivre blanc
Faon ▌ 400 g de faon (gigot ou morceaux de râble) ▌ 1 œuf ▌ 100 g de chapelure et 100 g de farine pour paner ▌ Persil fraîchement haché ▌ Saindoux pour frire ▌ Sel, poivre
Présentation ▌ 200 g de roquette

Salade de pommes de terre et roquette ▌ Laver et cuire les pommes de terre, les laisser ensuite refroidir légèrement, les peler et les couper en tranches. Préparer une vinaigrette avec le vinaigre, l'huile, le sel, le poivre et le sucre. Couper les oignons en dés fins et ajouter aux pommes de terre avec la vinaigrette. Bien mélanger et laisser mariner à température ambiante pendant ½ heure, puis assaisonner de nouveau, les pommes de terre absorbant fortement les arômes.

Faon ▌ Découper le faon en parts et les aplatir, assaisonner avec le sel, le poivre et le persil. Le passer successivement dans la farine, l'œuf battu et la chapelure puis le cuire dans le saindoux chaud.

Présentation ▌ Dresser la salade de pommes de terre sur une assiette, disposer les morceaux de faon par-dessus et garnir de roquette.

Gigot de sanglier braisé à la sauce lard-lentilles, avec Knödel de brioche Palfy au persil-racine
Ingrédients pour 8–10 personnes I Photo Page 88

Gigot I 1 gigot de sanglier I 1 cuillère à soupe de baies de genévrier I 2 cuillères à soupe d'huile I 2 oignons I 4 carottes I 3 racines de persil tubéreux I 2 branches de thym I 1 feuille de laurier I 2 cuillères à soupe de Xérès I 1 cuillère à soupe de miel I 1 l de fond de gibier I Sel, poivre
Sauce lard-lentilles I 100 g de lard maigre fumé I 3 échalotes I 1 gousse d'ail I 4 cl de vinaigre balsamique I 90 g de lentilles rouges I ¼ l de fond de légumes I ¼ l de crème I 20 g de beurre Sel, poivre, persil
Persil-racine I 4 racines de persil tubéreux I 2 cuillères à soupe d'huile d'olive I 1 cl de vinaigre de vin blanc I 6 cl de fond de bœuf I 50 g de persil I Sel, poivre
Knödel de brioche Palfy I 250 g de brioche rassie I 150 ml de lait I 100 ml de crème I ½ oignon 40 g de beurre I 4 œufs I 15 g de crème fouettée I Sel, poivre, muscade

Jambon I Frotter le gigot avec le sel, le poivre et les baies de genévrier hâchées. Chauffer l'huile dans une poêle et bien saisir le gigot des deux côtés. Cuire au four à 220 degrés pendant 30 minutes.
Laver les oignons, les carottes et le persil-racine, les éplucher et les couper en gros dés. Répartir les légumes et les épices autour du gigot, y ajouter un peu de fond de gibier et réduire la chaleur à 180 degrés. Cuire à point pendant 1 heure environ en arrosant régulièrement la viande avec son propre jus. Si nécessaire, verser encore un peu de fond de gibier.
Sortir le gigot, le tenir 10 minutes au chaud et augmenter la chaleur du four à 250 degrés. Dégraisser le fond de rôti, le mouiller avec un peu d'eau et le laisser fortement épaissir. Le passer à travers une passoire et assaisonner avec du Xérès. Enduire de miel le gigot, le remettre dans la poêle et le laisser glacer quelques minutes au four. Assaisonner avec le poivre fraîchement moulu.
Sauce lard-lentilles I Couper en dés le lard, les échalotes et l'ail, faire revenir un peu le lard, ajouter les échalotes et l'ail et les faire suer jusqu'à ce qu'ils soient transparents, mouiller avec le vinaigre balsamique et réduire. Y verser le fond de légumes et la crème et assaisonner avec le sel et le poivre. Laisser de nouveau épaissir. Délayer le beurre au fouet. Faire tremper les lentilles, les laisser égoutter et incorporer le persil hâché avant de servir.
Persil-racine I Eplucher les racines de persil tubéreux et les couper en morceaux. Chauffer l'huile d'olive et faire revenir les racines. Mouiller avec le vinaigre de vin blanc, saler et poivrer. Incorporer le persil hâché avant de servir.
Knödel (quenelles) de brioche Palfy I Couper la brioche en dés, mélanger avec le lait et la crème. Faire fondre les oignons finement hachés dans du beurre jusqu'à ce qu'ils soient transparents. Battre les œufs dans un saladier et incorporer aux dés de brioche mélangés à la crème fouettée. Assaisonner avec le sel, le poivre et la muscade. Bien malaxer et laisser reposer pendant ½ heure. Former de petites quenelles à partir du mélange, faire cuire 12 minutes à petit feu dans de l'eau bouillante salée.
Présentation I Trancher le gigot de sanglier, dresser les lentilles et servir avec les quenelles et les bâtonnets de persil-racine.

Rôti de mou de cerf dans un gâteau à la broche avec gnocchis aux marrons et pruneaux
Ingrédients pour 4 personnes I Photo Page 90

Rôti de mou de cerf I 600 g de rôti de mou de cerf I 150 g de gâteau à la broche I 50 g de farce de veau I 4 feuilles de pâte à Strudel I 2 cuillères à soupe d'huile I Sel, poivre et baies de genévrier
Gnocchis aux marrons et pruneaux I 100 g de pommes de terre I 100 g de purée de marrons 20 g de de fécule de pommes de terre I 1 cuillères à soupe de beurre I 1 jaune d'œuf I 25 g de pruneaux I Sel, poivre
Présentation I Coings confits I Bouillon de gibier (voir recette de base page 78) I 250 ml de sauce de cerf

Rôti de mou de cerf I Nettoyer le rôti de mou de cerf, le couper en quatre morceaux de même grosseur et assaisonner. Découper la pâte à Strudel en quatre morceaux de 15 x 15 centimètres, couper le gâteau à la broche en tranches fines et les disposer en éventail. Recouvrir avec la farce et mettre par-dessus le rôti de mou de cerf. Enrouler et saisir dans l'huile de tous les côtés, pour terminer cuire à point à 180 degrés pendant 5 minutes et laisser reposer 5 minutes à 80 degrés.
Gnocchis aux marrons et pruneaux I Cuire les pommes de terre dans leur peau, les laisser sécher quelques instants, les peler, les passer encore chaudes au presse-purée et mélanger à la purée de marrons. Ajouter la fécule de pommes de terre, le beurre et le jaune d'œuf et malaxer jusqu'à obtenir une pâte. Hacher finement les pruneaux, former des petites boules et les congeler. Dès qu'ils sont durs, former les gnocchis et les fourrer avec les boules de pruneaux. Faire cuire quelques minutes dans de l'eau chaude salée.
Présentation I Dresser les gnocchis avec les coings confits et le bouillon de gibier, placer le rôti de mou de cerf et ajouter la sauce de cerf.

Millefeuille à la mousse de yogourt et myrtilles
Ingrédients pour 10 parts I Photo Page 92

Crème à la vanille I 125 g de sucre I 60 g de poudre pour flan I 100 g de jaunes d'œufs I 500 ml de lait I 250 ml de crème fouettée
Gelée de myrtilles I 250 g de concentré de myrtilles I 25 g de sucre I 2 feuilles de gélatine
Glace à la crème brûlée I 375 ml de crème I 375 ml de lait I 2 gousses de vanille I 7 jaunes d'œuf 60 g de sucre I 50 g de sucre roux
Mousse de yogourt I 250 g de yogourt I 25 g de sucre I 2 feuilles de gélatine I 125 ml de crème
Sauce aux myrtilles I 200 g de myrtilles I 25 g de sucre I Jus d'un citron
Pâte I 500 g de pâte feuilletée I Un peu de sucre I Un peu de sucre glace
Présentation I Baies fraîches

Crème à la vanille I Battre le sucre, la poudre pour flan et les jaunes d'œufs, jusqu'à ce que le mélange soit clair et épais. Porter le lait à ébullition et le verser sur le mélange, transvaser dans une casserole et le porter de nouveau à ébullition. Mettre au froid, puis incorporer la crème fouettée. Remplir une poche à douille à embout lisse et réserver au froid.
Gelée de myrtilles I Porter le concentré de myrtilles et le sucre à ébullition, ajouter la gélatine ramollie et bien mélanger. Verser sur une plaque à pâtisserie recouverte de papier sulfurisé et mettre au frais. A l'aide d'un petit emporte-pièces de forme ronde, découper 50 ronds.
Glace à la crème brûlée I Porter à ébullition la crème, le lait, les graines de vanille grattées ainsi que les gousses. Battre les jaunes d'œufs et le sucre jusqu'à obtenir un mélange blanchâtre et mélanger avec la préparation précédente. Retirer les gousses et verser le mélange sur une plaque à bords hauts. Cuire au four à 90 degrés pendant 1 heure environ. Saupoudrer ensuite de sucre roux et caraméliser à l'aide d'un chalumeau ou d'une lampe à souder. Verser la crème brûlée dans un saladier et bien mixer. Remplir les moules Pacojet et congeler. Remuer avec le Pacojet avant emploi.
Mousse de yogourt I Mélanger le yogourt avec le sucre, y ajouter la gélatine ramollie et pressée puis bien mélanger. Incorporer la crème fouettée, remplir à moitié des verres à cocktail avec la mousse et réserver au froid.
Sauce aux myrtilles I Faire cuire à l'étouffée les fruits et le sucre. Bien mixer et ajouter le jus d'un citron et passer à travers une passoire à trous fins.
Pâte I Etaler la pâte feuilletée sur une épaisseur de 3 millimètres environ, la mettre sur une plaque à pâtisserie recouverte de papier sulfurisé et saupoudrer avec un peu de sucre. Cuire à 175 degrés pendant 20 à 25 minutes environ. A mi-cuisson, recouvrir avec une autre plaque à pâtisserie. Pour terminer, mettre au froid et couper en morceaux de 4 ½ x 4 ½ centimètres. Séparer les feuilles, saupoudrer avec un peu de sucre glace et caraméliser à l'aide d'un chalumeau ou d'une lampe à souder (env. 10 feuilles par parts).
Présentation I Avant de servir, faire mariner les myrtilles dans une assiette avec la sauce aux myrtilles. Monter en alternance les feuilles de pâte feuilletée et la crème à la vanille et ajouter en plus un rond de gelée de myrtilles, un étage sur deux. Décorer les assiettes avec la sauce aux myrtilles selon ses envies, et déposer la glace sur le millefeuille. Dresser joliment les baies sur la mousse.

Dessert aux abricots, cardamome et amandes
Ingrédients pour 10 parts I Photo Page 94

Croquant à la cardamome I 100 g de sucre roux I 250 g de farine I 125 g de beurre I 1 jaune d'œuf I Un peu de cardamome moulue
Tuiles I 30 g de beurre I 100 g de sucre roux I 50 g de blancs d'œufs I 75 g de farine
Abricots poêlés I 20 abricots frais I 25 g de sucre I 25 g de beurre I 1 cuillère à café de miel I Un peu de cardamome moulue
Brioche I 1 Brioche I 25 g de beurre I 1 pincée de sucre
Mousse d'amande I 200 ml de lait I 100 g de pâte d'amandes I 50 g de calissons (confiserie du sud de la France) I 2 feuilles de gélatine I 2 gouttes d'arôme d'amande amère I 125 ml de crème
Sorbet d'abricots I 500 g d'abricots mûrs I 160 g de sucre I 50 g de glucose I Jus d'un citron
Glace aux amandes I 500 ml de lait I 185 g de sucre I 6 jaunes d'œufs I 150 g d'amandes concassées grillées I 100 ml de crème
Mousse d'abricots et cardamome I 200 g de concentré d'abricots I 100 g de crème légère I 25 g de sucre I 1 feuille de gélatine I 1 pincée de cardamome

Croquant à la cardamome I Mettre tous les ingrédients dans un mixeur à lame horizontale et travailler jusqu'à obtenir une poudre. Répartir sur une plaque à pâtisserie recouverte de papier sulfurisé et réserver au froid.
Tuiles I Faire fondre le beurre et le faire brunir légèrement. Mélanger le sucre, le blanc d'œuf, la farine et le beurre. A l'aide d'une spatule, étaler en fines couches (3 x 18 centimètres) sur une plaque à pâtisserie recouverte de papier sulfurisé, ajouter le croquant à la cardamome et cuire au four à 180 degrés, jusqu'à ce que les tuiles deviennent dorées. Enrouler les tuiles encore tièdes autour d'un rouleau à pâtisserie.
Abricots poêlés I Dénoyauter les abricots et les couper en huit, faire fondre le beurre dans la poêle, ajouter le sucre, le miel et laisser caraméliser légèrement. Y ajouter les abricots, saupoudrer de cardamome, laisser doucement poêler, puis réserver au froid.
Brioche I Couper la brioche en tranches de 5 millimètres d'épaisseur et découper des anneaux de la taille du diamètre du rouleau à pâtisserie. Faire revenir dans du beurre légèrement sucré.
Mousse d'amande I Porter le lait à ébullition, ajouter la pâte d'amandes et les calissons. Faire ramollir la gélatine, la presser et l'y ajouter. Arômatiser, mixer le tout et le mettre au froid jusqu'à ce qu'il se fige un peu. Incorporer la crème au mélange encore liquide.
Verser dans un cadre à pâtisserie (8 x 20 centimètres). Mettre au frais jusqu'à ce que le mélange devienne ferme et découper à la taille de la brioche.
Sorbet d'abricots I Dénoyauter les abricots, les mettre dans une casserole, ajouter le sucre et le glucose. Lorsque les abricots sont cuits, ajouter le jus de citron, mixer finement et passer à travers une passoire. Remplir un moule Pacojet et congeler. Remuer avec le Pacojet avant emploi.
Glace à l'amande I Porter le lait et le sucre à ébullition, ajouter les jaunes d'œufs et confectionner une crème anglaise au bain-marie à 84 degrés, en mélangeant constamment. Incorporer les amandes et la crème, mélanger, remplir un moule Pacojet et congeler. Remuer avec le Pacojet avant emploi.
Mousse d'abricots et cardamome I Porter le concentré d'abricots à ébullition, ajouter le sucre, la cardamome et la gélatine ramollie. Bien mélanger, puis mettre au froid. Incorporer la crème légère au mélange et en remplir une bouteille iSi.
Présentation I Pour terminer, mettre la mousse sur les brioches posées dans les tuiles, déposer les abricots poêlés dessus et recouvrir de mousse d'abricots. Remplir un petit pot de mousse d'amande et décorer avec la glace et le sorbet.

Dessert au chocolat, whisky et café
Ingrédients pour 10 parts I Photo Page 96

Biscuit au chocolat I 150 g de beurre I 100 g de chocolat noir à 66% de cacao I 120 g d'œufs I 180 g de sucre I 80 g de farine
Ganache au chocolat I 250 ml de crème I 175 g de chocolat «Pur Caraïbe»
Feuilles de filo caramélisées I 3 feuilles de pâte filo I 50 g de beurre I 20 g de sucre glace I 10 g de cacao en poudre
Crème au chocolat I 25 g de sucre I 50 g de jaunes d'œufs I 125 ml de lait I 125 ml de crème I 140 g de chocolat au lait Jivara
Mousse au whisky I 25 g de sucre I 25 g de jaunes d'œufs I 125 ml de lait I 1 feuille de gélatine I 65 ml de crème I 15 g de whisky
Parfait au café I 150 g de chocolat de couverture blanc I 20 g de sucre I 40 g de jaunes d'œufs I 100 ml de lait I 100 ml de crème I 1 feuille de gélatine I 5 g de Nescafé
Tuiles en sucre I 75 g de fondant I 75 g de glucose I 75 g d'isomalt I 1 fève Tonka

Biscuit au chocolat I Faire fondre le beurre et le chocolat dans le micro-ondes. Battre légèrement les œufs et le sucre. Mélanger les deux préparations, ajouter la farine et étaler sur 2 centimètres de hauteur environ sur une plaque à pâtisserie beurrée et farinée. Cuire au four à 180 degrés pendant 12 minutes environ, couper en morceaux de 6 x 6 centimètres.
Ganache I Porter la crème à ébullition et la verser sur le chocolat. Bien mélanger le tout jusqu'à obtenir un mélange homogène et souple. Laisser refroidir et mettre dans une poche à douille à embout lisse.
Feuilles de filo caramélisées I Couper les feuilles en 20 carrés de 8 x 8 centimètres. Faire fondre le beurre, mélanger avec le sucre glace et le cacao en poudre et tartiner les morceaux de pâte avec ce mélange. Les mettre sur une plaque à pâtisserie recouverte de papier sulfurisé, couvrir d'un deuxième papier sulfurisé et recouvrir avec une autre plaque à pâtisserie. Cuire au four à 160 degrés, jusqu'à ce que les feuilles soient bien caramélisées.
Crème au chocolat I Battre le sucre et les jaunes d'œufs jusqu'à ce que le mélange soit clair et épais. Porter le lait avec la crème à ébullition, verser sur le mélange œufs-sucre, transvaser dans une casserole et chauffer de nouveau à 86 degrés. Ajouter le chocolat, incorporer et bien mélanger. Mettre au frais et en remplir une poche à douille à embout étoilé pour le dressage.
Mousse au whisky I Battre le sucre et les jaunes d'œufs jusqu'à ce que le mélange soit clair et épais. Porter le lait à ébullition, verser sur le mélange œufs-sucre, transvaser dans une casserole et chauffer à 86 degrés. Ajouter la gélatine ramollie, la crème et le whisky, bien mélanger et verser dans une bouteille iSi.
Parfait au café I Faire fondre le chocolat blanc. Battre le sucre et les œufs, jusqu'à ce que le mélange soit clair et épais. Porter le lait avec la crème à ébullition, verser sur le mélange œufs-sucre, transvaser dans une casserole et chauffer à 86 degrés. Incorporer la gélatine ramollie et le chocolat. Y ajouter le Nescafé et bien mélanger le tout. Poser des moules cylindres (diamètre 3 centimètres, hauteur 5 centimètres) sur un papier sulfurisé, les remplir avec le mélange, puis les mettre à congeler.
Tuiles I Mettre le fondant, le glucose et l'isomalt dans une casserole et chauffer à 165 degrés. Répartir sur une feuille à pâtisserie en silicone et laisser sécher. Emietter le mélange et mixer finement au mixeur. Répartir de nouveau sur la feuille à pâtisserie en silicone et râper dessus la fève Tonka à l'aide d'une râpe à noix de muscade. Cuire au four à 190 degrés jusqu'à ce que le sucre soit bien fondu. Laisser durcir et couper en morceaux souhaités.
Présentation I Mettre la ganache sur le fond de biscuit. Y déposer une feuille de filo et dresser une couche de crème au chocolat dessus. Couvrir avec une autre feuille de filo et déposer une autre couche de crème au chocolat. Déposer le parfait sur le dessus, décorer avec les tuiles et un jet de mousse au whisky.

Barre de nougat, glace au thé matcha et banane
Ingrédients pour 10 personnes I Photo Page 98

Dacquoise de noisettes I 85 g de sucre glace I 85 g de noisettes râpées I 100 g de blancs d'œufs I 30 g de sucre
Mousse au nougat I 100 ml de lait I 2 feuilles de gélatine I 200 g de pâte de nougat I 250 ml de crème I 150 g de beurre de cacao I 300 g de chocolat blanc
Glace au thé matcha I 125 g de sucre I 100 g de jaunes d'œufs I 500 ml de lait I 100 ml de crème I 10 g de thé matcha sous forme de poudre
Compote de bananes I 250 g de bananes I 25 g de sucre roux I Jus et zestes d'1 limette
Gelée au lait I 125 ml de lait I 20 g de sucre I 1 feuille de gélatine
Gelée au citron I 125 g de glaçure neutre I 65 ml de jus de citron I Zestes d'1 limette

Dacquoise de noisettes I Mixer finement le sucre glace et les noisettes. Battre les blancs d'œufs et le sucre. Incorporer les noisettes et étaler le mélange sur une plaque à pâtisserie recouverte de papier sulfurisé sur une épaisseur de 3 millimètres. Cuire au four pendant 10–12 minutes à 180 degrés, laisser refroidir et couper en morceaux de 9 x 3 centimètres.
Mousse au nougat I Porter le lait à ébullition, y dissoudre la gélatine ramollie, le verser sur la pâte de nougat et mixer finement jusqu'à ce que le mélange soit refroidi à 35 degrés. Battre la crème et l'incorporer. Remplir des moules à parois souples (9 x 3 centimètres), y poser la dacquoise de noisettes et réserver au frais.
Mélanger le beurre de cacao et le chocolat blanc, laisser fondre à 40 degrés. Remplir dans un pistolet airbrush, et vaporiser ce mélange sur la mousse froide démoulée. Puis réserver de nouveau au frais.
Glace au thé matcha I Battre le sucre et les jaunes d'œufs, jusqu'à ce que le mélange soit clair et épais. Porter le lait avec la crème à ébullition et verser sur le mélange œufs-sucre, transvaser dans une casserole et porter de nouveau à ébullition. Remplir les moules Pacojet et congeler. Remuer avec le Pacojet avant emploi.
Compote de bananes I Couper les bananes en petits morceaux, les mettre avec les autres ingrédients dans une casserole et chauffer. Couvrir avec un couvercle et laisser mijoter à faible température, jusqu'à ce que les bananes soient cuites. Travailler avec une spatule, jusqu'à ce que le mélange soit homogène.
Gelée au lait I Porter le lait et le sucre à ébullition. Y incorporer la gélatine ramollie et la dissoudre. Sur une plaque, étaler le mélange sur une hauteur de 3 centimètres environ et mettre au frais. Découper de tous petits dés de gelée solidifiée (3 x 3 millimètres).
Gelée au citron I Porter à ébullition la glaçure avec les zestes de limette et le jus de citron.
Présentation I Dresser la mousse, les gelées et la glace sur une assiette. Garnir les barres de nougat de compote de bananes à l'aide d'une poche à douille.

Tarte aux cerises, aux pêches et aux pistaches
Ingrédients pour 10 parts I Photo Page 100

Pâte sablée bretonne I 75 g de beurre mou I 75 g de sucre I 2 g de sel I 30 g de jaune d'œufs I 100 g de farine I 3 ½ g de levure chimique
Confiture de pêches I 100 g de pêches I 150 g de sucre I Un peu de jus de citron I ½ gousse de vanille
Cerises au vin I 100 g de vin rouge I 15 g de sucre I Mélange d'épices à base de vanille, poire, cardamome et cannelle I 50 g de concentré de cerises aigres I 60 de cerises
Pistaches I 25 g de sucre I 7 g d'eau I 15 g de pistaches râpées I 2 g de beurre
Mousse de pistaches I 125 g de lait I 25 g de jaunes d'œufs I 25 g de sucre I 15 g poudre pour flan I 25 g de concentré de pistaches I 1 feuille de gélatine I 75 g de crème légère
Sorbet aux pêches I 240 ml d'eau I 120 g de sucre I 500 g de concentré de pêches I 60 g de glucose I 25 ml de jus de citron
Tuiles I 12 ½ g de glucose I 25 g de fondant I 50 g de poudre de pistaches
Croquettes I 125 g de griottes au sirop I 125 g de concentré de cerises aigres I 2 g d'Agar-agar 1 œuf I 100 g de farine I 100 g de chapelure I Huile pour friture

Pâte sablée bretonne I Mélanger le beurre, le sucre et le sel et pétrir avec les jaunes d'œufs jusqu'à obtenir une consistance crémeuse. Ajouter la farine, la levure chimique et malaxer le tout jusqu'à obtenir une pâte. Former une boule et l'enrouler dans un film transparent. La laisser reposer 30 minutes au réfrigérateur. Etaler ensuite la pâte sur une épaisseur d'1 centimètre environ, découper des cercles avec des emporte-pièces ronds (diamètre 6 centimètres) et les déposer avec les emporte-pièces sur une plaque à pâtisserie recouverte de papier sulfurisé. Cuire au four à 160 degrés pendant 8 minutes environ. Retirer immédiatement les emporte-pièces à l'aide d'un couteau.
Confiture de pêches I Eplucher les pêches, les couper en deux, enlever le noyau et mélanger avec la moitié du sucre et du jus de citron. Gratter la gousse de vanille et ajouter aussi bien les graines que la gousse. Faire mijoter le tout, puis incorporer la deuxième moitié du sucre, retirer la gousse de vanille et réserver.
Cerises au vin I Réduire le vin de moitié, ajouter le sucre et les épices selon les goûts. Ajouter le concentré de cerises aigres et laisser macérer. Passer à travers une passoire à trous fins et ajouter les cerises dénoyautées. Cuire à petit feu les cerises jusqu'à ce qu'elles soient «al dente», les retirer et les mettre au froid. Réduire le sirop restant jusqu'à ce qu'il épaississe et le réserver pour la décoration.
Pistaches I Mélanger le sucre, l'eau et chauffer à 121 degrés. Ajouter les pistaches et mélanger jusqu'à ce qu'elles soient bien recouvertes de sucre. Ajouter le beurre, mélanger et étaler le mélange sur une plaque à pâtisserie recouverte de papier sulfurisé. Laisser dorer légèrement au four à 160 degrés.
Mousse de pistaches I Porter le lait à ébullition, battre les jaunes d'œufs, le sucre et la poudre pour flan jusqu'à ce que le mélange soit clair et épais. Verser le lait sur le mélange et porter de nouveau à ébullition. Incorporer le concentré de pistaches, la gélatine dissoute et laisser refroidir. Incorporer ensuite la crème légère fouettée. Remplir une poche à douille à embout lisse et réserver au froid.
Sorbet aux pêches I Confectionner un sirop à partir de l'eau, du sucre et du glucose. Ajouter au sirop chaud le concentré de pêches et le jus de citron. Mixer finement, remplir un moule Pacojet, laisser refroidir et congeler. Remuer avec le Pacojet avant l'emploi.
Tuiles I Chauffer le glucose et le fondant à 155 degrés et étaler très finement sur une plaque à pâtisserie huilée. Laisser refroidir, casser en morceaux et mixer finement au mixeur avec la poudre de pistaches. Répartir cette poudre sur le papier sulfurisé en la tamisant à travers une passoire à trous fins et cuire à 190 degrés pendant 10 minutes environ. Laisser refroidir et casser les tuiles.
Croquettes I Mélanger les griottes et le concentré de cerises aigres, porter à ébullition et ajouter l'Agar-agar. Remplir des moules à parois souples en forme de demi-sphères et congeler. Avant de présenter le plat, paner et faire frire les demi-sphères congelées.
Présentation I Dresser la confiture de pêches au centre de la pâte sablée, disposer les cerises tout autour et réchauffer brièvement au four. Déposer les tuiles dessus et dresser la mousse de pistaches. Garnir avec les pistaches caramélisées, dresser le sorbet aux pêches, disposer les croquettes à côté, puis décorer avec le sirop de vin.

Chocolats pralinés à la nougatine
Ingrédients pour 25 pièces ▮ Photo Page 102

Garniture ▮ 125 g de nougat ▮ 50 g de chocolat au lait ▮ 125 g de pailleté feuilletine (par ex. Pailleté feuilletine de Barry)
Glaçage ▮ 300 g de chocolat noir à 66 %
Garniture ▮ Faire fondre le nougat et le chocolat au lait à 32 degrés, y ajouter le pailleté feuilletine. Bien mélanger et remplir un cadre à pâtisserie sur une hauteur de 1 centimètre environ. Laisser figer à température ambiante et découper des dés de 2 x 2 centimètres.
Glaçage ▮ Faire chauffer le chocolat noir à 50 degrés, puis refroidir à 27 degrés et réchauffer de nouveau à 32 degrés. Dès que la bonne température est atteinte, plonger la garniture dans le chocolat et laisser reposer pendant au moins 12 heures à température ambiante sur des feuilles alimentaires spéciales pour le chocolat. Servir.

Tartelettes de cheesecake à l'ananas et à la noix de coco
Ingrédients pour 75 mini tartelettes ▮ Photo Page 102

Pâte brisée ▮ 250 g de sucre glace ▮ 250 g de beurre ▮ 4 jaunes d'œufs ▮ 500 g de farine
Mélange pour le cheesecake (gâteau au fromage) ▮ 600 g de fromage frais ▮ 2 œufs ▮ 1 jaune d'œuf ▮ 125 g de sucre ▮ 40 ml de crème ▮ 50 g de farine
Présentation ▮ 1 ananas ▮ 1 petit sachet de noix de coco râpée

Pâte brisée ▮ Mélanger le sucre glace et le beurre jusqu'à obtenir une consistance crémeuse, y ajouter les jaunes d'œufs et la farine puis mélanger jusqu'à obtenir une pâte lisse. Envelopper dans un film transparent et mettre au frais pendant ½ heure.
Abaisser la pâte et la précuire au four à 170 degrés pendant environ 10 minutes, jusqu'à ce qu'elle soit légèrement dorée.
Mélange pour le cheesecake ▮ Mélanger tous les ingrédients jusqu'à obtenir une consistance crémeuse. Etaler sur la pâte précuite et cuire au four à 120 degrés pendant 30 minutes environ.
Présentation ▮ Eplucher l'ananas, le découper en petits bâtonnets et rouler ceux-ci dans la noix de coco râpée. Découper en petits dés le cheesecake terminé et le décorer avec les bâtonnets d'ananas-noix de coco.

Macarons
Ingrédients pour 100 macarons ▮ Photo Page 102

250 g de sucre glace ▮ 250 g de poudre d'amandes ▮ 300 g de sucre ▮ 150 ml d'eau ▮ 200 g de blancs d'œufs ▮ Colorant alimentaire ▮ Arômes, par ex. noix de coco râpée, vanille liquide, selon les goûts

Mixer très finement le sucre glace et la poudre d'amandes et passer à travers une passoire. Chauffer le sucre et l'eau à 118 degrés. Battre en neige ferme mais souple la moitié des blancs d'œufs tout en incorporant le mélange sucre-eau. Bien mélanger le reste des blancs d'œufs avec le sucre glace-amandes. Mélanger les deux préparations et ajouter les couleurs et les arômes souhaités. Remplir une poche à douille lisse et former de petits cercles sur une plaque à pâtisserie recouverte de papier sulfurisé. Cuire au four à 160 degrés pendant 12 minutes environ. Le temps de cuisson peut varier en fonction du four utilisé.
Les macarons peuvent être remplis avec de la confiture ou de la pâte de fruits.

Nonnettes à l'orange
Ingrédients pour 50 nonnettes ▮ Photo Page 102

Nonnettes ▮ 150 g de sucre glace ▮ 150 g de beurre ▮ Zestes d'1 orange ▮ 3 œufs ▮ 190 g de farine ▮ 5 g de levure en poudre ▮ Un peu de sel
Présentation ▮ Confiture d'oranges pour la garniture ▮ Framboises, fraises, raisins noirs ▮ Sucre glace
Nonnettes ▮ Battre en mousse le beurre et le sucre et mélanger avec le reste des ingrédients. A l'aide d'une poche à douille, remplir de pâte des caissettes (en papier). Faire cuire au four à 190 degrés pendant 7 minutes environ.
Présentation ▮ Laisser refroidir, faire un petit trou et remplir de confiture d'orange à l'aide d'une poche à douille. Décorer avec les fruits et saupoudrer de sucre glace.

Brioches fourrées de crème à la vanille
Ingrédients pour 10 parts ▮ Photo Page 102

Pâte ▮ 250 g de farine ▮ 35 g de sucre ▮ 5 g de sel ▮ 50 ml de lait ▮ 10 g de levure fraîche ▮ 3 œufs ▮ 80 g de beurre mou
Crème à la vanille ▮ 50 g de sucre ▮ 30 g de poudre pour flan à la vanille ▮ 50 g de jaunes d'œufs ▮ 250 ml de lait ▮ 75 g de beurre

Pâte ▮ Mélanger la farine, le sucre et le sel. Mélanger également le lait, la levure et les œufs et verser dans le mélange farine-sucre. Y ajouter le beurre et pétrir dans le robot ou à la main jusqu'à obtenir une pâte lisse.
Laisser reposer jusqu'à ce que le volume de la pâte ait doublé. Etaler sur 1 centimètre de hauteur sur une plaque à pâtisserie recouverte de papier sulfurisé et laisser dorer légèrement au four à 180 degrés. Couper la pâte en dés de 3 x 3 centimètres.
Crème à la vanille ▮ Battre le sucre, la poudre pour flan et les jaunes d'œufs jusqu'à ce que le mélange soit clair et épais. Porter le lait à ébullition et le verser sur le mélange, le transvaser dans une casserole et le porter de nouveau à ébullition. Retirer du feu et y délayer le beurre.
Présentation ▮ Couper les dés de brioche en deux, les garnir avec la crème et décorer selon ses envies.

Catering

LOGISTIQUE ET LANGOUSTES

Comment Mörwald, chef d'entreprise, cuisinier et traiteur,
proposer à une clientèle toujours croissante d'habitués,
des produits culinaires de grande noblesse.

Les convives sont tous là, le champagne est servi. Le maître de maison fait alors asseoir les invités et demande leur attention. Il souhaite leur présenter l'homme qu'il a spécialement engagé pour cette soirée. Il s'agit de Toni Mörwald qui ce soir fera la cuisine spécialement pour ce petit cercle d'éminents gourmets.

Le menu est digne d'un restaurant gastronomique de haut niveau : velouté de homard aux écrevisses, foie d'oie glacé à la provençale, flétan poché au fenouil et, comme plat principal, des aiguillettes de canard à l'orange. Le dessert se compose d'une mousse au nougat à la menthe et aux fraises fraîches.

L'apparition n'a pas manqué son effet. Les convives ont déjà l'eau à la bouche, et les maîtres de maison semblent eux aussi parfaitement détendus. Au lieu de mettre eux-mêmes la main à la pâte, ils peuvent se consacrer à leurs invités pendant toute la soirée. Le service aussi est assuré par le personnel de Mörwald. Vers minuit, cuisiniers et serveurs font une dernière apparition pour recevoir des applaudissements enthousiastes.

Ce service s'appelle «Rent a Cook», il permet aux gourmets de faire appel à un professionnel pour faire la cuisine dans leurs propres murs sans devoir mettre le tablier, et ceci avec une qualité comme seuls les temples gourmets peuvent en offrir.

Le business du «Rent a Cook» est en plein essor. L'intervention mobile en cuisine d'éminents virtuoses du fourneau est devenue un service à la mode qui connaît une demande sans cesse croissante. «Nos carnets de commande sont pleins», dit Mörwald. «Ce domaine de prestations est récemment devenu très prospère.»

Cela fait maintenant des années que Mörwald a fait de ce service un secteur propre au sein de son empire culinaire – avec un tarif officiel et des prix fixes. L'entreprenant restaurateur arrive avec des véhicules spécialement équipés, se charge de l'ensemble des achats et, si nécessaire fournit même la vaisselle, les couverts, les verres et tous les ustensiles de cuisine nécessaires. «Nous venons au préalable examiner la cuisine et nous apportons ce qui manque», explique Mörwald. «S'il le faut nous avons une cuisine entièrement équipée dans notre véhicule».

Rent a Cook ne constitue toutefois qu'une partie du service Catering de Mörwald. Outre les interventions chez les particuliers, il prend aussi en charge des manifestations de toutes sortes. Qu'il s'agisse de réceptions, de cocktails ou de galas, l'équipe de Mörwald fournit tout le matériel et accomplit pratiquement tout ce qui est nécessaire. Depuis la nourriture jusqu'à l'équipement, du vin à la décoration, du savoir-faire culinaire aux serviettes, rien n'est laissé au hasard.

La cuisine étoilée n'est pas la seule à avoir sensiblement évolué au cours du temps. Les exigences envers un catering moderne sont elles aussi bien différentes de ce qu'elles étaient. On ne peut plus se maintenir longtemps sur ce marché fortement concurrentiel en se contentant d'une qualité moyenne.

Toni Mörwald le sait et il a reconnu depuis longtemps que le catering est plus que la simple restauration du plus grand nombre possible de personnes lors d'une soirée ou d'une fête. En tant que chef étoilé, il garantit déjà avec son seul nom une qualité exceptionnelle, et son art culinaire ne se contente pas de rassasier les convives mais ravit aussi les palais les plus exigeants.

Raviolis aux crevettes et à la ricotta
Ingrédients pour 10 personnes ∎ Photo Page 116

Raviolis ∎ 250 g de Ricotta ∎ 125 g de crevettes ∎ Fines herbes fraîches selon les goûts (persil, ciboulette, basilic, etc.) ∎ 2 œufs ∎ 200 g de pâte à pâtes fraîches ∎ 1 jaune d'œuf ∎ Sel, poivre blanc
Sauce ∎ Jus d'1 limette ∎ 125 ml de vin blanc ∎ 125 g de beurre froid ∎ 1 branche de menthe poivrée ∎ Sel, poivre, sucre
Présentation ∎ Zestes et tranches d'1 limette

Raviolis ∎ Mélanger la Ricotta, les crevettes, les fines herbes finement hachées et l'œuf. Abaisser finement la pâte, répartir la farce sur une moitié, badigeonner avec le jaune d'œuf, refermer la pâte, bien appuyer sur les bords et découper des raviolis. Faire cuire les raviolis dans de l'eau salée bouillante pendant 4 minutes environ.
Sauce ∎ Donner un bouillon au mélange de jus de limette et vin blanc, les monter avec le beurre, assaisonner avec le sel, le poivre et le sucre, puis incorporer les petites feuilles de menthe hachées.
Présentation ∎ Arroser les raviolis avec la sauce au vin blanc, garnir avec les zestes et les tranches de limette avant de servir.

Mou de veau au Riesling
Ingrédients pour 4 personnes ∎ Photo Page 118

Mou au Riesling ∎ 500 g de mou de veau (poumon et cœur) ∎ ½ oignon ∎ 1 carotte ∎ ½ poireau ∎ ¼ de céleri ∎ 1 feuille de laurier ∎ Quelques grains de poivre ∎ 1 cuillère à café de moutarde forte ∎ Jus d'un citron ∎ 1 cuillère à soupe de vinaigre de vin ∎ 1 petit cornichon ∎ 1 cuillère à café de câpres ∎ 1 cuillère à soupe de beurre ∎ ¼ l de Riesling ∎ 125 ml de crème ∎ 1 gousse d'ail ∎ 1 bouquet de persil ∎ Sel, poivre blanc
Knödel en serviette ∎ 400 g de croûtons ∎ ¼ de lait ∎ 4 œufs ∎ 20 g de persil haché ∎ 1 cuillère à soupe de beurre ∎ Sel, poivre, muscade
Présentation ∎ 4 œufs

Mou au Riesling ∎ La préparation du mou de veau constitue la majeure partie du travail, mais lorsque celle-ci est terminée, tout se déroule alors rapidement et facilement. Retirer la trachée, les gros tendons et le gras, faire tremper dans de l'eau froide pendant au moins 2 heures (ou plus si possible), afin de bien le faire dégorger. Changer l'eau plusieurs fois et remuer de temps en temps le mou de veau.
Nettoyer, ou peler le cas échéant, l'oignon, la carotte, le poireau et le céleri. Couper la moitié en gros morceaux et réserver l'autre moitié. Faire bouillir les légumes coupés grossièrement, la feuille de laurier et quelques grains de poivre écrasés dans une casserole suffisamment grosse, dans 2 litres d'eau environ. Y ajouter le mou dégorgé et cuire à couvert pendant 40 minutes environ. A ce stade de cuisson, il se peut que le mou soit déjà tendre. Le cœur a besoin habituellement de 10 à 15 minutes de plus. Retirer le mou du bouillon. Filtrer l'eau de cuisson et la réserver pour le mouillage ultérieur. Retirer les grosses veines du mou, mettre à refroidir dans un grand saladier, couvrir avec une planche et des assiettes et laisser reposer quelques heures.
Découper le mou en fines lamelles en retirant les gros cartilages. Mélanger avec la moutarde, le citron, le vinaigre, le cornichon haché menu et les câpres. Saler et poivrer, puis laisser mariner pendant 2 heures environ, toute une nuit étant l'idéal.
Pour terminer la préparation du mou, couper les légumes réservés en fines lamelles, les cuire dans de l'eau salée jusqu'à ce qu'ils soient «al dente», puis les passer sous l'eau froide. Chauffer le beurre dans une poêle suffisamment grande, y faire suer l'oignon, mouiller avec le vin blanc et faire réduire de moitié par rapport à la quantité initiale. Y ajouter les lamelles de légumes restantes ainsi que celles de mou, remplir avec le fond de mou et faire bouillir. Verser la crème et laisser réduire. Assaisonner avec le sel, le poivre blanc fraîchement moulu et l'ail pressé. Incorporer le persil haché !
Knödel en serviette ∎ Ramollir les croûtons dans le lait. Incorporer les œufs et le persil et assaisonner avec le sel, le poivre et la muscade. Enrouler le mélange à knödel dans un film transparent résistant à la chaleur en le serrant bien et pocher au bain-marie à 80 degrés pendant 40 minutes. Sortir de l'eau et mettre au frais. Enlever le film transparent, couper en tranches et faire frire des deux côtés dans le beurre.
Présentation
Déposer le mou de veau sur une assiette et dresser les knödel en serviette de façon décorative. Coiffer d'un œuf au plat.

Beignets au punch
Ingrédients pour 20 beignets environ ∎ Photo Page 120

Génoise ∎ 10 jaunes d'œufs ∎ 40 g de sucre glace ∎ 1 pincée de sucre vanillé ∎ 1 pincée de sel ∎ Zestes de 2 citrons ∎ 10 blancs d'œufs ∎ 200 g de sucre ∎ 250 g de farine
Fourrage au punch ∎ 200 g de confiture d'abricots ∎ 125 ml de rhum ∎ 40 ml de sirop de sucre ∎ 50 g de chocolat noir ∎ Zestes d'1 citron et d'1 orange ∎ 1 pincée de cannelle
Garniture ∎ 50 g environ de confiture d'abricots ∎ 250 g de fondant coloré avec du colorant alimentaire rose ∎ 20 griottes ∎ 20 feuilles de menthe ∎ Quelques feuilles d'or alimentaire

Génoise ∎ Battre en mousse les jaunes d'œufs et le sucre glace, incorporer le sucre vanillé, le sel et les zestes. Monter les blancs d'œufs en neige avec le sucre. Mélanger délicatement les deux préparations, tamiser la farine et l'incorporer. Préchauffer le four et faire cuire deux fonds à 200 degrés pendant 10 minutes en étalant le moitié sur deux plaques recouvertes de papier sulfurisé. Découper chaque fond en un rectangle de 20 x 25 centimètres et réserver le reste pour le remplissage.
Garniture au punch ∎ Emietter le reste de pâte à génoise dans un saladier et mélanger avec la confiture d'abricots, le rhum ainsi que le sirop de sucre. Ajouter le chocolat râpé, les zestes d'orange et de citron ainsi que la cannelle. Malaxer jusqu'à obtenir un mélange homogène.
Présentation ∎ Etaler la confiture d'abricots sur un des fonds, mettre celui-ci dans un cadre à dessert et le recouvrir de garniture au punch. Recouvrir avec le deuxième fond de génoise, couvrir d'un poids et mettre au frais pendant quelques heures.
Démouler la génoise et la couper en 20 dés de 5 x 5 centimètres. Napper les côtés et le dessus de confiture d'abricots légèrement réchauffée et laisser refroidir. Glacer ensuite avec le fondant réchauffé. Orner à votre gré de griottes, de feuilles de menthe ou de feuilles d'or alimentaire.

Rouleaux de neige
Ingrédients pour une quinzaine de rouleaux ∎ Photo Page 120

500 g de pâte feuilletée ∎ 4 blancs d'œufs ∎ 280 g de sucre glace, plus une petite quantité pour le saupoudrage

Étaler la pâte au rouleau sur une épaisseur de 3 millimètres env. A l'aide d'une roulette, couper des bandes de 1,5 centimètres de largeur ; les enrouler autour des moules à rouleaux. Les faire cuire 10–12 minutes au four à 160 degrés. Les détacher des moules lorsqu'ils sont encore chauds et les laisser refroidir. Monter les blancs d'œufs en neige très ferme au bain-marie très chaud (vapeur d'eau) avec le sucre glace. Verser cette mousse dans une poche à douille et en remplir les rouleaux.
Présentation ∎ Saupoudrer les rouleaux de sucre glace.

Zur Traube

ORIGINES ET TRADITIONS

Où Mörwald a débuté dans sa carrière
et où il s'inspire encore aujourd'hui des traditions.

Sans la renommée de Mörwald, Feursbrunn serait resté un petit village idyllique parmi d'autres. Cette commune de 700 âmes, est aujourd'hui le rendez-vous des gourmets d'Autriche et de l'étranger. Ils arrivent des quatre coins du monde, attirés à la fois par l'idylle campagnarde et les hauts-lieux gastronomiques. Le nom de Mörwald a donné à Feuersbrunn une nouvelle identité, unique et incomparable, et pour les gens du pays, Toni Mörwald est devenu le grand gourou des plaisirs de la bouche au royaume duquel la source des gourmandises ne se tarit jamais. C'est ici, à Feuersbrunn que sa carrière a commencé, c'est en partant d'ici qu'il a réussi en un temps record à ériger un empire gastronomique basé sur plusieurs restaurants de haute gastronomie, une école de cuisine à succès et un lucratif service de catering. Les établissements de Mörwald ont obtenu pas moins de sept toques dans le Gault-Millau et deux étoiles au Guide Michelin. Sa détermination dans la mise en œuvre de ses idées lui ont valu de remporter les titres convoités tels que «Wirt des Jahres» (aubergiste de l'année), «Gastronom des Jahres» ou «Grand Chef de Cuisine Europe».

C'est sa tante Rikki qui est responsable de tout cela. Pendant longtemps, elle a tenu une petite auberge dans le village de Feuersbrunn. Un beau jour, un agriculteur du Waldviertel apparut, l'épousa et l'enleva pour l'emmener vers les rudes climats de son haut-plateau. Du jour au lendemain, Feuersbrunn se retrouva sans auberge, une véritable catastrophe!

Les villageois se tournèrent alors vers le beau-frère de Rikki la renégate, qui n'était autre que le père de Toni Mörwald. Ils le pressèrent de reprendre aussi vite que possible l'auberge orpheline, car cette situation de village sans auberge ne pouvait durer.

Lasse de résister à tous ces assauts, la famille Mörwald décida de relever le défi. Papa Mörwald fit rénover l'auberge de fond en comble, sa femme Erika se mit aux commandes de la cuisine tandis que Grand-Maman tenait le bar dans la journée.

C'est dans cette ambiance que grandit le jeune Toni Mörwald, fasciné dès son jeune âge par les talents culinaires maternels. Lorsqu'il dut choisir un métier, il ne voulut pas quitter cet univers de senteurs et de saveurs: il choisit de devenir cuisinier.

Après avoir fait son apprentissage auprès du grand chef autrichien Reinhard Gerer, il alla se perfectionner en France, à Monaco, puis suivirent l'Italie, l'Espagne et la Chine. En 1989, il reprit le restaurant familial Zur Traube. Peu après, il reçut sa première toque du Gault-Millau, devenant ainsi le plus jeune cuisinier toqué d'Autriche.

En raison des remarquables performances de ce chef de cuisine prometteur, il fallut bientôt réserver des semaines à l'avance pour manger au restaurant Zur Traube. Tout Feuersbrunn se demandait d'où pouvaient bien sortir tous ces gens.

Aujourd'hui, l'établissement offre une ambiance contemporaine dans des espaces organisés au gré des phases de transformation de la maison. Outre l'auberge restée classique, le prestigieux restaurant gastronomique Toni M., un salon «Kräuterzimmer», une terrasse, trois salons-jardins, une véranda et une salle de banquets, le restaurant possède également une vinothèque richement approvisionnée en vins de sélection et une cuisine dotée d'équipements modernes dans laquelle des stages de cuisine sont proposés chaque mercredi et jeudi. Mais Zur Traube a conservé dans certaines pièces la sympathique atmosphère d'une hostellerie enracinée dans la tradition locale. Le maître des lieux y tient beaucoup. Car cette auberge permet à Mörwald de rester en contact avec ses racines culinaires. C'est ici que tout a commencé et aujourd'hui le chef François Laliberté propose des plat autrichiens raffinés – un contraste idéal à la cuisine gastronomique internationale de l'empire culinaire de Toni Mörwald.

Langue de veau tiède marinée aux légumes racines, raifort et huile de pépins
Ingrédients pour 4 personnes I Photo Page 134

Sauce I 125 ml de crème I 125 ml de bouillon de bœuf I 100 g de fines herbes hachées (persil, estragon, cerfeuil) I 50 g de beurre I Sel, poivre
Légumes racines I 2 carottes I 1 rave jaune I 1 poireau I 6 cl d'huile de noix I 3 cl de vinaigre balsamique I Sel, poivre
Présentation I 400 g de langue de veau cuite I ½ bouquet de ciboulette I 100 ml d'huile de pépins I ½ racine de raifort

Sauce I Porter à ébullition la crème mélangée au bouillon de bœuf, incorporer les fines herbes et le beurre, puis saler et poivrer. Passer à travers une passoire à trous fins.
Légumes racines I Couper finement les carottes, le rave jaune et le poireau, les blanchir «al dente» dans de l'eau salée, les refroidir, les tamponner pour les sécher puis les faire mariner dans l'huile de noix, le vinaigre balsamique, le sel et le poivre.
Présentation I Découper la langue de veau en tranches de 2 millimètres d'épaisseur et les poser à plat sur les assiettes réchauffées, ajouter les légumes racines par-dessus et napper de sauce. Pour terminer, dresser les assiettes avec la ciboulette finement coupée, l'huile de pépins et le raifort fraîchement râpé.

Salade de haricots avec langoustines et pêches de vigne
Ingrédients pour 4 personnes I Photo Page 136

Salade de haricots I 50 g de haricots blancs I 50 g de haricots rouges I 50 g de haricots verts I 1 pêche de vigne I 1 cuillère à café de graines de moutarde I 1 cuillère à soupe de vinaigre de vin blanc I 3 cuillères à soupe d'huile d'olives I 1 cuillère à soupe de ciboulette ciselée I Sel, poivre, sucre
Langoustines I 8 langoustines fraîches I Jus d'½ limette I ½ bouquet de ciboulette I Sel
Salade de haricots I Faire cuire séparément chaque variété de haricots. Couper les pêches en morceaux décoratifs.
Faire cuire trois fois les graines de moutarde dans 125 ml d'eau. Préparer une vinaigrette avec la moitié des graines, le vinaigre et 2 cuil. à soupe d'huile d'olives. Laisser mariner les haricots et les morceaux de pêche dans cette vinaigrette. Saler, poivrer et rectifier avec un peu de sucre.
Langoustines I Décortiquer les langoustines et retirer les intestins. Les faire mariner avec le sel, le jus de limette, 1 cuil. à soupe d'huile d'olives, le reste des graines de moutarde cuites et la ciboulette fraîchement ciselée.
Présentation I Dresser la salade avec les langoustines et les pêches de vigne.

Velouté de châtaignes avec pruneaux lardés
Ingrédients pour 4 personnes I Photo Page 138

Velouté I 13 châtaignes I 3 cuillères à soupe de beurre froid I ½ l de fond de volaille I 125 ml de crème fleurette I 50 g de crème fouettée I Sel, poivre
Pruneaux I 12 pruneaux I 12 tranches de lard maigre

Velouté I Entailler les châtaignes en croix, à l'aide d'un petit couteau bien aiguisé et les faire cuire 10 à 15 minutes sur une plaque au four préchauffé à 200 degrés. Les asperger d'eau froide à mi-cuisson, afin que l'enveloppe se détache plus facilement de la chair du fruit. Eplucher les châtaignes et les couper en petits morceaux. Dans une large poêle faire mousser 2 cuillères à soupe de beurre jusqu'à ce qu'il prenne une couleur noisette, y ajouter les châtaignes et les faire revenir rapidement. Mouiller avec le fond de volaille et laisser mijoter pendant 15 minutes. Ajouter la crème, donner un nouveau bouillon et réduire en purée à l'aide d'un mixeur tout en ajoutant le reste du beurre froid. Saler et poivrer, incorporer la crème fouettée et servir.
Pruneaux I Enrouler les tranches de lard autour des pruneaux et les faire griller dans une poêle avec revêtement antiadhésif jusqu'à ce qu'ils soient croustillants.
Présentation I Verser le velouté dans des assiettes à soupe, dresser chaque assiette avec trois pruneaux et servir.

Truite rouge sauvage de Mariazell rôtie avec pappardelle au persil et chou-rave à la crème
Ingrédients pour 4 personnes I Photo Page 140

Pâte à pâtes fraîches au persil I 100 g de persil I 1 œuf I 1 jaune d'œuf I ½ cuillère à café d'huile d'olive I Un peu d'eau minérale I 200 g de farine I 1 filet d'huile d'olive I Sel
Truite rouge sauvage I 400 g de filets de truite rouge sauvage de Mariazell I Jus d'un citron I 1 cuillère à soupe d'huile I 1 cuillère à café de beurre I Sel, poivre
Chou-rave à la crème I 200 g de chou-rave I 125 ml de crème I Sel, poivre, muscade I Un peu de persil plat I 40 g de beurre

Pâte au persil I Laver le persil et le tamponner pour le sécher, l'équeuter et le réduire finement en purée au mixeur avec l'œuf, le jaune d'œuf, l'huile, l'eau minérale et le sel. Verser dans un saladier, ajouter peu à peu la farine et malaxer jusqu'à ce que la pâte se détache des bords du saladier. Former une boule, l'envelopper dans un film transparent et mettre au réfrigérateur 30 minutes.
Etaler la pâte à l'aide de la machine et couper des pappardelle de 2 centimètres de largeur.
Truite rouge sauvage I Assaisonner la truite rouge sauvage avec le sel, le poivre et le jus de citron. Chauffer de l'huile dans une poêle et y faire griller les filets de truite jusqu'à ce qu'ils soient croustillants. En fin de cuisson, ajouter un flocon de beurre, tourner les truites du côté de la chair et laisser mijoter un court instant.
Chou-rave à la crème I Eplucher et râper le chou-rave, le faire cuire «al dente» dans la crème et assaisonner avec le sel, le poivre et la muscade. Couper le persil en lamelles et l'incorporer avec le beurre.
Présentation I Cuire les pappardelle «al dente» dans de l'eau salée, les égoutter, les remettre dans la casserole et mélanger avec un filet d'huile d'olive. Enrouler les pappardelle et déposer 3 portions sur chaque assiette. Dresser le chou-rave à la crème entre les pâtes et coiffer d'un filet de truite rouge.

Jarret de veau lardé dans une sauce à la moutarde et aux câpres avec champignons de Paris et riz Basmati
Ingrédients pour 4 personnes I Photo Page 142

Jarret de veau I 1 kg de jarret de veau I 100 g de lard gras I 3 cuillères à soupe de beurre fondu I 1 carotte I 1 rave jaune I 1 oignon I ¼ l de vin blanc I ¼ l de fond de veau ou bouillon de bœuf I 2 feuilles de laurier I Sel, poivre
Champignons I 200 g de champignons de Paris I 2 cuillères à soupe de beurre I 125 ml de crème I 1 cuillère à soupe de moutarde de Pommery I 1 cuillère à soupe de câpres I Un peu de persil I Sel
Présentation I 200 g de riz Basmati I 1 cuillère à soupe de beurre I Sel

Jarret de veau I Découper le lard en bandes très minces de ½ x 10 centimètres et larder le jarret. Faire chauffer le beurre fondu dans une poêle, saisir le jarret de tous les côtés, le retirer de la poêle, saler et poivrer. Couper la carotte, la rave jaune et l'oignon en gros dés, les faire revenir dans le fond de cuisson, puis remettre le jarret de veau salé dans la poêle, verser le vin blanc et le fond de veau, laisser réduire quelques instants et ajouter les feuilles de laurier. Laisser cuire doucement au four pendant une heure et demie environ, en arrosant régulièrement avec le fond. Retirer du fond le jarret, les feuilles de laurier, puis presser les légumes avec le jus de cuisson à travers un chinois.
Champignons de Paris I Nettoyer les champignons, les laver et les couper en tranches pas trop fines. Les faire sauter rapidement dans le beurre moussant, saler légèrement et les ajouter au jus de cuisson. Ajouter la crème et laisser mijoter 10 minutes environ. Ajouter la moutarde de Pommery et les câpres pour terminer. La sauce peut être affinée avec du persil finement haché.
Présentation I Rincer le riz Basmati sous l'eau courante. Le cuire «al dente» dans de l'eau salée, l'égoutter et le faire revenir dans le beurre. Mettre le jarret de veau dans la sauce, chauffer de nouveau rapidement et dresser sur les assiettes avec un peu de sauce et le riz Basmati.

Suprême et cuisse de canard sauvage sur chou aigre-doux à la livèche
Ingrédients pour 4 personnes ❙ Photo Page 144

Canard sauvage ❙ 2 canards sauvages entiers ❙ 1 l de fond de légumes ❙ Sel, poivre
Chou à la livèche ❙ 1 chou blanc (environ 500 g) ❙ 1 cuillère à soupe d'huile ❙ 2 cuillères à soupe de sucre glace ❙ 1 cuillère à soupe de livèche grossièrement hachée ❙ 3 cuillères à soupe de vinaigre balsamique ❙ ¼ l de fond de légumes ❙ Sel

Canard sauvage ❙ Mettre les canards sauvages dans une poêle à frire, verser le fond de légumes sur une hauteur de 2 doigts environ et cuire lentement à l'étouffée dans le four à 120 degrés pendant 1 heure et demie à 2 heures environ. Détacher les blancs et les cuisses. Hacher finement les os et les faire bouillir dans le fond de cuisson sur le feu pendant 15 minutes environ. Pour terminer, filtrer le fond, réduire fortement et assaisonner. Mettre les suprêmes et les cuisses sur une plaque à pâtisserie, la peau tournée vers le haut. Cuire à four moyen (chaleur par le haut) jusqu'à ce qu'ils soient croustillants et dorés.
Chou à la livèche ❙ Enlever le trognon du chou blanc et couper les feuilles en gros copeaux de 4 x 4 centimètres. Les faire revenir à la poêle dans de l'huile chaude, saler, saupoudrer de sucre glace et laisser légèrement caraméliser. Mouiller avec le vinaigre balsamique, verser le fond de légumes et faire mijoter le chou à l'étouffée. Incorporer la livèche.
Présentation ❙ Dresser un morceau de suprême et une cuisse sur chaque assiette. Y ajouter le chou à la livèche et servir avec le fond réduit.

Crêpes soufflées au fromage blanc
Ingrédients pour 4 parts (8 crêpes) ❙ Photo Page 146

Pâte à crêpes ❙ 100 g de farine ❙ 200 g de lait ❙ 2 œufs ❙ 1 pincée de sel ❙ Beurre pour la cuisson
Garniture ❙ 125 g de fromage blanc ❙ 75 g de crème aigre ❙ 2 œufs ❙ 25 g de sucre glace ❙ 15 g de sucre vanillé ❙ 20 g de poudre pour flan à la vanill) ❙ 1 cl d'Amaretto ❙ 1 cl d'eau-de-vie de cerise ❙ 2 cuillères à soupe de raisins secs ❙ 70 g de crème fouettée
Présentation ❙ Fruits frais

Crêpes ❙ Mélanger la farine, le lait, les œufs et une pincée de sel jusqu'à obtenir une pâte lisse. Cuire 8 crêpes dans un peu de beurre.
Garniture ❙ Préchauffer le four à 160 degrés. Passer le fromage blanc et le mélanger avec les autres ingrédients. Pour terminer, incorporer la crème fouettée.
Badigeonner les crêpes avec la garniture. Les déposer sur une plaque à pâtisserie graissée et les faire cuire au four pendant 10 minutes environ.
Présentation ❙ Servir 2 crêpes accompagnées de fruits frais dans chaque assiette.

Villa Katharina

HEBERGEMENT POUR EPICURIENS ET SENS DE L'HOSPITALITE

Où Mörwald reçoit ses visiteurs dans un hôtel raffiné,
selon la plus pure tradition d'hospitalité villageoise.

La Villa Katharina est un véritable hôtel pour épicuriens situé à Feuersbrunn, juste en face du restaurant Zur Traube, la maison mère de Mörwald. Cet hébergement pour gourmets est stratégiquement fort bien placé pour servir de point de départ à de nombreux itinéraires gastronomiques. La première étape sera naturellement le restaurant voisin Zur Traube avec toutes ses déclinaisons – depuis les salles rustiques de l'auberge campagnarde jusqu'à la zone de haute gastronomie Toni M, un restaurant dans le restaurant à l'ambiance futuriste et à l'extraordinaire décoration.

La Villa Katharina est également l'endroit idéal à partir duquel on peut explorer toute la région viticole de la Wagram, avec ses ruelles bordées de caves romantiques et ses nombreux grands viticulteurs dont les vins, peu connus jusqu'à récemment, jouissent maintenant d'une excellente renommée. C'est aussi pour cette raison que Toni Mörwald a donné à chacune des dix chambres de l'hôtel le nom d'un cépage particulier, ces cépage jouant tous un rôle essentiel dans la région : du Grüner Veltliner au Chardonnay en passant par le Riesling.

Feuersbrunn est aussi situé à proximité de la célèbre Wachau; c'est pourquoi de nombreux clients profitent de l'occasion pour visiter ce paysage culturel unique des bords du Danube. Non seulement la Wachau est inscrite sur la liste du patrimoine mondial de l'UNESCO, mais c'est encore une des régions les plus belles et les plus fascinantes d'Autriche. Elle est riche en rendez-vous culinaires à la mode, avec de nombreux grands restaurants mais aussi avec des vignerons de renommée internationale. De nombreux viticulteurs de la Wachau sont mondialement connus, un bon nombre d'entre eux sont des amis personnels de Toni Mörwald, c'est pourquoi ce dernier aime à organiser pour ses clients des excursions sur le thème de «Quand Wagram rencontre Wachau».

En réservant un week-end hédoniste dans la Villa Katharina on en aura pour son argent en matière de gastronomie et d'œnologie. La liste des activités liées à ces domaines est longue et commence dès le matin par du sport à Feuersbrunn: un jogging dans l'une des ruelles bordées de caves et à travers le vignoble. Puis un petit déjeuner gourmet au restaurant Traube avec un Sekt de chardonnay («champagne» autrichien) et de la bonne charcuterie. Pendant la journée, les hôtes peuvent visiter le vignoble et parler avec des vignerons; le midi ils dégusteront un repas copieux avec des produits locaux de la campagne environnante.

Pour finir, le soir, dans la salle à manger Korab du restaurant Zur Traube, Toni Mörwald leur servira un menu de «Cuisine Freestyle» plein de surprises. La soirée se terminera la plupart du temps à la lueur des chandelles dans la vinothèque – et bien sûr à déguster des vins sélectionnés.

Toni M.

OASIS POUR GOURMETS ET TEMPLE ETOILE

Où Mörwald dirige un «restaurant dans le restaurant»
pour lequel il obtient année après année les plus hautes récompenses.

Salade de carottes sauvages, céleri et filet de bœuf limousin. Omelette aux truffes noires. Consommé de faisan et raviolis d'oie. Mou de veau au riesling et œufs de caille. Aiguillettes de canard sauvage avec rôti de sanglier sur un lit de tendres lentilles Beluga et dés de lard. Soufflé de marrons et noix avec chocolat d'Aschaffenbourg sur sabayon au vin de glace.

Voici quelques-uns des plats typiques du restaurant Toni M. à Feuersbrunn. Toni M. c'est une philosophie gastronomique tout à fait personnelle et c'est l'apothéose des plaisirs culinaires. Quant on dîne à l'élégant Toni M. on peut être assuré que chaque plat a été créé par le maître en personne et qu'il en a lui-même contrôlé la qualité. Son ambiance architecturale exceptionnelle fait déjà de cette salle un endroit particulier. C'est un restaurant de luxe élégant et contemporain au cœur d'une auberge de campagne, un restaurant dans le restaurant. Ce concept est certes inhabituel, mais son succès est indéniable. Depuis des années, la critique gastronomique rend hommage à Toni Mörwald pour cette réalisation, en le gratifiant des plus hautes distinctions.

Pour son restaurant Toni M., Mörwald a créé une cuisine fusionnelle, terme qui prête souvent à confusion. Il ne s'agit pas ici de combiner différents styles culinaires de tous les coins du monde selon son bon vouloir. Bien au contraire : Mörwald tient à respecter les canons de la culture autrichienne et, tout en conservant l'idée de base de la cuisine classique, il la fait fusionner avec une méthode de préparation moderne. Ce qui lui importe c'est la légèreté, le raffinement et l'élégance, c'est un style de cuisine moderne basé sur des produits de base régionaux sélectionnés pour leur qualité.

L'un des atouts les plus remarquables de Toni Mörwald est la faculté qu'il a de dénicher sans arrêt de nouveaux fournisseurs pour ses délicieuses spécialités régionales. Ce sont tous des idéalistes, comme par exemple Alexander Quester avec sa truite rouge sauvage de Mariazell ou Robert Paget, ce maître fromager de Basse-Autriche. Mörwald achète ses escargots chez des éleveurs au sud de Vienne et même les pâtes qu'il sert, spaghetti ou tagliolini, ne viennent plus exclusivement d'Italie mais également d'un producteur du Waldviertel.

Pour ses fournisseurs, Mörwald est bien plus qu'un simple partenaire commercial important. En préparant les spécialités régionales pour en faire des plats délicieux servis dans son restaurant Toni M., il met les noms et les denrées de ces producteurs sur toutes les lèvres – au sens propre du terme.

Cuisses de grenouilles au confit de citron, légumes glacés et velouté de raifort fumé
Ingrédients pour 4 personnes I Photo Page 168

Confit de citron I 1 citron I 30 cl de sirop de sucre (voir recette de base page 78)
Velouté I 2 échalotes I 2 cuillères à soupe d'huile d'olive I 5 cl de vin blanc I 5 cl de fumet de poisson I 150 ml de crème I 2 cuillères à soupe de purée de raifort fumé I 2 cuillères à café de jus de citron I Sel, poivre
Légumes I 100 g de baby poireaux I 1 fenouil I 100 g de baby carottes I 4 radis I 6 échalotes I 1 cuillère à soupe de beurre I 200 ml de fond de légumes
Cuisses de grenouille I 24 cuisses de grenouilles I 1 cuillère à soupe de farine I 100 g de beurre I 1 cuillère à soupe d'huile d'olive I 2 gousses d'ail I 3 cuillères à soupe de fines herbes hachées (par ex. estragon, ciboulette, persil, cerfeuil, pimprenelle) I Sel, poivre
Présentation I Pointes de fines herbes (par ex. aneth, cerfeuil, ciboulette)

Confit de citron I Éplucher le citron et le fileter. Faire bouillir le sirop de sucre 2 à 3 minutes. Y ajouter les filets de citron et laisser macérer pendant la nuit.
Velouté I Couper les échalotes en brunoise et les faire revenir 4 à 6 minutes dans l'huile d'olive à feu moyen. Déglacer avec le vin puis réduire jusqu'à ce que le vin soit complètement évaporé. Ajouter alors le fumet de poisson et réduire de moitié. Ajouter la crème et le raifort puis laisser épaissir la sauce jusqu'à ce qu'elle ait une consistance crémeuse. Passer au chinois, assaisonner avec le sel, le poivre et le jus de citron.
Légumes I Couper les baby poireaux en morceaux de 3 centimètres de longueur, couper le fenouil en fines lamelles, nettoyer les baby carottes, couper les radis et les échalotes en quatre. Faire fondre le beurre dans une poêle à feu moyen, y ajouter les légumes et les faire revenir pendant 2 minutes. Mouiller avec le fond de légumes, laisser mijoter les légumes « al dente ».
Cuisses de grenouille I Fariner très légèrement les cuisses de grenouille avec très peu de farine. Faire fondre la moitié du beurre dans une poêle à feu moyen et mélanger à l'huile d'olive. Y mettre les cuisses de grenouille et les faire dorer des deux côtés. Saler et poivrer légèrement pendant la cuisson, couper l'ail en brunoise, y ajouter les fines herbes fraîchement hachée et 20 grammes de beurre en petits morceaux. Retirer les cuisses de grenouille et les réserver sur un plat préchauffé. Verser le beurre de cuisson, déglacer le fond de cuisson avec le vin, y ajouter la moitié des fines herbes et laisser revenir quelques secondes. Ajouter le reste du beurre, verser sur les cuisses de grenouilles et saupoudrer avec les fines herbes restantes.
Présentation I Mélanger les filets de citron aux légumes chauds et les dresser sur les assiettes, disposer les cuisses de grenouille dessus, à côté ou bien tout autour. Ajouter le velouté et servir parsemé de fines herbes.

Escargots des vignes dans une réduction de Bourgogne avec œufs pochés
Ingrédients pour 4 personnes I Photo Page 170

Escargots I 100 g de carottes finement coupées I 100 g de poireau finement coupé I 3 feuilles de laurier I 1 cuillère à café de grains de poivre I 1 citron non traité I 500 ml de vin blanc (Sauvignon blanc) I 24 escargots des vignes I 25 g de dés d'échalotes I 20 g de beurre I 1 cuillère à soupe de persil et de ciboulette hachés
Réduction de Bourgogne I 60 g de dés d'échalotes I 20 ml d'huile d'olive I 5 g de poivre noir concassé I 1 branche de thym I 1 feuille de laurier I 2 bouteilles de Pinot Noir I 200 ml de jus de bœuf I 100 g de moelle de bœuf découpée en dés fins
Echalotes I 8 petites échalotes rondes ou 12 oignons perlés I 10 g de sucre I 25 g de beurre I Sel, poivre
Œufs pochés I 4 œufs I 2 cuillères à soupe de vinaigre de table I Sel, poivre
Présentation I 40 g de lard à l'ail autrichien

Escargots I Porter à ébullition dans une casserole 700 millilitres d'eau avec les carottes, le poireau, les feuilles de laurier et les grains de poivre. Diminuer le feu et laisser mijoter. Couper le citron en deux, presser le jus et le mettre dans une casserole avec les moitiés de citron et le vin blanc.
Ajouter les escargots et laisser mijoter 5 à 6 heures. Puis sortir les escargots et les faire suer avec les dés d'échalotes et le beurre. Après 5 à 6 minutes, ajouter les fines herbes, saler et poivrer.
Réduction de Bourgogne I Faire suer les échalotes avec l'huile d'olive et 1 cuillère à café de poivre. Y ajouter le thym, la feuille de laurier et mouiller avec la moitié d'une bouteille de vin rouge. Laisser réduire jusqu'à obtenir un mélange bien lié. Ajouter le jus et la moelle de bœuf à la réduction de vin rouge et laisser macérer. Faire bouillir à part l'autre moitié de la bouteille de vin rouge, flamber et laisser réduire jusqu'à obtenir un sirop épais. Y verser la moitié de l'autre bouteille, épaissir de nouveau jusqu'à obtenir la consistance d'un sirop et procéder de la même façon avec le vin restant. Ajouter la réduction de vin rouge à la moelle de bœuf et laisser macérer avec le reste du poivre.
Echalotes I Mettre les échalotes avec le sucre, 200 millilitres d'eau, le beurre, le sel et le poivre dans une casserole, couvrir et laisser cuire jusqu'à ce que les échalotes soient caramélisées.
Œufs pochés I Peu avant la fin du temps de cuisson, pocher les œufs. Pour cela, porter l'eau, le vinaigre et le sel à ébullition dans une autre casserole et faire glisser les œufs dans l'eau bouillante à l'aide d'une louche. Au bout de 3 à 4 minutes, le blanc d'œuf coagule alors que le jaune reste liquide.
Présentation I Découper le lard en tranches fines et les faire griller jusqu'à ce qu'elles soient croustillantes. Dresser les escargots en cercle sur l'assiette et déposer l'œuf poché au centre. Ajouter les échalotes et le lard, puis napper avec la réduction de vin rouge.

Aiguillettes de homard breton, dans une réduction de pomélo et miel, épinards et pommes Maxim's
Ingrédients pour 4 personnes I Photo Page 172

Homard I 2 homards bretons de 800 à 1000 g I 2 branches de thym I 1 gousse d'ail I 2 cuillères à soupe de beurre salé I Poivre
Réduction de pomélo et miel I 600 ml de jus de pomélo ou de pamplemousse I 2 cuillères à soupe de miel de fleurs ou de miel de forêt I 4 cuillères à soupe d'huile d'olive native extra I Sel, poivre
Epinards I 1 gousse d'ail I 30 g de beurre I 600 g d'épinards frais I Sel, poivre, muscade
Pommes Maxim's I 1 grosse pomme de terre I 125 ml de beurre liquide I Sel marin

Homard I Cette recette requiert des homards frais, c'est-à-dire vivants. Lors de l'achat ils doivent bouger énergiquement et leur queue doit être cambrée. Ils doivent être plongé dans l'eau bouillante un à un, afin de leur assurer une mort rapide.
Tenir le homard par le dos et le brosser minutieusement dans de l'eau froide. Brider la tête et la queue, de telle sorte que le homard entier ainsi que la queue restent tendus. Retirer les élastiques qui maintiennent les pinces. Porter l'eau à ébullition. Afin que le homard soit tué aussi rapidement que possible en lui gardant ses qualités, le plonger la tête la première dans l'eau bouillante. Donner quelques bouillons puis laisser mijoter 8 à 10 minutes (sans bouillir). La carapace du homard va se teinter de rouge à l'extérieur.
Couper le homard dans le sens de la longueur, retirer l'estomac (masse beige et crémeuse, souvent remplie de sable) et faire revenir chaque moitié dans le beurre avec le thym et l'ail.
Réduction de pomélo et miel I Réduire le jus de pomélos à 100 millilitres. Assaisonner avec le miel, le sel et le poivre puis monter avec l'huile d'olive.
Epinards I Faire revenir rapidement dans du beurre la gousse d'ail coupée en dés, y ajouter les épinards, remuer jusqu'à ce qu'ils soient chauds puis assaisonner avec le sel, le poivre et la muscade.
Pommes Maxim's I Préchauffer le four à 150 degrés. Éplucher la pomme de terre et la râper en tranches très fines. Mélanger les tranches au beurre et les déposer sur un papier sulfurisé ou mieux, sur un tapis en silicone. Saupoudrer de sel marin.
Faire dorer les tranches de pomme de terre au four pendant 1 heure environ, jusqu'à ce qu'elles soient bien croustillantes.
Présentation I Bien égoutter les épinards, en dresser les deux tiers sur les assiettes, farcir les homards avec le dernier tiers. Placer un demi-homard sur chaque portion d'épinards, napper avec la réduction de pomélo et miel, servir garni de pommes Maxim's.

Rognons de veau rôtis au chou pointu de printemps, girolles et sauce Robert

Ingrédients pour 4 personnes I Photo Page 174

Rognons de veau I 2 rognons de veau I 1 branche de thym I 1 branche de romarin I 50 g de beurre I 200 ml de jus de veau I Sel, poivre
Chou pointu I 1 chou pointu I 50 g de beurre I 100 ml de crème I Sel, poivre
Girolles I 30 g d'échalotes I 400 g de girolles I 40 g de beurre I 1 cuillère à soupe de ciboulette finement coupée I Sel, poivre
Sauce Robert I 50 g d'échalotes I 30 g de beurre I 100 ml de vin blanc I 250 ml de jus de veau I 3 cuillères à soupe de moutarde de Pommery I 15 g de beurre très froid

Rognons de veau I Faire revenir les rognons dans le beurre avec le thym et le romarin à feu moyen, jusqu'à ce qu'ils soient rosés. Réduire le fond de veau.
Chou pointu I Couper très finement le chou pointu et le faire cuire à l'étuvée dans le beurre. Saler, poivrer et lier avec la crème, afin d'obtenir une consistance onctueuse.
Girolles I Couper les échalotes en brunoise et les faire revenir dans le beurre avec les girolles. Assaisonner avec le sel, le poivre et la ciboulette.
Sauce Robert I Couper finement les échalotes et les faire suer dans le beurre, mouiller avec le vin blanc et laisser complètement évaporer. Ajouter le jus de veau, laisser mijoter 15 minutes. Ajouter la moutarde. Monter avec le beurre et passer.
Présentation I Dresser le chou pointu sur les assiettes. Découper les rognons en tranches de 1 centimètre d'épaisseur, les placer sur le chou pointu, saler, poivrer, puis napper avec le jus de veau réduit. Déposer les girolles et servir avec la sauce Robert.

Panse de porc aux langoustines et salade de petits pois

Ingrédients pour 4 personnes I Photo Page 176

Panse de porc I 1 panse de porc, env. 2 kg I 2 cuillères à soupe d'huile I 100 g de carottes I 100 g de navet I 100 g d'oignons I 100 g de poireau I 1 bulbe d'ail I 1 l de vin blanc I 2 l de jus de veau I 4 feuilles de laurier I 4 g de grains de poivre I Sel, poivre
Langoustine I 16 queues de langoustines I 30 g de beurre I 1 cuillère à café de brunoise de zestes de limettes I Sel, poivre
Salade de petits pois I 100 g de petits pois blanchis I 50 g de feuilles de petits pois I 50 ml de vinaigre d'abricot I 100 ml d'huile d'amande I 20 ml de miel I Sel, poivre
Présentation I 50 ml de beurre fondu

Panse de porc I Saler et poivrer la panse de porc des deux côtés, la rouler en un épais rouleau et la ficeler. Faire revenir le rouleau dans l'huile de tous les côtés, jusqu'à ce qu'il soit bien croustillant. Couper les légumes et l'ail en petits morceaux et les faire dorer. Déposer le rouleau dessus, mouiller avec le vin blanc et laisser cuire à feu moyen, jusqu'à ce que tout le vin se soit évaporé. Verser le jus de veau, y ajouter les épices et laisser cuire pendant 2 heures environ, jusqu'à ce que la viande soit tendre. Retirer le rouleau, enlever la ficelle et placer la panse de porc à plat entre deux plaques à pâtisserie. Passer la sauce. Laisser la panse de porc reposer une nuit au réfrigérateur.
Langoustine I Nettoyer les queues de langoustines, les faire revenir dans une poêle avec le beurre et assaisonner en fin de cuisson avec le sel, le poivre et les zestes de limettes.
Salade de petits pois I Mettre les petits pois et les feuilles dans un saladier. Mélanger le reste des ingrédients et en napper les petits pois.
Présentation I Découper la panse de porc en gros dés et les faire rôtir de tous les côtés dans le beurre fondu. Faire chauffer la sauce. Dresser en alternance les langoustines et la panse de porc sur les assiettes, servir avec la sauce et la salade de petits pois.

Joues de bœuf braisées, échalotes fondues, lard à l'ail de Kamptal, jus de roquette et Powidl

Ingrédients pour 4 personnes I Photo Page 178

Joues de bœuf I 4 joues de bœuf de180 à 200 g I 100 g de carottes I 100 g de navet I 100 g d'oignons I 100 g de poireau I 1 bulbe d'ail I 1 l de vin rouge I 4 g de grains de poivre I 4 feuilles de laurier I 200 g de farine ronde I 500 ml d'huile de table I 1 l de jus de veau I Sel
Echalotes I 24 échalotes I 25 g de beurre I Env. 150 ml de bouillon de bœuf ou de légumes Sel, poivre
Jus de roquette I 20 g de beurre I 200 g de roquette I Sel, poivre
Présentation I 8 tranches fines de lard à l'ail de Kamptal I 4 cuillères à soupe de Powidl (pâte de quetsches à tartiner)

Joues de bœuf I Laisser mariner les joues de bœuf avec les légumes grossièrement hachés, le vin rouge, les grains de poivre et les feuilles de laurier pendant 48 heures.
Tamponner ensuite les joues de bœuf avec un tissu, saler, poivrer, paner avec la farine ronde et les faire rôtir jusqu'à ce qu'elles soient croustillantes.
Chauffer environ 2 cuillères à soupe d'huile dans une casserole et y faire dorer les légumes égouttés. Mouiller avec le vin rouge, ajouter les joues de bœuf, napper avec le jus de veau et laisser cuire à l'étuvée pendant 2 à 3 heures. Retirer les joues de bœuf lorsqu'elles sont tendres, les réserver au chaud et passer la sauce.
Echalotes I Mettre les échalotes pelées avec le reste des ingrédients dans une casserole et les faire cuire jusqu'à ce que le bouillon se soit évaporé. Verser encore un peu de bouillon, si toutefois les échalotes n'étaient pas encore tout à fait moelleuses.
Jus de roquette I Faire bouillir 75 millilitres d'eau dans une casserole, y ajouter le beurre et la roquette, réduire en purée pendant 1 minute dans un mixeur, puis passer à travers une passoire. Saler et poivrer.
Présentation I Préchauffer le four à 150 degrés. Déposer les tranches de lard à plat les unes à côté des autres sur une plaque à pâtisserie et les faire cuire au four pendant une heure jusqu'à ce qu'elles soient croustillantes. Dresser les joues de bœuf au centre de l'assiette, verser la sauce de cuisson. Servir garni de jus de roquette, d'1 cuillère à soupe de Powidl et de tranches de lard.

Soufflé aux limettes avec sorbet de framboises & sabayon à l'Amaretto

Ingrédients pour 4 soufflés I Photo Page 180

Sorbet de framboises I 125 g de sucre I 125 g d'eau I 500 g de concentré de framboises I Jus de 2 citrons
Sabayon à l'Amaretto I 3 jaunes d'œufs I 40 g de sucre I 40 g d'eau I 20 g d'Amaretto
Soufflé I Beurre pour les moules
Mélange 1 I 4 jaunes d'œufs I 30 g de sucre I 60 g de crème aigre I Zestes de 2 limettes
Mélange 2 I 120 g de blancs d'œufs I 80 g de sucre I 4 moules à soufflé de 8 cm de diamètre

Sorbet I Faire bouillir l'eau et le sucre, dissoudre le sucre en écumant la mousse éventuellement. Y ajouter le concentré de framboises et le jus des citrons. Remplir un moule Pacojet et congeler. Remuer avec le Pacojet avant emploi.
Sabayon I Battre énergiquement tous les ingrédients dans un saladier au-dessus de la vapeur d'eau, jusqu'à obtenir une crème onctueuse.
Soufflé I Beurrer les moules à soufflé.
Pour le mélange 1, battre le sucre et le jaune d'œuf, jusqu'à ce que le mélange devienne blanc et épais. Ajouter la crème aigre et les zestes de limettes.
Pour le mélange 2, battre légèrement les 2 blancs d'œufs et le sucre.
Incorporer délicatement le mélange 2 au mélange 1 et remplir au ¾ les moules préparés. Cuire au four à 190 degrés pendant 8 minutes environ.
Présentation I Dresser immédiatement le soufflé avec le sorbet et le sabayon. Décorer selon les goûts avec des framboises et des tuiles.

Ecole de cuisine

MAITRE D'APPRENTISSAGE ET APPRENTISSAGE MAGISTRAL

Comment Mörwald en tant que maître d'apprentissage, soumet les cuisiniers amateurs intéressés à un apprentissage culinaire magistral.

Auberge de village Zur Traube à Feuersbrunn: le seigneur des lieux, Toni Mörwald, fait son apparition à 17 heures précises. Un petit groupe de dix personnes attend déjà le célèbre chef. Comme presque chaque mercredi à la même heure, des cuisiniers amateurs se rencontrent ici pour découvrir comment faire une soupe, réaliser un fond de gibier, lever des filets sur les poissons ou comment découper les cailles ou les poulets, tout cela Mörwald l'explique lors de ses stages de cuisine réguliers. Une cuisine contemporaine ultramoderne a été spécialement aménagée à cet effet dans le restaurant Zur Traube. Mörwald: »Nous trouvons ici tout ce qu'il nous faut, chacun peut s'en donner à cœur joie.«

Des écoles de cuisine comme celle-ci sont très prisées. La demande est énorme. Femmes, hommes, étudiants, employés de banque, patrons d'entreprise ou cadres supérieurs, tous s'appliquent à faire rissoler et mijoter leurs plats, et les cours de cuisine sont pour eux aussi naturels qu'un week-end dans un centre de remise en forme.

Toni Mörwald est le leader autrichien dans ce domaine. C'est lui qui, de loin, organise le plus grand nombre de stages; depuis plus de 20 ans, il propose des thèmes variant chaque semaine. Le large éventail va de la «cuisine méditerranéenne» jusqu'à la typique «cuisine viennoise», une autre fois ce sera le tour des «poissons d'eau de mer et crustacés», de la «cuisine naturelle« ou du »poulet bio bouilli, rôti, farci et cuit à point».

Au programme aujourd'hui: «Sushi et cuisine japonaise». Impatient de se mettre au travail, chacun noue son tablier puis sirote nerveusement son verre de champagne. Prost, santé, et on y va.

Le premier plat s'appelle «Thuna-Sushi avec sauce chili et poivre vert». Mörwald explique chaque étape du travail: comment détailler correctement un poisson, préparer une sauce chili, comment choisir le bon riz et le faire cuire. Ensuite il présente le saumon bio pour un «Sashimi de saumon sauvage au Wasabi». Le fier animal est examiné sous toutes ses coutures et admiré avant d'être découpé en filets.

Les cours de cuisine de Mörwald sont devenus des incontournables. Certains participants enchaînent un cours après l'autre, certains ont déjà suivi 20 ou 30 stages. «L'important pour moi», dit Mörwald «c'est que les gens s'amusent et apprennent des techniques ludiques.»

Avec plus de mille cours, l'école de cuisine de Mörwald est bien l'institut le plus renommé pour la communication de connaissances de base et d'astuces facilitant aux cuisiniers amateurs la vie devant le fourneau et leur faisant découvrir «une nouvelle envie de cuisiner».

Tous les plats sont dégustés sur place à la fin des cours par les participants et Mörwald sert les vins allant avec les mets. Finalement chaque élève cuisinier reçoit un classeur de recettes, un tablier et un certificat qu'il affichera chez lui: une distinction devenue, chez les cuisiniers amateurs, presque aussi prisée que les toques et les étoiles chez les virtuoses professionnels du fourneau.

Pâtes fines au citron et caviar Ossietra
Ingrédients pour 4 personnes ∎ Photo Page 194

Pâtes ∎ 200 g de pâte à pâtes fraîches (voir recette de base page 78) ∎ 1 citron ∎ 3 cuillères à soupe de beurre ∎ Un peu d'eau ou un fond de bœuf doux ∎ 2 cuillères à soupe de dés de beurre réfrigéré ∎ 2 cuillères à soupe de crème fraîche ∎ 2 cuillères à soupe de crème fouettée
Présentation ∎ 4 cuillères à soupe de caviar Ossietra

Pâtes ∎ Abaisser finement la pâte à l'aide de la machine à pâtes et la découper avec le disque de coupe le plus fin (vérifier la forme des pâtes sur la photo des aliments).
Laver les citrons, en extraire des zestes très fins puis presser le reste du citron. Blanchir les zestes dans de l'eau bouillante pendant 1 minute, les verser dans une passoire et bien les égoutter. Cuire les pâtes dans de l'eau abondamment salée pendant 15 secondes environ, les verser dans une passoire et les plonger rapidement dans de l'eau très froide.
Faire mousser le beurre dans la poêle, y ajouter les zestes de citron, faire revenir brièvement. Y ajouter les pâtes et un peu d'eau ou le fond de bœuf doux, chauffer et assaisonner avec le sel et le poivre. Incorporer du beurre froid en mélangeant sans cesse, afin que les pâtes deviennent «grasses». Ajouter la crème fraîche et le jus de citron et, pour terminer, incorporer la crème fouettée.
Présentation ∎ Dresser dans des assiettes à soupe chaudes et couronner de caviar.

Blanc de poulet jaune fermier
au risotto de girolles et vinaigre de groseilles noir
Ingrédients pour 4 personnes ∎ Photo Page 196

Poulet jaune fermier ∎ 4 blancs de poulet jaune fermier de 150 g ∎ 2 cuillères à soupe d'huile de tournesol ∎ 1 branche de thym ∎ Sel, poivre
Risotto ∎ 2 échalotes ∎ 50 g de beurre ∎ 200 g de riz pour risotto ∎ 60 ml de vin blanc ∎ ½ l de fond de légumes (voir recette de base page 76) ∎ 150 g de girolles ∎ 40 g de parmesan râpé ∎ Sel, poivre
Présentation ∎ ¼ l de jus de volaille ∎ 4 cl de vinaigre de cassis

Poulet jaune fermier ∎ Saler et poivrer les blancs de poulet et bien les saisir à la poêle des deux côtés. Ajouter le thym et cuire au four à 180 degrés pendant 5 minutes environ.
Risotto ∎ Hacher finement les échalotes, les faire suer dans le beurre, y ajouter le riz et laisser suer l'ensemble pendant 1 minute. Mouiller avec le vin blanc puis réduire complètement. Verser un peu de fond de légumes tout en remuant et laisser mijoter. Procéder de la même façon avec la totalité du fond. Le riz doit prendre une consistance crémeuse mais rester «al dente». Saler et poivrer. Couper les girolles en morceaux et les ajouter au risotto ou bien les faire sauter et les servir séparément. Terminer la préparation du risotto en ajoutant le parmesan.
Présentation ∎ Faire bouillir quelques instants le jus de volaille avec le vinaigre de groseilles et dresser le poulet jaune fermier avec le risotto et, le cas échéant, avec les girolles sautées.

Brioches au pavot du Waldviertel
avec pommes poêlées et crème glacée
Ingrédients pour 30 mini brioches environ ∎ Photo Page 198

Crème glacée ∎ 50 ml d'eau ∎ 180 g de sucre ∎ Zestes de 2 limettes ∎ 500 g de crème aigre
Pommes poêlées ∎ 3 pommes ∎ 25 g de beurre ∎ 2 cuillères à soupe de miel
Garniture au pavot ∎ 125 g de pavot en poudre ∎ 70 g de chapelure ∎ 100 ml de lait ∎ 30 g de sucre ∎ Un peu de miel ∎ 1 trait de rhum ∎ Zestes d'1 citron ∎ 1 pincée de cannelle ∎ 50 g de chocolat blanc ∎ 1 jaune d'œuf
Pâte ∎ 500 g de farine ∎ 75 g de sucre ∎ 10 g de sel ∎ 300 g d'œufs entiers ∎ 1 dé de levure fraîche 300 g de beurre mou ∎ 75 g de beurre liquide

Glace ∎ Faire bouillir l'eau et le sucre en sirop, ajouter les zestes, laisser refroidir et passer. Ajouter la crème, bien mixer et verser dans un moule Pacojet. Mettre à congeler et remuer avec le Pacojet avant emploi.
Pommes poêlées ∎ Peler les pommes, les couper en quartiers, les épépiner puis les couper en tranches fines et les faire cuire «al dente» dans le beurre. Ajouter le miel et terminer la cuisson.
Garniture ∎ Mélanger le pavot et la chapelure. Faire bouillir le lait avec le sucre, un peu de miel, le rhum, les zestes de citron et la cannelle. Retirer du feu et mélanger à la préparation de pavot et chapelure. Faire fondre le chocolat et le mélanger avec le jaune d'œuf, mettre quelques instants au réfrigérateur.
Brioches ∎ Mélanger la farine, le sucre et le sel dans un saladier. Ajouter les œufs un à un, tout en continuant de mélanger. Émietter la levure dans le saladier et bien malaxer le tout. Lorsque la pâte est homogène, ajouter petit à petit le beurre mou et mélanger jusqu'à obtenir une pâte lisse. Mettre le mélange dans un saladier fariné et laisser reposer jusqu'à ce que le volume ait doublé. Abaisser sur une surface farinée et découper des cercles de 7 centimètres de diamètre. Mettre une cuillère à café de garniture sur chaque morceau, bien refermer sur le dessus et les poser côté à côte sur une plaque à pâtisserie. Laisser reposer encore une fois, bien badigeonner de beurre liquide et cuire au four à 170 degrés pendant 20 minutes environ.
Présentation ∎ Servir les brioches au pavot avec les pommes poêlées et la crème glacée.

Viticulture Mörwald

TRADITION VIGNERONNE ET REGION VINICOLE

Où la famille Mörwald élève des vins sélects selon des méthodes traditionnelles.

Le Wagram est une région viticole dans laquelle les gens ont conservé un certain flegme. Ils ne craignent rien plus qu'un tourisme qui leur ravirait leur identité. C'est pourquoi cette charmante région a jusqu'ici conservé sa tranquillité. Son climat favorable permet à de grands vins de prospérer ici, même s'ils ne sont pas aussi connus que ceux de la Wachau située à proximité. On trouve par exemple quelques-uns des meilleurs Grüner Veltliner du pays sur les puissantes couches de Lœss orientées au sud.

La viticulture a ici une tradition séculaire et nombre de ses caves des origines sont aujourd'hui encore en service. C'est dans cette sympathique région que la famille Mörwald pratique la viticulture depuis des générations, plus exactement depuis 1860. Le vignoble est aujourd'hui dirigé par Erhard Mörwald et femme Angelika. L'entreprise familiale possède plus de 14 hectares de vignes et 40 hectares de terres agricoles sur lesquelles on a planté des vergers pour la production maison d'alcools nobles.

Les Mörwald peuvent s'enorgueillir d'une belle gamme de produits œnologiques: cépages à vins blancs tels que Veltliner, Frühroter Veltliner, Sauvignon blanc, Weißburgunder, Riesling et Gelber Muskateller; et pour les rouges, les Blauer Zweigelt, Cabernet Sauvignon, Merlot et autres Blauburgunder.

Le frère de Toni, Erhard Mörwald, est un vinificateur subtil possédant une grande intuition pour mêler à bon escient méthode traditionnelle et technique moderne. C'est pourquoi tous ses vins ont un caractère propre, tout à fait spécifique.

Comme tous les vins, les vins de la Wagram sont fortement imprégnés des propriétés géologiques du terroir. Le Grüner Veltliner prospère particulièrement bien sur les sols de Lœss de la Wagram mais, parmi les spécialités régionales, on compte aussi le Roter Veltliner. Le Riesling quant à lui pousse sur des sols caillouteux situés plus en altitude, ce qui rend les raisins particulièrement aromatiques. La Wagram est également connue pour ses vins rouges à la texture particulièrement délicate.

A coté des vins, la maison Mörwald propose une variété d'eaux-de-vie et d'alcools maison. La gamme des alcools est vaste, de l'abricot à la framboise et la cerise, en passant par la poire Williams, la pomme et la corme. Quelques uns de ces distillats de grande qualité, comme par exemple l'excellent marc de Veltliner en fût, ont été distingués par les milieux spécialisés.

Et parce que chez les Mörwald, quel que soit le domaine, la tradition ne doit pas marquer le pas derrière l'innovation, Erhard Mörwald n'oublie pas ses bons vieux alcools maison. Parce que si le légendaire alcool de noix – eau-de-vie ou liqueur – venait à manquer soudain, beaucoup des fidèles clients de Mörwald monteraient aussitôt sur les barricades.

Schloss Grafenegg

IDYLLE PRINCIERE ET PLAISIR ARTISTIQUE

Où Mörwald gère un relais-château
pour les spectateurs d'un festival international de musique.

Ce fut l'idée royale d'un prince. Lorsque, au début des années quatre-vingt-dix, le prince Franz Albrecht Metternich Sandor, souhaitant engager un grand chef pour son relais-château de Grafenegg en Basse-Autriche, s'adressa à Mörwald, ce dernier commença par refuser. Puis le scepticisme des débuts se transforma rapidement en enthousiasme croissant pour une aventure qui lui parut au final extraordinairement séduisante. Car le château de Grafenegg en Basse-Autriche n'est pas un endroit quelconque. A plus ample examen, ce que le prince offrait finit par l'impressionner: Un grand, un immense parc. En toile de fond, un château prestigieux digne de ses cousins français. Face à lui un élégant restaurant donnant sur un jardin magique. Un joyau fascinant au cœur de la Basse-Autriche. Habituellement, on ne trouve de tels ensembles architecturaux qu'en France, où il n'est pas rare qu'ils soient dédiés à la grande gastronomie. Conclusion: Mörwald accepta. Aujourd'hui, le château de Grafenegg ne se contente pas d'être le rendez-vous des gourmets exigeants, cet endroit abrite également un festival de musique célèbre au-delà des frontières. Ainsi, tout à côté de la Schlosstaverne Mörwald, on trouve la salle de concert contemporaine «Auditorium» et, diamétralement opposée, la scène à ciel ouvert «Wolkenturm». Chaque année, des ensembles célèbres et des solistes de renom international s'y produisent. Le festival international de musique de Grafenegg est devenu rapidement un événement culturel innovant, accueillant des artistes de haut niveau.

Un restaurant dans un tel endroit profite donc d'un cadre exceptionnel. Outre son charme aristocratique, la Schlosstaverne est aussi remarquable à d'autres points de vue. Sous la direction du chef Thomas Törpel, l'équipe de Toni Mörwald sert ici une cuisine régionale irréprochable et sans fioritures qui utilise exclusivement des produits de base autrichiens. Pas de turbot d'Atlantique, mais de la truite rouge sauvage de Mariazell, pas de bœuf argentin mais du Limousin de Waldviertel, même le caviar provient d'un éleveur d'esturgeons de Salzbourg et non de Russie ou d'Iran.

Cette ligne de conduite stricte a été honorée par la critique culinaire: en 2009, la Schlosstaverne de Grafenegg a obtenu à nouveau une toque dans le Gault-Millau et 80 points sur 100 dans le guide autrichien Falstaff.

Un hôtel a depuis été ajouté au complexe. Il offre aux spectateurs des concerts et aux clients du restaurant la possibilité de passer tout un week-end à Grafenegg. Avec un peu de chance du côté de la météo, on peut aussi réserver un pique-nique en plein air – dans le cadre soigné du parc du château, avec des spécialités culinaires et un décor que l'on ne sera pas près d'oublier. C'est la symbiose incomparable entre les beaux-arts et l'art culinaire et, comme on le voit, l'idée véritablement royale d'un prince.

Ecrevisses de Mariazell frites
avec pommes pailles sur tripes de veau et persil
Ingrédients pour 4 personnes ❙ Photo Page 222

Tripes ❙ 1 carotte ❙ ½ céleri-branche ❙ 400 g de tripes de veau cuites ❙ 2 échalotes ❙ 100 g de beurre ❙ 1 l de fond de veau ❙ ½ l de crème
Ecrevisses ❙ 8 écrevisses ❙ 2 grosses pommes de terre ❙ 1 blanc d'œuf ❙ Huile pour friture
Présentation ❙ ½ bouquet de persil ❙ Huile pour friture ❙ 4 fagotins de cornichons

Tripes ❙ Couper en brunoise les carottes et le céleri. Couper finement les tripes cuites et les faire rissoler dans un peu d'huile avec les échalotes coupées en dés. Y ajouter le fond de veau et réduire. Incorporer la crème et laisser mijoter quelques instants. Pour terminer, rajouter la brunoise de carottes et céleri et laisser mijoter encore un peu.
Ecrevisses ❙ Faire bouillir les écrevisses et les décortiquer. Couper les pommes de terre en fine julienne et les mélanger au blanc d'œuf. En recouvrir les écrevisses et faire frire.
Présentation ❙ Faire frire le persil dans l'huile. Mettre les tripes dans les assiettes, les persiller, dresser les écrevisses par-dessus et disposer les fagotins de cornichons, en guise de garniture.

Rouleau de sandre frite
à la purée persillée et au beurre blanc de légumes
Ingrédients pour 4 personnes ❙ Photo Page 224

Sandre ❙ 400 g de sandre ❙ 80 g de truite saumonée marinée ❙ 100 g de farce de poisson (voir recette de base page 78) ❙ 4 feuilles d'épinard ❙ 150 g de chapelure ❙ 10 g de graines de sésame ❙ 1 l d'huile
Beurre blanc aux légumes ❙ 1 l de vin blanc ❙ 250 g de beurre ❙ Fenouil et coriandre ❙ 100 g de brunoise de légumes mixte (carotte, céleri-branche, poireau) ❙ Sel, piment de Cayenne
Purée persillée ❙ 200 g de persil racine ❙ 1 pomme de terre ❙ 100 g de persil ❙ 1 cuillère à soupe de crème fraîche ❙ Sel, poivre
Présentation ❙ ¼ l de lait ❙ Zeste d'1 citron ❙ 4 cuillères à café de caviar de saumon, selon les goûts ❙ Vert de fenouil ❙ Sel

Sandre ❙ Aplatir légèrement le filet de sandre, le recouvrir de farce de poisson. Couper les truites saumonées en belles tranches, les envelopper dans les feuilles d'épinard blanchies, les mettre sur la farce puis rouler la sandre dans un film transparent bien tendu. Congeler quelques instants les morceaux, puis enlever le film transparent, mélanger la chapelure et les graines de sésame, puis paner les rouleaux. Frire dans un bain d'huile.
Beurre blanc de légumes ❙ Réduire le vin à 125 millilitres et le monter avec le beurre, y ajouter les fines herbes, les épices et les légumes, laisser bouillir un court instant, assaisonner et retirer du feu.
Purée persillée ❙ Eplucher les persils racines et les pommes de terre, les couper en gros dés, les faire cuire puis les presser. Y ajouter le persil finement haché, saler, poivrer et aérer avec la crème fraîche.
Présentation ❙ Faire bouillir quelques instants le lait avec le sel et les zestes puis monter en mousse avec le mixeur. Dresser la purée persillée au centre de l'assiette, poser dessus le rouleau de sandre, ajouter le beurre blanc, garnir avec le caviar et le fenouil puis décorer avec le lait monté en mousse.

Foie de veau rosé rôti aux cerises cuites
au vinaigre, girolles sautées et purée de pommes de terre
Ingrédients pour 4 personnes ❙ Photo Page 226

Foie de veau ❙ 500 g de foie de veau ❙ Un peu de farine ❙ 4 tranches de lard ❙ 10 g de gros poivre ❙ 10 g de fleur de sel ❙ 10 g de persil haché
Purée de pommes de terre ❙ 5 pommes de terre de taille moyenne ❙ ½ gousse d'ail ❙ 1 branche de romarin ❙ 1 branche de thym ❙ Un peu de fleur de sel ❙ Un peu d'huile d'olive
Cerises au vinaigre ❙ 20 cerises ❙ 0,2 l de jus de cerise ❙ 1 cuillère à soupe de vinaigre balsamique ❙ 1 branche de thym ❙ 1 cuillère à soupe de miel ❙ Un peu de beurre
Girolles ❙ 300 g de girolles ❙ 1 cuillère à café de beurre ❙ 1 cuillère à café de ciboulette hachée ❙ 1 pincée de poudre de paprika ❙ Sel, poivre
Présentation ❙ Dés de légumes blanchis, selon les envies

Foie de veau ❙ Nettoyer le foie de veau (retirer la peau et les vaisseaux) et le couper en 8 portions de même taille. Les tourner dans un peu de farine et les faire griller lentement dans un peu d'huile. Les retirer de la poêle et les faire cuire 3 minutes au four à 180 degrés. Laisser reposer à faible température, afin que la viande reste tendre.
Purée de pommes de terre ❙ Faire cuire les pommes de terre avec les herbes, les éplucher, les écraser avec une fourchette puis assaisonner avec la fleur de sel et l'huile d'olive.
Cerises au vinaigre ❙ Faire revenir rapidement les cerises dénoyautées dans le jus puis les retirer. Ajouter le thym et le miel au jus et laisser réduire. Ajouter le vinaigre balsamique juste avant la fin et monter avec le beurre, bien laquer les cerises avec ce coulis.
Girolles ❙ Faire sauter les girolles dans le beurre et assaisonner avec la ciboulette, le sel et le poivre.
Présenter ❙ Dresser le foie de veau, déposer la purée de pommes de terre, garnir avec les girolles et les dés de légumes. Disposer les cerises laquées et napper avec le jus réduit.

Cailles lardées au foie gras d'oie truffé et petite salade des prés

Ingrédients pour 4 personnes ❙ Photo Page 228

Cailles lardées ❙ 2 cailles ❙ 100 g de farce de volaille (voir recette de base page 78) ❙ 8 tranches de truffes noires ❙ 4 feuilles d'épinards ❙ 4 tranches de jambon Serrano
Foie gras d'oie truffé ❙ 240 g de foie gras d'oie mariné ❙ 10 g de truffe noire râpée ❙ 20 g de Pumpernickel – pain de seigle au levain traditionnel – sec et moulu ❙ 20 g de chapelure ❙ 10 g de pistaches hachées ❙ Huile pour friture
Salade des prés ❙ Ciboulette, basilic, persil, cerfeuil, lavande, estragon, trèfle selon les goûts ❙ 1 petite salade frisée ❙ 2 cuillères à soupe d'huile de noix ❙ Sel, poivre
Présentation ❙ 4 œufs de caille ❙ 4 têtes de champignons découpées de façon décorative ❙ Quelques fleurs comestibles

Cailles lardées ❙ Désosser les cailles et les enduire d'un peu de farce de volaille. Revêtir de truffes et de feuilles d'épinard, puis barder de jambon Serrano. Faire griller à température modérée, puis cuire au four à 180 degrés pendant 5 minutes. Laisser reposer.
Foie gras d'oie truffé ❙ Bien malaxer le foie gras d'oie mariné avec la truffe râpée et former des petites quenelles. Les paner avec le Pumpernickel, la chapelure et les pistaches puis les faire frire rapidement dans un bain d'huile brûlante.
Salade des prés ❙ Equeuter les fines herbes et les laver, les mélanger avec la salade frisée, assaisonner avec l'huile, le sel et le poivre.
Présentation ❙ Cuire les œufs de caille 3 minutes dans de l'eau bouillante, puis les couper en deux. Dresser les cailles, le foie gras d'oie truffé, la salade des prés sur les assiettes, garnir avec les œufs de caille, les champignons et les fleurs comestibles.

Gâteau maison « Metternich »
Ingrédients pour un gâteau I Photo Page 230

Fond I 150 g de beurre mou I 100 g de sucre en poudre I 6 jaunes d'œufs I 6 blancs d'œufs I 110 g de sucre glace I 120 g de chocolat noir I 150 g de farine
Crème I 250 g de beurre mou I 300 g de nougat semi-liquide I 150 g de sucre glace I 4 jaunes d'œufs I 2 cuillères à soupe d'Amaretto
Garniture I 200 g de pâte d'amandes à la pistache I 12 décors en ganache I 12 boules creuses chocolatées I 100 g de nougatine

Fond I Battre le beurre en mousse et incorporer au fur et à mesure le sucre ainsi que les jaunes d'œufs. Battre les blancs d'œufs en neige ferme, en incorporant lentement le sucre glace. Faire fondre le chocolat, mélanger avec la préparation à base de sucre et de jaunes d'œufs et y verser doucement la farine. Pour terminer, incorporer délicatement les œufs en neige, mettre la pâte dans un moule à charnières avec revêtement antiadhésif et cuire au four à chaleur tournante à 180 degrés.
Crème I Battre le beurre en mousse, incorporer le sucre glace et le nougat. Faire chauffer lentement les jaunes d'œufs, en remuant sans cesse au-dessus de la vapeur d'eau à 72 degrés. Retirer de la source de chaleur, sans cesser de battre, ajouter l'Amaretto et le mélange à base de nougat, puis battre à froid.
Garniture I Couper le fond refroidi en trois morceaux, recouvrir chaque morceau avec un quart de la crème, les empiler les uns sur les autres et napper le pourtour avec le reste de la crème. Mettre au réfrigérateur 1 heure environ, puis habiller la couche supérieure de crème avec de la pâte d'amandes. Décorer le gâteau avec la ganache, les boules creuses chocolatées et la nougatine.

m.kunst.genuss

ART CULINAIRE ET BEAUX-ARTS

Comment Mörwald, avec sa »m.-Linie«,
offre aux visiteurs du musée et aux gens
de radio une cuisine rapide dans l'air du temps.

Avec ses restaurants Zur Traube, Schloss Grafenegg et Kloster Und et leurs nombreuses toques et étoiles, Toni Mörwald satisfait essentiellement aux exigences culinaires d'une clientèle de fins gourmets.

Mais point n'est besoin de fréquenter ces hauts-lieux de la gastronomie pour se régaler. Il faut savoir réserver aux grands jours le homard et le caviar. C'est dans cette optique que Mörwald a conçu sa ligne apurée, la «m.-Linie». Il s'agit ici d'établissements qui souhaitent répondre à une demande de cuisine rapide à des prix intéressants, sans aucun compromis quant à la qualité.

Le café-restaurant du musée des beaux-arts Kunsthalle Krems est la réponse adéquate à ce concept. L'enseigne m.kunst.genuss de Michael Mayr y propose bien plus que ce que l'on attendrait d'une simple cafétéria de musée. Ainsi, non seulement l'ambiance est en totale adéquation avec l'architecture du musée, mais encore les visiteurs des expositions y trouvent une restauration parfaitement adaptée à leurs besoins. La gamme proposée comprend des petits déjeuners, des snacks, des menus économiques et un grand nombre de plats méditerranéens, sans compter le café et les viennoiseries, le tout d'un haut niveau qualitatif.

Depuis 2003, le restaurant d'entreprise m.hitradio.genuss permet à Mörwald de choyer l'équipe de »Ö3«, la station de radio la plus écoutée d'Autriche. Il lui a fallu, pour cela aussi, faire œuvre de pionnier en matière culinaire. Car un restaurant dans une station de radio, c'est encore plus de rapidité, de créativité et d'innovations gastronomiques. Pour citer Mörwald: «Nous voulons atteindre dans le domaine de la restauration d'entreprise ce que certaines compagnies aériennes ont réalisé pour leur service de bord. Nous avons ici un secteur tout à fait sous-estimé du point de vue gastronomique.»

Le troisième établissement de la «m.-Linie» est le plus enraciné dans la tradition: il s'agit de l'auberge m.wirts.haus dans la maison mère de Feuersbrunn. Mörwald souhaite y faire la preuve qu'une cuisine d'auberge traditionnelle à base de produits régionaux peut également trouver preneur selon des critères contemporains. Le client se voit offrir ici une cuisine paysanne avec des produits régionaux de haute qualité dont le prix est intéressant et qui, au besoin, peut être rapidement préparée et servie.

Au contraire, quant on peut se permettre de prendre son temps, on a tout loisir de s'abandonner à l'atmosphère agréable de cette auberge de village et de savourer longuement chaque plat.

Raviolis au fromage frais et à l'ail des ours avec asperges et sabayon de cerfeuil
Ingrédients pour 4 personnes I Photo Page 240

Raviolis à l'ail des ours I 50 g de jeunes oignons coupés en rondelles I 1 gousse d'ail I Beurre I 200 g d'ail des ours I 1 pomme de terre farineuse I Un peu de lait I 150 g fromage frais I 200 g de pâte à pâtes fraîches (voir recette de base page 78) I Sel, poivre, noix de muscade

Sabayon de cerfeuil I 2 échalotes I 40 g de beurre I 2 pommes de terre farineuses I 500 ml de fond de volaille I 3 jaunes d'œufs I Cerfeuil selon les goûts I Sel, poivre, piment de Cayenne, noix de muscade
Asperges I 12 asperges vertes I 1 petit pain rassis pour la cuisson I Sel, poivre, sucre, beurre
Présentation I Beurre brun

Raviolis à l'ail des ours I Couper les jeunes oignons en rondelles, les faire revenir dans du beurre avec l'ail des ours et l'ail coupé en dés. Les retirer du feu et les hacher finement. Les mettre dans un saladier, écraser la pomme de terre, ajouter un trait de lait et le fromage frais et bien mélanger. Assaisonner avec le sel, le poivre et la noix de muscade.
Abaisser finement la pâte, découper des cercles, les badigeonner avec l'œuf, déposer sur les cercles l'équivalent d'une cuillère à café du mélange à l'ail des ours, refermer en demi-cercle et appuyer fermement sur les bords.
Sabayon de cerfeuil I Couper finement les échalotes, couper les pommes de terres en fines rondelles, les faire revenir dans du beurre sans les colorer. Assaisonner avec le sel, le poivre, le piment de Cayenne et la noix de muscade.
Verser le fond de volaille et laisser réduire pendant 15 minutes environ. Mixer et passer à travers une passoire à trous fins. Laisser refroidir quelques instants.
Mettre le fond avec les jaunes d'œufs dans un saladier cul de poule et battre en mousse épaisse au-dessus d'un bain-marie très chaud. Hacher le cerfeuil et réserver quelques feuilles pour la décoration. Assaisonner le sabayon de façon relevée et incorporer le cerfeuil haché.
Asperges I Couper les queues des asperges, éplucher éventuellement les parties fibreuses. Faire bouillir de l'eau salée, y ajouter le beurre, le sucre et le petit pain. Faire cuire les asperges «al dente», les refroidir dans de l'eau glacée et les laisser égoutter sur un papier absorbant.
Présentation I Cuire les raviolis dans de l'eau salée frémissante pendant 4 minutes environ. Réchauffer les asperges dans le fond d'asperges. Faire revenir les raviolis cuits dans le beurre brun. Dresser les asperges sur une assiette, y ajouter les raviolis et recouvrir avec le sabayon de cerfeuil. Garnir avec les feuilles de cerfeuil restantes.

Ragoût de chamois aux airelles rouges et pâtes aux champignons
Ingrédients pour 6 personnes I Photo Page 242

Ragoût I 900 g d'épaule de chamois I 4 à 5 baies de genévrier I 1 carotte I 1 rave jaune I ½ céleri I 2 feuilles de laurier I 2 cuillères à soupe d'huile de tournesol I 1 cuillère à soupe de concentré de tomates I 4 cl de gin I ½ l de vin rouge I ½ l de fond de gibier I ½ l de crème I 2 cuillères à soupe d'airelles rouges I Sel, poivre blanc
Pâtes I 200 g de pâtes larges I 50 g de champignons I 50 g de pleurotes I 50 g de champignons Shitake I ½ oignon I 1 cuillère à soupe de beurre I 1 brin de romarin I Un peu de persil I Sel, poivre

Ragoût I Retirer les gros tendons et la peau de l'épaule de chamois. La couper en morceaux de même taille, saler et poivrer, frotter avec les baies de genévrier concassées et laisser reposer 1 heure au réfrigérateur.
Couper la carotte, la rave jaune et le céleri en morceaux d'1 centimètre et les faire revenir avec les feuilles de laurier dans une casserole dans de l'huile chaude jusqu'à ce qu'ils prennent une couleur marron clair. Ajouter le concentré de tomates, faire rissoler rapidement avec les légumes, mouiller avec le gin et le vin rouge, réduire de moitié et ajouter le fond de gibier. Y ajouter les morceaux d'épaule de chamois et laisser cuire à petit feu pendant 1–2 heures. Retirer la viande, ajouter la crème et les airelles rouges au fond de gibier, puis réduire à nouveau de moitié. Passer à la moulinette et remettre la viande dans cette sauce. Donner un bouillon et, si nécessaire, rectifier l'assaisonnement avec le sel, le poivre et les baies de genévrier.
Pâtes aux champignons I Faire cuire les pâtes «al dente» dans de l'eau salée. Couper les champignons en petits morceaux, les oignons en dés fins. Faire chauffer le beurre dans la poêle, y faire sauter les oignons et les champignons. Saler et poivrer, hacher finement le romarin et le persil puis mélanger.
Présentation I Dresser les pâtes sur l'assiette, ajouter les champignons, déposer un morceau de chamois et encercler de sauce.

Mörwald en privé

L'OREILLE AU TELEPHONE ET LA MAIN AU FOURNEAU

Comment Toni Mörwald,
cuisinier parmi les plus grands et patron d'un empire gastronomique,
trouve sa source d'énergie pour décrocher les étoiles.

L'occupation préférée de Toni Mörwald est le téléphone. Pas une minute ne passe sans qu'on le voit avec un portable à l'oreille. Mais la plupart du temps, il ne se contente pas d'utiliser un seul téléphone portable. Il en a souvent un second collé à l'autre oreille et parle à deux personnes à la fois. Mörwald est passé maître en l'art des appels synchronisés, et il a acquis au fil du temps un grand niveau de virtuosité dans cette discipline. Sa devise est la suivante: ce que tu ne peux pas liquider immédiatement ne se réalise pour ainsi dire jamais. C'est pourquoi il a un téléphone en service de façon quasi permanente et il n'est pas rare qu'il en ait deux.

Mörwald ne connaît pas de compromis non plus en ce qui concerne la conduite automobile. Pour gérer la marche des nombreuses branches de son empire composé de plusieurs restaurants et établissements en Basse-Autriche et à Vienne, ainsi qu'une école de cuisine et un service de catering, il doit forcément passer énormément de temps dans l'une de ses voitures. Certains jours, il parcourt jusqu'à 500 kilomètres, et on est en droit de penser qu'il profite aussi des avantages du téléphone portable lorsqu'il est au volant.

Ce n'est pas un adepte de la conduite nonchalante. Le passager de Toni Mörwald se croirait plutôt en avion qu'en voiture. En tout cas, Mörwald essaie de raccourcir autant que faire se peut le délai entre démarrage et atterrissage et, dans ces moments-là, le chef étoilé subtil et sensible se transforme en pilote intrépide aux commandes d'un jet de combat auquel il voudrait faire franchir le mur du son.

Toni Mörwald quant à lui, trouve cela absolument normal. Il ne connaît pas l'hésitation, il ne fait pas dans la demi-mesure. Mörwald c'est du vif-argent, du condensé d'énergie comme il n'y en a guère. Mais comment se maintenir actif en permanence, comment faire le plein d'énergie et compenser l'énorme stress auquel il est soumis sans arrêt? L'une de ses principales sources de ressourcement est sa famille. Sa femme Eva et ses trois filles Antonia, Johanna et Theresia sont pour Toni Mörwald le point central de l'existence. «Une vie de famille intacte est pour moi plus importante que tout le reste» dit Mörwald, «elle me donne l'ancrage dont j'ai besoin, c'est mon centre d'équilibre intérieur.»

Mais c'est aussi dans l'exercice de sa profession que Mörwald fait le plein d'énergie. Il peut sembler absurde au premier abord, que celui qui prône sans cesse à ses clients: «Prenez le temps de déguster, car le temps passé à table est le meilleur temps de vie», soit justement quelqu'un qui ne cesse de courir d'un rendez-vous à l'autre. Or c'est bien dans cette contradiction apparente que réside le phénomène Mörwald. La mise en œuvre permanente d'idées est une source intarissable de motivation, et cela dans une branche qui a pour marchandise principale le plaisir de déguster. C'est ainsi que, pour Toni Mörwald, s'estompent les limites entre vie professionnelle et vie privée. Même certains jours particulièrement trépidants, on peut le voir prendre le temps d'un long repas de midi. Que ce soit pour des raisons professionnelles ou privées. Chez lui également, non loin de Feuersbrunn, il célèbre ce même style de vie qu'il vend avec tant de succès. Dans sa maison, il apprécie de festoyer avec sa famille et ses amis. C'est là-bas aussi que sont régulièrement filmées ses diverses apparitions télévisées.

Toni Mörwald est un bon vivant pur et dur. Mais, à la différence de beaucoup d'autres, point n'est besoin pour lui de douloureux efforts pour parvenir au plaisir, puisqu'il en vit, comme patron, comme cuisinier et dans la vie privée.

Recettes de base

Beurre persillé
100 g de beurre ∎ 100 g feuilles de persil blanchies ∎ Sel

Mettre le beurre et le persil dans un moule Pacojet, mixer, saler, former un rouleau, l'envelopper dans un film alimentaire transparent et le mettre au frais.

Bouillon de gibier
250 ml de fond de gibier clair ∎ 250 ml de crème ∎ 100 g de beurre ∎ Sel

Faire bouillir le fond de gibier avec la crème et réduire de moitié. Retirer la casserole du feu et incorporer le beurre en petits morceaux. Passer la sauce à travers une passoire à trous fins, saler et bien faire mousser.

Chips d'artichauts
1 à 2 artichauts ∎ Huile pour friture

Nettoyer les artichauts, les couper à la machine en fines tranches de 1 millimètre, les blanchir, les tamponner pour les sécher et les faire frire dans l'huile.

Epinards à la crème
300 g de feuilles d'épinards ∎ 125 ml de crème ∎ Sel, poivre, muscade

Nettoyer les épinards, les blanchir dans de l'eau salée bouillante pendant 2 minutes environ et les faire refroidir dans de l'eau glacée. Les égoutter et les réduire finement en purée à l'aide d'un mixeur. Epaissir avec la crème jusqu'à obtenir une consistance onctueuse, assaisonner avec le sel, le poivre et la muscade.

Farce de poisson
250 g de sandre ∎ 1 œuf ∎ 250 ml de crème ∎ Jus d'un ½ citron ∎ Sel, piment d'Espelette

Enlever la peau du filet de sandre et retirer les arêtes. Couper la chair en petits morceaux, les mettre dans un moule Pacojet et saler. Verser la crème sur le poisson, laisser cailler au congélateur puis mixer dans le Pacojet. Passer la farce à travers une passoire à trous fins, assaisonner avec le jus de citron, le sel et le piment d'Espelette.

Farce de volaille
250 g de viande de volaille ∎ 1 œuf ∎ 250 ml de crème ∎ Sel, poivre blanc

Couper finement la viande de volaille et la mettre dans un moule Pacojet. Verser la crème et laisser cailler au congélateur. Y ajouter l'œuf et mixer dans le Pacojet. Passer la farce à travers une passoire à trous fins, saler et poivrer.

Fumet de poisson
500 g d'arêtes de poisson (p.ex. turbot, lotte) ∎ 2 échalotes ∎ 2 champignons ∎ 1 céleri-branche ∎ 1 poireau ∎ 2 cuillères à soupe de beurre ∎ 5 grains de poivre ∎ 250 ml de vin blanc ∎ 250 ml de Noilly Prat ∎ Sel

Piler les arêtes de poisson et les mettre dans un saladier. Passer sous l'eau froide du robinet, jusqu'à ce que l'eau qui s'écoule soit complètement claire. Peler les échalotes et les couper en quatre, nettoyer les champignons et les couper également en quatre. Laver le céleri et le poireau et les couper en dés. Faire revenir les échalotes dans le beurre chaud ; lorsqu'elles sont transparentes, ajouter les arêtes de poisson, les légumes et les épices, ainsi que le Noilly Prat et 1 litre d'eau froide. Laisser mijoter 15 minutes à feu moyen dans une casserole non couverte et, si nécessaire, écumer la mousse. Passer le bouillon à travers une passoire à trous très fins ou une étamine.

Nage de poisson au Champagne
250 ml de fumet de poisson ∎ 100 ml de Champagne ∎ 300 ml de crème ∎ 100 g de beurre ∎ Sel

Faire bouillir le fumet de poisson avec le Champagne et la crème et réduire de moitié. Retirer la casserole du feu et incorporer le beurre en petits morceaux. Passer la sauce à travers une passoire à trous fins, saler et bien faire mousser.

Pâte à pâtes fraîches
200 g de farine ∎ 2 œufs ∎ Sel

Pétrir lentement tous les ingrédients jusqu'à obtenir une pâte souple, l'envelopper dans un film transparent et laisser reposer ½ heure.

Purée de petits pois
500 g de petits pois ∎ 250 ml de fond de volaille ou fond de légumes ∎ 250 ml de crème ∎ 125 g de beurre brun ∎ Sel, poivre

Blanchir les petits pois et les refroidir dans de l'eau glacée. Les mixer finement avec le reste des ingrédients et les passer à travers une passoire à trous fins.

Purée de potiron
500 g de potiron ∎ Brunoise de 2 échalotes ∎ 3 cuillères à soupe d'huile d'olive ∎ 3 à 4 gousses d'ail pressées ∎ 1 branche de thym ∎ Sel, poivre

Préchauffer le four à 160–180 degrés. Diviser le potiron avec l'écorce en morceaux grossiers, l'envelopper avec le reste des ingrédients dans une feuille d'aluminium et faire cuire au four pendant 20 à 25 minutes.
Sortir le potiron de la feuille d'aluminium, gratter la pulpe de l'écorce et bien mixer. Presser dans une étamine, jusqu'à ce qu'il n'y ait plus de liquide.

Sirop de sucre
150 g de sucre

Mettre dans une casserole le sucre avec 150 millilitre d'eau, porter à ébullition tout en remuant. Remuer jusqu'à ce que le sucre soit complètement dissout dans l'eau et écumer, le cas échéant, la mousse se formant pendant la cuisson.

Le compagnon

AMITIES SINCERES ET SYNERGIES COLLEGIALES

Comment Mörwald
fait bouger son monde
tout en cherchant la richesse
du contact humain.

Toni Mörwald possède un véritable talent d'animateur. Qu'il s'agisse de rendez-vous d'affaires ou d'une rencontre avec ses amis et confrères, l'ennui n'est jamais de la partie. Car Toni fait du plaisir une affaire personnelle ; pour lui «le temps passé à table est du temps de vie». Cette maxime dont il a fait sa devise, il la met en pratique avec toute l'obstination et l'énergie dont il dispose. L'inspiration et la critique constructive profitable à sa créativité, Mörwald ne les trouve pas seulement dans la douce intimité de sa famille. Il passe sa vie à rencontrer des amis et des collègues qui ont ceci de commun avec lui : l'amour de la cuisine et des plaisirs de la table. C'est avec reconnaissance et attachement que Toni Mörwald se souvient des compagnons de ces dernières années : des gourmets de tous les horizons, appartenant à sa propre profession mais aussi aux domaines de l'art, de la culture, de la science et de la recherche.